Embedded Cryptography 3

SCIENCES

Computer Science,
Field Directors – Jean-Charles Pomerol

Cryptography, Data Security,
Subject Head – Damien Vergnaud

Embedded Cryptography 3

Coordinated by
Emmanuel Prouff
Guénaël Renault
Matthieu Rivain
Colin O'Flynn

iSTE

WILEY

First published 2025 in Great Britain and the United States by ISTE Ltd and John Wiley & Sons, Inc.

ISTE Ltd
27-37 St George's Road
London SW19 4EU
UK

www.iste.co.uk

John Wiley & Sons, Inc.
111 River Street
Hoboken, NJ 07030
USA

www.wiley.com

Library of Congress Control Number: 2024945144

British Library Cataloguing-in-Publication Data
A CIP record for this book is available from the British Library
ISBN 978-1-78945-215-0

ERC code:
PE6 Computer Science and Informatics
PE6_5 Security, privacy, cryptology, quantum cryptography

Contents

Preface

Emmanuel PROUFF[1], Guénaël RENAULT[2], Matthieu RIVAIN[3] and Colin O'FLYNN[4,5]

[1] *LIP6, Sorbonne Université, Paris, France*
[2] *Agence nationale de la sécurité des systèmes d'information, Paris, France*
[3] *CryptoExperts, Paris, France*
[4] *Dalhousie University, Halifax, Canada*
[5] *NewAE Technology Inc, Halifax, Canada*

The idea for this project was born during a discussion with Damien Vergnaud. Damien had been asked to propose a series of volumes covering the different domains of modern cryptography for the SCIENCES series. He offered us the opportunity to take charge of the *Embedded Cryptography* books, which sounded like a great challenge to take on. In particular, we thought it was perfectly timely as the field was gaining increasing importance with the growing development of complex mobile systems and the internet of things.

The field of embedded cryptography, as a research domain, was born in the mid-1990s. Until that time, the evaluation of a cryptosystem and the underlying attacker model were usually agnostic of implementation aspects whether the cryptosystem was deployed on a computer or on some embedded hardware like a smart card. Indeed, the attacker was assumed to have no other information than the final results of a computation and, possibly, the corresponding inputs. In this black-box context, defining a cryptanalytic attack and evaluating resistance to it essentially consisted of finding flaws in the abstract definition of the cryptosystem.

In the 1990s, teams of researchers published the first academic results highlighting very effective means of attack against embedded systems. These attacks were based on the observation that a system's behavior during a computation strongly depends on the values of the data manipulated (which was previously known and exploited by intelligence services). Consequently, a device performing cryptographic computation does not behave like a black box whose inputs and outputs are the only known factors. The power consumption of the device, its electromagnetic radiation and its running time are indeed other sources that provide the observer with information on the intermediate results of the computation. Teams of researchers have also shown that it was possible to disrupt a computation using external energy sources such as lasers or electromagnetic pulses.

Among these so-called *physical attacks*, two main families emerge. The first gathers the (passive) side-channel attacks, including timing attacks proposed by Kocher in 1996 and power analysis attacks proposed by Kocher et al. in 1999, as well as the microarchitectural attacks that have considerably developed after the publication of the Spectre and Meltdown attacks in 2018. This first family of attacks focuses on the impact that the data manipulated by the system have on measurable physical quantities such as time, current consumption or energy dissipation related to state changes in memories. The second family gathers the (active) fault injection attacks, whose first principles were introduced by Boneh et al. in 1997. These attacks aim to put the targeted system into an abnormal state of functioning. They consist, for example, of ensuring that certain parts of a code are not executed or that operations are replaced by others. Using attacks from either of these families, an adversary might learn sensitive information by exploiting the physical leakage or the faulted output of the system.

Since their inception, *side-channel attacks* and *fault injection attacks*, along with their countermeasures, have significantly evolved. Initially, the embedded systems industry and a limited number of academic labs responded with ad-hoc countermeasures. Given the urgency of responding to the newly published attacks, these countermeasures were reasonably adequate at the time. Subsequently, the invalidation of many of these countermeasures and the increasing sophistication of attack techniques highlighted the need for a more formalized approach to security in embedded cryptography. A community was born from this observation in the late 1990s and gathered around a dedicated conference known as *cryptographic hardware and embedded systems* (CHES). Since then, the growth of this research domain has been very significant, resulting from the strong stake of the industrial players and the scientific interest of the open security issues. Nowadays, physical attacks involve state-of-the-art equipment capable of targeting nanoscale technologies used in the semiconductor industry. The attackers routinely use advanced statistical analyses or signal processing, while the defenders designing countermeasures calls on concepts from algebra, probability theory, or formal methods. More recently, and notably with the publication of the *Spectre* and *Meltdown* attacks, side-channel attacks have extended to so-called microarchitectural attacks, exploiting very common optimization techniques in modern CPUs such as out-of-order execution or speculative execution. Twenty-five years after the foundational work, there is now a large community of academic and industrial scientists dedicated to these problems. Embedded cryptography has gradually become a classic topic in cryptography and computer security, as illustrated by the increasing importance of this field in major cryptography and security conferences besides CHES, such as CRYPTO, Eurocrypt, Asiacrypt, Usenix Security, IEEE S&P or ACM CCS.

Pedagogical material

For this work, it seemed important to us to have both scientifically ambitious and pedagogical content. We indeed wanted this book to appeal not only to researchers in embedded cryptography but also to Master's students interested in the subject and curious to take their first steps. It was also important to us that the concepts and notions developed in the book be as illustrated as possible and therefore accompanied by a pedagogical base. In addition to the numerous illustrations proposed in the chapters, we have made pedagogical material available (attack scripts, implementation examples, etc.) to test and deepen the various concepts. These can be found on the following GitHub organization: https://github.com/embeddedcryptobook.

Content

This book provides a comprehensive exploration of embedded cryptography. It comprises 40 chapters grouped into nine main parts, and spanning three volumes. The book primarily addresses side-channel and fault injection attacks as well as their countermeasures. Part 1 of Volume 1 is dedicated to *Software Side-Channel Attacks*, namely, timing attacks and microarchitectural attacks, primarily affecting software; whereas Part 2 is dedicated to *Hardware Side-Channel Attacks,* which exploit hardware physical leakages, like power consumption and electromagnetic emanations. Part 3 focuses on the second crucial family of physical attacks against embedded systems, namely, *Fault Injection Attacks*.

A full part of the book is dedicated to *Masking* in Part 1 of Volume 2, which is a widely used countermeasure against side-channel attacks and which has become an important research topic since their introduction in 1999. This part covers a variety of masking techniques, their security proofs and their formal verification. Besides general masking techniques, efficient and secure embedded cryptographic implementations are very dependent on the underlying algorithm. Consequently, Part 2, *Cryptographic Implementations*, is dedicated to the implementation of specific cryptographic algorithm families, namely, AES, RSA, ECC and post-quantum cryptography. This part also covers hardware acceleration and constant-time implementations. Secure embedded cryptography needs to rely on secure hardware and secure randomness generation. In cases where hardware alone is insufficient for security, we must rely on additional software techniques to protect cryptographic keys. The latter is known as white-box cryptography. The next three parts of the book address those aspects. Part 3, Volume 2, *Hardware Security*, covers invasive attacks, hardware countermeasures and physically unclonable functions (PUF).

Part 1 of this volume is dedicated to *White-Box Cryptography*: it covers general concepts, practical attack tools, automatic (gray-box) attacks and countermeasures as well as code obfuscation, which is often considered as a complementary measure to white-box cryptography. Part 2 is dedicated to *Randomness and Key Generation* in embedded cryptography. It covers both true and pseudo randomness generation as well as randomness generation for specific cryptographic algorithms (prime numbers for RSA, random nonces for ECC signatures and random errors for post-quantum schemes).

Finally, we wanted to include concrete examples of real-world attacks against embedded cryptosystems. The final part of this series of books contains those examples of *Real World Applications*. While not exhaustive, we selected representative examples illustrating the practical exploitation of the attacks presented in this book, hence demonstrating the necessity of the science of embedded cryptography.

Acknowledgments

This series of books results from a collaborative work and many persons from the embedded cryptography community have contributed to its development. We have tried to cover (as broadly as possible) the field of embedded cryptography and the many research directions related to this field. This has not been an easy task given the dynamism and growth of the field over the past 25 years. Some experts from the community kindly shared their insights on the preliminary plan of the book, namely Sonia Belaïd, Pierre-Alain Fouque, Marc Joye, Victor Lomné and Yannick Sierra. We would like to thank them for their insightful comments.

For each of the identified topics, we wanted the book to cover, we have called upon expert researchers from the community, who have honored us by joining this project. The essence of this work is theirs. Dear Guillaume Barbu, Lejla Batina, Sonia Belaïd, Davide Bellizia, Florent Bernard, Begül Bilgin, Eleonora Cagli, Łukasz Chmielewski, Jessy Clédière, Brice Colombier, Jean-Sébastien Coron, Jean-Luc Danger, Lauren De Meyer, Cécile Dumas, Jean-Max Dutertre, Viktor Fischer, Pierre Galissant, Benedikt Gierlichs, Louis Goubin, Vincent Grosso, Sylvain Guilley, Patrick Haddad, Laurent Imbert, Ján Jančár, Marc Joye, Matthias Kannwischer, Stefan Katzenbeisser, Victor Lomné, José Lopes-Esteves, Ange Martinelli, Pedro Massolino, Loïc Masure, Nele Mentens, Debdeep Mukhopadhyay, Camille Mutschler, Ruben Niederhagen, Colin O'Flynn, Elisabeth Oswald, Dan Page, Pascal Paillier, Louisa Papachristodoulou, Thomas Peeters, Olivier Peirera, Thomas Pornin, Bart Preneel, Thomas Prest, Jean-René Reinhard, Thomas Roche,

Francisco Rodríguez-Henríquez, Franck Rondepierre, Eyal Ronen, Melissa Rossi, Mylene Rousselet, Sylvain Ruhault, Ulrich Ruhrmair, Sayandeep Saha, Patrick Schaumont, Sebastian Schrittwieser, Peter Schwabe, Richa Singh, Sergei Skorobogatov, François-Xavier Standaert, Petr Svenda, Marek Sys, Akira Takahashi, Abdul Rahman Taleb, Yannick Teglia, Philippe Teuwen, Adrian Thillard, Medhi Tibouchi, Mike Tunstall, Aleksei Udovenko, David Vigilant, Lennert Wouters, Yuval Yarom and Rina Zeitoun: thank you so much for the hard work!

To accompany these authors, we also relied on numerous reviewers who kindly shared their remarks on the preliminary versions of the chapters. Their behind-the-scenes work allowed us to greatly improve the technical and editorial quality of the books. We express our gratitude to them, namely, Davide Alessio, Sébastien Bardin, Sonia Belaïd, Eloi Benoist-Vanderbeken, Gaëtan Cassiers, Jean-Sebastien Coron, Debayan Das, Cécile Dumas, Julien Eynard, Wieland Fischer, Thomas Fuhr, Daniel Genkin, Dahmun Goudarzi, Eliane Jaulmes, Victor Lomné, Loïc Masure, Bart Mennink, Stjepan Picek, Thomas Pornin, Thomas Prest, Jurgen Pulkus, Michaël Quisquater, Thomas Roche, Franck Rondepierre, Franck Salvador, Tobias Schneider, Okan Seker, Pierre-Yves Strub, Akira Takahashi, Abdul Rahman Taleb, Mehdi Tibouchi, Aleksei Udovenko, Gilles Van Assche, Damien Vergnaud, Vincent Verneuil and Gabriel Zaid.

October 2024

PART 1

White-Box Cryptography

1

Introduction to White-Box Cryptography

Pierre GALISSANT and Louis GOUBIN
Laboratoire de Mathématiques de Versailles, UVSQ, CNRS, Université Paris-Saclay, France

1.1. Introductory remarks

In 1883, Auguste Kerckhoffs' article, *La cryptographie militaire*, was published in the *Journal des sciences militaires*, in which he stated six design rules for military ciphers. Here they are, translated from French:

1) The system must be practically, if not mathematically, indecipherable.

2) It should not require secrecy, and it should not be a problem if it falls into enemy hands.

3) It must be possible to communicate and remember the key without using written notes, and correspondents must be able to change or modify it at will.

4) It must be applicable to telegraph communications.

5) It must be portable and should not require several persons to handle or operate.

6) Lastly, given the circumstances in which it is to be used, the system must be easy to use and should not be stressful to use or require its users to know and comply with a long list of rules.

The second rule, now known as Kerckhoffs's principle, has been completely taken into account in the modern cryptography concepts. More precisely, it is usually

Embedded Cryptography 3,
coordinated by Emmanuel PROUFF, Guénaël RENAULT,
Matthieu RIVAIN and Colin O'FLYNN.

assumed, in most security models, that the attacker has a complete knowledge of the formal specifications of the cryptographic algorithms that are used to secure the communications or the storage of sensitive data.

On top of that, to make security possible, we must assume that the legitimate users (traditionally called Alice and Bob in the two-party scenarios) know a secret data which gives them an advantage over a potential adversary (usually called Charlie). Since this secret *key* has to be involved in the cryptographic computations, and must still remain hidden from the attacker, the classical security model in cryptography makes the assumption that it is not only the key but also the explicit implementation of the algorithm (which includes the key) which cannot be accessed by the attacker. This is the *black-box* model.

Nevertheless, cryptographic algorithms are increasingly deployed in various applications embedded on connected devices, such as smartphones and tablets. In this environment, the capabilities of the adversary can be greatly enhanced, and we should consider an adversary who can access the binary code, modify its execution, tamper with the memory and use existing reverse engineering tools such as debuggers to recover the hidden secrets. This *white-box* model is of course more demanding, and white-box cryptography aims at providing the same security guarantees as in the black-box model, despite this huge new advantage given to the adversary.

In the following sections, we will be able to provide precise security notions that capture this idea of cryptographic security in a white-box model. However, we give here some preliminary remarks to highlight the subtleties which can arise when trying to formalize white-box cryptography.

As a first tentative goal, let us consider the problem of providing an implementation of a block cipher algorithm E_K for which the secret key K is computationally difficult to extract from the given implementation.

If no further constraints are given, it is not difficult to build such a block cipher algorithm, together with a white-box implementation. Indeed, we can choose E defined by:

$$E_K = E'_{h(K)}$$

where E' is a standard block cipher (for instance, AES) and h is a one-way function (for instance, h can be built with a standard hash function). It is obviously easy to build an implementation such that $h(K)$ is easy to recover, but not K. This shows that the difficulty of extracting the key does not completely capture the intuitive notion we have for white-box cryptography.

Another natural idea follows from this first remark: Can we make it computationally difficult, from the implementation of E_K (i.e. the code of the function $x \mapsto E_K(x)$), to find a decomposition of the form:

$$E_K(x) = F(x, G(K)),$$

for which we can explicitly obtain the code of F and the code of G? Note that in this framework, G can contain several elements. For instance, block ciphers typically use a key schedule mechanism such as $G(K) = (K_1, \ldots, K_r)$, with *subkeys* K_i $(1 \leq i \leq r)$, so that we have:

$$E_K(x) = F(x, K_1, ..., K_r)$$

A typical example that would not satisfy this definition is a "one-way" key schedule:

$$K_i = h(K||i) \quad (1 \leq i \leq r),$$

where h is a one-way function (that can easily be built from a standard hash function).

In summary, it seems a good definition of white-box cryptography should forbid the following situation: "the code is independent of K, except constants which depend on K in a deterministic way".

At first sight, we could fear all cryptographic implementations would therefore be forbidden! Fortunately, the possibility remains that G has, among its inputs, an external value r:

$$E_K(x) = F(x, G(K, r))$$

This construction is reminiscent of the randomness used in side-channel countermeasures and historically appeared to be a key idea in the seminal proposals of white-box DES and AES implementations (Chow et al. 2002), where:

$$G(K, r) = \text{tables that depend on } K \text{ and } r.$$

Note that this also opens the way to a useful application: *traitor tracing*. If someone reveals $G(K, r)$, we can recover r (in the extreme case, by exhaustive search on r). This relies on the assumption that it is difficult to deduce $G(K, r')$ from $G(K, r)$ (and a fortiori K from $G(K, r)$).

We can also remark that such a construction can be done in the context of the RSA primitive. The fundamental idea is the following: if the encryption function is built upon $x \mapsto y = x^e \bmod n$, the decryption function is based on $y \mapsto x = y^d \bmod n$ (where d is the inverse of e modulo $\varphi(n)$) and can be implemented as $y \mapsto x = y^{d'} \bmod n$, where d' is an arbitrary large integer such that $d' \equiv d \bmod \varphi(n)$, namely, $d' = d + r\varphi(n)$. For this construction to make sense, we have to assume that e is also a secret exponent (if not, a well-known argument can be used to deduce the factorization of n from d'), so that what we obtain is an example of white-box symmetric algorithm:

$$\begin{cases} K = (e, d, p, q) \\ E_K(y) = y^{d'} \bmod n \\ E_K^{-1}(x) = x^e \bmod n \end{cases}$$

Here, which instructions are executed (or not) may depend on K (typically in the case of *square and multiply*: "if $d'_i = 1$ then $x := x \times y \bmod n$"). However, the knowledge of these executed instructions is equivalent to the knowledge of n and d', which does not allow us to recover $K = (e, d, p, q)$.

1.2. Basic notions for white-box cryptography

The basic security requirement for a white-box implementation is to resist key extraction. However, we should expect more from white-box cryptography and consider various security properties for the white-box implementations; and hopefully we provide formal definitions and security notions for white-box cryptography. In particular, Delerablée et al. (2014) defined some concrete white-box security notions for symmetric encryption schemes. For example, *unbreakability*, *one-wayness*, *incompressibility* and *traceability* are derived from folklore intuitions behind white-box cryptography.

1.2.1. *Unbreakability*

The notion of unbreakability is a very intuitive security notion for white-box cryptography and has been studied since the seminal paper of Chow et al. (2002).

Let us describe the game for unbreakability of a white-box compiler $\mathcal{C}_\mathcal{S}$ corresponding to a given cryptographic algorithm $\mathcal{S}$:

– draw at random key k in private keyspace $K_\mathcal{S}$;

– the adversary $\mathcal{A}$ gets the program $\mathcal{C}_\mathcal{S}(k)$ from the compiler;

– the adversary $\mathcal{A}$ returns a key guess $\hat{k}$ in time, and τ knows $\mathcal{C}_\mathcal{S}(k)$;

– the adversary $\mathcal{A}$ succeeds if $k = \hat{k}$.

DEFINITION 1.1.– Let $\mathcal{S}$ be a cryptographic algorithm, $\mathcal{C}_\mathcal{S}$ a white-box compiler for this algorithm $\mathcal{S}$ and let $\mathcal{A}$ be any adversary. We define the probability of the adversary $\mathcal{A}$ to succeed in the unbreakability game by:

$$Succ_{\mathcal{A},\mathcal{C}_\mathcal{S}} := \mathbb{P}[k \leftarrow K; \mathcal{P} = \mathcal{C}_\mathcal{S}(k), \mathcal{A}(\mathcal{P}) = \hat{k}; k = \hat{k}]$$

We say that $\mathcal{C}_\mathcal{S}$ is (τ,ϵ)-unbreakable if for any adversary $\mathcal{A}$ running in time τ, $Succ_{\mathcal{A},\mathcal{C}_\mathcal{S}} \leq \epsilon$.

1.2.2. *Incompressibility*

The notion of incompressibility is a stronger security notion, first formally defined by Delerablée et al. (2014), where the study of this notion is motivated as a software countermeasure against code-lifting attacks.

We now describe, for any $\sigma > 0$, the game for incompressibility for a white-box compiler $\mathcal{C}_\mathcal{S}$ corresponding to a given cryptographic algorithm $\mathcal{S}$:

– draw at random a key k in private keyspace $K_\mathcal{S}$;

– the adversary $\mathcal{A}$ gets the program $\mathcal{C}_\mathcal{S}(k)$ from the compiler;

– the adversary $\mathcal{A}$ returns a program $\mathcal{P}$ knowing $\mathcal{C}_\mathcal{S}(k)$;

– the adversary $\mathcal{A}$ succeeds if $\mathcal{P} \approx \mathcal{C}_\mathcal{S}(k)$ and $size(\mathcal{P}) \leq \sigma$.

DEFINITION 1.2.– Let $\mathcal{S}$ be a cryptographic algorithm, $\mathcal{C}_\mathcal{S}$ a white-box compiler for this algorithm $\mathcal{S}$ and let $\mathcal{A}$ be any adversary. We define the probability of the adversary $\mathcal{A}$ to succeed in the σ-incompressibility game by:

$$Succ_{\mathcal{A},\mathcal{C}_\mathcal{S}} := \mathbb{P}[k \leftarrow K; \mathcal{P} = \mathcal{A}(\mathcal{C}_\mathcal{S}(k))\,; \mathcal{P} \approx \mathcal{C}_\mathcal{S}(k);\ (size(\mathcal{P}) \leq \sigma)]$$

Moreover, we say that $\mathcal{C}_\mathcal{S}$ is (σ,τ,ϵ)-incompressible if for any adversary $\mathcal{A}$, Time($\mathcal{A}$)+Time($\mathcal{P}$) $< \tau$ implies $Succ_{\mathcal{A},\mathcal{C}_\mathcal{S}} \leq \epsilon$.

REMARK 1.1.– In a more general case, the definition can include a parameter δ that allows the program $\mathcal{P}$ to agree with the targeted function with probability δ.

REMARK 1.2.– Note that if a compiler is incompressible, then it is unbreakable for reasonable security levels: the key-recovery is indeed an extreme compression of a white-box implementation.

The definition of incompressibility we state here is a slightly modified version from the initial definition of Delerablée et al. (2014). Indeed, the latter does not constrain the running time of the program $\mathcal{P}$, which leaves the possibility of a trivial way of compressing any white-box algorithm, namely, by using brute force: an attacker can compute a few (plaintext, ciphertext) pairs and code the brute-force attack on the primitives that are white-boxed, and then code the computation of the primitive, including the obtained key. This program can be made with few lines of code and is functionally equivalent to the initial white-box implementation, but has an unreasonable running time. The definition above makes use of a new time constraint: the sum of the running time of the attacker and the produced program must be less than a constant τ representing the whole computation time allowed.

REMARK 1.3.– The previous modification does not necessarily invalidate all the proofs found in the literature for incompressibility. Indeed, in some of these proofs, the programs produced by the attacker are restrained by a model (for example, Ideal Group Model), whereas the program we mentioned here does not fit into this kind of model.

1.2.3. *One-wayness*

Let us describe the game for one-wayness of a white-box compiler $\mathcal{C}_\mathcal{S}$ corresponding to a given symmetric encryption algorithm $\mathcal{S}$:

– draw at random a key k in private keyspace $K_\mathcal{S}$;

– the adversary $\mathcal{A}$ gets the program $\mathcal{C}_\mathcal{S}(k)$ from the compiler;

– the adversary $\mathcal{A}$ gets the ciphertext c corresponding to a randomly selected plaintext m;

– the adversary $\mathcal{A}$ returns a guess $\hat{m}$ in time τ knowing $\mathcal{C}_\mathcal{S}(k)$;

– the adversary $\mathcal{A}$ succeeds if $m = \hat{m}$.

DEFINITION 1.3.– Let $\mathcal{S}$ be a symmetric encryption algorithm, $\mathcal{C}_\mathcal{S}$ a white-box compiler for this algorithm $\mathcal{S}$ and let $\mathcal{A}$ be any adversary. We define the probability of the adversary $\mathcal{A}$ to succeed in the one-wayness game by:

$$\mathcal{S}ucc_{\mathcal{A},\mathcal{C}_\mathcal{S}} := \mathbb{P}[k \leftarrow K, m \leftarrow M; \mathcal{P} = \mathcal{C}_\mathcal{S}(k), c = \mathcal{S}(m), \mathcal{A}(\mathcal{P}, c) = \hat{m}; m = \hat{m}]$$

We say that $\mathcal{C}_\mathcal{S}$ is (τ,ϵ)-one-way if for any adversary $\mathcal{A}$ running in time τ, $\mathcal{S}ucc_{\mathcal{A},\mathcal{C}_\mathcal{S}} \leq \epsilon$.

REMARK 1.4.– This one-wayness has the following consequence: the cryptographic algorithm can be used as a public-key cryptosystem. It is indeed possible to see the obtained white-box implementation as a public key, and the key K of the algorithm as the private key. The one-wayness property implies that the public key can only be used to encrypt messages, whereas the decryption requires the knowledge of the private key. This illustrates the power of this security notion.

1.3. Proposed (and broken) solutions

1.3.1. *Block ciphers*

Many attempts have been made to construct white-box implementations for standard block ciphers in recent years.

DES obfuscation methods were first proposed by Chow et al. (2002) at the DRM 2002 workshop. The simplest method ("naked DES") was cryptanalyzed by Chow et al. (2003) themselves at the SAC 2002 conference; an improved method was also cryptanalyzed by Jacob et al. (2002) and by Link and Neuman (2004); the strongest known method ("nonstandard-DES") was also cryptanalyzed independently by Wyseur et al. (2007) and by Goubin et al. (2007) at the SAC 2007 conference.

A specific obfuscation method for AES was proposed by Chow et al. (2002) at SAC 2002, and later cryptanalyzed by Billet et al. (2004) at SAC 2004 (see also Billet (2005); PhD Thesis, defended in December 2005).

Further construction attempts followed, for instance, by Link and Neumann (2004), Bringer et al. (2006), Xiao and Lai (2009), and by Karroumi (2010), but they were also shown to be insecure sooner or later, by De Mulder et al. (2010) at INDOCRYPT, De Mulder et al. (2012) at SAC, Lepoint et al. (2013) at SAC, De Mulder et al. (2013), and Lepoint and Rivain (2013). The WhibOx 2017 and 2019 contests showed that even with hidden designs, producing unbreakable and one-way AES implementations in pure software is a difficult open problem.

This illustrates that reaching the *unbreakability* property – and a fortiori the *incompressibility* property – are already difficult when implementing standard block ciphers such as 3DES or AES.

Concerning the *one-wayness* security notion, we already mentioned that it allows us to tranform a (symmetric) block cipher into a public-key cryptosystem, which gives a first hint that it is probably even more difficult to obtain than unbreakability.

More precisely, for usual block ciphers, the one-wayness problem appears to have a close relationship with the problem of "functional decomposition". Standard block ciphers are indeed built from several rounds (for instance, 16 rounds for DES or 10 rounds for AES), which leads to typical implementations as a loop corresponding to a functional decomposition:

$$E_K = f_r \circ \ldots \circ f_1$$

Hence, inverting E_K boils down to inverting each f_i, which is likely to be an easy task.

REMARK 1.5.– A natural idea would be to compute functional compositions of the type $f_i \circ f_j$, such that the "functional decomposition" is computationally hard. However, the problem for classical block ciphers is that the algebraic degree of such compositions grows quickly. This can even be seen as an unavoidable consequence of the fundamental principle stated by Shannon (1949) paper: breaking a "good" cipher should require "as much work as solving a system of simultaneous equations in a large number of unknowns of a complex type". Therefore, the composition cannot be done via the representation as polynomial systems, and new strategies seem to be required here.

REMARK 1.6.– White-box constructions (with the unbreakability and one-wayness properties) are possible if we are allowed to choose an (ad hoc) block cipher. This is reminiscent of public-key cryptography and can easily be illustrated in the context of multivariate cryptography. In a nutshell, a multivariate algorithm makes use of a function A that can be represented as a system of n multivariate polynomials in n variables and can be easily inverted. In the asymmetric setting, the secret key comprises two secret invertible linear (of affine) functions s and t, and the corresponding public key is obtained as $t \circ A \circ s$, one of the security assumptions being that recovering A from this public key in computationally difficult (this is usually called the "Isomorphism of polynomials with two secrets" problem).

This construction can be converted into a symmetric block cipher:

$$\begin{cases} K = (s, t, A) \\ E_K(y) = (t \circ A \circ s)(y), \text{where } t \circ A \circ s \text{ is given as a system of polynomials} \\ E_K^{-1}(x) = s^{-1} \circ A^{-1} \circ t^{-1}(x) \end{cases}$$

In summary, the idea here is that multivariate cryptography can make K difficult to extract from the implementation of E_K, without having a huge algebraic degree for the "global" (and public) description of E_K.

1.3.2. *Asymmetric algorithms*

While many candidates have been publicly proposed to construct white-box implementations of block ciphers, almost no white-box implementations for public-key algorithms have been published up to now, in spite of numerous research efforts.

In their works, Feng et al. (2020) and Zhang et al. (2020), claim to achieve unbreakability for asymmetric cryptosystems. However, their proposals require a non-standard verification process, which makes them irrelevant for genuine public-key applications.

To the best of our knowledge, the first candidate that does not change the underlying scheme is due to Barthelemy (2020a, 2020b), who proposed a white-box implementation of a scheme suggested by Aguilar Melchior et al. (2016) whose (black-box) security is based on the computational difficulty of the RLWE (ring learning with errors) problem over the cyclotomic ring $R_q = \mathbb{Z}/q\mathbb{Z}[X]/(X^n + 1)$.

Lucas Barthelemy's implementation of the decryption algorithm makes use of the NTT transformation and RNS representations to reduce the computation to small look-up tables, which can in turn be transformed using ideas dating back to the SAC 2002 seminal paper of Chow et al. (2020), together with additive of multiplicative masking based on homomorphic properties of the cryptographic scheme. However, a fatal flaw was found (and acknowledged by Lucas Barthelemy in his PhD thesis): the core part of the white-box implementation consists of trying to prevent the key extraction for a function of the form $\alpha_2 - \alpha_1 \cdot sk$, where (α_1, α_2) is the ciphertext we want to decrypt, and sk is the secret key. This function is linear in α_1 and α_2, and this linear dependence on the elements coming from the ciphertext remains true, even after applying the NTT transformations and using the representations RNS. It is therefore very easy for an attacker to find the coefficients of these linear transformations (which depend on sk), then sk itself.

The WhibOx 2021 contest showed that for the ECDSA algorithm, even with hidden design, getting an unbreakable implementation is out of reach: all the implementations proposed were quickly broken. In-depth analyses of the generic attacks and problems these implementations suffered were provided by Barbu et al. (2022) and Bauer et al. (2022).

Galissant and Goubin (2022) proposed a concrete white-box implementation for the well-known hidden field equations (HFE) signature algorithm (a signature algorithm belonging to the multivariate family of public key algorithms) for a specific set of internal polynomials, providing the first white-box implementation of a public key algorithm, together with an extensive security analysis providing strong arguments for both unbreakability and incompressibility. For a security level 2^{80}, the public key size is approximately 62.5 MB and the white-box implementation of the signature algorithm has a size of approximately 256 GB.

This is a promising research direction and some variants are currently being investigated to improve the size of the white-box implementation and adapt it to various security levels.

1.4. Generic strategies to build white-box implementations

1.4.1. *DCA and countermeasures*

In the white-box model, the attacker has access all the details of the implementation of a (known) cryptographic algorithm, including a given secret key, and the goal of the attacker is to recover the secret key. Up to now, most candidate implementations (of DES, AES, substitution linear-transformation ciphers, etc.) have been broken. Most of the time, the attacks use various cryptanalytic techniques, which require knowledge and understanding of all the implementation principles and details.

In the past years, *generic attacks* have emerged that apply to white-box implementations, irrespective of their (secret) designs and which consist of translating usual hardware attacks to the white-box setting. In particular, Sanfelix et al. (2015), Bos et al. (2016) at CHES, described differential computational analysis (DCA), whose principle is to apply side-channel analysis (SCA) techniques to so-called *computational traces* composed of all the intermediate results of the computation (bus transfers, register allocations, memory addresses, etc.). More precisely, a dynamic binary instrumentation (DBI) framework can be used to build software traces and then mount an analogue of differential power attack (DPA) on these software traces. The advantage of this technique is that – as DPA in the case of smart card implementations – the attacker does not need to know (and to analyze) the very details of the implementation. The attack can be launched in an automated way on candidate white-box implementations.

For instance, Bos et al. (2016) describe several examples illustrating the power of this DCA: the authors show that their method can break many challenge implementations, which utilize many of the ideas used up to now to build white-box implementations. This shows that an already stated principle (namely, a whitebox implementation must in particular resist all kinds of side-channel attacks) had probably not been considered seriously enough.

The lack of random source in a white-box implementation (at run-time) is a reason for the weakness against DCA, but theoretically this does not rule out the possibility of resistant white-box implementations. Therefore, a first challenge is to provide a theoretical explanation of the fact that white-box implementations, based on look-up tables, can be attacked by SCA, even when they are "hidden" by randomly chosen bijections (e.g. in DES and AES implementation by Chow et al. (2002)).

A second challenge consists of elaborating specific countermeasures against this new kind of attack.

REMARK 1.7.– As noted by Jacob et al. (2002), and Sanfelix et al. (2015), differential fault analysis (DFA) can also be directly applied to the white-box setting, so that resisting these attacks is also a challenge for future research.

1.4.2. *Using fully homomorphic encryption (FHE)*

When considering DCA, we have to limit the power of the attacker, usually by bounding the "order" of such attacks. Classical ways of protecting the key are making use of the *secret sharing* principle, leading to so-called *masking* countermeasures.

In the white-box setting, such a limit is less relevant. We cannot expect noise to make the complexity of the attack grow exponentially with the DCA order. Is it therefore natural to push DCA to its limits, and try to obtain "infinite order" countermeasures? The intuition can be viewed as follows. DCA-type masking countermeasures of order n are based on the idea that the attacker cannot control more than n values, so that computing the algorithm with a "multiparty computation"-like implementation can prevent the attack. In the context of delegated computations, when no limit is assumed about the number of parties controlled by the attacker, multiparty computation is not sufficient any more, and has to be replaced by FHE.

For the more general problem of obfuscation, methods based on hard computational problems have indeed been derived from fully homomorphic encryption and the universal oblivious Turing machine. Pippenger and Fischer (1979) proved that a two-tape oblivious Turing machine can simulate any non-oblivious Turing machine with only logarithmic slowdown. The idea is then to homomorphically run the universal oblivious Turing machine, with two inputs:

$$Prog' = FHE.Encrypt(Prog),$$

where $Prog$ is the program to be computed in an obfuscated way. Of course, the program does not appear in the form $Prog$ but only in the form $Prog'$, pre-computed during the creation of the obfuscated software.

$$x' = FHE.Encrypt(x),$$

where x is the input of $Prog$.

To resist partial evaluation attacks and mixed input attacks, as noticed by Garg et al. (2013), the final decryption of the result has to be conditional. The condition is twofold:

– Check the proof of computation of the universal oblivious Turing machine that testifies that the program $Prog'$ was indeed run (in an FHE way) on the input x', and also that $x' = FHE.Encrypt(x)$ was correctly computed.

– Verify a digital signature of $Prog'$, so as to authentify the executed program.

This idea can directly be adapted to the white-box context by using FHE to encrypt only K instead of the whole program $Prog$. For the conditional decryption, two possibilities arise. Conditional decryption can be executed within a dedicated tamper-resistant hardware, as illustrated by Bitansky et al. (2011) and Döttling et al. (2011). One more challenging direction consists of replacing this hardware part by an obfuscated (software) program. To achieve this, a line of research – starting from a paper by Garg et al. (2013) that develops a complex design based on branching programs and multilinear maps – aims at obtaining generic obfuscation methods (which here would only use the fact that the conditional decryption can be written as a NC^1 circuit). However, they are still highly non-practical.

1.4.3. *White-box solutions with the help of a (small) tamper-resistant hardware*

Alpirez Bock et al. (2020) considered (at ASIACRYPT) an alternative use of such a tamper-resistant hardware. They build a hardware-bound white-box key derivation function (WKDF) on top of a standard (black-box) key derivation function (KDF). In a nutshell, if the adversary uses its hardware access, they are able to evaluate the WKDF, but if they have no access to the relevant hardware values, for example, in case of a code-lifting attack, then they learn nothing about the WKDF values. The design, based on techniques published by Sahai and Waters (2014), requires puncturable pseudorandom functions (PRFs, which are equivalent to one-way functions) and indistinguishability obfuscation (*iO*). Although interesting from a theoretical point of view, the current state of the art of *iO* makes the construction highly impractical.

In comparison, as described in section 1.4.2, white-box resistance can be achieved using FHE together with a (relatively small) tamper-resistant hardware that computes the conditional decryption operation. The performance overhead due to FHE is rather high, but the solution remains realistic in case we really need a single call to the hardware at the end of the computation.

Other ways of using a secure hardware component have been considered in the context of white-box cryptography (seen as a particular case of software obfuscation). For instance, Anderson (2008) described the following idea. The program to be obfuscated can be written on the encrypted memory tape of a Turing machine. Each time an operation has to be executed, the whole tape is sent to the hardware component, which decrypts it, executes the next instruction, reencrypts the tape and sends it back to the software part. This is of course very time consuming and requires a huge number of exchanges between the software and the hardware token.

A more efficient solution was described by Goyal et al. (2010). By building on techniques from resettably secure computation (due to Goyal and Sahai (2009)), they gave a general positive result for stateless oblivious reactive functionalities under standard cryptographic assumption. This result also provides the first general feasibility result for program obfuscation using stateless tokens. As a side result, they also propose constructions of non-interactive secure computation for general reactive functionalities with stateful tokens, which can be adapted to hardware-aided white-box constructions.

1.5. Applications of white-box cryptography

Real-world applications of white-box cryptography are numerous. Below are some typical examples illustrating potential use cases of white-box cryptography, either in a symmetric model or in a public key setting.

1.5.1. *EMV payments on NFC-enabled smartphones without secure element*

In recent years, the payment industry has shown great interest in the extension of the EMV specifications to mobile transactions via near field communication (NFC). In that scenario, the usual contactless smart card is emulated by an NFC-compliant mobile phone or wearable device such as a smart watch. This is referred to as *host card emulation* (HCE). Unfortunately, however, mobile platforms do not provide access to a secure element to third-party applications: the SIM card belongs to the telecommunication operator and handset manufacturers keep any form of trusted hardware for their own needs. These emerging applications are therefore facing the challenge of being as secure as a tamper-resistant hardware, although being totally based on software. White-box cryptography is currently the only approach to secure these applications and compensate the security risks inherent to common embedded operating systems such as Android. By hard-coding the EMV keys into the application code itself, as suggested in the EMVCo requirements documentation in 2019, white-box cryptography tries to achieve a notion of *tamper-resistant software*. Similarly, Mastercard Cloud-Based Payments (MCBP) is a secure and scalable software-based solution developed to digitize card credentials and enable both contactless and remote payment transactions. In this context, in 2017, Mastercard specifically recommended the use of white-box implementation for the secure storage of payment tokens.

1.5.2. *Software DRM mechanisms for digital contents*

Digital right management (DRM) is a set of techniques whereby subscribers get access to protected content under a number of conditions (access rights). Video on-demand and mobile TV are typical examples of DRM-protected services. Here again, in the absence of a hardware cryptographic module, a white-box implementation of the content decryption algorithm under an individual user key prevents the key from being recovered and re-used by third-parties (piracy based on key sharing and redistribution).

1.5.3. *Mobile contract signing*

The eIDAS regulation (EU Reg. No. 910/2014) came into force on July 1, 2016 in the 28 member states of the EU, and introduced the *end of the smart card dogma*, in the sense that the signing capability can now be implemented by purely software means as long as they fulfill specific requirements through a qualification procedure. Electronic signatures also become legal evidence that cannot be denied by sovereign authorities or in court. By relaxing constraints on the signing utility, the eIDAS regulation opens the way to software-only solutions for digital signatures. As a result, a rapid emergence of mobile contract signing is anticipated in the near future. The user experience is straightforward: a contract (or any form of document in that respect) is downloaded on the mobile device, reviewed by the human user, digitally signed locally and the legally binding signature is returned to a back-end server in the cloud, where it is validated and archived. Now, the need for the signing application to be eIDAS-qualified imposes (depending on the qualification level) resisting security threats pertaining to mobile platforms and most particularly logical attacks where some form of external control is exerted through malware, typically in an attempt to steal the signing key(s) stored on the device. White-box cryptography is the only approach that effectively puts the signing key(s) out of reach of logical attacks on the operating system. Combined with countermeasures against code lifting, white-box cryptography is expected to take a major role in the adoption and deployment of eIDAS-based services in the EU.

1.5.4. *Cryptocurrencies and blockchain technologies*

Most solutions to store cryptocurrencies and perform transactions on the blockchain are today based on a hardware token (USB stick, smart card) or on a mobile application. While the former provide adequate security, it is inconvenient for the wider usage. For the latter case on the other hand, the security often relies on the operating system of the mobile device and the principle of application sandboxing. Given the wide variety of mobile OS versions on the field, strictly relying on the operating system to protect critical assets (such as money) is very hazardous and should always be avoided. This raises a strong need for the design of security solutions for pure-software cryptocurrency wallet against all kind of threats such as stealing malwares. In order to protect the cryptographic keys intrinsically involved in cryptocurrencies and blockchain technologies, white-box cryptography is essential. As concerns digital signatures, ECDSA is currently the most used algorithm (for instance, Bitcoin and Ethereum), but alternatives are considered, either for other cryptocurrencies or to prepare for the post-quantum era.

1.6. Notes and further references

From a historical perspective, the term "white-box cryptography" was introduced by Chow et al. (2002, 2003) in their seminal papers in relation to the following situation: "When the attacker has internal information about a cryptographic implementation, choice of implementation is the sole remaining line of defense" (Chow et al. 2003).

– Section 1.1. Auguste Kerckhoffs published his seminal paper in Kerckhoffs (1883a). See also Kerckhoffs (1883b), entitled *La cryptographie militaire, ou les chiffres usités en temps de guerre, avec un nouveau procédé de déchiffrement applicable aux systèmes à double clef.*

– Section 1.2. The paper by Delerablée et al. (2014) about white-box definitions was published in 2013 in the procedings of the SAC conference. The seminal paper of Chow et al. (2002) was published in the proceedings of the DRM 2002 workshop; see also their paper at SAC 2002 (Chow et al. 2003).

– Section 1.3. DES obfuscation methods, first proposed by Chow et al. (2002), were cryptanalyzed by Chow et al. (2003), Jacob et al. (2002), Link and Neumann (2004), Goubin et al. (2007) and Wyseur et al. (2007).

The white-box implemention for AES by Chow et al. (2003) was later cryptanalyzed by Billet et al. (2004) (see also Billet (2005)). Other constructions were proposed by Link and Neumann (2004), Bringer et al. (2006), Xiao and Lai (2009) and Karroumi (2011), but were all broken by De Mulder et al. (2010, 2013a, 2013b), Lepoint and Rivain (2013); Lepoint et al. (2014), Lepoint and Rivain (2013); Lepoint et al. (2014). During the WhibOx Organizing Committee (2017) and WhibOx Organizing Committee (2019) contests, all the AES proposals were eventually broken.

In his famous paper "Communication theory of secrecy systems" (Shannon 1949), Claude Shannon discussed cryptography from an information theory point of view, thus providing foundations of modern cryptography.

In the asymmetric context, white-box implementations were claimed by Feng et al. (2020) and Zhang et al. (2020), but they have to modify the verification process, so that the cryptosystem does not fit the original public key framework. Lucas Barthelemy's candidate (Barthelemy 2020b) is a white-box implementation of a public key encryption scheme, a variant of a scheme suggested by Aguilar Melchor et al. (2016). The white-box implementation uses ideas from Chow et al. (2003), but flaws were acknowledged by Barthelemy in his PhD thesis (Barthelemy 2020a): the linear dependences allowing us to recover the secret key can be seen in the equations in section 4.2.

During the WhibOx Organizing Committee (2021) contest, all of the proposed ECDSA white-box implementations were eventually broken. Detailed analyses of the attacks were given by Barbu et al. (2022) and Bauer et al. (2022).

The recent proposal by Galissant and Goubin (2022) is a white-box implementation of a variant of HFE, a signature algorithm belonging to the multivariate family of public key algorithms.

– Section 1.4. The idea of differential computational analysis (DCA) was introduced by Sanfelix et al. (2015) and Bos et al. (2016). Its principle originates in side-channel analysis (SCA) techniques (see, for instance, Kocher et al. (1999) or Brier et al. (2004)), applied to computational traces, instead of power (or electro-magnetic) traces.

The idea of using differential fault analysis (DFA) in the context of white-box implementations was mentioned by Jacob et al. (2002) and Sanfelix et al. (2015). Basic notions about DFA can be found in the well-known papers of Boneh et al. (1997) and Biham and Shamir (1997).

A detailed survey of fully homomorphic encryption can be found in Marcolla et al. (2022). The property that a two-tape oblivious Turing machine can simulate any non-oblivious Turing machine with only logarithmic slowdown is due to Pippenger and Fischer (1979).

The idea of using a conditional decryption operation to resist partial evaluation attacks and mixed input attacks was described by Garg et al. (2013) at FOCS. This operation can in turn be executed either in a tamper-resistant hardware, as illustrated by Bitansky et al. (2011) and Döttling et al. (2011), or in an obfuscated way, following a line of research initiated by Garg et al. (2013).

A construction of a hardware-bound white-box key derivation function (WKDF) was proposed at ASIACRYPT 2020 by Alpirez Bock et al. (2020). It is based on an idea of Sahai and Waters (2014), according to which white-box can be obtained from puncturable pseudorandom functions (PRFs) and indistinguishability obfuscation (iO).

Other constructions using a secure hardware component to obtain obfuscation properties were proposed by Anderson (2008) and at TCC 2010 by Goyal et al. (2010). The latter is based on techniques from resettably secure computation, due to Goyal and Sahai (2009) at EUROCRYPT.

– Section 1.5. The extension of the EMV specifications to mobile transactions via near field communication (NFC) was specified in EMVCo (2008). In 2019, the EMVCo requirements documentation (EMVCo 2019) suggested to hard-code the EMV keys into the application code itself. In the same spirit, Mastercard Cloud-Based Payments (MCBP) (Mastercard 2014) aims at digitizing card credentials, and Mastercard has specifically recommended the use of white-box implementation for the secure storage of payment tokens (Mastercard 2017).

1.7. References

Aguilar Melchor, C., Barrier, J., Guelton, S., Guinet, A., Killijian, M.-O., Lepoint, T. (2016). NFLlib: NTT-based fast lattice library. In *CT-RSA 2016*, Sako, K. (ed.). Springer, Heidelberg.

Alpirez Bock, E., Brzuska, C., Fischlin, M., Janson, C., Michiels, W. (2020). Security reductions for white-box key-storage in mobile payments. In *ASIACRYPT 2020*, Moriai, S. and Wang, H. (eds). Springer, Heidelberg.

Anderson, W.E. (2008). On the secure obfuscation of deterministic finite automata. Cryptology ePrint Archive, Report 2008/184 [Online]. Available at: https://eprint.iacr.org/2008/184.

Barbu, G., Beullens, W., Dottax, E., Giraud, C., Houzelot, A., Li, C., Mahzoun, M., Ranea, A., Xie, J. (2022). ECDSA white-box implementations: Attacks and designs from WhibOx 2021 contest. Report 2022/385, Cryptology ePrint Archive [Online]. Available at: https://eprint.iacr.org/2022/385.

Barthelemy, L. (2020a). A first approach to asymmetric white-box cryptography and a study of permutation polynomials modulo 2^n in obfuscation. PhD Thesis, Sorbonne Université, Paris.

Barthelemy, L. (2020b). Toward an asymmetric white-box proposal. Cryptology ePrint Archive, Report 2020/893 [Online]. Available at: https://eprint.iacr.org/2020/893.

Bauer, S., Drexler, H., Gebhardt, M., Klein, D., Laus, F., Mittmann, J. (2022). Attacks against white-box ECDSA and discussion of countermeasures – A report on the WhibOx contest 2021. Report 2022/448, Cryptology ePrint Archive [Online]. Available at: https://eprint.iacr.org/ 2022/448.

Biham, E. and Shamir, A. (1997). Differential fault analysis of secret key cryptosystems. In *CRYPTO'97*, Kaliski, B.S. Jr. (ed.). Springer, Heidelberg.

Billet, O. (2005). Cryptologie multivariable. PhD Thesis, Université de Versailles-Saint-Quentin-en-Yvelines, Versailles.

Billet, O., Gilbert, H., Ech-Chatbi, C. (2004). Cryptanalysis of a white box AES implementation. In *SAC 2004*, Handschuh, H. and Hasan, A. (eds). Springer, Heidelberg.

Bitansky, N., Canetti, R., Goldwasser, S., Halevi, S., Kalai, Y.T., Rothblum, G.N. (2011). Program obfuscation with leaky hardware. In *ASIACRYPT 2011*, Lee, D.H. and Wang, X. (eds). Springer, Heidelberg.

Boneh, D., DeMillo, R.A., Lipton, R.J. (1997). On the importance of checking cryptographic protocols for faults (extended abstract). In *EUROCRYPT'97*, Fumy, W. (ed.). Springer, Heidelberg.

Bos, J.W., Hubain, C., Michiels, W., Teuwen, P. (2016). Differential computation analysis: Hiding your white-box designs is not enough. In *CHES 2016*, Gierlichs, B. and Poschmann, A.Y. (eds). Springer, Heidelberg.

Brier, E., Clavier, C., Olivier, F. (2004). Correlation power analysis with a leakage model. In *CHES 2004*, Joye, M. and Quisquater, J.-J. (eds). Springer, Heidelberg.

Bringer, J., Chabanne, H., Dottax, E. (2006). White-box cryptography: Another attempt. Cryptology ePrint Archive, Report 2006/468 [Online]. Available at: https://eprint.iacr.org/2006/468.

Chow, S., Eisen, P.A., Johnson, H., van Oorschot, P.C. (2002). A white-box DES implementation for DRM applications. In *Security and Privacy in Digital Rights Management*. Springer, Heidelberg.

Chow, S., Eisen, P.A., Johnson, H., van Oorschot, P.C. (2003). White-box cryptography and an AES implementation. In *SAC 2002*, Nyberg, K. and Heys, H.M. (eds). Springer, Heidelberg.

De Mulder, Y., Wyseur, B., Preneel, B. (2010). Cryptanalysis of a perturbated white-box AES implementation. In *INDOCRYPT 2010*, Gong, G. and Gupta, K.C. (eds). Springer, Heidelberg.

De Mulder, Y., Roelse, P., Preneel, B. (2013a). Cryptanalysis of the Xiao-Lai white-box AES implementation. In *SAC 2012*, Knudsen, L.R. and Wu, H. (eds). Springer, Heidelberg.

De Mulder, Y., Roelse, P., Preneel, B. (2013b). Revisiting the BGE attack on a white-box AES implementation. Cryptology ePrint Archive, Report 2013/450 [Online]. Available at: https://eprint.iacr.org/2013/450.

Delerablée, C., Lepoint, T., Paillier, P., Rivain, M. (2014). White-box security notions for symmetric encryption schemes. In *SAC 2013*, Lange, T., Lauter, K., Lisonek, P. (eds). Springer, Heidelberg.

Döttling, N., Mie, T., Müller-Quade, J., Nilges, T. (2011). Basing obfuscation on simple tamper-proof hardware assumptions. Cryptology ePrint Archive, Report 2011/675 [Online]. Available at: https://eprint.iacr.org/2011/675.

EMVCo (2008). Integrated circuit card specifications for payment systems. Book 2. Security and Key Management. Version 4.2 [Online]. Available at: www.emvco.com.

EMVCo (2019). EMV mobile payment: Software-based mobile payment security requirements. Technical Report [Online]. Available at: https://www.emvco.com/wp-content/uploads/documents/EMVCo-SBMP-16-G01-V1.2SBMPSecurityRequirements.pdf.

Feng, Q., He, D., Wang, H., Kumar, N., Choo, K.R. (2020). White-box implementation of Shamir's identity-based signature scheme. *IEEE Syst. J.*, 14(2), 1820–1829. doi: 10.1109/JSYST.2019.2910934.

Galissant, P. and Goubin, L. (2022). Resisting key-extraction and code-compression: A secure implementation of the HFE signature scheme in the white-box model. Cryptology ePrint Archive, Report 2022/138 [Online]. Available at: https://eprint.iacr.org/2022/138.

Garg, S., Gentry, C., Halevi, S., Raykova, M., Sahai, A., Waters, B. (2013). Candidate indistinguishability obfuscation and functional encryption for all circuits. In *54th FOCS*. IEEE, Berkeley.

Goubin, L., Masereel, J.-M., Quisquater, M. (2007). Cryptanalysis of white box DES implementations. In *SAC 2007*, Adams, C.M., Miri, A., Wiener, M.J. (eds). Springer, Heidelberg.

Goyal, V. and Sahai, A. (2009). Resettably secure computation. In *EUROCRYPT 2009*, Joux, A. (ed.). Springer, Heidelberg.

Goyal, V., Ishai, Y., Sahai, A., Venkatesan, R., Wadia, A. (2010). Founding cryptography on tamper-proof hardware tokens. In *TCC 2010*, Micciancio, D. (ed.). Springer, Heidelberg.

Jacob, M., Boneh, D., Felten, E.W. (2002). Attacking an obfuscated cipher by injecting faults. In *Security and Privacy in Digital Rights Management*. Springer, Heidelberg.

Karroumi, M. (2011). Protecting white-box AES with dual ciphers. In *ICISC 10*, Rhee, K.H. and Nyang, D. (eds). Springer, Heidelberg.

Kerckhoffs, A. (1883a). La cryptographie militaire. *Journal des sciences militaires*, 9, 5–38.

Kerckhoffs, A. (1883b). *La cryptographie militaire, ou les chiffres usités en temps de guerre, avec un nouveau procédé de déchiffrement applicable aux systèmes à double clef.* Librairie Militaire de L. Baudoin, Paris.

Kocher, P.C., Jaffe, J., Jun, B. (1999). Differential power analysis. In *CRYPTO'99*, Wiener, M.J. (ed.). Springer, Heidelberg.

Lepoint, T. and Rivain, M. (2013). Another nail in the coffin of white-box AES implementations. Cryptology ePrint Archive, Report 2013/455 [Online]. Available at: https://eprint.iacr.org/2013/455.

Lepoint, T., Rivain, M., De Mulder, Y., Roelse, P., Preneel, B. (2014). Two attacks on a white-box AES implementation. In *SAC 2013*, Lange, T., Lauter, K., Lisonek, P. (eds). Springer, Heidelberg.

Link, H.E. and Neumann, W.D. (2004). Clarifying obfuscation: Improving the security of white-box encoding. Cryptology ePrint Archive, Report 2004/025 [Online]. Available at: https://eprint.iacr.org/2004/025.

Marcolla, C., Sucasas, V., Manzano, M., Bassoli, R., Fitzek, F.H.P., Aaraj, N. (2022). Survey on fully homomorphic encryption, theory, and applications. *Proceedings of the IEEE*, 110(10), 1572–1609.

Mastercard (2014). Mastercard cloud-based payments – Mobile payment application functional description. Version 1.0.

Mastercard (2017). Mastercard mobile payment SDK security guide for MP SDK v1.0.6. Version 2.0. Technical Report [Online]. Available at: https://developer.mastercard.com/media/32/b3/b6a8b4134e50bfe53590c128085e/mastercard-mobile-payment-sdk-security-guide-v2.0.pdf.

Pippenger, N. and Fischer, M.J. (1979). Relations among complexity measures. *J. ACM*, 26(2), 361–381. doi: 10.1145/322123.322138.

Sahai, A. and Waters, B. (2014). How to use indistinguishability obfuscation: Deniable encryption, and more. In *46th ACM STOC*, Shmoys, D.B. (ed.). ACM Press, New York.

Sanfelix, E., de Haas, J., Mune, C. (2015). Unboxing the white-box: Practical attacks against obfuscated ciphers. Presentation, BlackHat Europe [Online]. Available at: https://www.blackhat.com/eu-15/briefings.html.

Shannon, C.E. (1949). Communication theory of secrecy systems. *Bell Systems Technical Journal*, 28(4), 656–715.

WhibOx Organizing Committee (2017). CHES 2017 CTF challenge – WhibOx contest [Online]. Available at: https://whibox.io/contests/2017/.

WhibOx Organizing Committee (2019). CHES 2019 CTF challenge – WhibOx contest [Online]. Available at: https://whibox.io/contests/2019/.

WhibOx Organizing Committee (2021). CHES 2021 CTF challenge – WhibOx contest [Online]. Available at: https://whibox.io/contests/2021/.

Wyseur, B., Michiels, W., Gorissen, P., Preneel, B. (2007). Cryptanalysis of white-box DES implementations with arbitrary external encodings. In *SAC 2007*, Adams, C.M., Miri, A., Wiener, M.J. (eds). Springer, Heidelberg.

Xiao, Y. and Lai, X. (2009). A secure implementation of white-box AES. In *2009 2nd International Conference on Computer Science and its Applications*. IEEE, Jeju.

Zhang, Y., He, D., Huang, X., Wang, D., Choo, K.R., Wang, J. (2020). White-box implementation of the identity-based signature scheme in the IEEE P1363 standard for public key cryptography. *IEICE Trans. Inf. Syst.*, 103-D(2), 188–195.

2

Gray-Box Attacks against White-Box Implementations

Aleksei UDOVENKO
CryptoExperts and SnT, University of Luxembourg, Luxembourg

2.1. Introduction

Secure white-box implementations of existing symmetric ciphers, such as the AES block-cipher, is a long-standing open problem in cryptography. The table-based implementations from seminal works of Chow et al. (2003a, 2003b) and their variants were broken by a variety of attacks. Recently, it was even noticed that classic side-channel attacks, such as differential power analysis (DPA) and differential fault attacks (DFA), can be adapted to easily break most existing white-box designs. What is special about these attacks is that they are generic and automated; they do not require a complete understanding of the design behind the implementation being attacked. This effectively reduces the cost for an attacker, removing or minimizing the human-driven reverse-engineering step (see Chapter 4 of this volume about code obfuscation techniques).

This observation leads to important questions: why are state-of-the-art *white-box* implementations susceptible to *gray-box* attacks? How different is the *white-box* setting from the *gray-box* setting with respect to these attacks? Can we apply the knowledge of protecting implementations against side-channel attacks to the white-box setting?

Embedded Cryptography 3,
coordinated by Emmanuel PROUFF, Guénaël RENAULT,
Matthieu RIVAIN and Colin O'FLYNN. © ISTE Ltd 2025.

Since the white-box model gives more power to adversaries, it is natural to further extend the usual gray-box model arising from the classic side-channel setting. As outlined above, we are interested in attacks that are sufficiently generic and automatic.

In this chapter, we will investigate these questions. Our hope is to give the reader an understanding of the close but complex relationships between the white- and gray-box models. Compared to Chapter 3 of this volume, this chapter shifts focus toward theoretical aspects of attacks and countermeasures. In addition, we only analyze attacks arising specifically in the white-box setting, thus skipping the DCA (as a reformulation of DPA) and the DFA attacks. We nonetheless emphasize the strength of these two attack classes against white-box designs.

– *Designer perspective*: to give more concrete feeling to this chapter, we suggest to keep in mind the following AES-based scenario as an example. A white-box designer selects a random AES-128 master key and creates an implementation performing single-block AES-128 encryption. The primary goal of the designer is to prevent the extraction of the master key from this implementation. In this chapter, we will not consider additional security requirements discussed in Chapter 1 of this volume, and we will only consider white-box implementations without external encodings, that is, implementing unaltered functionality of the cipher.

– *Adversarial perspective*: an adversary obtains the white-box implementation and attempts to extract the master key. In the general white-box setting, the adversary has full access to the implementation and is not restricted in methods. In this chapter, however, the adversary will be applying (or be limited to) particular attack methods. At a high level, the adversary will choose arbitrary inputs (plaintexts), record and analyze *computational traces* (see section 2.2), inject faults in the intermediate computations and record and analyze faulty outputs (ciphertexts) (see section 2.3).

– *Chapter overview*: specifics of the white-box setting are discussed in section 2.2. Section 2.3 shows how fault injections can be used to simplify white-box implementations and remove unprotected pseudorandomness, weakening possible gray-box countermeasures. Section 2.4 describes a simplification of the DPA attack arising from the absence of measurement noise in the white-box setting. Section 2.5 exhibits a recent cryptanalysis technique based on linear algebra for bypassing linear masking protections of an arbitrarily large order, and section 2.6 overviews known countermeasures against the algebraic attack.

2.2. Specifics of white-box side-channels

Gray-box attacks in the white-box model get more powerful, due to *determinism*, absence of inherent *measurement noise* and exposition of the *data-dependency graph* (DDG). In this section, we will briefly discuss these sources of increased power and also define *models of computation*, *computational traces* and *sensitive/predictable functions*.

2.2.1. *Determinism*

From the attacker's viewpoint, implementations in the white-box model are fully *deterministic*. Even if some inputs may play the role of randomness (required, for example, to implement a randomized encryption scheme), the adversary can easily fix these inputs to arbitrary constants. There are two important consequences of this fact.

First, all the countermeasures relying on randomness (such as masking and shuffling) have to derive it solely from the inputs (*pseudorandomly*). More importantly, this derivation has to be itself secure, obscure and robust to faults. In the spirit of this chapter, it should at least not be susceptible to generic and automated methods of randomness prediction or removal.

Second, determinism amplifies the impact of *fault* attacks. The same location in the code, time and/or memory can be faulted with full precision on multiple inputs. This makes fault attacks much easier to mount. In addition, fault injections can be used to detect randomness, or even to locate and group multiple shares of each value protected by masking schemes (see section 2.3).

2.2.2. *Precise measurements*

Compared to power analysis attacks, values computed in the white-box setting can be inspected and recorded precisely, without any measurement noise. This opens paths to advanced data-analysis attacks, such as the linear decoding analysis/algebraic attacks (see section 2.5). In addition, faster variants of DPA are possible based on exact value lookups, rather than on pairwise correlation computations (see section 2.4).

2.2.3. *Data-dependency graph and attack windows*

A white-box implementation gives out a DDG of computed values, which is the structure of the data flow inside the program. It leaks relations between computed values. The main purpose of DDG *analysis* is to focus attacks on small cohesive parts of the implementation (called *windows*), one at a time. This makes attacks of very high orders possible.

EXAMPLE 2.1.– Consider a multiplication gadget of any ISW-like masking scheme (see Chapter 2 of Volume 2). Let values x, y be shared as:

$$x = x_1 + \ldots + x_l \quad \text{and} \quad y = y_1 + \ldots + y_l$$

respectively. Then, the product $x \times y$ can be expressed as:

$$(x_1 + \ldots + x_l) \times (y_1 + \ldots + y_l) = x_1 y_1 + x_1 y_2 + \ldots + x_1 y_l + \ldots + x_l y_l.$$

The ISW-like masking schemes first *compute* products of all pairs $x_i y_j$ of shares, and then group them into shares of the resulting value $x \times y$ (together with extra random values).

Observe that all of the shares of the second operand form a subset of all multiplicands of each share of the first operand. For example, $y_1, \ldots, y_l$ are all multiplicands of x_1, because all products $x_1 y_1, \ldots, x_1 y_l$ are computed *explicitly*. This data-dependency information can be used to mount high-order attacks efficiently by focusing them on sets of multiplicands of single variables or by performing further analysis on multiple variables.

DEFINITION 2.1 (Attack Window).– *Attack window* is a (small) attacked part of the analyzed implementation. The window's size (in the number of included intermediate values) is denoted by n.

EXAMPLE 2.2.– Consider an implementation computing N values and some hypothetical "heavy" attack taking time $\mathcal{O}(n^3)$ on a window of size n. Running it on the full implementation would take time $\mathcal{O}(N^3)$. If the implementation is split into N/n windows of size n, the complexity becomes $\mathcal{O}(\frac{N}{n} n^3) = \mathcal{O}(Nn^2)$. The gain is tremendous: in an implementation with $N = 10^6$ instructions and an attack requiring window $n = 100$, the time goes from 10^{18} down to 10^{10}! Although in practice the windows should overlap significantly in order to cover all possible combinations of values, multiplying the optimized time by a small factor, the overall improvement is still very strong and gets better with heavier attacks (e.g. higher order correlation attacks or higher degree algebraic attacks).

Data-dependency analysis can be broadly classified by its scale. *Macroscopic* analysis includes automatic or manual (e.g. visual) location of high-level patterns in the DDG, such as iterative structures (encryption rounds) and clusters/communities (e.g. S-boxes). This bears similarities to visual inspection of memory access traces from Chapter 3 of this volume. *Microscopic* analysis covers low-level structures or patterns in the implementation, for example, identification of masking/obfuscation gadgets, higher order attacks on node siblings or small subgraphs.

2.2.4. *Computational model*

In order to make the presentation of attacks and countermeasures more concrete while still general, we need to choose an appropriate model of computations, that is, how the implementations are *defined*.

– *Random-access machine (RAM)*: the most realistic model is the RAM computational model, where programs consist of simple instructions such as arithmetic operations, reading from and writing into memory by constant or *dynamically* computed addresses. Word sizes can be bounded as in real-world CPUs. Specifics of the RAM model are studied in the context of real-world white-box implementations and code obfuscation in Chapters 3 and 4 of this volume.

– *Boolean/arithmetic circuits*: a much simpler model is given by *computational circuits*, defined over the binary field $\mathbb{F}_2 = \{0, 1\}$ or over any other field or ring (e.g. a prime field $\mathbb{F}_p$, an extension field such as the AES field $\mathbb{F}_{2^8}$, or the ring of integers $\mathbb{Z}$). Usually represented by directed acyclic graphs (DAGs), they also have an equivalent *static single assignment* (SSA) form, which is a program where each variable is assigned exactly once. The key differences of Boolean circuit-induced SSA programs from RAM programs are the absence of dynamic addressing of operands and, more importantly, the absence of control flow structures, such as conditional jumps and loops. While RAM programs can be simulated by Boolean circuits (up to a predetermined execution time), the cost of doing so may be non-negligible.

In this chapter, for the ease of exposition, we will mostly focus on and assume the Boolean circuits model (i.e. with variables and arithmetic operations over the field $\mathbb{F}_2$).

However, in most generic attacks/countermeasures, we will use $\mathbb{F}$ to denote an arbitrary field if it does not introduce technical difficulties.

NOTATION 2.1.– In figures illustrating circuits, we shall use $+/-$ to denote addition/subtraction in the field (which are both equal to the *"exclusive or"* (XOR) operation for the binary field $\mathbb{F}_2$) and $\times$ to denote multiplication in the field. An example of such a figure is given in Figure 2.1.

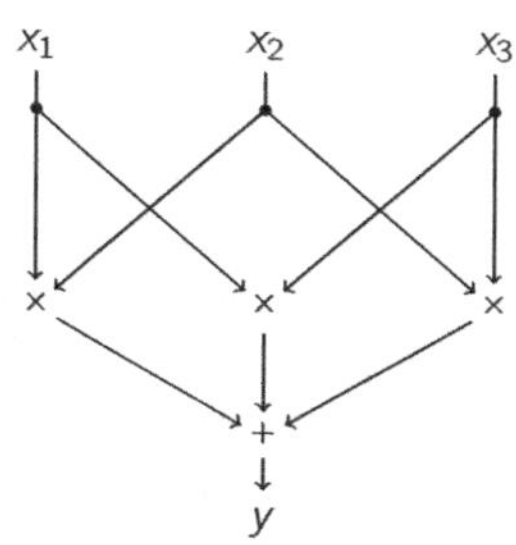

Figure 2.1. *Example of a Boolean circuit for computing the 3-bit majority function* $y = Maj(x_1, x_2, x_3) = x_1x_2 + x_1x_3 + x_2x_3$

2.2.5. Computational traces

One of the key tools used in gray-box attacks on white-box implementations is the recording of *computational traces*. While playing the same role as classic power or EM radiation traces, computational traces record *exact* values computed in an actual execution. Moreover, computational traces of programs allow easier synchronization across multiple executions: points of interest can be linked to instructions in the code, execution time in cycles, memory addresses or any combination of those. In this chapter, we will abstract from these details and assume that traces are already synchronized. This simplification is especially natural in Boolean circuit implementations. For practical details on recording, processing, synchronization and analysis of computational traces, we refer to Chapter 3 of this volume.

DEFINITION 2.2 (Computational Traces).– Let $C : \mathbb{F}^m \to \mathbb{F}^{m'}$ and I_C be an implementation of C, computing $n = |I_C|$ values in total (including inputs, intermediate values and outputs). Given a list $X \in (\mathbb{F}_2^m)^t$ of t inputs, the *computational trace* of I_C on X is a $t \times n$ matrix M, where the entry $M_{i,j}$ is equal to the jth computed value in I_C on the ith input from X. The matrix M is denoted by $\mathrm{Trace}(I_C, X)$.

EXAMPLE 2.3.– Consider the example circuit given in Figure 2.1. Let us define the computation order to be $I_C(x) = (x_1, x_2, x_3, x_1x_2, x_1x_3, x_2x_3, x_1x_2+x_1x_3+x_2x_3)$. Then, we can write:

$$X = \begin{pmatrix} x_1 = (0,0,0) \\ x_2 = (0,0,1) \\ x_3 = (0,1,0) \\ x_4 = (0,1,1) \\ x_5 = (1,0,0) \\ x_6 = (1,0,1) \\ x_7 = (1,1,0) \\ x_8 = (1,1,1) \end{pmatrix}, \quad \mathrm{Trace}(I_C, X) = \left(\begin{array}{ccc|ccc|c} 0 & 0 & 0 & 0 & 0 & 0 & 0 \\ 0 & 0 & 1 & 0 & 0 & 0 & 0 \\ 0 & 1 & 0 & 0 & 0 & 0 & 0 \\ 0 & 1 & 1 & 0 & 0 & 1 & 1 \\ 1 & 0 & 0 & 0 & 0 & 0 & 0 \\ 1 & 0 & 1 & 0 & 1 & 0 & 1 \\ 1 & 1 & 0 & 1 & 0 & 0 & 1 \\ 1 & 1 & 1 & 1 & 1 & 1 & 1 \end{array}\right) \qquad [2.1]$$

The ith row of the trace matrix corresponds to the computational trace on the input x_i. The jth *column* of the trace matrix corresponds to the jth (out of $n = 7$) component of $I_C(x)$ computed on all $m = 8$ chosen inputs, including the inputs themselves (the first three columns), the intermediate values (the next three columns) and the outputs (the last column). Although in this case the set X consists of all possible 3-bit inputs, in practice, it is only feasible to consider a relatively small subset of all inputs, chosen at random or according to some criteria.

2.2.6. Sensitive/predictable functions

A large number of gray-box attacks on white-box implementations can be formulated as solving the following problem.

PROBLEM 2.1 (Informal).– Given an implementation I_C of a function $C : \mathbb{F}^m \to \mathbb{F}^{m'}$, and a function $f : \mathbb{F}^m \to \mathbb{F}$, decide whether I_C computes functions "related" to f.

This problem is usually instantiated with f being a "sensitive function", which is a function that, if detected, leaks secret information about the implementation. In white-box implementations of encryption schemes, a sensitive function is typically an intermediate value computed in the *reference* implementation and depending on a small chunk of the secret (sub)key. The classic example is the output of an S-box in the first round of the AES block cipher. However, this problem can be interpreted more generally in the context of (cryptographic) obfuscation, where the role of the secret is played by the whole reference implementation.

NOTATION 2.2.– The set of k candidate sensitive functions to test (as in Problem 2.1) is denoted by $S \in (\mathbb{F}^{\mathbb{F}^m})^k$, where m is the size of the implementation's input and $\mathbb{F}^{\mathbb{F}^m}$ is the set of all functions mapping $\mathbb{F}^m$ to $\mathbb{F}$ (i.e. $s : \mathbb{F}^m \to \mathbb{F}$ for all $s \in S$).

Different gray-box attacks in the white-box model solve the problem for different definitions of the "relation" to f:

– *Equality*: the simplest is to define the relation to be "equality". That is, the sensitive function f has to be computed in the white-box implementation precisely, in a single intermediate value (e.g. in a node in a Boolean circuit). However, this means that the implementation does not protect f at all. This type of attack and its generalization to implementations protected with low-order Boolean masking are described in section 2.4.

– *Correlation*: defining the relation to be "high correlation" leads to classic DPA/DCA attacks. In DPA attacks (the gray-box model), the necessity to use correlation instead of exact matching stems from inherently noisy measurements. In DCA attacks (the white-box model), the advantage of using correlation is that it allows us to break weak nonlinear encodings, such as 4-bit random encodings in the classic white-box AES proposal by Chow et al., or, for example, linear encodings using non-uniform random masks. We refer to Chapter 3 of this volume for more practical details on the DCA attack.

– *Algebraic*: the relation can be defined to be "algebraic", requiring existence of a multi-variate polynomial of low-degree connecting intermediate values in the implementation and the sensitive function. The respective attack is called LDA (linear decoding analysis) or simply algebraic attack and is described in section 2.5.

Finally, we remark that the mix of the two paradigms – correlation and algebraic – is possible, resulting in LPN-based attacks[1], which however were not demonstrated in practice yet and will not be discussed in this chapter.

1 Learning parity with noise, the problem of solving noisy (erroneous) linear systems.

– *On fake sensitive functions*: in principle, a positive answer to Problem 2.1 does not guarantee that the detected sensitive function performs its genuine role in the white-box implementation. It may be used as pseudorandomness, be a part of fault countermeasures, or simply be added to confuse attackers and lead them into wrong paths. For example, in the case of white-box AES, the implementation may compute AES encryptions of the input under multiple dummy keys and discard them in the end, keeping only the real one. The adversary may then be forced to consider sensitive functions deeper in the implementation, such as S-box outputs after two rounds of encryption. It is an interesting unstudied question, whether dummy keys (or, in general, dummy computations of sensitive functions) can provide viable protection against attacks. In this chapter, we will focus solely on solving Problem 2.1 and assume absence of dummy sensitive functions.

The rest of the chapter is dedicated to specific attacks. Section 2.3 focuses on white-box-specific fault attacks. Section 2.4 presents an exact matching attack, based on computational traces. Section 2.5 describes a generic and powerful linear algebraic attack/linear decoding analysis, and section 2.6 overviews existing countermeasures against the algebraic attack. For protections against faults and the exact matching attack, we refer to general methods (see Chapters 7 and 12 of Volume 1, Part 1 of Volume 2, and also relevant is Chapter 8 of Volume 2).

Section	Type	Attack
2.3.1	Fault injection	Removal of pseudorandomness and dummy values
2.3.2		Location of linear shares
2.4.1	Exact matching	First-order matching (targets unprotected implementations)
2.4.2		Higher-order matching (targets low-order masked implementations)
2.5.1	Algebraic (LDA)	Linear algebraic (targets linear masking)
2.5.2		Differential algebraic (targets dummyless shuffling and linear masking)

Table 2.1. *Summary of attacks described in the chapter*

2.3. Fault injections

Fault injection becomes a very powerful tool in the white-box setting. The most powerful application is the *differential fault attack* (DFA). In Chapter 3 of this volume, the reader will learn about existing software tools allowing us to inject faults into programs. Part 3 of Volume 1 is fully dedicated to fault attacks and includes all relevant information and examples. The only difference in the white-box setting is that it is much easier to inject faults in the software setting. Therefore, in this section, we will ignore the basic DFA and assume that the implementation is not vulnerable to it, that is, it contains countermeasures preventing direct application of the attack. The focus thus will be on new applications such as pseudorandomness removal.

2.3.1. *Locating and removing pseudorandomness and dummy values*

A big difficulty for white-box designs is the absence of a reliable source of randomness. This prevents direct usage of standard countermeasures such as masking or shuffling. The natural idea is to use *pseudorandomness* generated solely from the input. In order for it to be unpredictable for any adversary, the pseudorandomness generator (PRG) must involve a secret, embedded at the compilation time. However, how should we protect *this* secret? This becomes a chicken-or-egg problem!

While it may sound desperate, a similar problem was already considered in the side-channel setting, more precisely, in the t-probing model. Since a true random number generator (TRNG) is very costly, a so-called *robust* pseudorandom number generator can be used, which requires only a negligible amount of true randomness for seeding. For more details, the reader can refer to Chapters 5 and 6 of this volume. Another possible advantage for the white-box designer is the ability to create non-standard PRGs. Here, the focus would be not on the *secrecy of the design*, but rather on greater *variability* of PRG instances with respect to different (fixed) secret keys. Nonetheless, the problem of a secure embedding of a PRG in a white-box implementation (even with respect to just extended gray-box attacks) is still a big open problem.

Besides the security of the PRG itself, another issue is the *integration* of the PRG with the main part of the implementation. Here, fault injections become a powerful tool for detecting and removing randomness. The basic idea is simple: *if modifying the same computed entry does not affect the output (on a large set of inputs), this entry in the implementation can be replaced by a constant, and operations involving it can be further pruned.* Such a step, if successful, simplifies the implementation and weakens any present countermeasures. Seemingly simple, it has a variety of options.

– *Node or wire?* It is important to distinguish *nodes* and *wires* in the implementations. A *node* corresponds to a computed value as a result of an operation. Faulting a *node* modifies its value *immediately* after its computation for *all* consequent uses. A *wire* corresponds to a single *use* of a computed value and can be faulted separately.

– *Absolute or relative change?* Another choice is whether the faulted value has to be set to a fixed value or modified by a fixed offset. This question is meaningful, even in Boolean circuits, where the only option might seem to be to flip the value. For example, a fault setting the value to 0 differs from this option by actually *not* injecting faults into executions where the value is already 0.

We shall illustrate the different variants on examples.

EXAMPLE 2.4.– Consider the following implementation of addition obfuscated with a dummy value. For a color version of this example, see www.iste.co.uk/prouff/cryptography3.zip.

Require: $x, y \in \mathbb{F}$
Ensure: $z = x + y$
1: $r \overset{\$}{\leftarrow} \mathbb{F}$ $\quad\triangleright$ possibly pseudorandom
2: $x' \leftarrow x + r$
3: $z' \leftarrow x' + y$
4: $z \leftarrow z' - r$
5: **return** z $\quad\triangleright z = x + y$

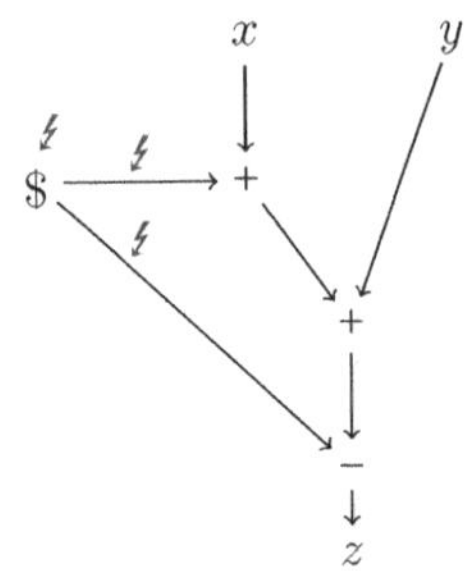

This is a simple example of obfuscation of arithmetic expressions. While such *local* examples can be easily deobfuscated by symbolic expression analysis (see Chapter 4 of this volume), fault injection is an alternative that can capture complex and/or non-local cases. For example, assume that x' and r are encrypted and decrypted after the line 2 by a function that is too complex for symbolic analysis, before being used in lines 3–5. This would prevent removal of the dummy value r by symbolic analysis.

On the other hand, any fault injection in r on line 1 (node fault) would not affect the output of the implementation, showing that r value is a dummy value and operations using it can be simplified. In the hypothetical case described above (encryption and decryption between lines 2 and 3), the first step would be to remove line 2 as redundant (letting $x' = x$). The input of the hypothetical encryption however would take the constant value $r = 0$, and would produce the same constant in the output to be used in line 4. This constant can be detected statistically or by another fault injection, allowing us to finally simplify line 4.

Injecting a fault into any single *wire* (lines 2, 4) would modify the output of the gadget, potentially affecting the output of the implementation, not leading to simplification. Faulting both *wires* however would show that the two wires only have to be equal and can be set to 0 (i.e. removed). This is particularly useful if r is used in other computations (i.e. has other outgoing wires) and cannot be faulted as a node. Here, the two wires have to be chosen from the outgoing wires of a single node, leading to much smaller combinatorial complexity than in the case, where the wires are chosen from the full implementation or even from a relatively small window. This emphasizes the usefulness of the DDG. See section 2.3.2 for an alternative single-wire fault attack.

EXAMPLE 2.5.– Consider a simple refresh gadget of 2-share linear masking. For a color version of this example, see www.iste.co.uk/prouff/cryptography3.zip.

Require: $x_1, x_2 \in \mathbb{F}$
Ensure: $x_1', x_2' \in \mathbb{F}, x_1' + x_2' = x_1 + x_2$
$r \overset{\$}{\leftarrow} \mathbb{F}$ ▷ possibly pseudorandom
$x_1' \leftarrow x_1 + r$
$x_2' \leftarrow x_2 - r$
return (x_1', x_2')

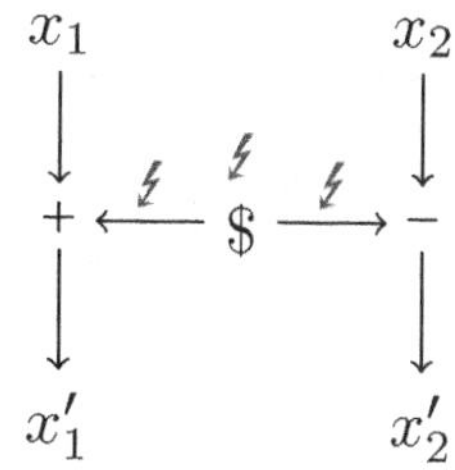

This example is completely analogous to the previous one. Note that symbolic analysis is not applicable here, since we first need to detect irrelevance of the values of x_1, x_2 separately and the relevance of the value of $x_1 + x_2$, which cannot be done locally (i.e. solely from this code fragment).

EXAMPLE 2.6.– Consider the following dummy operation. For a color version of this example, see www.iste.co.uk/prouff/cryptography3.zip.

Require: $x \in \mathbb{F}$
Ensure: $x' \in \mathbb{F}, x' = x$
generate $r, r' \in \mathbb{F}$ such that $r \cdot r' = 0$
▷ (possibly pseudorandom)
$x' \leftarrow x + r \cdot r'$
return x'

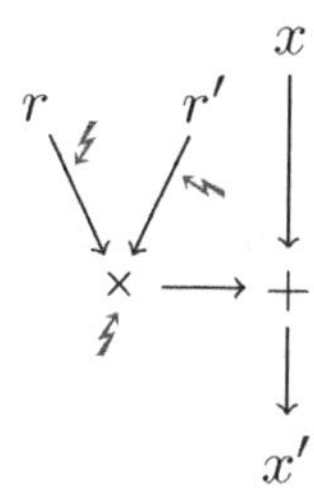

Consider fault injection in r when $r = 0, r' = 1$. Replacing $r = 0$ with $r = 1$ will result in $r \cdot r' = 1$, breaking the invariant $r \cdot r' = 0$ and corrupting the value x from main computations, failing to detect the dummy operation. On the other hand, setting r to 0 never corrupts the value of x. In addition, replacing r with 0 in the circuit would make it obvious that $r \cdot r' = 0$ can be removed altogether, allowing us to remove the full dummy operation.

2.3.2. *Detecting linear shares from output collisions*

In this section, we describe an interesting fault injection technique based on analysis of outputs of the attacked implementation. Indeed, a faulty output may often provide useful information about the injected fault. The idea is as follows.

Consider an implementation protected by a linear masking scheme, where some intermediate value $s \in \mathbb{F}$ is represented by a vector $(z_1, \ldots, z_l) \in \mathbb{F}^l$ such that:

$$z_1 + \ldots + z_l = s. \qquad [2.2]$$

Let us also assume, for simplicity, that the implementation detects faults in the protected value s and, when a fault is detected, outputs $H(s||r(x))$, where $r(x)$ is pseudorandomness computed from the implementation's input x and H is a cryptographic hash function.

Consider additive fault injection in any of the shares, that is,

$$z_i \leftarrow z_i + c,$$

for some integer $i, 1 \leq i \leq l$ and a constant $c \in \mathbb{F}, c \neq 0$. By [2.2], the effective value of s is changed to $s + c$ and the output of the implementation is equal to h given by:

$$h = H((s + c)||r).$$

Note that it is independent of the share index i, meaning that the implementation would always output h when the additive fault c is injected into a linear share of s on the global input x.

– *Attack outcome*: the main outcome of the attack is the *clusterisation* of intermediate functions in the implementation (i.e. nodes). Ideally, the resulting clusters should be small (but not singletones), precisely leaking closely related intermediate values, such as shares of the same protected value. Small clusters can further be used for deeper analysis and higher order attacks, including detection of linear shares, which is the main inspiration for the attack.

Detecting and removing linear shares can be done in a way similar to 2-wire fault injections from section 2.3.1. More precisely, let $z_1, \ldots z_l$ be a discovered cluster. Then, inject faults $z_i \leftarrow z_i + c, z_j \leftarrow z_j - c$ for some indexes $i \neq j$ and $c \in \mathbb{F}, c \neq 0$. If the output is not faulty (for a sufficiently large number of inputs), then the implementation can be rewritten into $z_i \leftarrow z_i + z_j, z_j \leftarrow 0$ (because there is a value of c equivalent to this rewrite). While a new addition operation is added, the redundancy and pseudorandomness of the implementation decreases. In addition, the replacement $z_j \leftarrow 0$ would likely lead to simplifications of the consequent operations having z_j as an operand. Again, repeating the procedure for all pairs in the cluster has potential to remove the linear masking completely, significantly simplifying the implementation.

– *False positives*: the described attack is not perfect and may produce false positives – group intermediate values that do not actually play the role of additive shares of the same protected value. Those may occur for various reasons, including specifics of the underlying implementation, used countermeasures, etc. False positives occurring due to "coincidental" equivalences in the underlying data (especially relevant for small fields $\mathbb{F}$, e.g. $\mathbb{F} = \mathbb{F}_2$) may be easily detected and removed by repeating the fault injections on discovered clusters.

For example, if the implementation computes $s'' = s \cdot s'$ and outputs $H(s''||r)$, and each of s, s' are shared as in [2.2], an additive fault injected into a share of s leading to $s = 0$ would produce the same output $h = H(0||r)$ as a fault injection into a share of s' leading to $s' = 0$. However, repeating the procedure on various inputs would allow us to exclude this false positive.

Another source of false positives may be due to low-entropy output (or, more generally, conditional entropy of the output on the (faulted) intermediate values s given the input x). In particular, a fault-detection countermeasure that returns a fixed output (e.g. all zeros) would group all faults in one bin, not leaking any information on the internal structure of the implementation.

– *Countermeasures*: one weakness that the attack highlights is that detecting faults in the underlying masked values may not be enough: shares themselves should be protected in some way.

On the other hand, this attack shows that seemingly random faulty output of the implementation may still convey a lot of information to the attacker. A possible conclusion could be that *it is best to return a special fixed output (e.g. all zeros) on a fault detection*, rather than a corrupted/randomized output.

For general countermeasures against fault attacks, we refer the reader to Chapter 12 of Volume 1.

2.4. Exact matching attack

In this section, we describe a simple yet powerful attack exploiting the absence of measurement noise in white-box designs, called the *exact matching attack*. This aims to solve the outlined Problem 2.1. While it is applicable in fewer scenarios than the generic correlation attacks (DPA/DCA), it is much faster in those few cases. In particular, it is probably the fastest way to break unprotected implementations or implementations protected by low-order (up to 4) Boolean masking schemes. For masking schemes of even higher order, better performance is achieved by the linear algebraic attack (section 2.5).

2.4.1. *First-order exact matching attack*

In classic first-order correlation attacks (DPA/DCA), each point of interest in the power traces is evaluated against all possible (partial) key candidates, by computing a correlation over all recorded traces with predicted values of the selected function. This leads to complexity at least proportional to nkt (trace size $\times$ key size $\times$ number of traces). Another way to look at it is to consider two sets containing n and k t-bit vectors, respectively. The correlation attacks aim to find a pair of vectors, one from each set, which have the highest correlation. However, in an unprotected white-box implementation, predicted vectors from the second set would appear in the first set in full, without any measurement noise. The problem then reduces to intersecting two sets of vectors, which can be done much faster using hash tables. The complexity of this method is $\mathcal{O}(nt + kt)$. Usually, $k < n$ and thus the complexity of the first-order exact matching attack is proportional to nt, which is k times faster than standard DCA. The attack procedure is detailed in Algorithm 2.1.

Algorithm 2.1. First-order exact matching attack

Require: an implementation I_C of $C : \mathbb{F}^m \to \mathbb{F}^{m'}$
Require: a list of k sensitive function candidates $S \in (\mathbb{F}^{\mathbb{F}^m})^k$ ($s : \mathbb{F}^m \to \mathbb{F}$ for $s \in S$)
Ensure: $\tilde{S} \subseteq S$ - candidate functions computed in I_C

1: $X = (x_1, \ldots, x_t) \xleftarrow{\$} (\mathbb{F}^m)^t$ ▷ choose t random inputs
2: $D \leftarrow$ hash-map $\{(s(x_1), \ldots, s(x_t)) \rightsquigarrow s \mid s \in S\}$ ▷ traces of sensitive functions
3: $T \leftarrow \text{Trace}(I_C, X) \in \mathbb{F}^{t \times n}$ ▷ record computational traces
4: $\tilde{S} \leftarrow \emptyset$
5: **for** each column c of T, $c \in \mathbb{F}^t$ **do**
6:     **if** $c \in D$ **then**
7:         $\tilde{S} \leftarrow \tilde{S} \cup \{D[c]\}$
8:     **end if**
9: **end for**
10: **return** $\tilde{S}$

– *Complexity*: step 2 has time complexity $\mathcal{O}(kt)$ evaluations of a sensitive function. Step 3 and the loop on Steps 5–9 both have time complexity $\mathcal{O}(nt)$, which is typically dominating. Again, this provides significant improvement over the DCA complexity $\mathcal{O}(nkt)$ by a factor of k. For example, in the case of a classic attack on the first round of AES, the complexity is reduced by a factor of 256 per each S-box (the number of candidate keys). Furthermore, the DCA attack analyzes each S-box separately, effectively multiplying the complexity by a factor of 16. In the exact matching attack, on the other hand, we can put the candidate functions for all S-boxes in one hash table, increasing only the $\mathcal{O}(kt)$ complexity part by a factor of 16. For typical large white-box implementations, this does not affect the overall complexity $\mathcal{O}(nt)$. This means that the overall gain of the exact matching attack over the standard DCA on an unprotected implementation is about a factor of $4096 = 2^{12}$. The gain increases further if the attacker considers more sensitive functions, for example, each of the output bits of the S-boxes, or even their linear combinations.

The downside of the exact matching attack is that it is less powerful than the DCA attack, as it essentially requires an unprotected implementation or a serious flaw in implementation exhibiting a sensitive function in clear. In the following, we will show that it can be used to also attack masked implementations.

2.4.2. *Higher order exact matching attack*

This method easily generalizes to attack implementations protected with linear masking. Consider the masking equation:

$$x_1 + x_2 + \ldots + x_l = s,$$

where s is a sensitive value. The idea is to rewrite the equation as:

$$x_1 + \ldots + x_h = -(x_{h+1} + \ldots + x_l) + s,$$

where h can be set, for example, to $\lceil l/2 \rceil$. Now, computational traces of candidates for the left-hand side of the equation can be put into a hash table, and computational traces of candidates for the right-hand side of the equations can be iteratively checked for a match in the table. This requires enumerating all $\binom{n}{h}$ choices of h shares in the implementation (window) in the first step, and enumerating all $\binom{n}{l-h}$ choices of $l - h$ shares in the second step. Note that the side to put in the table (the left-hand side or the right-hand side) can be chosen to minimize the memory complexity, and the choice does not affect the time complexity. The case of the left-hand side is described in Algorithm 2.2.

– *Complexity*: we naturally assume $h \ll n$ (i.e. the implementation is much larger than the attacked number of shares), so that $\binom{n}{h}$ can be well approximated by $\frac{n^h}{h!}$. This attack is superseded by the LDA attack (section 2.5) for the number of shares $l \geq 5$. Therefore, for simplicity, we can ignore the factor $\frac{1}{h!}$ (note that $h \leq l \leq 4$). The complexity of the first stage (table generation) is thus $\mathcal{O}(n^h t)$, and the complexity of the second stage (table lookups) is $\mathcal{O}(n^{l-h} kt)$. In order to minimize the overall complexity, h can be set to:

$$h = \left\lceil \frac{1}{2}(l + \log_n k) \right\rfloor.$$

When the number of sensitive functions is small ($k \ll n$), this leads to the setting $h = \lceil l/2 \rfloor$. The resulting complexities for $l \leq 4$ are given in Table 2.2. We recall that the memory complexity is given by the table size, which can be chosen to be the smallest value of $\mathcal{O}(n^h t)$ and $\mathcal{O}(n^{l-h} kt)$.

Algorithm 2.2. Higher-order exact matching attack

Require: an implementation I_C of $C : \mathbb{F}^m \to \mathbb{F}^{m'}$
Require: a list of k sensitive function candidates $S \in (\mathbb{F}^{\mathbb{F}^m})^k$ ($s : \mathbb{F}^m \to \mathbb{F}$ for $s \in S$)
Require: integers $h, l, 0 \le h \le l$
Ensure: $\tilde{S} \subseteq S$ - candidate functions computed in I_C

$X \overset{\$}{\leftarrow} (\mathbb{F}^m)^t$ ▷ choose t random inputs
$T \leftarrow \text{Trace}(I_C, X) \in \mathbb{F}^{t \times n}$ ▷ record computational traces
$S' \leftarrow \{(s, (s(x_1), \ldots, s(x_t)))) \mid s \in S\}$ ▷ precompute sensitive function values
$D \leftarrow \emptyset$
for each combination $(c_1, \ldots, c_h)$ of h columns of T, $c_i \in \mathbb{F}^t$ **do**
  $D \leftarrow D \cup \{(c_1 + \ldots + c_h)\}$
end for
$\tilde{S} \leftarrow \emptyset$
for each combination $(c_1, \ldots, c_{l-h})$ of $l - h$ columns of T, $c_i \in \mathbb{F}^t$ **do**
  for each $(s, v) \in S'$ **do**
    $c \leftarrow v + c_1 + \ldots + c_{l-h}$
    if $c \in D$ **then**
      $\tilde{S} \leftarrow \tilde{S} \cup \{s\}$
    end if
  end for
end for
return $\tilde{S}$

l	h	Time complexity	Memory	Comment
1	1	$O(nt + kt)$	$O(kt)$	section 2.4.1
2	1	$O(nkt)$	$O(nt)$	same time complexity as first-order DCA
3	2	$O(n^2t + nkt)$	$O(nkt)$	feasible for small attack windows
4	2	$O(n^2kt)$	$O(n^2t)$	feasible for small attack windows

Table 2.2. *Time complexities of the exact matching attack for masking order l up to 4*

– *Countermeasures*: countermeasures against the exact matching attack are not white-box specific. The attack's complexity is exponential in the number of shares; therefore, linear masking schemes of a sufficiently larger order should ensure security (see Part 1 of Volume 2 dedicated to masking). It is important however to distinguish the source of hardness in the two cases: in the side-channel setting, the complexity arises from the measurement noise, amplified when multiple measurements are combined; in the white-box exact matching attack, the complexity arises from the combinatorial explosion of possible locations of shares in the attacked windows.

2.5. Linear decoding analysis/algebraic attacks

This section presents *the linear decoding analysis* (LDA), also called *the (linear) algebraic attack*. It can be seen as a natural continuation of the exact matching attack from section 2.4, as it also exploits the absence of measurement noise in the white-box model.

NOTE.– The linear algebraic attack was first used to break the longest surviving challenge of the WhibOx 2017 competition of white-box AES implementations. The core part of that implementation was protected using first-order masking. However, the surprising power of the algebraic attack is that it is capable of breaking *any* kind of linear masking *of any order*, given that all the shares are present in one of the attacked windows.

The main idea comes from the observation that the (higher order) exact matching attack finds a small subset of columns of the matrix of computational traces that sums to a given candidate vector of values of the target sensitive function. The requirement on the size of the subset can be lifted by increasing the number of traces (the number of rows in the matrix), which should decrease the chances of false positive solutions to stay. Then, the problem is simply about solving a system of linear equations: given the trace matrix $T \in \mathbb{F}_2^{t \times n}$ and a vector $s \in \mathbb{F}_2^t$ (a candidate sensitive function computed on the traced set of inputs), find a vector $z \in \mathbb{F}_2^n$ such that:

$$T \times z = s.$$

The *existence* of a solution is itself a solution of Problem 2.1 in the case of the sensitive function in the implementation being split into (an arbitrary amount of) linear shares. Furthermore, a solution $z \in \mathbb{F}_2^t$ indicates the *location* of shares in the implementation.

In section 2.5.1, we will discuss more deeply the basic algebraic attack, possible optimisations and its improvement by restriction of inputs. Then, in section 2.5.2, we will describe how *differential LDA* can efficiently break basic shuffling, even combined with linear masking. Finally, in section 2.6, we will study how to protect against the algebraic attack.

2.5.1. *Basic algebraic attack*

The basic LDA attack (solving Problem 2.1) is described by pseudocode in Algorithm 2.3.

– *Complexity*: since $t \approx n$, the complexity of solving a system of t linear equations in n variables is given by the matrix multiplication constant ω, which for practical purposes is given by the Strassen's matrix multiplication algorithm with $\omega = 2.8$. The complexity of the attack is thus $\mathcal{O}(n^{\omega}) = \mathcal{O}(n^{2.8})$.

Algorithm 2.3. First-order LDA / linear algebraic attack

Require: an implementation I_C of $C : \mathbb{F}^m \to \mathbb{F}^{m'}$
Require: a sensitive function candidate $s : \mathbb{F}^m \to \mathbb{F}$
Ensure: True if the candidate function is detected in I_C (possibly split into linear shares), or False otherwise

$t \leftarrow n + \varepsilon$, for a small integer ε
$X \overset{\$}{\leftarrow} (\mathbb{F}^m)^t$ ▷ choose t random inputs
$\tilde{s} \leftarrow (s(x_1), \ldots, s(x_t)) \in \mathbb{F}^t$ ▷ compute the sensitive function on X
$T \leftarrow \text{Trace}(I_C, X) \in \mathbb{F}^{t \times n}$ ▷ record computational traces
return [the matrix equation $T \times v = s$ has a solution in v]

– *Batch testing candidates*: usually, the attacker needs to test multiple candidates for a sensitive function. The naive approach would be to test each candidate one by one. This leads to complexity $\mathcal{O}(n^{2.8}k)$ for testing k candidate functions. However, solving the same linear system (defined by T) for multiple different target vectors $\tilde{s}$ can be optimized.

The idea is to compute the parity check matrix K (i.e. a basis of the left kernel of T):

$$K \in \mathbb{F}^{\varepsilon' \times t} : \text{rowspan}\, K = \ker T^{\top} = \{v \in \mathbb{F}^t \mid v \times K = 0\},$$

where $T^{\top}$ is the transpose of T and $\varepsilon' \geq \varepsilon$ is the left nullity of T. Observe that:

$$K \times s = K \times T \times v = 0$$

for all s having solution $T \times v = s$. It follows that a candidate sensitive vector s can be checked by a matrix multiplication by K from the left. Note that each row K_i of K filters a wrong candidate s with probability $1/|\mathbb{F}|$. Therefore, testing a candidate s by each single row of K would require on average $1 + 1/|\mathbb{F}| + 1/|\mathbb{F}|^2 + \ldots \leq 2$ inner product calculations (i.e. $\langle K_i, s \rangle$), each having time complexity $\mathcal{O}(t) = \mathcal{O}(n)$. Since the parity check matrix can be computed in time $\mathcal{O}(n^{\omega})$, the total time complexity is $\mathcal{O}(n^{2.8} + nk)$. The optimized batch algorithm is illustrated in Algorithm 2.4.

2.5.2. *Differential algebraic attack against shuffling*

In this section, we will study how the algebraic attack can be tweaked into a *differential* algebraic attack to break the classic shuffling countermeasure (see Chapter 7 of Volume 1).

Algorithm 2.4. First-order LDA / linear algebraic attack (batched version)

Require: an implementation I_C of $C : \mathbb{F}^m \rightarrow \mathbb{F}^{m'}$
Require: a list of k sensitive function candidates $S \in (\mathbb{F}^{\mathbb{F}^m})^k$ $(s : \mathbb{F}^m \rightarrow \mathbb{F}$ for $s \in S)$
Ensure: $\tilde{S} \subseteq S$ - candidate functions computed in I_C

$t \leftarrow n + \varepsilon$, for a small integer ε
$X \xleftarrow{\$} (\mathbb{F}^m)^t$ ▷ choose t random inputs
$\tilde{s} \leftarrow (s(x_1), \ldots, s(x_t)) \in \mathbb{F}^t$ ▷ compute the sensitive function on X
$T \leftarrow \text{Trace}(I_C, X) \in \mathbb{F}^{t \times n}$ ▷ record computational traces
$K \leftarrow \ker T^\top \in \mathbb{F}^{\varepsilon' \times t}$ ▷ parity check matrix
$\tilde{S} \leftarrow \emptyset$
for each $s \in S$ **do**
  for each row r of K **do**
    if $\langle r, s \rangle \neq 0$ **then**
      break
    end if
  end for
  if no break **then**
    $\tilde{S} \leftarrow \tilde{S} \cup \{s\}$
  end if
end for
return $\tilde{S}$

Recall that shuffling permutes a group of identical computations on different inputs, such as the 16 AES S-boxes in one round. In terms of gray-box attacks in the white-box model, this countermeasure effectively permutes a subset of entries in computational traces on each execution. We will not rely on the implementation details of shuffling and only exploit the described shuffling effect on the computational traces.

First, note that shuffling leaks the sum of shuffled values as a linear function of computed values. Indeed, assume q slots are shuffled using a permutation σ. If the original computed values were:

$$x_1, \ldots, x_q,$$

then a computational trace would contain

$$x_{\sigma(1)}, \ldots, x_{\sigma(q)}.$$

Observe that:

$$\sum_{i=1}^{q} x_{\sigma(i)} = \sum_{i=1}^{q} x_i$$

is a linear function of the computed values (e.g. memory cells storing shuffled values) equal to the sum of all x_i, independently of the shuffling permutation σ. This leakage is independent of the shuffling method and it follows from the shuffling property itself.

The sum leakage can be exploited efficiently using a *chosen-plaintext attack*, namely, *differential* LDA. The idea is to encrypt two pairs of plaintexts following a chosen difference, record the two computational traces, subtract them and run LDA on the resulting differential trace. To do this, an attacker needs to compute the *difference* of the candidate sensitive function on the two inputs, which can be much simpler to do than to compute the candidate sensitive function on one input. We will illustrate this method on the case of AES.

– *Example application to AES*: consider AES implemented with shuffled S-boxes and, possibly, protected with linear masking of an arbitrary order. As noticed above, shuffling leaks the sum of shuffled values. In particular, the sum of all S-box outputs in the first round is leaked by a linear function of the computed values. As this sensitive function depends on 16 key bytes, a standard LDA attack is not possible. To mount differential LDA, we encrypt a pair (p, p') of plaintexts differing in one byte (say, the first byte) and record the respective computational traces $T_1, T_1' \in \mathbb{F}_2^n$. Then, there exists a linear function, defined by (unknown) $\alpha \in \mathbb{F}_2^n$, such that:

$$\langle \alpha, T_1 \rangle = S(p_1 \oplus k_1) \oplus \ldots \oplus S(p_{16} \oplus k_{16}), \qquad [2.3]$$

$$\langle \alpha, T_1' \rangle = S(p_1' \oplus k_1) \oplus \ldots \oplus S(p_{16}' \oplus k_{16}), \qquad [2.4]$$

where S is some chosen output bit of the AES S-box. Since $p_i = p_i'$ for all i except $i = 1$, we have:

$$\langle \alpha, T_1 \rangle \oplus \langle \alpha, T_1' \rangle = \langle \alpha, T_1 \oplus T_1' \rangle = S(p_1 \oplus k_1) \oplus S(p_1' \oplus k_1).$$

Repeating the pair encryption step for t pairs, we obtain computational trace matrices $T, T' \in \mathbb{F}_2^{t \times n}$ such that:

$$\alpha \times (T \oplus T') = s, \qquad [2.5]$$

where $s \in \mathbb{F}_2^t$ is such that:

$$s_i = S(p_{i,1} \oplus k_1) \oplus S(p_{i,1}' \oplus k_1),$$

and $p_{i,1}$ and $p'_{i,1}$ are first bytes of the respective plaintexts from the ith pair. Solving the linear system [2.5] allows us to test a candidate sensitive function, which depends only on k_1 (the first key byte).

This method efficiently breaks a combination of classic shuffling and linear masking.

2.6. Countermeasures against the algebraic attack

The LDA attack being powerful against standard gray-box countermeasures, a natural question arises: How to protect implementations against this class of attacks? In this section, we will give a brief look over available methods.

> This section only provides a high-level and not comprehensive overview of existing countermeasures against the algebraic attacks, which is a recent and ongoing topic in white-box cryptography research. Yet the section is rather technical. The reader is encouraged to follow the references in the end of the chapter for more details.

Box 2.1. *Section note*

2.6.1. *Security model sketch*

The first step is to define a security model. For example, in the side-channel field, most often the t-probing model is used: it is assumed that an attacker may probe (read) at most t different wires during a computation. However, in the LDA attack, the adversary may read *all* wires, but only combine the resulting values using linear combinations (or with functions of degree at most d, in the case of generalized degree-d algebraic attacks). The crucial difference is that, in the t-probing model, the adversary has limited information but is not limited in what they can do with it; in the security model for algebraic attacks, we cannot limit the information, and thus, we have to restrict the range of an adversary's manipulations on the available data. Roughly speaking, an adversary may only collect computational traces and run the LDA attack on them against sensitive function candidates.

How could we define sensitive function candidates generally? Intuitively, these are functions that an adversary may *compute* on any input, aiming to find them in the given obfuscated implementation (in the sense of Problem 2.1). As we should not limit the adversary's analysis of a reference implementation and possible choices of sensitive functions, we cannot answer this question definitively. Instead, we can formalize the element of *unpredictability* by an attacker: we can allow the use of *randomness*, similarly to how it is done in the side-channel field. This idea is rather fragile in the white-box model, where randomness is under the adversary's control. Hypothetically, the randomness for countermeasures has to be generated as pseudorandomness, computed from the input in a secure and obscure way, so that it cannot be detected and removed. However, this is already beyond the state of the art in white-box cryptography. Importantly, the introduction of randomness allows us to define a security model for *encoded computations*: assuming a secure input encoding step and a source of randomness, we can define and construct countermeasures against the LDA attack.

A countermeasure in such a model can be formalized as a *scheme*.

DEFINITION 2.3 (Scheme).– Let $f : \mathbb{F}^m \to \mathbb{F}^{m'}$ be a function. A *scheme* S *computing* f consists of

1) an *encoding function* $\mathsf{S.enc}(x, r_e) : \mathbb{F}^m \times \mathbb{F}^{\tau_e} \to \mathbb{F}^{m_e}$;
2) an *implementation* $\mathsf{S.comp}(x', r_c) : \mathbb{F}^{m_e} \times \mathbb{F}^{\tau_c} \to \mathbb{F}^{m_c}$;
3) a *decoding function* $\mathsf{S.dec}(y') : \mathbb{F}^{m_c} \to \mathbb{F}^{m'}$.

It is required that for all $x \in \mathbb{F}^m, r_e \in \mathbb{F}^{\tau_e}, r_c \in \mathbb{F}^{\tau_c}$

$$\mathsf{S.dec}(\mathsf{S.comp}(\mathsf{S.enc}(x, r_e), r_c)) = f(x).$$

Here, the encoding and decoding functions are assumed to be secure and the attacker is not allowed to attack them in the model. The critical part is the main implementation $\mathsf{S.comp}$, which takes an encoded input and randomness, and computes an encoded output *securely from algebraic attacks*. The security is formalized by the following definition.

DEFINITION 2.4 (Algebraically secure scheme).– A scheme S is said to be *algebraically secure* if, for any nonconstant linear combination of intermediate functions in $\mathsf{S.comp}$), its composition with $\mathsf{S.enc} = \mathsf{S.enc}(x, r_e)$ on the first input is nonconstant for any *fixed* $x \in \mathbb{F}^m$:

$$\forall f \in \text{span}\,(\mathsf{S.comp}), f \text{ non-constant}, \quad \forall x \in \mathbb{F}^m \qquad [2.6]$$

$$g : (r_e, r_c) \mapsto f(\mathsf{S.enc}(x, r_e), r_c) \text{ is non-constant.} \qquad [2.7]$$

REMARK.– This simplified definition does not *quantify* security, that is, limit success probability of a linear algebraic attack. Detailed analysis and the generalized case of higher degree attacks is out of scope of this book.

The definition requires all possible linear combinations of functions in the main circuit to depend on randomness (unpredictable to adversaries), *for any fixed main input*. This prevents linear algebraic attacks as an adversary cannot (reliably) compute *any* sensitive function candidate that would be accepted by the attack on any subset of inputs.

We are now ready to study concrete countermeasures, namely, *nonlinear masking* and *dummy shuffling*.

2.6.2. *Nonlinear masking*

The algebraic/LDA attack exploits the fact that classic masking schemes are linear. It is natural therefore to use *nonlinear* masking schemes. We first show how to define a masking-based scheme (as in Definition 2.3).

DEFINITION 2.5.– Given a masking scheme $\mathcal{M}$ and an implementation I_C of $C : \mathbb{F}^m \to \mathbb{F}^{m'}$, the algebraic countermeasure scheme S is defined as follows:

1) S.enc(x, r_e) uses $\mathcal{M}$.enc to encode each element of x using an independent chunk of randomness from r_e.

2) S.comp(x', r_c) computes the implementation I_C on x' and independent chunks of randomness from r_c using gadgets from $\mathcal{M}$ (operating on encoding values).

3) S.dec(y', r_e) uses $\mathcal{M}$.dec to decode each element of y'.

The simplest nonlinear masking scheme is based on the decoding function:

$$(a, b, c) \mapsto ab \oplus c.$$

It is called *minimalist quadratic masking scheme* (MQMS). The respective encoding, decoding and XOR/AND gadget implementations are provided in Algorithm 2.5. The resulting scheme is algebraically secure; however, security analysis of this masking scheme is highly non-trivial and is out of scope of this book.

It is important to mention that *algebraic security* is not directly related to *probing security*. Indeed, standard linear masking schemes are probing secure but not algebraically secure. The MQMS scheme is a counter-example for the other direction, which should be a simple exercise to the reader.

EXERCISE 2.1.– Show that the encoding function $(x, r_a, r_b) \mapsto (r_a, r_b, r_a r_b \oplus x)$ is not secure against correlation attacks (with r_a, r_b sampled independently and uniformly at random).

The decoding formula of the minimalist quadratic masking scheme can be generalized to the following form:

$$(x_1, x_2, \ldots, x_d, x'_1, \ldots, x'_t) \mapsto x_1 x_2 \ldots x_d \oplus x'_1 \oplus \ldots \oplus x'_t.$$

Algorithm 2.5. Minimalist Quadratic Masking

function $\mathcal{M}$.enc(x, r_a, r_b)
    return $(r_a, r_b, r_a r_b \oplus x)$
end function

function $\mathcal{M}$.dec(a, b, c)
    return $ab \oplus c$
end function

function $\mathcal{M}$.gadgetNOT(a, b, c)
    return $(a, b, c \oplus 1)$
end function

function $\mathcal{M}$.gadgetXOR($(a, b, c), (d, e, f), (r_a, r_b, r_c), (r_d, r_e, r_f)$)
    $(a, b, c) \leftarrow \text{REFRESH}((a, b, c), (r_a, r_b, r_c))$
    $(d, e, f) \leftarrow \text{REFRESH}((d, e, f), (r_d, r_e, r_f))$
    $x \leftarrow a \oplus d$
    $y \leftarrow b \oplus e$
    $z \leftarrow c \oplus f \oplus ae \oplus bd$
    return (x, y, z)
end function

function $\mathcal{M}$.gadgetAND($(a, b, c), (d, e, f), (r_a, r_b, r_c), (r_d, r_e, r_f)$)
    $(a, b, c) \leftarrow \text{REFRESH}((a, b, c), (r_a, r_b, r_c))$
    $(d, e, f) \leftarrow \text{REFRESH}((d, e, f), (r_d, r_e, r_f))$
    $m_a \leftarrow bf \oplus r_c e$
    $m_d \leftarrow ce \oplus r_f b$
    $x \leftarrow ae \oplus r_f$
    $y \leftarrow bd \oplus r_c$
    $z \leftarrow am_a \oplus dm_d \oplus r_c r_f \oplus cf$
    return (x, y, z)
end function

function REFRESH($(a, b, c), (r_a, r_b, r_c)$)
    $m_a \leftarrow r_a \cdot (b \oplus r_c)$
    $m_b \leftarrow r_b \cdot (a \oplus r_c)$
    $r_c \leftarrow m_a \oplus m_b \oplus (r_a \oplus r_c)(r_b \oplus r_c) \oplus r_c$
    $a \leftarrow a \oplus r_a$
    $b \leftarrow b \oplus r_b$
    $c \leftarrow c \oplus r_c$
    return (a, b, c)
end function

This expression can be viewed as a merge of the linear masking scheme (the part $x'_1 \oplus \ldots \oplus x'_t$) and the nonlinear masking scheme (the part $x_1 x_2 \ldots x_d$). It allows us to achieve more efficient gadgets than a simple composition of the two masking schemes (one applied on top of the other). However, provably secure gadgets for such decoding functions are known only for $d \leq 3$ (providing security against degree-2 algebraic attacks) and arbitrary t. We invite the interested reader to follow the references at the end of the chapter.

2.6.3. *Dummy shuffling*

Classic side-channel countermeasures include masking and shuffling. As we have seen, linear masking is susceptible to the algebraic attack. Shuffling procedure is highly nonlinear in its nature; therefore, it is a good protection candidate against LDA. Unfortunately, basic shuffling is leaking *the sum of shuffled values*, preventing it being a universal countermeasure. Even the classic combination of linear masking plus shuffling is not secure, since linear masking is "transparent" to algebraic attacks. Furthermore, differential LDA (section 2.5.2) can exploit the sum leakage efficiently.

Fortunately, shuffling can be "repaired" to provide provable algebraic security. The main missing component is the addition of *dummy* slots: shuffling slots that contain dummy (random) values, freshly generated on each execution. This prevents the sum leakage as the sum of all slots would be corrupted by the dummy values. Another missing component is modification of the circuit being protected, making it more robust, ensuring that there are no sensitive functions that are predictable with high probability. This robustness is related to the quantification of algebraic security, omitted in Definition 2.4 for simplicity of exposition.

IMPORTANT.– *Besides enhancing security, dummy slots also enhance applicability. Dummyless shuffling may only protect parallel identical subfunctions. With dummy slots, we always have an option of replicating full implementation.*

We begin by defining dummy shuffling in the framework of computational circuits. This means that shuffling/unshuffling steps are explicitly performed on data slots, avoiding implementation details such as shuffling by time or by memory.

DEFINITION 2.6 (Dummy shuffling).– Given an implementation I_C of a function $C\colon \mathbb{F}^m \rightarrow \mathbb{F}^{m'}$ and two integers $w_{\text{main}}, w_{\text{dummy}}$, *dummy shuffling* defines an implementation $I'_C\colon (\mathbb{F}^m)^{w_{\text{main}}} \times \$ \rightarrow (\mathbb{F}^{m'})^{w_{\text{main}}}$ consisting of three steps: input-shuffling, slots evaluation and output-selection (see Figure 2.2). Here, \$ stands for a randomness source (formally, equivalent to an implementation-dependent number of extra inputs).

– *Input-shuffling*: the w_{main} inputs are concatenated with w_{dummy} values sampled independently and uniformly at random from $\mathbb{F}$. All $w_{\text{main}}+w_{\text{dummy}}$ inputs are shuffled randomly.

– *Slots evaluation*: the implementation I_C is evaluated on each of $w_{\text{main}} + w_{\text{dummy}}$ shuffled values in parallel.

– *Output-selection*: the outputs are unshuffled (using the information from the input-shuffling step), and the main outputs are marked as the final outputs; the dummy outputs are omitted.

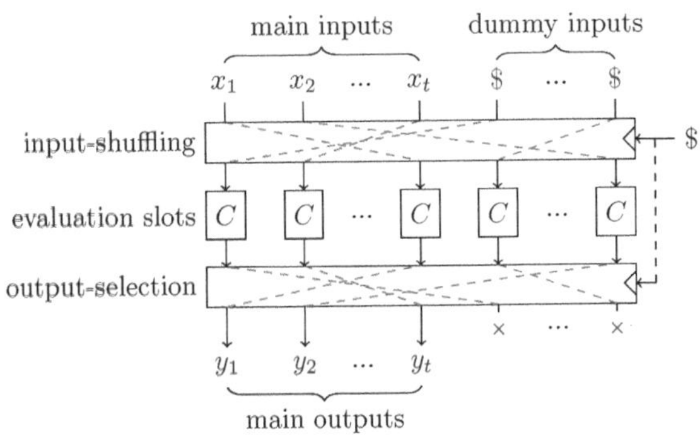

Figure 2.2. *Dummy shuffling. The notation $\$$ stands for a uniform and independent source of randomness. For a color version of this figure, see www.iste.co.uk/prouff/cryptography3.zip*

The state-of-the-art algebraic security model cannot analyze the full dummy shuffling procedure. However, it can analyze the algebraic security of the slots evaluation phase. To do this, we need to define the respective scheme (as in Definition 2.3), which is called the *evaluation-phase model.*

DEFINITION 2.7 (Evaluation-Phase Model).– Let I_C be an implementation of a function $C\colon \mathbb{F}^m \to \mathbb{F}^{m'}$. Let $w_{\text{main}}, w_{\text{dummy}}$ be positive integers, $w = w_{\text{main}} + w_{\text{dummy}}$. The *evaluation-phase model* analyzes the algebraic security (Definition 2.4) of the scheme $\mathsf{EPM}(I_C, w_{\text{main}}, w_{\text{dummy}}) = \mathsf{S}$, constructed as follows:

$\mathsf{S.enc}(x, r_e) : (\mathbb{F}^m)^{w_{\text{main}}} \times \mathbb{F}^{\tau_e} \to (\mathbb{F}^m)^w$
let $v \in (\mathbb{F}^m)^w$
for $i \in \{1, \ldots, w_{\text{main}}\}$ **do**
  $v_i \leftarrow x_i$
end for
$(r'_e, r''_e) \leftarrow r_e$
for $i \in \{w_{\text{main}} + 1, \ldots, w\}$ **do**
  $v_i \xleftarrow{r'_e} \mathbb{F}^m$
end for
return $x' \xleftarrow{r''_e} \mathsf{Shuffle}(v_1, \ldots, v_w)$

$\mathsf{S.comp}(x') : (\mathbb{F}^m)^w \to (\mathbb{F}^{m'})^w$
let $y' \in (\mathbb{F}^{m'})^w$
for $i \in \{1, \ldots, w\}$ **do**
  $y'_i \leftarrow C(x'_i)$
end for
return $y' \leftarrow (y'_1, \ldots, y'_w)$

$\mathsf{S.dec}(y', r''_e) : (\mathbb{F}^{m'})^w \to (\mathbb{F}^{m'})^{w_{\text{main}}}$
$y \xleftarrow{r''_e} \mathsf{Unshuffle}(y'_1, \ldots, y'_w)$
return $(y_1, \ldots, y_{w_{\text{main}}})$

The notation $\overset{r'_e}{\longleftarrow}$ ($\overset{r''_e}{\longleftarrow}$) means that r'_e (r''_e) is used as randomness to generate the value (sample uniformly from $\mathbb{F}^m$ or shuffle/unshuffle almost-uniformly).

Now, we can show that the evaluation-phase model is algebraically secure as long as there is at least one dummy slot. We provide a short insightful proof.

PROPOSITION 2.1.– Let I_C be an implementation of a function $C : \mathbb{F}^m \to \mathbb{F}^{m'}$. Let $w_{\text{main}}, w_{\text{dummy}}$ be positive integers. Then, $S = \mathsf{EPM}(I_C, w_{\text{main}}, w_{\text{dummy}})$ is algebraically secure.

Proof.– Let $f(x')$ be a non-constant function expressed as a linear combination of functions from $\mathsf{S.comp}$ (which consists of parallel applications of I_C). We omit r_c as it is not used in dummy shuffling. Without loss of generality, assume that f has form $g(x'_1) \oplus h(x'_2, \ldots, x'_{w_{\text{dummy}}+w_{\text{main}}})$. In other words, it is a linear combination of some functions computed in the I_C in the first slot (g) and some functions computed in the other slots (h). Furthermore, g must be a non-constant function. We need to prove that $g(\mathsf{S.enc}(x, r_e))$ is non-constant for all $x \in \mathbb{F}^n$. Indeed, when the first slot is dummy, its input x'_1 is sampled uniformly at random. Since g is non-constant, $g(\mathsf{S.enc}(x, r_e))$ is non-constant for all fixed x. More precisely, it depends on the part of r_e used for shuffling and also on the part of r_e used for generating dummy inputs. □

We remind the reader that the algebraic security defined in Definition 2.4 is simplified and does not *quantify* how close to constant functions the reachable functions can be, which is important to have concrete security guarantees against the LDA attack. Such a deep analysis is out of scope of this book.

We will only note that, with a certain preprocessing of the implementation being protected, dummy shuffling provides provable security against algebraic attacks of arbitrary predetermined degrees, with strong quantifiable security bounds.

2.7. Conclusions

Gray-box attacks are applicable in the white-box setting and they even become more powerful due to specifics of the white-box model: determinism, precise measurements and data-dependency information. These properties lead to a wide range of generic automated attacks. Besides classic key recovery attacks, fault injections may be used for simplification and weakening of the implementation via removal of pseudorandomness and dummy computations. Noise-free measurements allow the efficient exact matching attack and the powerful algebraic attack, defeating linear encodings or any order. DDGs allow us to mount correlation or algebraic attacks of very high orders. These and many other attacks make advances in white-box designing techniques very difficult. Although (practical) white-box cryptography is not yet achieved by the scientific community, the area of white-box cryptanalysis and countermeasures has many interesting results, which were not covered by this chapter. In the following, we provide a list of references, so that an interested reader may explore particular topics in depth.

2.8. Notes and further references

Recently, several WhibOx[2] competitions were held, where practical white-box designers and attackers were confronted. A few works related to these competitions targeting white-box AES implementations are due to Goubin et al. (2020a, 2020b) and Alpirez Bock and Treff (2020). The latest to date competition WhibOx 2021 targeted white-box ECDSA implementations and inspired a few reports with attacks and design ideas: Barbu et al. (2022), Bauer et al. (2022). Another analysis of white-box ECDSA is given by Dottax et al. (2021).

Recent doctoral theses on white-box cryptography provide a good overview of state-of-the-art (see Udovenko (2019); Rasoamiaramanana (2020); Wang (2020)).

– Section 2.2. The study of gray-box attacks (DCA and DFA) in the white-box setting includes works by Sanfelix et al. (2015), Ahn and Han (2016), Bos et al. (2016), Sasdrich et al. (2016), Banik et al. (2017), Alpirez Bock et al. (2018), Bock et al. (2019), Rivain and Wang (2019), Ranea and Preneel (2020), Goubin et al. (2020b) and Carlet et al. (2021). Several works applied side-channel masking protections to counter the attacks, including Lee (2017) and Lee and Kim (2020). Higher order DCA was analyzed in Bogdanov et al. (2019) and Maghrebi and Alessio (2020). Affine encodings were analyzed by Lee et al. (2018) and Derbez et al. (2018).

– Section 2.4. The exact matching attack was analyzed in Biryukov and Udovenko (2018).

– Sections 2.5 and 2.6. Algebraic/LDA attacks and countermeasures were developed in works by Biryukov and Udovenko (2018), Goubin et al. (2020a), Biryukov and Udovenko (2021) and Seker et al. (2021).

2.9. References

Ahn, H. and Han, D.-G. (2016). Multilateral white-box cryptanalysis: Case study on WB-AES of CHES challenge 2016. Cryptology ePrint Archive, Report 2016/807 [Online]. Available at: https://eprint.iacr.org/2016/807.

2 Available at: https://whibox.io.

Alpirez Bock, E. and Treff, A. (2020). Security assessment of white-box design submissions of the CHES 2017 CTF challenge. In *COSADE 2020*, Bertoni, G.M. and Regazzoni, F. (eds). Springer, Heidelberg.

Alpirez Bock, E., Brzuska, C., Michiels, W., Treff, A. (2018). On the ineffectiveness of internal encodings – Revisiting the DCA attack on white-box cryptography. In *ACNS 18*, Preneel, B. and Vercauteren, F. (eds). Springer, Heidelberg.

Banik, S., Bogdanov, A., Isobe, T., Jepsen, M.B. (2017). Analysis of software countermeasures for whitebox encryption. *IACR Trans. Symm. Cryptol.*, 2017(1), 307–328.

Barbu, G., Beullens, W., Dottax, E., Giraud, C., Houzelot, A., Li, C., Mahzoun, M., Ranea, A., Xie, J. (2022). ECDSA white-box implementations: Attacks and designs from WhibOx 2021 contest. Cryptology ePrint Archive, Report 2022/385 [Online]. Available at: https://eprint.iacr.org/2022/385.

Bauer, S., Drexler, H., Gebhardt, M., Klein, D., Laus, F., Mittmann, J. (2022). Attacks against white-box ECDSA and discussion of countermeasures – A report on the WhibOx contest 2021. Cryptology ePrint Archive, Report 2022/448 [Online]. Available at: https://eprint.iacr.org/2022/448.

Biryukov, A. and Udovenko, A. (2018). Attacks and countermeasures for white-box designs. In *ASIACRYPT 2018, Part II*, Peyrin, T. and Galbraith, S. (eds). Springer, Heidelberg.

Biryukov, A. and Udovenko, A. (2021). Dummy shuffling against algebraic attacks in white-box implementations. In *EUROCRYPT 2021, Part II*, Canteaut, A. and Standaert, F.-X. (eds). Springer, Heidelberg.

Bock, E.A., Bos, J.W., Brzuska, C., Hubain, C., Michiels, W., Mune, C., Gonzalez, E.S., Teuwen, P., Treff, A. (2019). White-box cryptography: Don't forget about grey-box attacks. *J. Cryptol.*, 32(4), 1095–1143.

Bogdanov, A., Rivain, M., Vejre, P.S., Wang, J. (2019). Higher-order DCA against standard side-channel countermeasures. In *COSADE 2019*, Polian, I. and Stöttinger, M. (eds). Springer, Heidelberg.

Bos, J.W., Hubain, C., Michiels, W., Teuwen, P. (2016). Differential computation analysis: Hiding your white-box designs is not enough. In *CHES 2016*, Gierlichs, B. and Poschmann, A.Y. (eds). Springer, Heidelberg.

Carlet, C., Guilley, S., Mesnager, S. (2021). Structural attack (and repair) of diffused-input-blocked-output white-box cryptography. *IACR TCHES*, 2021(4), 57–87.

Chow, S., Eisen, P., Johnson, H., Van Oorschot, P.C. (2003a). White-Box cryptography and an AES implementation. In *Selected Areas in Cryptography*, Nyberg, K. and Heys, H. (eds). Springer, Berlin, Heidelberg. doi: 10.1007/3-540-36492-7_17.

Chow, S., Eisen, P., Johnson, H., van Oorschot, P.C. (2003b). A White-Box DES implementation for DRM applications. In *Digital Rights Management*, Feigenbaum, J. (ed.). Springer, Berlin, Heidelberg. doi: 10.1007/978-3-540-44993-5_1.

Derbez, P., Fouque, P.-A., Lambin, B., Minaud, B. (2018). On recovering affine encodings in white-box implementations. *IACR TCHES*, 2018(3), 121–149.

Dottax, E., Giraud, C., Houzelot, A. (2021). White-box ECDSA: Challenges and existing solutions. In *Constructive Side-Channel Analysis and Secure Design: 12th International Workshop, COSADE 2021*. Springer-Verlag, Heidelberg. doi: 10.1007/978-3-030-89915-8_9.

Goubin, L., Paillier, P., Rivain, M., Wang, J. (2020a). How to reveal the secrets of an obscure white-box implementation. *Journal of Cryptographic Engineering*, 10(1), 49–66.

Goubin, L., Rivain, M., Wang, J. (2020b). Defeating state-of-the-art white-box countermeasures. *IACR TCHES*, 2020(3), 454–482.

Lee, S. (2017). A masked white-box cryptographic implementation for protecting against differential computation analysis. Cryptology ePrint Archive, Report 2017/267 [Online]. Available at: https://eprint.iacr.org/2017/267.

Lee, S. and Kim, M. (2020). Improvement on a masked white-box cryptographic implementation. *IEEE Access*, 8, 90992–91004.

Lee, S., Jho, N.-S., Kim, M. (2018). On the key leakage from linear transformations. Cryptology ePrint Archive, Report 2018/1047 [Online]. Available at: https://eprint.iacr.org/2018/1047.

Maghrebi, H. and Alessio, D. (2020). Revisiting higher-order computational attacks against white-box implementations. Report, Cryptology ePrint Archive [Online]. Available at: https://ia.cr/2019/1405.

Ranea, A. and Preneel, B. (2020). On self-equivalence encodings in white-box implementations. In *SAC 2020*, Dunkelman, O. and O'Flynn, C. (eds). Springer, Heidelberg.

Rasoamiaramanana, S. (2020). Design of white-box encryption schemes for mobile applications security. PhD Thesis, University of Lorraine, Nancy.

Rivain, M. and Wang, J. (2019). Analysis and improvement of differential computation attacks against internally-encoded white-box implementations. *IACR TCHES*, 2019(2), 225–255.

Sanfelix, E., Mune, C., de Haas, J. (2015). Unboxing the white-box. Practical attacks against obfuscated ciphers. Document, Black Hat Europe.

Sasdrich, P., Moradi, A., Güneysu, T. (2016). White-box cryptography in the gray box – A hardware implementation and its side channels. In *FSE 2016*, Peyrin, T. (ed.). Springer, Heidelberg.

Seker, O., Eisenbarth, T., Liskiewicz, M. (2021). A white-box masking scheme resisting computational and algebraic attacks. *IACR TCHES*, 2021(2), 61–105.

Udovenko, A.N. (2019). Design and cryptanalysis of symmetric-key algorithms in black and white-box models. PhD Thesis, University of Luxembourg, Luxembourg.

Wang, J. (2020). On the practical security of white-box cryptography. PhD Thesis, University of Luxembourg, Luxembourg.

3

Tools for White-Box Cryptanalysis

Philippe TEUWEN
Quarkslab, Paris, France

3.1. Introduction

While Chapter 2 covers theoretical aspects of attacks and countermeasures specific to the white-box setting, this chapter focuses on a few practical tools and their accessibility without requiring advanced knowledge, including techniques originating from the hardware side-channel and fault injection domains.

Until some years ago (circa 2015), the white-box cryptanalysis field was driven exclusively by academic papers. Industry could still offer white-box implementations and cope with a moderate threat of advanced attackers able to first reverse-engineer obfuscated programs, and then apply and adapt the mathematical methods described in such academic papers to the result of their de-obfuscation efforts.

Then, the so-called gray-box attacks, from side-channel cryptanalysis techniques presented in Chapters 5 and 10 of Volume 1, were transposed to the white-box domain. Theoretically, a white-box implementation – an implementation of a cryptographic algorithm meant to operate in a white-box attack model – is supposed to be resistant in such a powerful model (where an attacker can freely observe and tamper with an execution instance), which supersedes the gray-box model (where the attacker has much more limited capabilities, merely observing noisy leakages and injecting vaguely controlled faults). However, gray-box attacks approach the problem

Embedded Cryptography 3,
coordinated by Emmanuel PROUFF, Guénaël RENAULT,
Matthieu RIVAIN and Colin O'FLYNN.

in a radically different way, working surprisingly well on a variety of white-box implementations: Gray-box attacks are meant to be usable against hardware chips without knowledge of their processing and this remains true for their transposition to the white-box domain, enabling a class of less advanced attackers. Of course, the tools implementing such attacks are neither magical nor truly universal, but they are largely sufficient to tackle the "low-hanging fruits" and, with some practical experience, we can adapt and fine tune them to target more advanced white-box implementations as well.

Nowadays, industry has to take into account the existence of these tools when bringing new white-box designs to the market. It probably goes even further: a number of recent papers describe new attacks against implementations, without necessarily providing the corresponding tools. In this context, industry must assess the security of a white-box design in the event that someone, somewhere, implements these attacks or even publicly releases a new tool with an implementation of one of these attacks. By understanding the existing tools and their requirements and limitations, we can try to estimate if such a new tool would be easy to use or if it would still require a high level of expertise and reverse engineering. In short, industry must assess how an existing design would be impacted by the availability of new tools that implement already known attacks.

White-box cryptography can be applied to any cryptographic component, block cipher, message authentication code, public key scheme, etc. The vast majority of the currently existing tooling targets the most common white-box implementations – block ciphers, more specifically AES and DES. To guarantee accessibility, we cover exclusively tools that are available under open source licenses. For practicing, several publicly available white-box implementations have been collected in the Deadpool project, part of the SideChannelMarvels, an open source initiative to provide samples and tools related to white-box cryptography. The WhibOx competitions are also a great source of white-box implementations.

– *Chapter overview*: execution traces constitute the main source of side-channel information in the white-box context. Therefore, section 3.2 introduces various methods to trace the activity of a program. Section 3.3 illustrates how these traces can be exploited graphically to learn about the program structure. Section 3.4 explains how to acquire traces suitable for a number of cryptanalysis attacks and section 3.5 explains how to preprocess them. Sections 3.6 and 3.7 present two side-channel analyses on such traces. Section 3.8 details how to inject faults in a program execution and section 3.9 presents cryptanalysis attacks to exploit faulty results. Finally, section 3.10 discusses how to deal with white-box implementations protected by external encodings.

All links to the tools and additional references are available at the end of this chapter in section 3.12.

3.2. Tracing programs

In the gray-box attack model, side-channel information is extracted from a physical device by observing fluctuations in its power consumption or in its electromagnetic emanations; and a recording of these observations during a cryptographic operation is called a trace. The advantage of the white-box attack model is that, by definition, everything can be observed. In practice, what can be done to extract information from a targeted white-box executable, potentially obfuscated, in an automated fashion? We can record software execution traces: record the input, output and intermediate activity of the program such as executed instructions, memory reads and writes, as well as the content of the registers. It is not strictly required to record prior traces before running some of the attacks described in this chapter, but they provide an appreciable initial insight. These traces are useful to get a rough picture of the white-box implementation, its location in the program, identify some countermeasures and finally provide useful leakages to mount side-channel attacks, as will be seen in the next sections.

To acquire such traces, several approaches are possible depending on the nature of the targeted program. Simple debugger scripts (IDA, Ghidra, GDB, etc.) stepping through the code and recording data might be sufficient but, most of the time, DBI (*dynamic binary instrumentation*) tools are a better choice. These tools can monitor programs at the instruction level much more efficiently than a debugger. A few frameworks exist such as Intel PIN, Valgrind, DynamoRIO, Frida and its Stalker module or the newcomer QBDI. Each of them differs in performance and in supported operating systems, architectures and features (self-modifying code, multithreading, etc.), so we need to check which framework is suitable for a given target. Emulators providing hooks for instrumentation are also an option: there exist a number of them based on the open source emulator QEMU such as Qiling and Rainbow. If the targeted white-box design is not implemented in a native executable but in some intermediate bytecode (Java, ART, Python, etc.), it will be more valuable to instrument the bytecode or add instrumentation hooks in the virtual machine engine in order to record a trace of the bytecode execution rather than blindly tracing the engine itself. The more information gets recorded, the more storage and the more analysis time it will take.

IMPORTANT. Choose the available tracing tool that will offer the closest access to the important data, without being lost in extra information such as unrelated functions of the program, system libraries, OS or kernel and execution engine.

In rare cases, the white-box source code might be available (but obfuscated) like for the challenges of the WhibOx competitions. In such events, automating the injection of some `printf` calls in the code with the command `sed` and some regular expressions may fit the tracing needs.

When using DBI frameworks, we need to write little pieces of code telling us to trace each instruction in the desired functions and to record memory operations in the desired memory range. If instructions and memory ranges are unknown at first, we can trace the whole executable, possibly its libraries (but probably not the system libraries), at some extra cost. It is rarely required to trace the registers themselves, which is a quite storage- and time-consuming operation. To simplify the usage of some DBI frameworks in this context, the TracerPIN and TracerGrind plugins are available for Intel PIN and Valgrind, in the Tracer project, part of the SideChannelMarvels.

Tracing a program should be as undetectable as possible for the program, in order to avoid possible countermeasures, but it is also desirable to have the ability to reproduce or compare traces in the exact same environment. Some implementations may even use the environment entropy to add countermeasures such as random masking. Therefore, it is preferable to strictly control the environment by removing ASLR (*address space layout randomization*) support (see `setarch -R` under Linux) and intercepting and freezing sources of entropy such as `srand`, `gettimeofday` or `open("/dev/random")` (e.g. with the help of `LD_PRELOAD` under Linux).

As a first step, a single execution trace comprising instructions and memory operations should be enough to perform an initial visual inspection, as detailed in section 3.3. The Deadpool project contains numerous examples on how to install and use the TracerPIN and TracerGrind tools to get such a trace.

We choose the RHme3 *capture-the-flag* pre-qualification challenge as a typical white-box implementation example to demonstrate various tools all along this chapter. It comes with the following description: *here is a binary implementing a cryptographic algorithm. You provide an input and it produces the corresponding output. Can you extract the key?*

With TracerPIN, tracing it is as easy as the following.

```
$ Tracer -o rhme3.txt -- ./whitebox some_plaintext
```

The tool generates a human-readable file describing each instruction. This small excerpt from the core of the white-box implementation, slightly edited, illustrates what a software execution trace may give as information about one given execution. Instructions `[I]` and memory being read `[R]` and written `[W]` can be easily observed. Columns in this excerpt represent respectively the type of record, the number of the event being recorded, the instruction address and either the disassembled instruction or the memory address and value being read or written.

```
[R]    42963 0x0000000000463915    0x00000000006650f1 size=1 value=0x02
[I]    42963 0x0000000000463915    movzx edx, byte ptr [rdx]
```

```
[I]      42964 0x0000000000463918      movzx edx, dl
[I]      42965 0x000000000046391b      movsxd rdx, edx
[I]      42966 0x000000000046391e      movsxd rcx, ecx
[I]      42967 0x0000000000463921      shl rcx, 0x4
[I]      42968 0x0000000000463925      add rdx, rcx
[I]      42969 0x0000000000463928      add rdx, 0x6650c0
[R]      42970 0x000000000046392f      0x00000000006650e2 size=1 value=0x00
[I]      42970 0x000000000046392f      movzx edx, byte ptr [rdx]
[I]      42971 0x0000000000463932      movzx edx, dl
[I]      42972 0x0000000000463935      shl edx, 0x4
[I]      42973 0x0000000000463938      or edx, r8d
[I]      42974 0x000000000046393b      mov byte ptr [rax], dl
[W]      42974 0x000000000046393b      0x00007fffffffd930 size=1 value=0x03
```

With TracerGrind, we must determine the address range of the main executable to apply an address filter because, by default, Valgrind traces everything, including system libraries. The desired range is the `r.x` (read & execute) section of the executable and can be determined with the command `objdump`.

```
$ objdump -p whitebox |grep -A1 LOAD|grep -B1 "r.x"
    LOAD off    0x00000000 vaddr 0x00400000 paddr 0x00400000 align 2**21
         filesz 0x0006432c memsz 0x0006432c flags r-x
```

The executable section is loaded at 0x400000 and to trace the beginning of the execution of the RHme3 challenge, TraceGrind can be called with the following filter option:

```
$ valgrind --tool=tracergrind --filter=0x400000-0x410000 --output=rhme3.trace \
    ./whitebox some_plaintext
$ texttrace rhme3.trace rhme3.txt
```

In any case, there is a far easier way to analyze such a trace with graphical visualization, as detailed in the following section.

3.3. Target recognition

Before running actual attacks, it may be worth getting some insight on the white-box structure and location within the program, especially when the white-box algorithm is only a small part of a much larger application. This first recognition step is useful to limit the instruction address range and memory range to the interesting tidbits. Attacks will run faster and require less memory.

One way is to visualize a software execution trace with TraceGraph from the Tracer project mentioned in the previous section. The first step requires recording the trace in a database. With TracerPIN, this is achieved by adding the option "`--sqlite`".

```
$ Tracer --sqlite -o rhme3.sqlite -- ./whitebox some_plaintext
```

If TracerGrind is used, the trace is acquired as usual, then post-processed with "`sqlitetrace rhme3.trace rhme3.sqlite`". After that, we can load the trace in TraceGraph: "`tracegraph rhme3.sqlite`" and get an overview as shown in Figure 3.1(a).

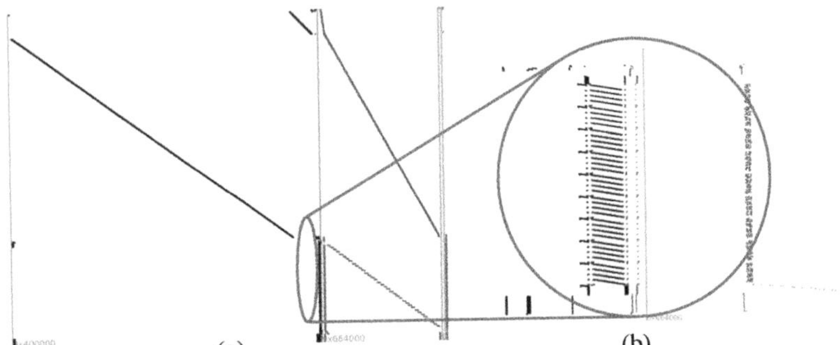

(a) (b)

Figure 3.1. *RHme3: software execution trace overview (a) and zoom on the white-box operations (b). For a color version of this figure, see www.iste.co.uk/prouff/cryptography3.zip*

The Y-axis is the events timescale, from top to bottom, while the X-axis is the memory address space, with executed instructions (in black) starting at `0x400000`, and some memory region allocated at `0x664000`, where data were first written (in red) and then read (in green).

Zooming on the second part of the instruction (Figure 3.1(b)), we clearly see the loops grouped in 9 × 4 patterns. This is an indication of a possible AES-128 and its nine rounds with a *MixColumns* operation working on each of the four columns. The tenth round lacks such *MixColumns* operation so the pattern repeats only nine times.

NOTE. Sometimes, no pattern is visible on the instructions plot, for example, on white-box instances where the loops are unrolled, but the stack can still reveal patterns.

Zooming further and clicking on individual events in TraceGraph will reveal the corresponding instruction, address and data value. Observing how a buffer of bytes is rewritten on the stack can even reveal operations like an AES *ShiftRows*, which would be a strong indication of an AES performing an encryption and not a decryption. Other white-box implementations will result in vastly different representations, but patterns can emerge and indicate where the white-box core operations are performed, whether it is based on static tables, dynamic tables or function stubs, if it is likely an AES-128 (with a 9×4 pattern), AES-192 (11×4), AES-256 (13×4) or DES (16). Sometimes, it is also possible to spot some countermeasures such as dummy rounds, artificial jittering in an attempt to desynchronize side-channel traces, obfuscation techniques, etc.

3.4. Acquiring traces for side-channel analysis

One of the possible automated attacks on a white-box implementation is the application of side-channel analysis techniques, well known in the hardware domain, to software execution traces.

The traces acquisition methods are very similar to those described in section 3.2 but with some specific tuning to get better performances. While we needed one single rich trace for visualization purposes, side-channel analysis requires us to record about a few dozen to a few thousand traces. To ease the analysis phase, it is worth limiting the acquisition to a promising scope. Fewer data require less storage and a shorter analysis time. Typically, we apply filters to instruction ranges or memory address ranges learned from the visual inspection to target the memory operations of the first few rounds of an AES algorithm. The data being read or written, but also the (least significant bytes of the) memory addresses, may be a source of leakage. Tracing the content of the registers might also be required.

Contrarily to hardware side-channel acquisitions, there is no need to acquire hundreds of thousands of traces because in the white-box model, traces are noiseless. Even individual bits are accessible, hence there is no need to use models such as the Hamming weight. It is as if we could probe all the lines of the memory bus and record them individually with a logic analyzer, rather than listening to the power supply fluctuations with an oscilloscope. It does not mean that an exploitable leakage exists in the acquired traces, but if an attack fails with a few thousand traces, it is highly unlikely that it will succeed with more traces.

An important point is that we need to also record the block cipher inputs or outputs *in clear* along the corresponding traces. Some implementations work on *encoded* inputs and outputs and this will be discussed in section 3.10.

Traces can be acquired for example with the framework provided in the Deadpool project. In the following example, we tell the framework to acquire 32 traces with TracerPIN over an instruction address range covering the loops identified in Figure 3.1. The address range is not a requirement but an optimization. Each white-box implementation has a different way to expect input and return output, therefore small processing functions `processinput` and `processoutput` need to be defined. More complex cases may even require us to instrument the executable with some hooks to capture input and output directly in memory.

```
#!/usr/bin/env python
from deadpool_dca import *

def processinput(iblock, blocksize):
    return (struct.pack(">QQ", iblock//(2**64), iblock%(2**64)), ["--stdin"])

def processoutput(output, blocksize):
    return int(b''.join(output.strip().split(b' ')), 16)

T=TracerPIN('./whitebox', processinput, processoutput, ARCH.amd64, 16,
            addr_range="0x462886-0x463D6C")
T.run(32)
```

The execution shows the acquisition progress, with the randomly generated inputs and the corresponding outputs.

```
$ ./trace_it.py
00000 2227820658040B26AB68DA370FC13820 -> 019A3D131A001711472D433E23AA5ED7
00001 B63E15444B8D17779DB6C74CDEE84A6F -> AB559AD34C10DAD5077CA51BA2405669
00002 659BDA21887A9AA54277AF950E1807A9 -> DF69FB4B1AF97916645507FD8ECFA6D0
...
```

By default, the script will produce a set of three files per execution: one record of the memory reads of one byte (`trace_mem_data_rw1_*`), one of the lower bytes of the address of such reads (`trace_mem_addr1_rw1_*`), useful to monitor some *lookup tables* inputs, and a last one of the memory writes of one byte on the stack (`trace_stack_w1_*`). Which type of data to record under which condition is entirely configurable. By analogy with the hardware side-channel traces, recorded data within a trace are called *samples*. The following are the files produced by the first three iterations of the script:

```
trace_mem_addr1_rw1_2227820658040B26AB68DA370FC13820_019A3D131A001711472D433E23AA5ED7.info
trace_mem_addr1_rw1_0000_2227820658040B26AB68DA370FC13820_019A3D131A001711472D433E23AA5ED7.bin
trace_mem_addr1_rw1_0001_B63E15444B8D17779DB6C74CDEE84A6F_AB559AD34C10DAD5077CA51BA2405669.bin
trace_mem_addr1_rw1_0002_659BDA21887A9AA54277AF950E1807A9_DF69FB4B1AF97916645507FD8ECFA6D0.bin
...
trace_mem_data_rw1_2227820658040B26AB68DA370FC13820_019A3D131A001711472D433E23AA5ED7.info
trace_mem_data_rw1_0000_2227820658040B26AB68DA370FC13820_019A3D131A001711472D433E23AA5ED7.bin
trace_mem_data_rw1_0001_B63E15444B8D17779DB6C74CDEE84A6F_AB559AD34C10DAD5077CA51BA2405669.bin
trace_mem_data_rw1_0002_659BDA21887A9AA54277AF950E1807A9_DF69FB4B1AF97916645507FD8ECFA6D0.bin
...
trace_stack_w1_2227820658040B26AB68DA370FC13820_019A3D131A001711472D433E23AA5ED7.info
trace_stack_w1_0000_2227820658040B26AB68DA370FC13820_019A3D131A001711472D433E23AA5ED7.bin
trace_stack_w1_0001_B63E15444B8D17779DB6C74CDEE84A6F_AB559AD34C10DAD5077CA51BA2405669.bin
trace_stack_w1_0002_659BDA21887A9AA54277AF950E1807A9_DF69FB4B1AF97916645507FD8ECFA6D0.bin
...
```

A `.info` file is also produced for the first trace of each set to ease the identification of a possible leakage. For example, if we develop a white-box design and manages to break it by some side-channel analysis, the developer wants to identify the source of the leakage. Each line of the `.info` file details the source of each sample. Therefore, once the samples responsible for the leakage have been identified, we can find which instruction and memory address it corresponds to. For example, if later it appears that an analysis can break the last byte of the key based on the 21st sample (byte) of the `trace_mem_addr1_rw1` set of traces, we can look at line 21 of `trace_mem_addr1_rw1_*.info`: `"[R] 459 4638A3 6650D7 1 06"` that indicates the sample is a byte produced by the event 459, which is an instruction located at address `0x4638A3` reading from address `0x6650D7`.

If the white-box implementation is compiled with debug information, we can even know which source code line is responsible for the leakage by providing the spotted instruction address to the command `addr2line`.

3.5. Preprocessing traces

We have seen how the Deadpool framework records traces intended for side-channel analysis. In section 3.6, we will see how Daredevil and Jlsca can analyze these traces and Deadpool has functions to convert traces to the format expected by Daredevil and to *trs*, a format supported by Jlsca. The exact format used to record traces may vary with other tools and we must be prepared to write little scripts to convert traces from one format to another, depending on the source and destination tools.

The Deadpool conversion functions include the following trick. On real hardware, a side-channel trace captures power variations, including effects of each bit being manipulated at the same time, which translates into using the Hamming weight or the Hamming distance in the leakage models. However, the software execution traces are 8-bit integers representing something fundamentally different: the true values of these manipulated bits, grouped in bytes which are by definition driven by their most significant bits. The trick is therefore to decompose the recorded bytes into a succession of individual bits, each bit becoming a new sample. Compared to an analog trace, samples no longer represent acquisitions at regular intervals, as the trace contains only data when a specific event – e.g. a memory read instruction – occurred, and as one event byte gets decomposed into multiple samples. However, this does not affect the logic of the attack, as we only need to record traces aligned across executions.

To convert the traces of our example in a format suitable for Daredevil, simply execute the function `bin2daredevil`.

```
#!/usr/bin/env python
from deadpool_dca import *
bin2daredevil()
```

It will spread the traced bytes into bits, regroup traces, inputs and outputs in three files per set and provide a configuration file template for each set. The following is the `mem_addr1_rw1` set of 32 traces of 7976 samples:

```
mem_addr1_rw1_32_7976.config
mem_addr1_rw1_32_7976.input
mem_addr1_rw1_32_7976.output
mem_addr1_rw1_32_7976.trace
```

For some white-box instances, traces can become quite large. If we use Jlsca instead of Daredevil, we can skip the bytes decomposition into bits as Jlsca can handle white-box traces (stored in `trs` format) and decompose them on-the-fly, if instructed with `addSamplePass(trs, BitPass())`. However, you can do even better by applying sample reduction techniques supported by Jlsca as well, which will remove many unneeded samples from the traces. One technique is the *duplicate column removal* (DCR), which eliminates repeating samples and their inverse. A second technique is the *conditional sample reduction* (CSR), which further compresses the traces by considering only a varying part of the input used to attack a part of the key and eliminating samples not affected by the varying input. Required storage, but also analysis time will be greatly improved as combining both techniques leaves only the samples relevant for recovering the targeted portion of the key. For a complete example using Jlsca and sample reduction technique against the RHme3 challenge, see the section, notes and further references.

3.6. Differential computation analysis

Once software execution traces got collected and preprocessed, it is time to perform the actual side-channel analysis. The most elementary analysis is to apply classical DPA (*differential power analysis*) or CPA (*correlation power analysis*) presented in Chapter 4 of Volume 1, on these preprocessed traces, a technique referred to as DCA (*differential computation analysis*), as it handles computation traces made of individual bits and not power traces. Technically, Daredevil, introduced in section 3.5, performs a CPA, but on such preprocessed traces, no actual Hamming weight is used and its results are identical to a DPA.

In our RHme3 example, we will call Daredevil with the three default sets and configuration files created in section 3.5.

```
$ daredevil -c stack_w1_32_2816.config
$ daredevil -c mem_data_rw1_32_7976.config
$ daredevil -c mem_addr1_rw1_32_7976.config
```

For this specific white-box design, processing the set of data being read from or written to memory (`mem_data_rw1`) and the set of writings on the stack (`stack_w1`) will not show any key candidate standing out, even if more traces get recorded. However, the set of addresses of the memory operations (`mem_addr1_rw1`), actually the lower byte of these addresses, returns a clear key candidate, with the highest cumulated correlation possible: 16 (one for each key byte).

```
Most probable key max(abs):
1: 16: 61316c5f7434623133355f525f6f5235
```

On other white-box designs, our mileage may vary. This white-box implementation was easy to break with a very low number of traces and a maximal correlation probably because the intermediate encodings, if any, did not properly mask the correlation with the output of a clear AES S-box. At least one bit of the address of data being read from memory correlated perfectly with one of the bits of the AES S-box output.

On several white-box implementations where internal encodings are chosen randomly, it has been observed that on average about 10 of the 16 key bytes could be recovered by correlating with the S-box output and a few hundred to a few thousand traces. However, internal encodings can also be carefully chosen to avoid any correlation with the S-box output.

Nevertheless, instead of computing correlation against each bit of the AES S-box output, we can check against all the 255 possible linear combinations of the S-box output bits in order to cover all possible 1-byte internal affine encodings. In practice, this can be achieved with Daredevil by telling in its configuration file to use one of the extended look-up tables provided with the tool in the LUT directory under the names `AES_AFTER_SBOX_x*`.

As discussed earlier, external sources of entropy can easily be intercepted and controlled by an attacker in the white-box context. Therefore, some white-box implementations are using the input itself as a source of randomness to apply various masking techniques. In the example presented above, the tool proceeded with random inputs, but in some cases, we may get better results by modifying one single byte of the input at once, up to a maximum of $256 \times 16 = 4,096$ inputs.

The RHme3 example is an AES-128 encryption and the presented DCA relied on the inputs in clear and the traces. Like the regular DPA on hardware traces, the

DCA can also be performed using the outputs in clear and leakages located in the last rounds, but also on decryption and on AES-192 or AES-256 white-box designs by attacking two successive round keys. In case the recovered round keys are not the first round keys, the tool `aes_keyschedule` from the Stark project will help rewinding the keyschedule back to the AES key.

The tutorial mentioned in the previous section notes covers the application of CPA against the RHme3 challenge using Jlsca as well.

To close this section, we would like to mention the availability of a new toolchain shortly before the finalization of this book: Whiteboxgrind, a fast implementation to obtain execution traces and apply the DCA on them, enabling attacks that were previously infeasible on large white-box implementations due to memory constraints.

3.7. Linear decoding analysis also known as algebraic attack

A new side-channel analysis technique presented in Chapter 2 of this volume is the *Algebraic Attack*, also referred to as LDA (*linear decoding analysis*), which is specific to computation traces as it takes advantage of the absence of noise, unlike physical power traces. LDA consists of trying to solve a linear algebra problem $M \times z = s$ with $M = [v_1 \| \dots \| v_n]$, where v_i is the vector of values collected in all traces at the same point i, M is the collection of n consecutive points over a window of the traces and z is a vector indicating locations of samples to recombine to match a predictable value s depending on a small part of the secret key. The attack is successful if the system has a solution only for one single predictable value s, so one single key hypothesis. To avoid false positives, it needs more traces than the width of the samples window, that is, the maximum distance between samples to recombine. Therefore, LDA can defeat linear masking schemes with arbitrary number of shares.

An implementation of the first-order LDA implemented in SageMath is available in the White-box Cryptography Design and Analysis kit wboxkit. The trace format is slightly different as each trace is stored in its own file triplet (samples, input and output) and it is quite straightforward to convert the traces already made for Daredevil. Once done, the LDA can be performed. For illustration purposes, LDA is executed against the same set of 32 traces `mem_addr1_rw1_32_7976` acquired in section 3.4 and converted in a `traces` directory, with a window of eight samples. Make sure `~/.sage/local/bin` is in your path.

```
$ sage -pip install wboxkit
$ sage -sh
(sage-sh) $ wboxkit.lda -T 32 -w 8 --masks 1 traces/
MATCH:
sbox #15,
```

```
lin.mask 0x01,
key 0x35='5',
negated? False,
indexes 160...160 (distance 0) [160]
[...]
Key candidates found:
S-Box #0: 0x61('a')
S-Box #1: 0x31('1')
S-Box #2: 0x6c('l')
[...]
Example: 61316c5f7434623133355f525f6f5235
```

Beyond this toy example, this tool demonstrates its real power on more complex white-box implementations with linear masking schemes of any high order involving recombinations over much larger windows. LDA is nicely complementary to DCA which, on its side, can break weak nonlinear encodings and variants of the seminal *CEJO* white-box by Chow et al.

3.8. Injecting faults

Another technique brought from the physical cryptographic attacks is DFA (*differential fault analysis*), as presented in Chapter 10 of Volume 1. Its prerequisite is to have access to the output in clear, to be able to replay the same input several times and to inject faults during the execution of the block cipher.

There are several strategies to inject a fault during the execution. If the white-box implementation does not have any integrity protection, the easiest way is to directly modify a copy of the white-box files statically, in its data or in its code sections. A visual analysis of a first trace as explained in section 3.3 may help targeting the right location for a fault injection.

For the classical *Piret and Quisquater* DFA against AES, the fault model is an unknown modification of a single byte of the state somewhere between the two last *MixColumns* operations for each execution. One advantage of this fault model is that it requires almost no control on the fault itself. It is helpful because white-box intermediate values are encoded and a modification of the encoded representation will lead to an unknown modification of the real value of the attacked byte. Moreover, faults can be injected blindly at arbitrary positions and the faulted outputs can be filtered later. Indeed, for a fault to be exploitable with this attack, it needs to be injected before the last *MixColumns*, and this is easily detectable by inspecting the output, as such a fault will propagate to exactly four bytes of the output. A fault injected too late will affect one single byte and a fault injected too soon will affect the whole output.

The Daredevil DFA framework implements strategies to automatically inject faults statically in a program or a data file. The framework starts by faulting large sections of the data, then it divides and explores sections where faults affect the output, until it reaches faults limited to individual bytes. It observes the fault patterns on the output to filter the results and keeps the potentially good faults. By observing fault patterns, we can even tell if the attacked AES is an encryption or a decryption. Of course, the framework must cope with possible crashes and infinite loops caused by the injected fault, especially when faulting the instructions. For performance reasons, it is preferable to run the tool from a virtual filesystem in random access memory (*tmpfs*).

The upper two-thirds of Figure 3.1(a) show the actual tables of the RHme3 example being initialized (in red) from immediate values in the code itself (in black, from 0x400000 to 0x45b000), before the execution of the rounds. Therefore, targeting the tables used in the one but last round can be achieved by attacking initialization code instructions around approximately 0x445000 to 0x455000 (corresponding to offsets 0x45000 to 0x55000 in the program file). We may skip specifying the code range to attack; the process will just become slower. The following example also includes some other fine-tuning parameters because the target to fault is a code section. The tool documentation explains their usage. When a white-box implementation allows it, faulting data section is typically much easier and faster.

```
#!/usr/bin/env python

import deadpool_dfa
import phoenixAES
import struct

def processinput(iblock, blocksize):
    return (struct.pack(">QQ", iblock//(2**64), iblock%(2**64)), ["--stdin"])

def processoutput(output, blocksize):
    return int(b''.join(output.strip().split(b' ')), 16)

engine=deadpool_dfa.Acquisition(
   targetbin='./whitebox', targetdata='./whitebox', goldendata='./whitebox.gold',
   dfa=phoenixAES, processinput=processinput, processoutput=processoutput, verbose=2,
   faults=[('nop', lambda x: 0x90)], maxleaf=1, minleaf=1, minleafnail=1,
   minfaultspercol=2, addresses=(0x45000,0x55000))

engine.run()
```

The tool outputs a line for each execution. The last ones are provided as illustration, slightly edited. These faulted outputs are to be compared to the reference output 896D983BEDC6275E0F7BBB18DF4AF219. Columns indicate respectively the *Level* (the tool proceeds in several passes, reducing progressively the area being faulted), the faulted memory range (on this last pass, it is a single byte), the type of fault (here each faulted byte is replaced by a NOP instruction), the result (either an output, an infinite loop or a crash) and if an output was collected, the last column indicates if it is faulty, and if the pattern of faulty bytes corresponds to a fault injected somewhere on a column before the last *MixColumns* operation (flagged as *GoodEncFault*).

```
...
Lvl 005 [0x00047934-0x00047935[ nop -> 896D983BEDC6275E0F7BBB18DF4AF219 NoFault
...
Lvl 005 [0x00047BC8-0x00047BC9[ nop -> Loop
...
Lvl 005 [0x00047BF3-0x00047BF4[ nop -> 2E9586D19558C9BCA8B14264A8045095 MajorFault
Lvl 005 [0x00047BF4-0x00047BF5[ nop -> Crash
Lvl 005 [0x00047BF5-0x00047BF6[ nop -> Crash
Lvl 005 [0x00047BF6-0x00047BF7[ nop -> AB6D983BEDC627E90F7B9718DFA4F219 GoodEncFault Col:0
Lvl 005 [0x00047BF7-0x00047BF8[ nop -> 896D982FEDC6BA5E0F51BB187B4AF219 GoodEncFault Col:3
Lvl 005 [0x00047BF7-0x00047BF8[ nop -> 896D982FEDC6BA5E0F51BB187B4AF219 GoodEncFault Col:3
Lvl 005 [0x00047BF8-0x00047BF9[ nop -> 896D223BED28275E7D7BBB18DF4AF28D GoodEncFault Col:2
Lvl 005 [0x00047BF8-0x00047BF9[ nop -> 896D223BED28275E7D7BBB18DF4AF28D GoodEncFault Col:2
Saving 9 traces in dfa_enc_9.txt
```

Two such *GoodEncFault* outputs are collected per faulted column in the saved file `dfa_enc_9.txt`, together with the reference output. This file is now ready for analysis as explained in section 3.9.

In case of an AES-192 or AES-256, the framework can target the previous round key once the last round key has been found.

If the white-box implementation has some integrity protection preventing static fault injection, or if some tables are uncompressed or decoded in RAM, it will be necessary to use dynamic fault injection techniques. Contrarily to the software execution traces, we need only very local binary instrumentation. To achieve that, a large set of tools is available: DBI frameworks seen in section 3.2 or even debugging scripts. In case of complex applications, it is interesting to consider execution snapshots: run the executable up to the few last rounds, make a reference snapshot of the memory and registers, and run all fault attempts from this snapshot. Depending on the executable, some anti-debugging routines might need patching as well.

3.9. Differential fault analysis

Once faulty outputs have been collected according to section 3.8, the next step is to apply the DFA itself. An implementation, phoenixAES, is available in the JeanGrey project.

```
#!/usr/bin/env python

import phoenixAES
phoenixAES.crack_file("dfa_enc_9.txt")
```

It instantaneously returns its result.

```
Last round key #N found:
4E44EACD3F54F5B54A4FB15E0710B974
```

As our example is an AES-128, the last round key is the tenth round key. Using `aes_keyschedule` introduced in section 3.6 against the recovered round key allows us to recover the AES key itself, which is identical to the initial round key.

```
$ aes_keyschedule 4E44EACD3F54F5B54A4FB15E0710B974 10
K00: 61316C5F7434623133355F525F6F5235
```

Some white-box implementations implement countermeasures against this classical DFA. In such a case, it is interesting to test fault injections one round earlier.

Faults will propagate to the whole output, as they are diffused by two *MixColumns* operations, but we can preprocess them as if they were affecting only one column at once, by rewriting each faulty output affecting all 16 bytes as four faulty outputs affecting only four bytes each.

This principle can be illustrated by using the logs of the previous DFA example and pretending it did not find the exploitable outputs flagged as *GoodEncFault*. The idea is to prepare a file based on the reference output and a collection of *MajorFault* outputs, that is, outputs where all bytes are faulty.

```
$ echo 896D983BEDC6275E0F7BBB18DF4AF219 > r8faults
$ grep MajorFault dfa_enc.log|cut -d " " -f 8 >> r8faults
```

Then, use phoenixAES to preprocess the file into a version as if the next round was targeted and analyze it.

```
#!/usr/bin/env python
import phoenixAES

phoenixAES.convert_r8faults_file("r8faults", "r9faults")
phoenixAES.crack_file("r9faults")
```

Again, the last round key was successfully recovered, but this time from faults injected one round earlier.

```
Last round key #N found:
4E44EACD3F54F5B54A4FB15E0710B974
```

There exist many more DFA variants and if the ones presented here do not work, it might be interesting to explore other ones. Nevertheless, we must keep in mind the specificities of white-box fault injection compared to attacking hardware: it is easy to reproduce faults or to generate more faults once a fault position has been identified, but it is hard to work with bitflip models as internal encodings are unknown. Therefore, it is usually better to favor fast analysis techniques with fewer constraints and to try many combinations at many locations.

We only covered AES in this section, but we invite the reader to also have a look at the WhibOx 2021 contest, which was a showcase of various fault injection attacks against white-box implementations of ECDSA signature.

3.10. Coping with external encodings

So far, we have covered tools that did not require much reverse engineering effort and, in best cases, could be fully automated. However, DCA requires that the input (or the output) is accessible in clear and DFA requires the output in clear. This sounds like a reasonable assumption when talking about cryptanalysis of a block-cipher, but because having access to the input or output in clear facilitates a number of attacks, including algebraic analysis methods preceding gray-box attacks, the notion of *external encodings* emerged very soon in the white-box cryptography field. The idea is that an extra layer of encodings (typically, a byte-wise random substitution layer) keeps input and output secret. The application using such white-box design would need to encode its input prior to sending it to the algorithm and would need to decode its output. In the case of a local application, reverse engineering could still probably find the clear data within the application. However, there are some situations where the external encoding layers are not within reach. For example, a proprietary client–server system: there is no need to exactly follow the AES standard in their protocol and the extra encoding/decoding can be handled by the server. Another example is local storage encryption, where standard AES interoperability is not required and data at rest could be stored encrypted *and* encoded.

Fortunately, there exists a variant of the DFA meant to cope with external encodings and DarkPhoenix is a tool implementing such a technique. It has stronger requirements than standard DFA as we must provide instrumentation or emulation able to inject faults in the three last *full* rounds (those with a *MixColumns*) for an AES-128. The number of executions and faults is also quite consequent: first, running about half a million times the white-box algorithm with random inputs to find sets able to enumerate each output byte, and then injecting about a million faults in total. In case we have access to both the white-box encryption and decryption implementations, the first step's complexity is drastically reduced as output bytes can directly be enumerated.

If we have reversed or extracted the white-box logic enough to be able to apply individual rounds on an AES state, it is possible to attempt the so-called BGE attack, referring to the authors of the initial version of this powerful algebraic technique: *Billet*, *Gilbert* and *Ech-Chatbi*. This attack is implemented in the BlueGalaxyEnergy tool and targets the classic design by Chow et al., which is (at least partially) reused in most white-box challenges.

3.11. Conclusion

As white-box designs moved from academic propositions to commercial implementations, it is important that white-box attacks, which were also confined to papers for quite a number of years, follow a similar path and develop into practical tools. Tools enable evaluations of these white-box implementations and help raise awareness for a larger public. Fortunately, the situation is changing with more and more researchers sharing their tools under open source licenses. Some of these can run almost fully automatically in the best scenarios, but acquiring more knowledge on the topic will help choosing and tuning the proper tools. Also, when none of the easy ways is working, mastering execution trace visualization and binary instrumentation will help the deobfuscation process and the extraction of features, which is a prerequisite of more advanced white-box cryptanalysis techniques.

3.12. Notes and further references

– Section 3.1. Resources for public white-box implementations and attacks.

- Deadpool project: https://github.com/SideChannelMarvels/Deadpool.
- WhibOx competitions: https://whibox.io/contests.

– Section 3.2. Tools for tracing programs:

- Intel PIN: http://www.intel.com/software/pintool.
- Valgrind: https://valgrind.org.
- DynamoRIO: https://dynamorio.org.
- Frida: https://frida.re/.
- QBDI: https://qbdi.quarkslab.com.
- Qiling: https://qiling.io/.
- Rainbow: https://github.com/Ledger-Donjon/rainbow.
- TracerPIN and TracerGrind: https://github.com/SideChannelMarvels/Tracer.

Usage examples against white-boxes are available among others for Rainbow: https://donjon.ledger.com/ctf-rainbow/; QBDI: https://www.romainthomas.fr/post/20-09-r2con-obfuscated-whitebox-part2/ and https://blog.quarkslab.com/

introduction-to-whiteboxes-and-collision-based-attacks-with-qbdi.html; and the SideChannelMarvels tools in general: https://github.com/SideChannelMarvels/Deadpool/wiki.

A copy of the RHme3 challenge is available at:

- https://github.com/SideChannelMarvels/Deadpool/tree/master/wbs_aes_rhme3_prequal.

– Section 3.3. Another possible visual aid is to generate a data dependency graph, which requires us to trace memory and registers as well (see, for example, Goubin et al. (2018)).

– Section 3.5. Tools for preprocessing traces are as follows:

- Daredevil: https://github.com/SideChannelMarvels/Daredevil.

- Jlsca: https://github.com/Keysight/Jlsca.

Sample reduction techniques are described in Breunesse et al. (2018). A tutorial using Deadpool DCA framework for trace acquisition, then Jlsca for trace reduction and analysis against the RHme3 example is available: https://github.com/ikizhvatov/jlsca-tutorials/blob/master/rhme2017-qual-wb.ipynb.

– Section 3.6.

- Stark: https://github.com/SideChannelMarvels/Stark.

- Extension of DCA to all 1-byte affine encodings is explained in Klemsa (2016).

- Whiteboxgrind: https://gitlab.lrz.de/tueisec/whiteboxgrind (as described in Holl et al. (2023)).

– Section 3.7. wboxkit: https://github.com/hellman/wboxkit containing the LDA tool along with tutorials based on the low-level circuit construction kit circkit https://github.com/CryptoExperts/circkit, allowing us to experiment with various white-box masking schemes. LAA is described in Biryukov and Udovenko (2018) and LDA is described in Goubin et al. (2018), together with a Mathematica proof-of-concept at https://github.com/junwei-wang/WhibOx-breaking-adoring-poitras/tree/master/lda.

– Section 3.9. JeanGrey: https://github.com/SideChannelMarvels/JeanGrey.

To better understand DFA, especially in the white-box context, see Alpirez Bock et al. (2019) and https://blog.quarkslab.com/differential-fault-analysis-on-white-box-aes-implementations.html. See also Lu (2019), which improves phoenixAES and relaxes the fault requirements. For fault attacks against ECDSA, see Barbu et al. (2022) and Bauer et al. (2022).

– Section 3.10.

- DarkPhoenix: https://github.com/SideChannelMarvels/Dark Phoenix.

- BlueGalaxyEnergy: https://github.com/SideChannelMarvels/BlueGalaxy Energy. See also Derbez et al. (2018), which provides a proof-of-concept at https://recovaffeq. github.io/ to attack all variants of the Chow white-box with external encodings, what is called the *CEJO framework*.

– Section 3.11. Tools or just proof-of-concepts and datasets are essential for scientific reproducibility and to demonstrate results. Open source licensing will allow anyone to contribute and build upon the existing, rather than having to start from scratch. Therefore, if you are a researcher, do not hesitate to publish your scripts as well, even if they are less polished than your papers!

3.13. References

Alpirez Bock, E., Bos, J.W., Brzuska, C., Hubain, C., Michiels, W., Mune, C., Gonzalez, E.S., Teuwen, P., Treff, A. (2019). White-box cryptography: Don't forget about grey-box attacks. *Journal of Cryptology*, 32(4), 1095–1143.

Barbu, G., Beullens, W., Dottax, E., Giraud, C., Houzelot, A., Li, C., Mahzoun, M., Ranea, A., Xie, J. (2022). ECDSA white-box implementations: Attacks and designs from WhibOx 2021 contest. Cryptology ePrint Archive, Report 2022/385 [Online]. Available at: https://eprint.iacr.org/2022/385.

Bauer, S., Drexler, H., Gebhardt, M., Klein, D., Laus, F., Mittmann, J. (2022). Attacks against white-box ECDSA and discussion of countermeasures – A report on the WhibOx 2021 contest. Cryptology ePrint Archive, Report 2022/448 [Online]. Available at: https://eprint.iacr.org/2022/448.

Biryukov, A. and Udovenko, A. (2018). Attacks and countermeasures for white-box designs. In *ASIACRYPT 2018*, Peyrin, T. and Galbraith, S. (eds). Springer, Heidelberg/Brisbane.

Breunesse, C.-B., Kizhvatov, I., Muijrers, R., Spruyt, A. (2018). Towards fully automated analysis of whiteboxes: Perfect dimensionality reduction for perfect leakage. Cryptology ePrint Archive, Report 2018/095 [Online]. Available at: https://eprint.iacr.org/2018/095.

Derbez, P., Fouque, P.-A., Lambin, B., Minaud, B. (2018). On recovering affine encodings in white-box implementations. *IACR TCHES*, 2018(3), 121–149.

Goubin, L., Paillier, P., Rivain, M., Wang, J. (2018). How to reveal the secrets of an obscure white-box implementation. Cryptology ePrint Archive, Report 2018/098 [Online]. Available at: https://eprint.iacr.org/2018/098.

Holl, T., Bogad, K., Gruber, M. (2023). Whiteboxgrind – Automated analysis of whitebox cryptography. In *Constructive Side-Channel Analysis and Secure Design*, Kavun, E.B. and Pehl, M. (eds). Springer, Cham.

Klemsa, J. (2016). Side-channel attack analysis of AES white-box schemes. PhD Thesis, Czech Technical University, Prague.

Lu, Y. (2019). Attacking hardware AES with DFA. *arXiv* [Online]. Available at: http://arxiv.org/abs/1902.08693.

4
Code Obfuscation

Sebastian SCHRITTWIESER[1] and Stefan KATZENBEISSER[2]
[1]*University of Vienna, Austria*
[2]*University of Passau, Germany*

4.1. Introduction

This chapter deals with practical techniques that try to "obfuscate" code, i.e. to make the code more difficult to understand for either a human analyst or an automated framework based on dynamic or static code analysis. Obfuscation has several application domains that range from intellectual property protection over code diversity up to hiding secrets like passwords or keys in software. In the chapter, we first define the task of obfuscation. Subsequently, we look at various attacker goals as well as attacker models, which largely restrict the type of software obfuscation that is applicable in certain application domains. Finally, we give examples of obfuscation methods, discuss their strength and outline applications.

4.1.1. *Definition of obfuscation*

Informally, code obfuscation tries to convert code – either in the form of source code or executable code – into code that is unintelligible in some form, either by a human observer or by an automated analysis tool. The development of code obfuscation techniques was mainly driven by the desire to hide the specific implementation of a program.

Malware authors, who aimed at hiding the malicious purpose of a program, were one of the main driving forces of the development of obfuscation techniques.

Embedded Cryptography 3,
coordinated by Emmanuel PROUFF, Guénaël RENAULT,
Matthieu RIVAIN and Colin O'FLYNN. © ISTE Ltd 2025.

Consequently, breaking obfuscations was a prerequisite for malware detection. Another important application in the early days of software obfuscation was the protection of license checks embedded in commercial software. Since then, software protection has developed more sophisticated obfuscation techniques to hide the behavior of the code, while analysts have been using increasingly complex code analysis techniques to defeat obfuscations. The demand from the malware economy is still one of the major driving forces behind the development of obfuscation techniques. The other leading application area of code obfuscation is the protection of commercial software against reverse engineering, which tries to extract some interesting secrets from a program or binary. This secret may be a cryptographic key, an algorithm considered a trade secret, or credentials for a remote service. Practical software obfuscation, as discussed in this chapter, aims to provide heuristics and practical solutions that make reverse engineering more difficult. This should be distinguished from provably secure obfuscation, which originated from the cryptographic community and aims to provide a solution for the software obfuscation problem whose security can be proven mathematically.

4.1.2. *Goals of obfuscation*

The precise goals of code obfuscation can vary between different application domains. In general, obfuscation aims to defend against a human or an automated analyst, which tries to perform one of the following tasks.

4.1.3. *Protecting against locating data*

In this scenario, an analyst aims to identify the presence of certain pieces of data: for example, are cryptographic keys, which can be extracted in order to break up some of the encryption routine, or constants used in cryptographic implementations, which give a hint to which algorithm was implemented.

4.1.4. *Protecting against locating code*

In this scenario, the analyst tries to identify a particular piece of code in a larger obfuscated software package. For example, of interest may be the entry point of a cryptographic software routine, so that it can be analyzed in more detail in a later step of the attack. More generally, the analyst may ask the question of whether a program implements a particular functionality (such as a particular cipher) or simply whether a program is malicious or not.

4.1.5. *Protecting against extraction of code*

Here, the analyst seeks to extract a "meaningful" piece of code from an obfuscated program. For example, their goal may be to extract the decryption routine of a Digital Rights Management system in order to be able to bypass any protections. In another application, the analyst seeks to extract fragments of code written by a commercial competitor. In some use cases, the code does not need to be extracted from the program and integrated into a separate executable as long as the functional component within the original executable can be accessed at runtime (called "in-situ reuse"). For example, instead of writing a dedicated decryption routine, we can bundle an existing obfuscated program with an attack software, as long as the decryption routine can be called.

4.1.6. *Protecting against understanding of code*

In this case, a human analyst seeks to "understand" the behavior of a piece of obfuscated code. This requires that the analyst must be able to "remove" the obfuscation techniques and gain an understanding of the original, non-obfuscated program or a nontrivial fragment of it. For example, the analyst may want to uncover the code of an unknown encryption scheme in use, to find vulnerabilities in existing programs, to correct flaws in software for which the source code is not available, and create new programs that are compatible with proprietary software. A major driving force here can be intellectual property theft.

4.1.7. *Attacker models*

Depending on the capabilities of the adversary, obfuscation methods have a largely varying strength. For example, a human reverse engineer who tries to understand a piece of code of a competitor may afford spending time and effort on highly complex and time-consuming analyses, while an antivirus vendor, who has to timely analyze hundreds of thousands of different malware samples each day, may be required to resort to very lightweight and thus limited analysis techniques. We can roughly distinguish the following different forms of analysis methods in increasing level of sophistication.

4.1.8. *Pattern matching*

This analysis is the simplest – and fastest – form of code analysis. It is a purely syntactic analysis on the program binary or byte code. For example, we may search for suspicious substrings or patterns, for example, encoded as regular expressions. The main benefit of this analysis technique is that it is very fast. It can however be easily defeated by stronger obfuscations.

4.1.9. *Automated static analysis*

In this method, code is analyzed without actually executing it. In contrast to syntactic pattern matching, static analysis reasons the program semantics. Typical forms of static analysis include disassemblers that interpret branch targets, or tools that reconstruct the control flow graph (CFG) of a program.

4.1.10. *Automated dynamic analysis*

This analysis method actually runs a program in a secure environment (e.g. a specially crafted sandbox) and observes its behavior. This allows it to collect a vast amount of data: from system calls to accessed memory locations. The advantage of this method is that it allows it to analyze a program with respect to executed traces. The downside is that data gathered from one or several runs of a program do not necessarily allow it to draw conclusions about the behavior of other runs or the entire program.

4.1.11. *Human-assisted analysis*

This analysis method is the most complex one. Here, a human analyst performs a tool-assisted exploration of a piece of code. This process is typically referred to as reverse-engineering, where the analyst aims to understand the program's structure and behavior.

4.2. Obfuscation methods

Obfuscation techniques can be roughly divided into three categories.

– *Data obfuscations* are used to modify data contained in software in such a way that it becomes difficult for an adversary to locate data based on its known structure. Thus, data obfuscations are primarily used to prevent simple pattern matching attacks.

– *Static obfuscations* make the code of software artificially more complex with the goal of rendering static code analysis – performed by a human analyst or an automated analysis program – more difficult. Static obfuscations essentially complicate the CFG of a program and make it harder accessible for analysis.

– *Dynamic obfuscations* modify code at runtime and are tailored against dynamic code analysis. Dynamic obfuscation aims to defend against attackers who have captured execution traces of the software at runtime.

Based on the protection goal and the security property, useful obfuscation techniques need to be determined by the obfuscator.

In the following, important obfuscation techniques of all three groups are presented and their protection concepts are briefly explained. For more details on these obfuscations, see Schrittwieser et al. (2016).

4.2.1. *Data obfuscation*

4.2.1.1. *Data encoding/encryption*

Data is converted into another representation using a special encoding or encryption function. At runtime, an inverse function is used to convert the data back to its plaintext representation. An advanced variant of this data obfuscation technique is mixed-Boolean arithmetic (MBA) where a simple expression is converted into a difficult-to-understand representation by combining arithmetic (e.g. ADD and SUB) and Boolean operations (e.g. AND, XOR and NOT). For example, the code fragment:

```
2 * (x & y) + (x ^ y)
```

is equivalent to

```
x + y
```

4.2.1.2. *Converting static data to procedures*

Instead of storing data in software (encoded, encrypted or in plaintext), it can also be calculated at runtime, thus effectively hiding it from static code analysis. White-box cryptography can be seen as an extreme form of this obfuscation technique, since the secret cryptographic key is not stored in the software, but is integrated into the program code as a complex sequence of operations (e.g. table lookups). For example, the stored constant:

```
let symbols = "abcdefghijklmnopqrstuvwxyz
    ABCDEFGHIJKLMNOPQRSTUVWXYZ0123456789";
```

can be converted to the following code fragment:

```
function generate_symbols() {
  let symbols = "";
  for (let i = 0; i < 26; i++) {
     symbols += String.fromCharCode(97 + i);
  }

  for (let i = 0; i < 26; i++) {
     symbols += String.fromCharCode(65 + i);
  }

  for (let i = 0; i < 10; i++) {
```

```
        symbols += String.fromCharCode(48 + i);
    }

    return symbols;
}
```

4.2.1.3. *Data transformation*

Data transformations do not directly change the appearance of data, but the sequence or composition in which they are stored. For example, data can be protected by splitting, merging or reordering in such a way that a simple search for known structures is prevented. For example, a cryptographic key with a length of 256 bit can be hidden by splitting it into two partial keys of 128 bits each. A search for a string of length 256 bit would not directly identify the partial keys:

```
let keyChunk1 = "01234567";
let keyChunk2 = "89abcdef";
let keyChunk3 = "01234567";
let keyChunk4 = "89abcdef";

function decryptData(data) {
    let key = keyChunk1 + keyChunk2 + keyChunk3 + keyChunk4;
    // Decrypt data using the key
    // ...
}
```

4.2.2. *Static obfuscation*

4.2.2.1. *Control flow obfuscations*

The CFG of a software is tremendously helpful for an adversary performing static code analysis. Methods for obfuscating the CFG can be divided into two categories. Control flow indirections work with program jumps, which are computed at run time only. Thus, a static reconstruction of the CFG is made more difficult as important flow information is not available before running the program. A well-known type of this protection is control flow flattening. In this technique, control flow is directed to a central dispatcher at each branch, which then determines the code block to be executed next:

```
function cfg_flattening() {
    int flow = 3;
    while(flow != 0) {
        switch(flow) {
```

```
            case 1:
                print "CFG"
                flow = 4;
                break;

            case 2:
                print "is"
                flow = 1;
                break;

            case 3:
                print "This"
                flow = 2;
                break;

            case 4:
                print "flattening!"
                flow = 0;
                break;
        }
    }
}
```

This turns the CFG into a flat but very wide graph, which does not contain information about the actual flow of a program. In contrast, control flow transformations change the CFG in such a way that it remains reconstructible by an adversary, but looks different.

4.2.2.2. *Junk code insertion*

Junk code insertion increases the code size without modifying the effect of the computation. Two variants of this technique exist: irrelevant and dead code insertion. Irrelevant code are sequences of instructions that do not have an effect on the execution of a program, while dead code describes code blocks that cannot be reached in the CFG of the software and thus never get executed. Both variants make the analysis of code more time consuming, since the amount of program code is artificially increased. For example, the code sequence:

```
mov eax, 0
mov ebx, 7
add ebx, eax
```

can be changed into:

```
mov eax, 0
```

```
mov ebx, 7
xor eax, eax
add ebx, eax
```

4.2.2.3. *Opaque predicates*

Opaque expressions are expressions whose value is known at obfuscation time, but difficult for an attacker to determine using static code analysis. Boolean-valued opaque predicates are widely used to construct fake branches where only one path gets actually executed at runtime. The other path can be considered as junk code that is hard to identify:

```
mov ebx, 5
xor eax, eax ; clear eax register
xor eax, ebx ; xor eax with ebx, resulting in a non-zero value
jz label     ; jump to label if zero flag is set (which it is not)
```

Opaque predicates are often used in combination with data obfuscation techniques (such as MBA) in order to make the analysis more difficult.

4.2.2.4. *Identifier renaming*

By substituting expressive names of variables or fuctions with random strings, semantic information, which can be important for a human analyst, is removed. Identifier renaming is primarily used for source and byte code obfuscation. While binary code usually does not contain identifier names anymore, byte code (e.g. Java) typically preserves some of the identifier names. For example:

```
function convertCurrency(amount, exchangeRate) {
    return amount * exchangeRate;
}
console.log(convertCurrency(100, 0.91)); // Output: 91
```

can be transformed to:

```
function _0x1234(_0x4321, _0x9876) {
    return _0x4321 * _0x9876;
}
console.log(_0x1234(100, 0.91)); // Output: 91
```

4.2.2.5. *Code diversity*

Software can be implemented in multiple ways. Thus, instructions or sequences of instructions can be replaced with syntactically different, yet semantically equivalent, code. As a simple example:

```
xor eax, eax
```

can be changed to

```
xor eax, 0
```

without altering the semantics of the program.

4.2.2.6. *Aliasing*

Inserting spurious aliases (i.e. pointers to memory locations) can make code analysis more complex as the number of possible ways for modifying data at a particular location in memory increases. These pointer references can also be used as indirections to complicate the reconstruction of the CFG of a program in static analysis scenarios. Consider the following code fragment:

```
int opaque(int* x, int* y) {
    *x = 1;
    *y = 2

    if ((*y - *y) == 0 ) {
        // dead code?
    }
}
```

At first sight, it seems the if-statement could never be true. However, if the function gets called with variables pointing to the same memory location, that is,

```
opaque(&var1, &var1)
```

the alleged dead code is executed.

4.2.2.7. *Code reordering*

Like data structures, expressions and statements can also be reordered to decrease locality. This concept can be taken even further to move parts of the code or functionality into different modules or programs. For example:

```
mov eax, 2
mov ebx, 3
add eax, ebx
```

can be replaced by:

```
mov ebx, 3
mov eax, 2
add eax, ebx
```

4.2.2.8. *Loop transformations*

This group of obfuscations modify the structure of loops. Loop unrolling, where the body of a loop is replicated one or multiple times to reduce the number of loop iterations, can be used to make the code more complex. For example:

```
for (var i = 1; i <= 10; i++) {
    console.log(i);
}
```

can be replaced by:

```
console.log("1");
console.log("2");
console.log("3");
console.log("4");
console.log("5");
console.log("6");
console.log("7");
console.log("8");
console.log("9");
console.log("10");
```

Furthermore, loop tiling breaks up the iteration space of a loop and creates nested loops. Loop fission splits a loop into two or more loops with the same iteration space and spreads the loop body over these new loops.

4.2.2.9. *Function and class transformations*

These obfuscations change the structure of functions (binary code) or classes (byte code) in order to generate more complex code. Important concepts are as follows:

– *Function cloning* splits the control flow in two or more different paths that look different to the analyst, while they are in fact semantically equivalent.

– *Function merging* combines the bodies of two or more (preferably unrelated) functions. The new method has a mixed parameter list of the merged functions and an extra parameter that selects the function body to be executed.

– *Overlapping functions* generate code so that the binary code of one function ends with bytes that also define the beginning of another function.

– *Class factoring* artificially splits up classes.

– *False refactoring* creates a misleading (abstract) parent class for classes that have no common behavior.

– *Class hierarchy flattening* removes all inheritance relations from object-oriented programs.

For example, function merging can merge the body of the two unrelated functions:

```
function printA() {
    console.log("A");
}

function printB() {
    console.log("B");
}
```

into one (more complex) function:

```
function printAorB(func) {
    if (func == "A") {
        console.log("A");
    } else {
        console.log("B");
    }
}
```

4.2.2.10. *Parallelization*

Parallel code tends to be harder to understand than sequential code. Adding dummy processes to a program or parallelizing sequential code blocks that do not depend on each other increases the complexity of the analysis.

4.2.2.11. *Library hiding*

Calls to libraries of programming languages (particularly ones with a high level of abstraction) offer useful information to an analyst, because they are called by their name and they cannot be obfuscated. By replacing standard libraries with custom versions, these calls can be removed. Other variants of this obfuscation method are to link libraries statically into the application or to combine many small libraries into a few large ones.

4.2.3. *Dynamic obfuscation*

4.2.3.1. *Virtualization*

Virtualization is one of the most advanced techniques for binary obfuscation. The functionality of a program is converted into byte code for a custom virtual machine interpreter that is bundled with the program. The virtual machine interpreter and payload can be different for each instance of the program (*polymorphism*).

4.2.3.2. *Anti-debugging*

Anti-debugging techniques actively oppose analysis attempts via disassembly or debugging. For example, attached debuggers can be detected based on timing and latency analysis or the identification of code modifications caused by software breakpoints. Another technique is the execution of undocumented instructions in order to confuse a code analysis tool or a human analyst. For example, the following code uses the Windows specific `fs` segment register to access the TEB (thread environment block) and check the value of the `BeingDebugged` flag:

```
; Check if the program is being debugged
mov eax, fs:[0x30]
movzx eax, byte ptr [eax + 2]
cmp al, 2
jz Debugged

; code to be executed if not debugged
; ...

jmp End

Debugged:
; code to be executed if debugged
; ...

End:
```

4.2.3.3. *Hardware-assisted obfuscations*

Hardware can be utilized in code obfuscation in two ways: *hardware tokens* bind hardware and software by making the execution of the software dependent on a value provided by a hardware token. Without this token, analysis of the software will fail, because important information such as jump targets is not available.

Hardware-based isolation mechanisms for trusted computation – for example, Intel SGX – allow an application to prevent other applications and even the operating system kernel from accessing certain memory regions. While not primarily designed for code obfuscation, such mechanisms are well-suited to protect code and data from runtime inspection and tampering.

4.2.3.4. *Environmental requirements*

This concept makes the correct execution of a program dependent on some environmental conditions (e.g. MAC address of network interface) and thus binds a program to a specific runtime environment.

4.2.3.5. *Packing and encryption*

Packing and encryption of program code is widely used by malware authors. The basic idea is to hide code by encoding or encrypting it as data so that it cannot be interpreted by static analysis. An unpacking routine turns the packed or encrypted data back into machine-interpretable code at runtime. By changing the encryption or encoding keys, packed program code can easily be rewritten upon distribution to complicate simple pattern matching analysis (polymorphism).

4.2.3.6. *Dynamic code modification*

With this protection, code is modified at runtime right before its execution. For example, we can correct intentionally erroneous code at runtime. Static analysis techniques fail to analyze such programs, as their correct functionality is available at runtime only.

4.2.3.7. *Server side code execution and code mobility*

With *server side code execution*, code to be protected is not directly included in a program, but is executed on a server and only the result of the execution is returned. This effectively prevents code analysis and also allows the execution of a program to be made dependent on additional conditions (e.g. the existence of a valid license).

In contrast, *code mobility* is a protection technique where pieces of code are downloaded on-demand from a remote system (e.g. a server) at runtime and then executed in the context of the program.

4.3. Attacks against obfuscation

4.3.1. *Principles of program analysis*

The security of obfuscation techniques is directly linked to the performance of program analysis methods. Programs can be analyzed statically or dynamically. Static analysis looks at the code of a program without actually executing it; for example, to extract the CFG. In contrast, dynamic analysis observes the runtime behavior of a program. In practice, both methods are often used in combination.

4.3.1.1. *Static analysis*

The foundation of static analysis is always the code of the program. This could either be source code, byte/intermediate code or binary code. Typical static analysis methods are disassembling, control flow analysis, data flow analysis, data dependence analysis, alias analysis, slicing and decompilation. All static analysis methodologies share the common characteristic that they generate conservative information. This means that everything that can be read from a static analysis is correct. For example, if a certain value is assigned to a variable at a given point in the code, it can be assumed with certainty that this will actually happen at runtime every time that code is executed.

However, static analysis is incomplete in general and always a trade-off between precision and analysis efforts. While some static analysis algorithms may collect imprecise information, but are fast, others may collect more precise information, but are slow.

4.3.1.2. *Dynamic analysis*

Dynamic analysis observes a program at runtime. This includes its internal state (e.g. memory and CPU register values) and the program's interaction with its environment (e.g. network connections and file system access). Typical dynamic analysis methods are debugging, profiling, tracing and emulation. The result from dynamic analysis is always nonconservative information. The existence of observable behavior (e.g. the assignment of a certain value to a variable) does not allow us to draw conclusions about the behavior in future program executions. Internal and external factors can lead to a completely different runtime behavior.

4.3.2. *Measuring the strength of obfuscations*

In contrast to cryptography, it is very difficult to make a precise statement about the strength of an obfuscation as it depends on a variety of parameters, including the motivation and creativity of a human analyst. We follow the proposal of Collberg et al. (1997) and define the strength of obfuscations in terms of four parameters: potency, resilience, cost and stealth.

4.3.2.1. *Potency*

Usually, the goal in software engineering is to make code less complex. In contrast, a potent obfuscating transformation makes code more complex. Thus, potency measures how much more obscure and unreadable an obfuscated representation of a program is for a human analyst. In practice, potency is often evaluated with software complexity metrics (e.g. counting textual properties of the source code and cyclomatic complexity).

4.3.2.2. *Resilience*

In contrast to potency, resilience measures the strength of a transformation against an automatic deobfuscator program. Both the programmer's effort (amount of time required to construct an automatic deobfuscator for a particular obfuscating transformation to effectively reduce its potency) and the deobfuscator's effort (execution time and space required to run the deobfuscator) are taken into consideration. Resilience tends to decrease with advances in the area of program analysis. As a general rule of thumb, static obfuscations can only be expected to be resilient against static analyses. In case an analyst applies dynamic analysis, static obfuscations tend to fail and one has to resort to dynamic obfuscations.

4.3.2.3. *Cost*

The application of obfuscations to a program has negative consequences on performance. Cost or efficiency measures the computational overhead (runtime, memory consumption, etc.) of an obfuscating transformation. Quantifying cost penalties of an obfuscation is easy compared to potency and resilience. However, cost is directly related to potency and resilience, as typically an increased strength of obfuscation results in higher costs.

4.3.2.4. *Stealth*

The stealth property indicates the extent to which obfuscated code can be distinguished from untransformed code. There exist two types of obfuscation stealth: with local stealth an adversary can not determine a particular instruction as being affected by an obfuscating transformation. In contrast, with steganographic stealth it is not possible to determine if a program has been transformed with a certain transformation or not.

4.4. Application of code obfuscation

4.4.1. *Digital rights management*

One of the first applications of code obfuscation was Digital Rights Management, where a content owner wants to retain control of the use of a certain piece of content distributed to a number of clients. The central idea was to encrypt the content with a (symmetric) cipher and issue a special license, which included the decryption key, to intended recipients. A piece of software at the side of the client was responsible to enforce the conditions of the license (enforcing the maximum number of views of the object). Only if the conditions in the license were met, the software would decrypt the content.

The obvious threat models in this scenario were attacks that extract the key embedded in the license so that the content could be decrypted without enforcing the conditions of the license. Note that this key has to be present in the player and can be extracted using code or memory inspection. Thus, code obfuscation was seen as a viable method to "hide" the key in software. The goal was thus to hide a piece of data in code.

A different strategy to generate a pirated player was to extract the decryption functionality without actually trying to extract the key. In this case, the existing player software including the key was interfaced with and called by the pirated player. This attack can be seen as an instance of code extraction. Regarding the security properties, we have to assume a human-assisted analysis.

4.4.2. *Intellectual property protection*

A key driver for the construction of obfuscation techniques was the desire to protect intellectual property (such as novel algorithms or proprietary configurations) within software. The goal here is twofold: for one, locating the desired piece of code in a large software package should be made difficult. This will certainly increase the effort for a human analyst. Second, the defender tries to make understanding of the code – and thus removing the obfuscations – more difficult.

Similar to the case of Digital Rights Management, we must assume that a human analyst is performing the task using special tools. Thus, this application puts high demands on the obfuscations employed.

4.4.3. *Malware obfuscation*

Virtually all newly discovered malware comes with some form of code obfuscation. Due to the large number of new malware variants, antivirus vendors have to timely analyze hundreds of thousands of different malware samples each day. Thus, they are required to resort to rather lightweight and thus limited analysis techniques, such as static or simple dynamic analysis. For this reason, rather lightweight obfuscations may still be effective.

4.4.4. *Hardware-software binding*

Binding a certain piece of software to an instance of hardware has been proposed as means to limit the impact of supply chain attacks and overproduction: since one instance of software runs only on one particular device, software cannot be copied between two devices. Even if the production of a pirated hardware instance would be possible, the necessary software will not run on them. Hardware-software binding thus allows to control the number of devices sold. Hardware-software binding has also been proposed as a means to enhance software security, as critical portions of the software (such as addresses of jump targets) can only be determined when an attacker has access to the appropriate hardware.

Methodologically, hardware-assisted obfuscation methods are popular in this domain. For the attacker model, one typically has to assume a human-assisted analyst, who has access to one piece of hardware.

4.4.5. *Software diversity*

Software diversity tries to enhance the security of software products by shipping syntactically different software packages to each client. The hope is that an exploit generated for one particular software instance will not run on the others and that an attacker thus has to attack every software instance individually, which hinders large-scale attacks. Technically, code diversification uses methods of software obfuscation to generate several syntactically different instances of software that share the same functionality.

4.5. Conclusions

In this chapter, practical code obfuscation has been discussed. This type of software protection intentionally makes code more complicated by adding irrelevant code, increasing the control flow complexity, encoding data structures, etc. As long as the exact method of complication (including its configuration such as random seeds, etc.) is not known to the attacker, it can make analysis significantly more difficult. However, no well-defined level of security exists here. To some extent, this can be attributed to the fact that attackers are human and, therefore, hard-to-measure characteristics such as motivation, creativity and persistence play a crucial role in the success of an attack. Also obfuscation resilience tends to decrease with advances in the area of program analysis. Thus, practical code obfuscation remains an arms race between defenders and attackers.

4.6. Notes and further references

In their book *Surreptitious Software*, Nagra and Collberg (2009) gave a scholarly introduction and overview of the topic of code obfuscation. Schrittwieser et al. (2016) classified goals of obfuscation as well as types of code analysis methods and generated *attack scenarios* by combining them.

– Section 4.1. The cryptographic obfuscation field originated from the work of Barak et al. (2001) and led to the development of the theory of "indistinguishability obfuscation" (e.g. see, Jain et al. (2021) and Garg et al. (2016)). However, no practical provably secure obfuscation has been provided so far.

– Section 4.2. In the literature, many complex and creative concepts for *code diversity* were proposed, such as shellcode, which looks like English prose (Mason et al. (2009)), functionality implemented through side effects of the processor (Schrittwieser et al. (2014)), or coding of programs as a sequence of MOV instructions (Dolan (2013)). Katzenbeisser et al. (2012) analyzed how *physically unclonable functions* (PUFs) can be used in the context of code obfuscation. Various advanced packing and encryption concepts have been proposed in the literature, for example, mimimorphism (Wu et al. 2010), which encodes packed code into a representation that looks like real program code and thus increases obfuscation stealth.

– Section 4.3. Collberg et al. (1997) first proposed the metrics potency, resilience, and stealth and conducted an evaluation of the strength of existing obfuscations. Ceccato et al. (2017) measured obfuscation potency through observing human reserve-engineers while they analyzed binary code.

– Section 4.4. Different concepts for *software diversity* were surveyed by Larsen et al. (2014). A *hardware-software binding* scheme based on control flow indirections and self-check summing using PUFs was proposed by Xiong et al. (2019).

4.7. References

Barak, B., Goldreich, O., Impagliazzo, R., Rudich, S., Sahai, A., Vadhan, S., Yang, K. (2001). On the (im)possibility of obfuscating programs. In *Advances in Cryptology – CRYPTO 2001: 21st Annual International Cryptology Conference*, Santa Barbara, 19–23 August. Springer, Berlin, Heidelberg.

Ceccato, M., Tonella, P., Basile, C., Coppens, B., De Sutter, B., Falcarin, P., Torchiano, M. (2017). How professional hackers understand protected code while performing attack tasks. In *2017 IEEE/ACM 25th International Conference on Program Comprehension (ICPC)*, Buenos Aires.

Collberg, C., Thomborson, C., Low, D. (1997). A taxonomy of obfuscating transformations. Technical Report, University of Auckland, Auckland.

Dolan, S. (2013). mov is Turing-complete. Lecture, University of Cambridge, Cambridge [Online]. Available at: https://www.slideshare.net/slideshow/mov-is-turing-complete/54328998#6.

Garg, S., Gentry, C., Halevi, S., Raykova, M., Sahai, A., Waters, B. (2016). Candidate indistinguishability obfuscation and functional encryption for all circuits. *SIAM Journal on Computing*, 45(3), 882–929.

Jain, A., Lin, H., Sahai, A. (2021). Indistinguishability obfuscation from well-founded assumptions. In *Proceedings of the 53rd Annual ACM SIGACT Symposium on Theory of Computing*. ACM, New York.

Katzenbeisser, S., Kocabaş, Ü., Rožić, V., Sadeghi, A.-R., Verbauwhede, I., Wachsmann, C. (2012). PUFs: Myth, fact or busted? A security evaluation of physically unclonable functions (PUFs) cast in silicon. In *Cryptographic Hardware and Embedded Systems – CHES 2012: 14th International Workshop*, Leuven, 9–12 September. Springer, Berlin, Heidelberg.

Larsen, P., Homescu, A., Brunthaler, S., Franz, M. (2014). Sok: Automated software diversity. In *2014 IEEE Symposium on Security and Privacy*, Berkeley.

Mason, J., Small, S., Monrose, F., MacManus, G. (2009). English shellcode. In *Proceedings of the 16th ACM Conference on Computer and Communications Security*. ACM, New York.

Nagra, J. and Collberg, C. (2009). *Surreptitious Software: Obfuscation, Watermarking, and Tamperproofing for Software Protection: Obfuscation, Watermarking, and Tamperproofing for Software Protection*. Pearson Education, London.

Schrittwieser, S., Katzenbeisser, S., Kieseberg, P., Huber, M., Leithner, M., Mulazzani, M., Weippl, E. (2014). Covert computation: Hiding code in code through compile-time obfuscation. *Computers & Security*, 42, 13–26.

Schrittwieser, S., Katzenbeisser, S., Kinder, J., Merzdovnik, G., Weippl, E. (2016). Protecting software through obfuscation: Can it keep pace with progress in code analysis? *ACM Computing Surveys (CSUR)*, 49(1), 1–37.

Wu, Z., Gianvecchio, S., Xie, M., Wang, H. (2010). Mimimorphism: A new approach to binary code obfuscation. In *Proceedings of the 17th ACM Conference on Computer and Communications Security*. ACM, New York.

Xiong, W., Schaller, A., Katzenbeisser, S., Szefer, J. (2019). Software protection using dynamic PUFs. *IEEE Transactions on Information Forensics and Security*, 15, 2053–2068.

PART 2

Randomness and Key Generation

5

True Random Number Generation

Viktor FISCHER[1,2], Florent BERNARD[1] and Patrick HADDAD[3]

[1] *Jean Monnet University, Saint-Étienne, France*
[2] *Czech Technical University in Prague, Czechia*
[3] *Rambus Cryptography Research, Rotterdam, Netherlands*

5.1. Introduction

Random numbers are essential in cryptography. They are used as encryption keys, padding values, nonces – numbers used once, and recently also as random masks in countermeasures against side-channel attacks. Random numbers (bits, bytes or other numerical values or their vectors or streams) aimed at cryptographic applications should have unpredictable values and good statistical properties, for example, they should not feature a pattern, and should be uniformly distributed.

Random numbers are generated by random number generators (RNGs). Their random behavior can be guaranteed by an unpredictable physical process in so-called (physical) true random number generators (TRNGs) or by a cryptographic algorithm that guarantees that it is computationally impossible to determine past or future generated numbers based on knowledge of the current generator output in the (deterministic) pseudorandom number generators (PRNGs).

While the underlying physical random process guarantees truly random behavior of the generator output, the TRNGs are usually slower and generated numbers are of

Embedded Cryptography 3,
coordinated by Emmanuel PROUFF, Guénaël RENAULT,
Matthieu RIVAIN and Colin O'FLYNN.

lower statistical quality. On the other hand, PRNGs are much faster and the generated numbers have perfect statistical parameters; however, despite the fact they are based on secure cryptographic algorithms, they can be vulnerable to side-channel attacks and hence predictable. For this reason, RNGs used in practice are mostly hybrid, that is, a combination of a TRNG and PRNG.

When the output bit rate is determined by the TRNG, we call it a hybrid TRNG (H-TRNG), while if the bit rate is determined by the PRNG, we call it a hybrid PRNG (H-PRNG). Indeed, in H-TRNGs, the output of the TRNG is post-processed by the PRNG and in H-PRNGs, the PRNG is seeded by the TRNG outputs.

In this chapter, we present and discuss the design and evaluation of RNGs and the characteristics of the generated numbers required depending on their applications in cryptography – as cipher keys in block and stream ciphers, as prime numbers and asymmetric keys in public key cryptography, as nonces in ECC, and as random errors in post-quantum schemes.

5.2. TRNG design

The cryptographic system is basically a deterministic system that implements algorithmic cryptographic primitives and protocols. Consequently, it is mostly implemented in logic systems – computers, embedded systems and logic devices. As one of the basic cryptographic primitives, a TRNG is very often an integral part of the cryptographic system. Implementing a (physical) TRNG that exploits some random physical phenomena that are essentially analog in nature, in purely digital devices, is a serious challenge. The problems are linked not only to the search for exploitable stationary sources of randomness, but particularly to their characterization, quantification and the conversion of their random analog quantities to output random numbers.

The block diagram of a typical TRNG aimed at cryptographic applications is presented in Figure 5.1. The randomness harvesting mechanism and digitization process extract randomness from one (or several) physical sources of randomness and convert the analog quantities into a stream of random numbers (bits or bit vectors). If the generated raw binary signal does not have enough entropy, it can be post-processed using an optional data compression algorithm that increases entropy at the expense of the bit rate. The security of the generator can be further enhanced using some cryptographically secure algorithm (usually a one-way function) that guarantees the unpredictability of the generated numbers when the source of randomness fails.

The security of the TRNG is also guaranteed by simple and fast online statistical tests that continuously or periodically test if the generator is operating correctly.

Finally, the security of the generator can be further enhanced by optional real time monitoring (quantification) of the source of randomness and comparison of measured values with thresholds obtained using a stochastic model to ensure that the entropy rate at output of the generator is sufficient and hence to guarantee the unpredictability of generated numbers.

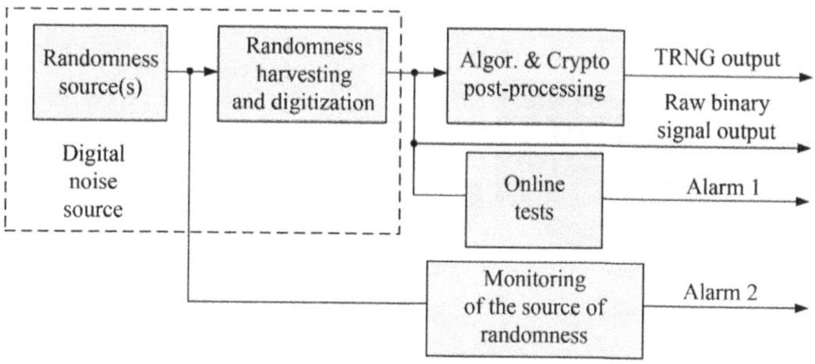

Figure 5.1. *Block diagram of a contemporary TRNG aimed at cryptographic applications*

In the following sections, we discuss the role of the individual TRNG blocks presented in Figure 5.1 and the design constraints on these blocks determined by data security requirements. We both theoretically and practically illustrate the workflow of the TRNG design on a widely spread TRNG principle: generators that exploit the jitter of multiple free-running oscillators, for example, ring oscillators.

5.3. Randomness and sources of randomness

Randomness is the quality or state of unpredictability of a system. In cryptography, designers look for sources of randomness that can be exploited in cryptographic systems. Two kinds of sources of unpredictability are usually used: nonphysical and physical sources, although physical sources largely dominate.

Non-physical sources such as the time between keyboard events, movements of the mouse, task scheduling and disk-head seek times are commonly used by software engineers. However, this approach can be risky when it uses computer-controlled events that can be manipulated by a clever attacker. For this reason, unpredictable physical phenomena are preferable for the construction of TRNGs for cryptography.

Physical sources of randomness in electronic devices are mainly linked to phenomena originating in quantum electronics. The number of physical sources of randomness available in logic devices is quite small: electric noises, random initial state of flip-flops, metastable events, the metastability of oscillations, etc. The most often used sources of randomness in logic devices are electric noises converted into a phase noise in free-running oscillators.

The phase noise of the generated clock signal mostly comes from an ensemble of electric noises of different origins and characteristics (see Figure 5.2): global noises, data-dependent noises, low-frequency noises and thermal noise.

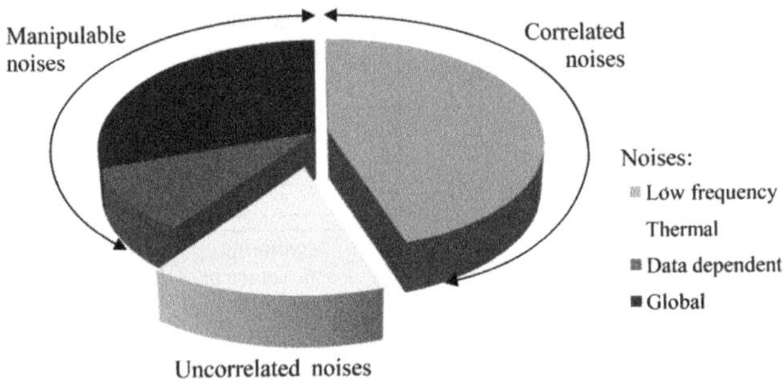

Figure 5.2. *Noise sources in logic devices*

Global noises can be caused by the power supply or electromagnetic emanations. They are therefore easy to manipulate, for example, by replacing the noisy power supply with a battery and/or enclosing the module in a metal shield during an attack on the generator, which accounts for global noises as sources of randomness. Data-dependent noises are unavoidable in cryptographic systems, since they can come from algorithms executed in the vicinity of the clock generator. Unfortunately, they can also be manipulated, for example, by stopping device activities during the generation of random numbers. Although low-frequency noises, such as flicker noise, are random noises, their contribution to the entropy rate is difficult to estimate, because they are autocorrelated and their stochastic model is not yet available. The most convenient source of the phase noise in the clock signals that is suitable for the generation of random numbers is thermal noise. Although thermal noise is temperature dependent, it is unavoidable in common temperature ranges, since it drops to zero only at 0°K. Further, the physical model of thermal noise has been well studied and its stochastic model based on the Wiener process exists. In general, all the above mentioned noises are practically unavoidable.

Unfortunately, the overall contribution of individual noises is not known, since it depends on the technology applied and on the hardware architecture. Thus, the role of the designer is to minimize the impact of global and data-dependent noises and to consider stationary thermal noise as the only contributor to the output entropy rate.

5.3.1. *Example: jitter of a clock signal as a source of randomness*

The jitter of the clock signals generated in free-running oscillators, namely, ring oscillators, is one of the most frequently used sources of randomness, because ring oscillators are very easy to implement in logic devices. A ring oscillator is a set of odd number of inverters connected in a ring structure. Figure 5.3 (left panel) shows a three-element ring oscillator and its waveforms. It shows that any time, only one event (rising or falling edge) is propagated across the ring. The mean period of the generated clock signal is thus $6t_d$, where t_d is the mean delay of the inverter. The right panel in Figure 5.3 illustrates the conversion of analog electric noises into timing instability: the output timing of the inverter depends on the time at which the input voltage u_1 crosses the noisy threshold voltage of the input comparator. Differences in the threshold voltages due to electric noises (Δ_{thr}) are thus converted into differences in the time delay at the inverter output (Δ_t). Note here that the threshold voltage includes all the electric noises present in Figure 5.2 and consequently, we can assume that the resulting clock jitter will have the same composition.

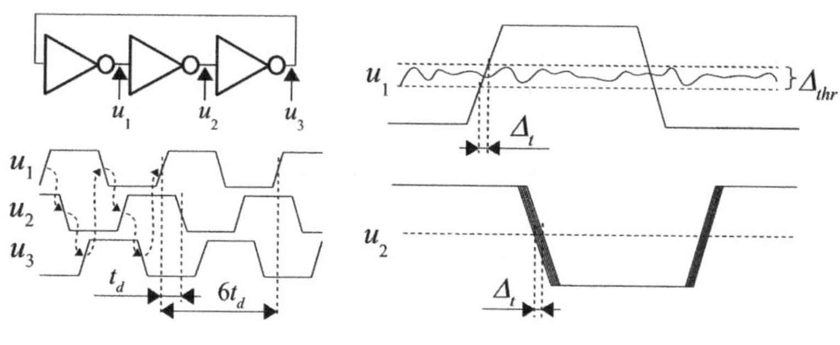

Figure 5.3. *Principle of the ring oscillator (left panel) and transformation of electric noises into timing instability at the output of the inverter (right panel)*

5.3.2. *Stochastic model of the phase of the jittered clock signal*

In the following, we consider only the contribution of the thermal noise to the clock jitter. All other noises can contribute to the jitter, but cannot reduce it. Consequently, the clock jitter coming from the thermal noise can be considered as the only contributor that determines the lower entropy bound.

The output signal $s(t)$ of a free running oscillator O can be modeled by a periodic function of time t having the form:

$$s(t) = f_\alpha(\omega(t + \xi(t))), \tag{5.1}$$

where f_α is a given real valued one-periodic function such that $f_\alpha(x) = 1$ for $0 < x < \alpha$, $f_\alpha(x) = 0$ for $\alpha < x < 1$, and $f_\alpha(0) = f_\alpha(\alpha) = 1/2$. Here, α is the duty cycle of the sampled oscillator. The term $\phi(t) = \omega(t + \xi(t))$ is the total phase of the oscillator, where ω is its mean frequency and ξ accounts for the timing jitter.

We can model the evolution of the total phase $\phi(t) = \omega(t + \xi(t))$ from equation [5.1], that is, the phase of a ring oscillator subject to a thermal noise, by a stationary Wiener stochastic process $\Phi(t)$ with drift $\mu > 0$ and volatility $\sigma^2 > 0$. In other words, for any time $t \geq t_0$, the phase $\Phi(t)$ conditioned by the value $\Phi(t_0) = \phi(t_0)$ follows a Gaussian distribution of mean $\phi(t_0) + \mu(t - t_0)$ and variance $\sigma^2(t - t_0)$. Equivalently, in terms of conditional probability density, we have for all t, t_0, x, x_0:

$$\frac{d}{dx}\mathbb{P}\{\Phi(t) \leq x \mid \Phi(t_0) = x_0\}$$
$$= \frac{1}{\sigma\sqrt{2\pi(t - t_0)}} \exp\left(\frac{-(x - x_0 - \mu(t - t_0))^2}{2\sigma^2(t - t_0)}\right). \qquad [5.2]$$

When we compare the definition of μ with equation [5.1], it is clear that $\mu = 2\pi/T$. Thus, the parameters needed to model the probabilistic evolution of the phase jitter component caused by the thermal noise in oscillator O are as follows:

- α: the duty cycle of the clock signal generated by the oscillator;
- T: its mean period;
- σ^2: the volatility of the associated Wiener process expressed in $[s^{-1}]$.

In the following, we term the triple (α, T, σ^2) the statistical parameters of oscillator O.

5.4. Randomness extraction and digitization

The role of the randomness extraction and digitization block is to convert analog source signals into digits. As we saw in the previous section, in the case of oscillator-based TRNGs, the phase noise of the clock signal represents an analog source of randomness, which needs to be converted into a raw binary signal. This conversion can be done in two ways at least: using a sampler or a counter.

Figure 5.4 presents the principle of converting of a jittered clock signal clk_1 into a random bit stream in an elementary oscillator-based TRNG (EO-TRNG). The conversion is based on the accumulation of the clock jitter presented in the left panel of Figure 5.4: the clock jitter accumulates during the accumulation period $\Delta t = DT_0$, after which the jittered clock signal is sampled in the D flip-flop (DFF). Since the standard deviation of the jitter after a sufficiently long accumulation period is comparable to (or bigger than) the period of the sampled signal, the DFF output behaves randomly.

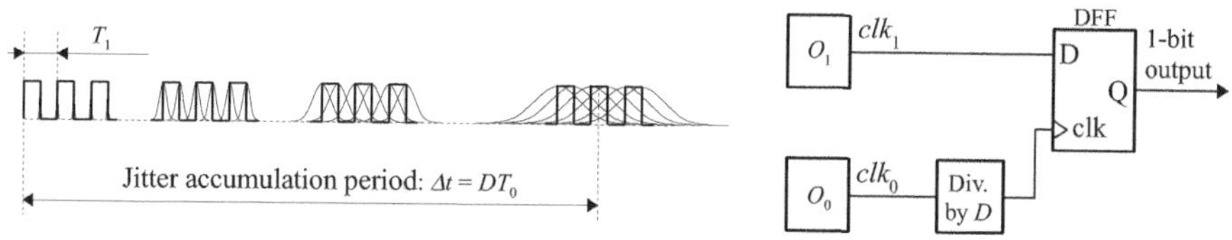

Figure 5.4. *Randomness extraction from a jittered clock signal by a D flip-flop (for sake of simplicity, flip-flop initialization and output validation signals are omitted)*

It is important to note that the impact of the global noise sources is reduced if the differential principle, which is based on the use of two oscillators featuring the same topology, is applied. The clock signals generated in two such rings are impacted by the global noises in the same way and the relative jitter between these clocks does not depend on global noises. Therefore, to avoid possible attacks, the reference clock clk_0 should never be generated using a quartz oscillator, which generates a clock signal with a fix frequency. Moreover, when characterizing the jitter, activities in blocks surrounding the TRNG should be stopped to avoid data-dependent noises. In this way, the accumulated clock jitter can be considered stationary with normal distribution $\mathcal{N}(0, \sigma^2)$ and variance $\sigma^2 = \sigma_{th}^2 + \sigma_{fl}^2$, where $\sigma_{th}^2 = K_1 \Delta t$ is the variance of the jitter coming from the thermal noise and $\sigma_{fl}^2 = K_2(\Delta t)^2$ is the variance of the jitter caused by the flicker noise. Constants K_1 and K_2 depend on the technology used and on the architecture and the topology of the rings.

Note that the TRNG entropy rate estimation should only be based on the contribution of the thermal noise. Unfortunately, as mentioned in the previous paragraph, the jitter caused by the flicker noise accumulates faster than the jitter caused by the thermal noise. Therefore, considering the total jitter in entropy computation using the model leads to significant entropy overestimation. It is therefore very important to determine the proportion of σ_{th}^2 on σ^2 at the end of the jitter accumulation period. This can be done off-line during the TRNG characterization procedure.

Another fact that needs to be taken into account is the presence of the period jitter (expressed in $[s]$) in both clk_0 and clk_1. Since we only account for the jitters caused by the thermal noises, which are known to be independent, we can consider one clock signal to be jitter-free, while the second one will feature jitter with variance $\sigma_{tot}^2 = \frac{T_0}{T_1}\sigma_1^2 + \sigma_0^2$.

Figure 5.5 presents two other ways of extracting randomness, both using a counter. In the generator presented in the left panel, the counter counts the number of periods of the jittered clock clk_1 during the jitter accumulation time Δt, whereas the generator in the right panel counts cases, when clk_1 is equal to one at the rising edges of clk_0 throughout the accumulation period.

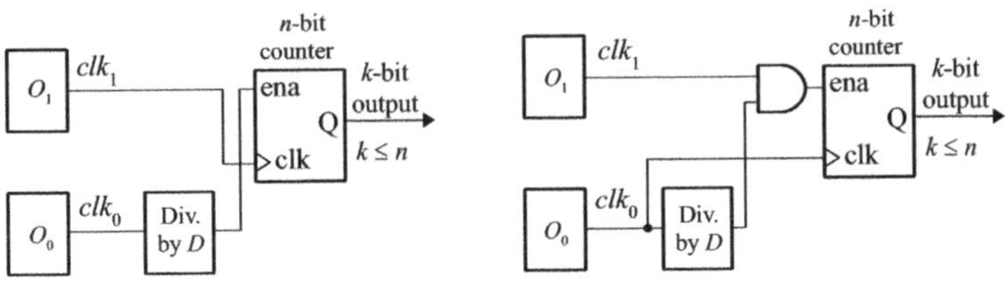

Figure 5.5. *Randomness extraction from a jittered clock signal using a counter that counts the number of clock periods (left) or the number of samples equal to one (right)*

Note that for the sake of simplicity, counter initialization and output validation signals are omitted from Figure 5.5. However, counter initialization is unavoidable to ensure independence of the generated random values. It is also important to stress that the three generators presented in Figures 5.4 and 5.5 use the same sources of randomness (phase noises of clk_0 and clk_1), but because of very different ways of randomness extraction, they have very different stochastic models and consequently different output entropy rates. In the rest of this chapter, we consider the generator in which the jittered clock signal is sampled on the rising edges of the reference clock signals (e.g. using the sampling method of randomness extraction presented in Figure 5.4).

5.4.1. *Example: oscillator-based TRNGs*

As mentioned above, we are studying the design of oscillator-based TRNGs, in which the jittered clock signal is sampled periodically at the end of each jitter accumulation period $\Delta t = DT_0$. The first generator to consider is the simplest version of this kind of generator – the elementary oscillator-based TRNG (EO-TRNG) presented in Figure 5.4. Clearly, the entropy at its output depends on the following parameters:

– clock periods T_0 and T_1;

– duty cycle α_1;

– variance $\sigma_{tot}^2 = \frac{T_0}{T_1}\sigma_1^2 + \sigma_0^2$ expressed as period jitter in $[s]$;

– accumulation time $\Delta t = DT_0$.

Intuitively, the output bit rate for a given entropy rate will depend on three parameters: periods T_0 and T_1 and division factor D, which can all be modified by the designer. Note that the duty cycle and jitter variance depend on the frequencies of the two clock signals and on the technology used, but also on the architecture and topology of the rings.

In this exercise, you can analyze the impact of input parameters of the EO-TRNG on the generator output. You can launch the application and observe how the duty cycle, the jitter variance and the accumulation time affect the randomness of the generated numbers. Randomness is analyzed by observing the distribution and the auto-correlation of generated 4-bit bit-vectors.

NOTE.– In the case of an ideal RNG, the distribution and the auto-correlation are in 99.9% of the cases between the red lines. Your goal is to find the smallest D for which the EO-TRNG would not be distinguishable from an ideal RNG. You should repeat the procedure for all possible $\frac{\sigma_{tot}}{T_1}$ and α_1 values.

Further explanations and the Python code are available at the following link:

https://github.com/patrickhaddadteaching/TRNG_ex1.

Box 5.1. *Impact of input parameters of the EO-TRNG on the generator output*

The EO-TRNG is, by its principle, the simplest generator to exploit free-running oscillators. However, its simplicity is offset by the impossibility to obtain a high entropy rate at its output. Indeed, the designer has very limited opportunities to increase it: (a) they can do so by increasing the frequency of the sampled clock to some extent (note that at high frequencies, the duty cycle tends to differ from the ideal value (0.5), which increases the output bias and reduces the entropy rate); (b) they can alternatively increase the value of the division factor D at the cost of the reduced output bit rate.

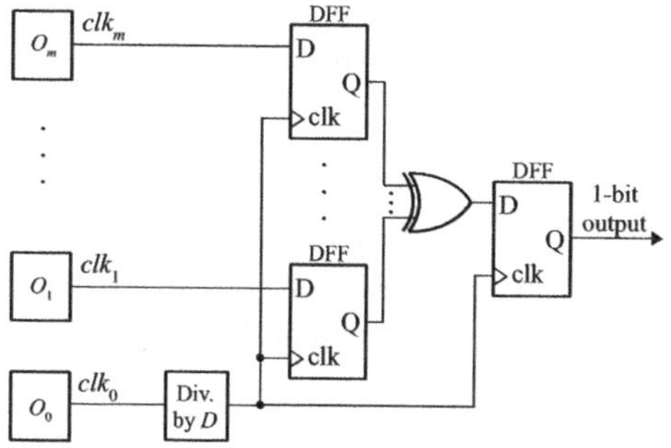

Figure 5.6. *Multi-oscillator-based TRNG (MO-TRNG)*

Another possible way to increase entropy is to use a larger number of sources of randomness, that is, number of oscillators. Figure 5.6 shows the resulting multi-oscillator based TRNG (MO-TRNG), in which outputs of m oscillators are sampled by m flip-flops and XOR-ed to obtain one output bit. This kind of generator can be considered as an ensemble of m EO-TRNGs.

In this exercise, we can analyze the impact of input parameters of the MO-TRNG on the generator output. Further explanations and the Python code are available at the link below. We can launch the application and observe how the number of oscillators, the jitter variance and the accumulation time affect the randomness of the generated numbers. The randomness is analyzed by observing the distribution and the auto-correlation of generated 4-bit bit-vectors.

NOTE.– In the case of an ideal RNG, the distribution and the auto-correlation are in 99.9% of the cases between the red lines. Your goal is to find the smallest D, for which the MO-TRNG would not be distinguishable from an ideal RNG. We should repeat the procedure for all possible $\frac{\sigma_{tot}}{T_1}$ and N values.

The exercise is available at the following link:

https://github.com/patrickhaddadteaching/TRNG_ex2.

Box 5.2. *Impact of input parameters of the MO-TRNG on the generator output*

5.5. Post-processing of the raw binary signal

According to the German standard AIS 20/31, the raw binary signal can be post-processed algorithmically and/or cryptographically. Algorithmic post-processing should make generated numbers statistically and computationally indistinguishable from the output of an ideal TRNG. Indeed, in a weak generator, the generated numbers may be biased (or not uniformly distributed), correlated, they may feature a pattern, etc. Algorithmic post-processing should remove all of the statistical weaknesses and (if possible) increase entropy.

The role of cryptographic post-processing is to guarantee the unpredictability of the generated numbers between the moment when the source of randomness fails and the instant when the alarm of the online tests is triggered. The cryptographic post-processing must be cryptographically secure – robust against cryptanalysis. Depending on implementation of the generator, the side-channel attacks should also be considered.

5.5.1. *Algorithmic post-processing*

The post-processing algorithm is sometimes called entropy conditioner or entropy extractor. As discussed above, its main objective is to convert the distribution of generated numbers into a uniform one. Let X denote a distribution of generated l-bit numbers and U_l denote a uniform distribution over $\{0,1\}^l$, then its *min-entropy* (see later) is $H_\infty(X) = l$.

We call the distribution of the n-bit data set S with distribution X and min-entropy k, an (n, k) distribution. The closeness of the distribution of generated numbers X (bit vectors) to the uniform distribution Y can be evaluated using a *statistical distance*:

$$\Delta(X,Y) = \max_{T \subset S} |\Pr[X \in T] - \Pr[Y \in T]|. \quad [5.3]$$

We say that X and Y are ε-close if $\Delta(X,Y) \leq \varepsilon$. Then, the deterministic entropy extractor called (k, ε)*-extractor* is defined as follows.

Extractor **Ext**: $\{0,1\}^n \rightarrow \{0,1\}^m$ takes an n-bit sample from a weak random source as an input and produces an m-bit output $(n > m)$ that is statistically ε-close to the uniform distribution U_m (i.e. m is close to k). In other words, the post-processing algorithm serving as entropy extractor compresses the n-bit bit-stream into a k-bit bit-stream, having a distribution that is sufficiently close to a uniform one. Next, we give two examples of the most frequently used entropy extractors: parity filter and von Neumann's corrector.

The parity filter breaks the input n-bit stream into m blocks of length $r = \lfloor n/m \rfloor$ and outputs the parity of each block. The filter can dramatically reduce the bias on the generator output but at the cost of reducing its bit rate r-times:

$$\Pr[Y = 1] = 0.5 - 2^{r-1} \left(\Pr[X = 1] - 0.5\right)^r = 0.5 - B, \quad [5.4]$$

where B is the bias. It is clear that if $\Pr[X = 1]$ differs from 0 or 1, the bias B converges toward 0 when r tends to infinity. However, we note that equation [5.4] is valid if the generated numbers (bits) are independent. If this is not the case, the parity filter can still be used, but is less efficient.

In the von Neumann's corrector, the biased output bit stream is broken into pairs of bits and, for each pair, the output bit is equal to 0 if the input pair was 01, to 1 if the pair was 10, and the pair is skipped if it was 00 or 11. The output bit rate is thus data dependent. The process will yield an unbiased random bit after $1/(2\Pr[X = 1](1 - \Pr[X = 1]))$ pairs on average.

5.6. Stochastic modeling and entropy rate management of the TRNG

Entropy is a measure of the uncertainty contained in an information unit, for example, a bit or vector of bits. In the context of RNG, it is a measure of guesswork and unpredictability. Several entropy definitions exist. The most general is the Rényi entropy:

$$H_\alpha(X) = \frac{1}{1-\alpha}\log_2\left(\sum_{i=1}^{n}(p_i)^\alpha\right), \qquad [5.5]$$

where $\alpha \geq 0$, $\alpha \neq 1$ and p_i =Pr$[X = x_i]$. Unfortunately, in practice, the Rényi entropy is difficult to assess. Consequently, two special cases of Rényi entropy are usually used: *min-entropy* and *Shannon entropy.*

Min-entropy is the most conservative entropy measure that can be obtained from the Rényi entropy definition for $\alpha \to \infty$. The min-entropy $H_\infty(X)$ is defined as follows:

$$H_\infty(X) = \inf_{i=1..n}(-\log_2(p_i)) = -\log_2 \sup_{i=1..n} p_i. \qquad [5.6]$$

The min-entropy is easy to handle if the generated numbers are not correlated.

The Shannon entropy is the most commonly used entropy measure in information theory. It can be obtained from the Rényi entropy definition for $\alpha \to 1$. The Shannon entropy $H(X) = H_1(X)$ is defined as follows:

$$H(X) = H_1(X) = -\sum_{i=1}^{n} p_i \log_2 p_i. \qquad [5.7]$$

The Shannon entropy is particularly useful if the generated numbers are somehow correlated. It is then computed as a so-called conditional entropy.

The entropy per bit of a TRNG should be close to 1 (according to AIS 20/31, for internal random numbers, $H(X) > 0.997$). A high entropy rate guarantees that the preceding or succeeding bits cannot be guessed with a probability different from 0.5. It is important to note that entropy is a property of random variables and not of observed realizations. Consequently, entropy cannot be measured, only estimated using the model.

The role of the stochastic model of a RNG is to determine probability that the output bit of the generator is equal to one, that is, Pr$(X = 1)$ or the probability of values of an n-bit vector, Pr$(X_1 = x_1, X_2 = x_2, ..., X_n = x_n)$ and from these probabilities to estimate entropy or so-called conditional entropy at the output. The probability expressions should depend on some measurable parameters used as the inputs of the stochastic model. Ideally, they should be measurable inside the cryptographic module. Comparison of the obtained values with those computed using the model can provide a basis for dedicated statistical tests.

5.6.1. *Example: a comprehensive stochastic model of the EO-TRNG*

The EO-TRNG in Figure 5.4 can be used as an example for the construction of a comprehensible stochastic model. Baudet et al. (2014) showed that the evolution of the oscillator phase can be modeled by an ergodic stationary Markov process. The probability of obtaining a sample $s(t)$ equal to one at time $t \geq 0$ that is conditioned by $\varphi(0)$ (the oscillator's phase at time 0) can be expressed as follows:

$$\Pr[s(t) = 1|\varphi(0) = x] \approx \frac{1}{2} - \frac{2}{\pi}\sin(2\pi(\mu t + x))e^{-2\pi^2\sigma^2 t}. \quad [5.8]$$

The probability of outputting a vector $\boldsymbol{b} = (b_1, ..., b_n) \in \{0, 1\}^n$ at sampling times $0, \Delta t, ..., (n-1)\Delta t$ is given as:

$$p(\boldsymbol{b}) = \Pr[s(0) = b_1, ..., s((n-1)\Delta t) = b_n] \approx \quad [5.9]$$

$$\approx \frac{1}{2^n} + \frac{8}{2^n\pi^2}\left(\sum_{j=1}^{n-1}(-1)^{b_j+b_{j+1}}\right)\cos(2\pi\nu)e^{-2\pi^2 Q},$$

where $Q = \sigma^2\Delta t = \frac{\sigma_{th}^2 DT_0}{(T_1)^3}$ is the quality factor and $\nu = \mu\Delta t = \frac{DT_0}{T_1}$ is the ratio between the frequencies of the sampled and sampling signals.

Finally, the entropy of an n-bit output vector $\boldsymbol{b}$ is then given as:

$$H_n = -\sum_{b\in\{0,1\}^n} p(b)\log p(b) \approx \quad [5.10]$$

$$\approx n - \frac{32(n-1)}{\pi^4 \ln(2)}\cos^2(2\pi\nu)e^{-4\pi^2 Q}.$$

Using this equation, the lower bound of the Shannon entropy rate per bit at the generator output is given as:

$$H_{min} \approx 1 - \frac{4}{\pi^2\ln(2)}e^{-4\pi^2 Q} = 1 - \frac{4}{\pi^2\ln(2)}e^{\frac{-4\pi^2\sigma_{th}^2 DT_0}{(T_1)^2 \cdot T_1}}. \quad [5.11]$$

The lower entropy bound is thus determined by measurable parameters:

1) jitter variance per the sampled clock period $((\sigma_{th}/T_1)^2)$;

2) ratio between DT_0 and T_1 (i.e. sampling period and sampled clock period).

We observe that the Shannon entropy rate of the EO-TRNG increases with jitter variance and with accumulation time and decreases with longer periods of the sampled clock signal.

5.6.2. Example: stochastic model of the MO-TRNG

To ensure an $H_{min} \geq 0.997$ in the EO-TRNG, with $\frac{T_1}{T_0} \approx 1$ and $\frac{\sigma_{th}}{T_1} \approx \frac{1}{1000}$, equation [5.11] shows that the division factor D should be greater than $133,000$. This condition must be fulfilled to ensure security but it drastically reduces the TRNG bitrate.

In order to overcome this low-throughput problem at the TRNG output, the generator can use several rings as multiple independent sources of randomness. This is the idea behind the multiple (ring) oscillator–based TRNG (MO-TRNG).

Assuming independence of rings, which can be obtained by their careful placement and routing, the EO-TRNG model from the previous section can be extended to the one characterizing MO-TRNG. In this case, the probability of obtaining a sample $s(t)$ equal to "1" at time $t \geq 0$ conditioned by the phase vector $\varphi(0) = (x_1, x_2, \ldots, x_m)$ at $t = 0$ is given by:

$$\Pr[s(t) = 1 | \varphi(0) = (x_1, x_2, \ldots, x_m)] =$$
$$\frac{1}{2} - \frac{2^{2m-1}}{\pi^m} \prod_{i=1}^{m} \sum_{N=0}^{+\infty} \frac{\sin(2\pi(\mu_i t + x_i)(2N+1))}{2N+1} e^{-2\pi^2\sigma_i^2 t(2N+1)^2}, \quad [5.12]$$

where:

– m is the number of sampled ROs in the MO-TRNG;

– σ_i^2 and μ_i are, respectively, the volatility and the drift of the Wiener process modeling the phase of the oscillator O_i.

Equation [5.12] is then used to compute an approximate lower bound of entropy (H_{La}) for the MO-TRNG after an accumulation time Δt and conditioned by $\varphi(0) = (x_1, x_2, \ldots, x_m)$:

$$H(s(\Delta t) = 1 | \varphi(0) = (x_1, x_2, \ldots, x_m)) =$$
$$\underbrace{1 - \frac{2^{3n-1}}{\pi^{2n}\ln(2)} e^{-4\pi^2 Q} - \frac{2^{5m-2}3^{m-1}}{\pi^{4m}\ln(2)} e^{-8\pi^2 Q}}_{H_{La}} + O(e^{-12\pi^2 Q}), \quad [5.13]$$

where $Q = \Delta t \sum_{i=1}^{m} \sigma_i^2$ is the sum of quality factors of oscillators O_i.

Using equation [5.13], it is possible to express the sum of quality factors Q as a function of H_{La}.

$$Q = \frac{-1}{4\pi^2} \ln\left(\frac{\pi^{4n}\ln(2)}{2^{5m-1}3^{m-1}}\left(-\frac{2^{3m-1}}{\pi^{2m}\ln(2)} + \sqrt{C(m, H_{La})}\right)\right), \quad [5.14]$$

where $C(m, H_{La}) = \left(\frac{2^{3m-1}}{\pi^{2m}\ln(2)}\right)^2 - 4\frac{2^{5m-2}3^{m-1}}{\pi^{4m}\ln(2)}(H_{La} - 1)$. Then, for a given threshold on H_{La} (e.g. $H_{La} \geq 0.997$)) and volatility σ_i^2, it is possible to determine how the number m of oscillators, the sampling frequency $f_s = \frac{1}{\Delta t}$ should be set, depending on the model, to ensure the desired security level.

In this exercise, you can study the impact of input parameters of the MO-TRNG on the output entropy rate. You can launch the application and observe how the number of oscillators, the jitter variance and the accumulation time affect Shannon entropy and min-entropy rate at the MO-TRNG output. Your goal is to find the smallest D for which the generator will produce random bits with a Shannon entropy rate higher than 0.997. You should repeat the procedure for all possible $\frac{\sigma_{tot}}{T_1}$ and N values.

Further explanations and the Python code are available at the following link:

https://github.com/patrickhaddadteaching/TRNG_ex3.

Box 5.3. *Impact of input parameters of MO-TRNG on the output entropy rate*

5.7. TRNG testing and testing strategies

Statistical tests are mathematical tools to evaluate the statistical quality of generated numbers. A common strategy in statistical testing is as follows: different statistical features of an *ideal RNG* are evaluated to then be compared with output values of a real RNG (= DUT) to check for a so-called *null hypothesis* – H_0. The null hypothesis is a statement of "no difference" between the tested generator and an ideal RNG. The number of statistical features to be evaluated (more or less complex) is practically unlimited (usually, up to 16 features are tested).

Two types of errors can occur in statistical testing: the generator functions correctly (it behaves as an ideal RNG, i.e. the null hypothesis is true), but the test rejects the null hypothesis. This type of error, which is called Type 1 error or *false reject*, is less security critical (see Table 5.1). It appears with probability α, called the significance level. The second type of error occurs when the null hypothesis is false (the generator is imperfect), but the test does not reject the null hypothesis. This kind of error, which is more dangerous, is called Type 2 error or *false accept* (see Table 5.1). It appears with probability β. Unfortunately, although more security critical, β is more difficult to assess than α. The results of statistical tests are evaluated depending on the testing strategy: according to the predefined significance level α (testing procedures in AIS 20/31) or according to the distribution of p-values (according to NIST SP 800-22b).

It should be stressed that the statistical testing of the generator is necessary, but is not sufficient to guarantee security. Namely, it cannot substitute cryptanalysis in the case of DRNGs and analysis of output entropy rate (unpredictability) in the case of TRNGs. Two testing strategies are applied to evaluate the statistical quality of generated numbers: online and offline testing. Both generic and dedicated statistical tests can be used. Dedicated tests are preferable in online testing, since they are simpler and faster. Generic tests are used in offline testing, since they are more accurate.

Test result	Null hypothesis is in fact true	Null hypothesis is in fact false
Test **rejects** the null hypothesis	Type 1 error (with probability α) – false reject	OK (correct decision)
Test **does not reject** the null hypothesis	OK (correct decision)	**Type 2 error** (with probability β) – false accept

Table 5.1. *Overview of types of errors in statistical tests. For a color version of this table, see www.iste.co.uk/prouff/cryptography3.zip*

5.7.1. *Generic (black-box) statistical tests used in cryptography*

The quality of generated random numbers is evaluated using generic statistical tests defined by security standards. Usually, generic statistical tests require huge amounts of data and long execution times. They are thus used mostly offline. Several sets of statistical tests exist. Their objectives vary depending on the application targeted. In general, the precision of statistical test suites is tightly linked to the amount of input data they require.

The *FIPS 140-1 test suite* is the simplest set of tests aimed at testing RNGs in cryptographic modules. The following four tests included in the FIPS 140-1 test suite require 20,000 bits as input:

– *Monobit test*: it tests the proportion of bits equal to “0” and “1” in the tested bit stream.

– *Poker test*: it tests the probabilities of 16 possible values of groups of four bits.

– *Runs test*: it tests the probabilities of runs of 1, 2, 3, 4, 5 and 6+ identical values.

– *Long runs test*: it searches for runs of length 34 or more (of either zeros or ones).

In this exercise, we can analyze the impact of the Monobit test parameters on the test results. We can launch the application and observe how the threshold and the block size affect Type 1 and 2 errors, which are introduced in section 5.6.

This test triggers an alarm if the number of bits equal to 1 is bigger than $\frac{Number\ of\ input\ bits}{2} + relative\ threshold$ or is smaller than $\frac{Number\ of\ input\ bits}{2}$ –

$relative\ threshold$. Our goal is to find the lowest $relative\ threshold$ that makes it possible for α to be bigger than 10^{-6} and we should note the highest Shannon entropy (H_1) for which β is smaller than 10^{-6}. This H_1 will be the lowest entropy rate at the TRNG output that will not trigger the alarm. We should repeat the procedure for $Block\ sizes = 4096, 8192, 16384, 32768$.

Now, can we answer the following question? Which parameter values of the Monobit test are required by the AIS 20/31 and FIPS 140-1 test suites? Further explanations and the Python code are available at the following link:

https://github.com/patrickhaddadteaching/TRNG_ex4.

Box 5.4. *Study of the Monobit test and its threshold setup*

The *DIEHARD test suite* was developed by Georges Marsaglia in 1993 to test PRNGs. The suite contains 15 tests requiring a total of 80 million bits. *Tests NIST SP 800-22b* were derived from the DIEHARD test suite. The NIST test suite contains 15 tests requiring 1,000 files of one million bits each.

Recently, American NIST and German BSI proposed dedicated test suites to test TRNGs. These are described in NIST SP 800-90B and AIS 20/31 national standards, respectively.

The role of the NIST SP 800-90B test suite is to check that the min entropy rate at the generator output claimed by the designer corresponds to claims. During testing, the evaluator has first to check that the generated random numbers are IID (independent and identically distributed). This is done using 11 statistical tests applied on 10,000 permutations of one million generated numbers and five additional chi-square tests. If the generated samples are shown to be IID, the min entropy is estimated using the *most common value* estimate. If the sample values are not IID, 10 specific estimators are calculated and the minimum of all of the estimates is taken as the entropy assessment of the entropy source.

The German AIS 20/31 standard requires testing raw random numbers and post-processed random numbers in two testing procedures. Procedure A aims to test internal random numbers (post-processed random numbers). The goal of this procedure is to check whether the generated numbers behave statistically inconspicuously. This includes one disjointness test (T0) and five simple statistical tests repeated 257 times. Four of these tests (T1–T4) correspond to the four FIPS 140-1 tests mentioned previously and test T5 is the autocorrelation test. For an ideal RNG, the probability that test procedure A finally fails is almost 0.

Test procedure B of AIS 31, which is composed of tests T6 to T8 (including several sub-tests), is usually applied to raw random numbers. The goal is to ensure the entropy rate is sufficiently high, that is, the Shannon entropy rate per output bit should be higher than 0.997. A small bias and slight one-step dependencies are permitted, but no significant longer dependencies are allowed. If these requirements are fulfilled and the one-step transition probabilities are negligible, Test T8 output value estimates the Shannon entropy rate at the generator output.

> In this exercise, we can analyze the impact of the MO-TRNG parameters on black-box statistical tests. We can launch the Python application and observe how the duty cycle, the variance and the accumulation time affect the results of the five black-box tests included in the AIS 20/31 test suite (four of which are also included in the FIPS 140-1). Our goal is to find the smallest D for which the generated data would pass all five black-box tests. We should repeat the procedure for all possible $\frac{\sigma_{tot}}{T_1}$ and N values.
>
> Further explanations and the Python code are available at the following link:
>
> https://github.com/patrickhaddadteaching/TRNG_ex5.

Box 5.5. *Impact of input parameters of MO-TRNG on generic tests*

5.7.2. *Online statistical tests*

Online tests are simple statistical tests that continuously (or periodically) evaluate the performance of the generator while it is operating. Online tests should preferably evaluate physical quantities, which serve as input parameters for the generator's stochastic model and compare the measured values with the thresholds determined using the model. These dedicated statistical tests, also called the white-box tests, are usually less expensive, faster and better suited for the detection of weaknesses of the generator than generic tests and are thus preferable for online TRNG testing.

While the NIST SP 800-90B standard requires two simple generic tests or their equivalents to be executed online (the repetition count and adaptive proportion tests), according to the AIS 20/31 standard, the designer is free to design online tests that respect the working principle of the generator. Two kinds of tests are required by the AIS 20/31 standard: a simple and very rapid test that detects the total failure of the source of randomness with a very small probability of false rejection and at least one efficient, and sufficiently rapid online test able to detect generator unacceptable failures.

5.7.3. *Example: dedicated online tests for the MO-TRNG*

As detailed above, online tests should preferably be based on the measurement and evaluation of the input parameters of the stochastic model. We remind the reader that, according to the models presented in sections 5.6.1 and 5.6.2, the MO-TRNG output entropy rate depends on clock periods T_0 and T_i, the total jitter variance σ_{tot}, the jitter accumulation time $\Delta t = DT_0$ and the number of oscillators. The generator can fail completely for one (or several) reasons:

– the reference clock and/or sampled clock generators stop oscillating;

– clock generators become interlocked or locked to an external signal;

– the total clock jitter drops to zero (this is only a hypothetical possibility).

Note that in all these cases the counter presented in Figure 5.5 would output a constant value. Counting the number of repetitions of the counter values can thus serve as a basis to test for total failure. Moreover, the same counter can be used to implement the online test. For example, we can calculate the Allan variance of the counter values and compare it with the threshold determined using the stochastic model of the generator.

5.8. Conclusion

In this chapter, we have presented a modern approach to generating true random numbers for cryptographic applications. We have illustrated the design of a secure TRNG on a particular type of generator – oscillator-based TRNGs. Practical exercises are included to show how to setup the generator parameters and how to evaluate the quality of the generated numbers. We recommend applying this new approach to all future TRNG designs to guarantee their security.

5.9. Notes and further references

Many oscillator-based TRNG architectures exist. An overview can be found in Fischer et al. (2016). Several randomness extraction methods including sampling and counter methods are presented and their efficiency is analyzed in Allini et al. (2018). An elementary oscillator-based TRNG and its comprehensible model were published by Baudet et al. (2011). An advanced version of the oscillator-based TRNG using multiple oscillators was published by Sunar et al. (2007) and enhanced by Wold and Tan (2008). The model of the multi-oscillator based TRNG derived from the model of Baudet et al. (2011) was then proposed by Wu et al. (2019).

The TRNG security evaluation standards NIST SP 800-90B and AIS 20/31, including description of corresponding statistical tests are presented in Killmann and Schindler (2011) and Turan et al. (2018), respectively. The NIST SP 800-22b generic statistical test suite is described in Rukhin et al. (2010). The FIPS 140-1 statistical test suite is described in National Institute of Standards and Technology (NIST) (1994).

5.10. References

Allini, E.N., Skórski, M., Petura, O., Bernard, F., Laban, M., Fischer, V. (2018). Evaluation and monitoring of free running oscillators serving as source of randomness. *IACR Transactions on Cryptographic Hardware and Embedded Systems*, 2018(3), 214–242. doi: 10.13154/tches.v2018.i3.214-242.

Baudet, M., Lubicz, D., Micolod, J., Tassiaux, A. (2011). On the security of oscillator-based random number generators. *Journal of Cryptology*, 24(2), 398–425.

Fischer, V., Haddad, P., Cherkaoui, A. (2016). Ring oscillators and self-timed rings in true random number generators. In *Oscillator Circuits: Frontiers in Design, Analysis and Applications*, Nishio, Y. (ed.). Institution of Engineering and Technology, Stevenage.

Killmann, W. and Schindler, W. (2011). AIS 20/31. A proposal for: Functionality classes for random number generators. Version 2.0 [Online]. Available at: https://www.bsi.bund.de/EN/Home/home_node.html.

National Institute of Standards and Technology (NIST) (1994). Federal Information Processing Standard (FIPS) 140-1. Security Requirements for Cryptographic Modules. Special Publication [Online]. Available at: http://csrc.nist.gov/publications/fips/fips140-1/fips1401.pdf.

Rukhin, A., Soto, J., Nechvatal, J., Smid, J., Barker, E., Leigh, S., Levenson, M., Vangel, M., Banks, D., Heckert, A. et al. (2010). A statistical test suite for random and pseudorandom number generators for cryptographic applications. NIST Special Publication, 800-22 Rev. 1a [Online]. Available at: https://nvlpubs.nist.gov/nistpubs/legacy/sp/nistspecialpublication800-22r1a.pdf.

Sunar, B., Martin, W., Stinson, D. (2007). A provably secure true random number generator with built-In tolerance to active attacks. *IEEE Transactions on Computers*, 109–119 [Online]. Available at: http://www.cacr.math.uwaterloo.ca/ dstinson/papers/rng-IEEE.pdf.

Turan, M.S., Barker, E., Kelsey, J., McKay, K.A., Baish, M.L., Boyle, M. (2018). Recommendation for the entropy sources used for random bit generation. NIST Special Publication, 800-90B. doi: 10.6028/NIST.SP.800-90B.

Wold, K. and Tan, C.H. (2008). Analysis and enhancement of random number generator in FPGA based on oscillator rings. In *2008 International Conference on Reconfigurable Computing and FPGAs*. IEEE, Cancun.

Wu, X., Ma, Y., Yang, J., Chen, T., Lin, J. (2019). On the security of TRNGs based on multiple ring oscillators. In *Security and Privacy in Communication Networks – SecureComm 2019*, Chen, S., Choo, K., Fu, X., Lou, W., Mohaisen, A. (eds). Springer, Cham.

6

Pseudorandom Number Generation

Jean-René REINHARD and Sylvain RUHAULT
Agence nationale de la sécurité des systèmes d'information, Paris, France

6.1. Introduction

In the previous chapter, we have seen that sequences of random numbers can be produced by extracting entropy from a physical random process, a noise source. When the noise source is well understood and operates nominally, a lower bound on its entropy rate is guaranteed, and it can provide an unbounded amount of randomness.

Regarding cryptographic mechanisms, the focus is generally on their computational security: if no adversary with bounded resources can threaten a security objective of a given cryptographic mechanism with more than negligible probability of success, this cryptographic mechanism is deemed to be secure. This principle can also be applied to the generation of random numbers, which can also be considered as a cryptographic mechanism. In other words, it is not strictly necessary to generate numbers that are fully random, as long as a bounded adversary is not able to distinguish the generator from an ideal source: the difference between the One-Time-Pad and streamciphers illustrates the same idea. While the One-Time-Pad adds to the plaintext a keystream of same length generated uniformly at random, streamciphers generate this keystream deterministically from a key of fixed size using a pseudorandom generator.

Adopting this principle for randomness generation leads to defining cryptographic schemes that will be referred to as *pseudorandom number generator*

Embedded Cryptography 3,
coordinated by Emmanuel PROUFF, Guénaël RENAULT,
Matthieu RIVAIN and Colin O'FLYNN.

(PRNG) or *deterministic random number generator* (DRNG). They enable to anchor the security assurance for random number generation in the assurance provided by well-studied cryptographic primitives.

In this chapter, we review the security properties of such schemes. After restating the classical security model of PRNG, we remark that their stateful nature calls for an adaptation of the model, and even further, its extension to allow for proper handling of their security in case of compromise of their internal state. In particular, *forward security*, that is, the property that a state compromise does not provide any information on past outputs of the generator, is expected.

These models assume the use of a perfect source of randomness to setup the PRNG state, and even refresh the PRNG state in the case of *PRNG with inputs* that have access to a noise source beyond their setup. An ideal noise source may not be available to PRNG implementations. To fill this gap, extended models have been developed, in which the PRNG is also able to *extract* seeds close to uniformly random from imperfect noise sources providing a sufficient amount of entropy. We discuss the difficulties associated with the modelization of extractors and express the *robustness* security property in the case where an underlying cryptographic primitive is idealized.

Finally, we also succinctly present SP800-90A DRNGs, which constitute the most widely accepted standard PRNGs with inputs. The proposed constructions predate the latest developments in the modelization of PRNGs with inputs, and their interfaces differ slightly from the models described in this chapter. However, the security models can be adapted to fit the specificities of these PRNGs with inputs, as shown by recently published works.

6.2. PRNG with ideal noise source

We shall start by reviewing security properties for PRNGs in the computational model. In this model a scheme has provable security if its security requirements can be stated formally in an adversarial model where the capabilities of the adversary, modeled as an efficient algorithm, are described with clear assumptions. We use the code-based game-playing framework of Bellare and Rogaway (2006).

A security game involves a challenger and an adversary denoted $\mathcal{A}$. The adversary is modeled as a probabilistic algorithm. The challenge of the adversary is to distinguish between two experiments, which are both indexed by a Boolean bit b. Interactions between the challenger and the adversary are modeled with procedures, marked **proc**. The arguments of the procedures are adversarially chosen. Procedures may output values to the adversary using the directive `OUTPUT`. The output of the security game is returned through directive `RETURN`, before the game terminates.

A security game is executed as follows. Firstly, the challenger executes a procedure initialize, where it generates a random bit b and its output are given as input to the adversary $\mathcal{A}$. Then, $\mathcal{A}$ executes and its oracle queries are answered by corresponding procedures of the security game. When $\mathcal{A}$ terminates, the finalize procedure of the game returns 1 if the output of $\mathcal{A}$ equals b, 0 otherwise. The advantage of $\mathcal{A}$ in the security game is given by:

$$\mathsf{Adv}_{\mathcal{A}} = \left|\mathsf{Pr}\left[\mathsf{GAME}^{\mathcal{A}} \Rightarrow 1\right] - \mathsf{Pr}\left[\mathsf{GAME}^{\mathcal{A}} \Rightarrow 0\right]\right|.$$

In this section, we start by describing security properties of PRNGs that have access to an ideal binary noise source, providing uniformly random bitstrings. This enables us to start describing the security properties that can be achieved by a PRNG, and the class of attacks it has to defend against, without going into the difficulties associated with processing inputs provided by imperfect noise sources. It is natural to view these PRNGs as cryptographic mechanisms or modes of operation. They are also practically relevant, since they describe cryptographic mechanisms appropriate for post-processing the outputs of true random number generators generating random bitstrings close to uniformly distributed.

The simplest security notion, referred to as *standard PRNG,* models a PRNG as an expanding function. This definition allows it to capture the simplest security property for a PRNG, that its output shall be undistinguishable from random. A second security notion, referred to as *stateful PRNG*, models a PRNG as a stateful algorithm. This is more in line with the lifecycle of PRNG implementations, which are instantiated and keep providing random inputs during the uptime of a system. This increased exposure calls for studying their security in the event of a compromise of their inner state. This definition then allows us to capture advanced properties as forward security. Both standard and stateful PRNG rely on the use of a unique random seed, which is not refreshed. Finally, the notion of *PRNG with inputs* is described. This notion models that a PRNG can be refreshed with new inputs during its lifecycle, enabling it to recover from a compromise of its internal state.

6.2.1. *Standard PRNG*

If a user has access to an ideal noise source, they can use a deterministic algorithm to expand its output to a longer sequence. We can define a security property in the computational model for this algorithm: no computationally bounded adversary who does not know the seed can distinguish an output from an uniformly randomly generated bitstring. This definition is adapted from Blum and Micali (1982) and Bellare and Yee (2003).

DEFINITION 6.1 (Standard PRNG).– Let s and ℓ be integers such that $\ell > s$. A (s, ℓ)-*standard PRNG* is a function $\mathbf{G} : \{0,1\}^s \to \{0,1\}^\ell$ that takes as input a bit string S of length s and outputs a bit string R of length ℓ.

In this situation, the seed of the generator is the most critical part of it since an adversary that has access to it can predict future outputs of the generator. Consider the security game PR described in Figure 6.1. In this security game, the challenger generates a random secret input S and challenges the adversary $\mathcal{A}$ on its capacity to distinguish the output of the generator from random.

proc. initialize	**proc.** next-ror	**proc.** finalize(b^*)
$S \xleftarrow{\$} \{0,1\}^s$;	$R_0 \leftarrow \mathbf{G}(S)$	IF $b = b^*$ RETURN 1
$b \xleftarrow{\$} \{0,1\}$;	$R_1 \xleftarrow{\$} \{0,1\}^\ell$	ELSE RETURN 0
	OUTPUT R_b	

Figure 6.1. *Procedures in security game* PR

DEFINITION 6.2 (Security for a standard PRNG).– Let n and ℓ be integers such that $\ell > n$. A (n, ℓ)-standard PRNG is (t, ε)-*secure* if for any adversary $\mathcal{A}$ running in time at most t, the advantage of $\mathcal{A}$ in game PR is at most ε.

6.2.2. *Stateful PRNG*

Bellare and Yee (2003) proposed a notion of *stateful PRNG* where the maximal number of outputs the PRNG is allowed to produce (named q_n hereafter) is a parameter of the generator. This notion is illustrated in Figure 6.2 and formalized in the following definition.

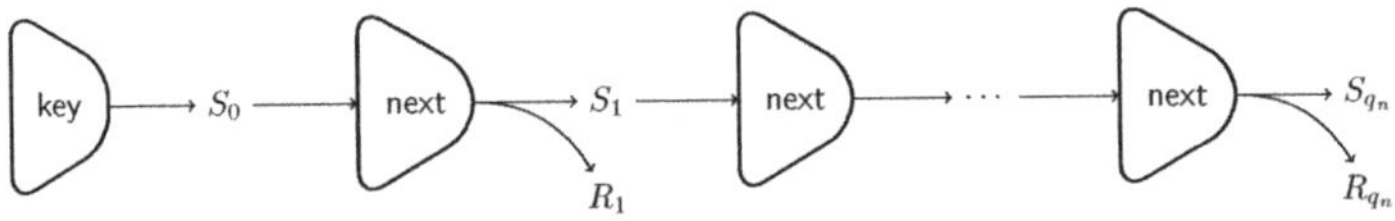

Figure 6.2. *Stateful pseudorandom number generator*

DEFINITION 6.3 (Stateful PRNG).– A *stateful PRNG* is a pair of algorithms (key, next) and an integer q_n, where key is a probabilistic algorithm that takes no input and outputs an initial state $S \in \{0,1\}^s$, next is a deterministic algorithm that, given the current state S, outputs a pair $(S', R) \leftarrow \text{next}(S)$ where S' is the new state and $R \in \{0,1\}^\ell$ is the output and q_n is the maximal number of outputs the PRNG is allowed to produce.

Consider the security game SPR described in Figure 6.3. In this security game, the challenger generates a random initial secret S and challenges the adversary $\mathcal{A}$ on its capacity to distinguish the real output of the PRNG from random. The difference with game PR is that here, successive calls to next-ror will produce different outputs that should all globally be indistinguishable from random.

proc. initialize	**proc.** next-ror	**proc.** finalize(b^*)
$S \stackrel{\$}{\leftarrow}$ key();	$(S, R_0) \leftarrow$ next(S)	IF $b = b^*$ RETURN 1
$b \stackrel{\$}{\leftarrow} \{0,1\}$	$R_1 \stackrel{\$}{\leftarrow} \{0,1\}^\ell$	ELSE RETURN 0
	OUTPUT R_b	

Figure 6.3. *Procedures in security game* SPR

DEFINITION 6.4 (Security for a stateful PRNG).– A stateful PRNG $\mathbf{G}$ = (key, next, q_n) is called (t, q_n, ε)-*secure*, if for any adversary $\mathcal{A}$ running in time at most t, making q_n calls to next-ror, the advantage of $\mathcal{A}$ in game SPR is at most ε.

Bellare and Yee (2003) proposed an extension of the previous model, where a stateful PRNG should be designed so that it is infeasible to recover any information on previous states or previous outputs from the compromise of the current state. To formalize this property, they proposed a dedicated security model where an adversary $\mathcal{A}$ chooses dynamically when to compromise the current state S. After this compromise, all *future* outputs are compromised, as they all deterministically depend on the compromised state, however, the expected security property is that the *past* outputs are computationally indistinguishable from random.

Consider the security game FWD described in Figure 6.4. In this security game, the challenger generates a random initial secret input S and challenges the adversary $\mathcal{A}$ on its capacity to distinguish the real output of the PRNG from random. In addition to the usual procedures, the adversary $\mathcal{A}$ is allowed to perform a final query to a get-state oracle that reveals the final value of the internal state S.

proc. initialize	**proc.** next-ror	**proc.** get-state	**proc.** finalize(b^*)
$S \stackrel{\$}{\leftarrow}$ key();	$(S, R_0) \leftarrow$ next(S)	*(final query)*	IF $b = b^*$ RETURN 1
$b \stackrel{\$}{\leftarrow} \{0,1\}$	$R_1 \stackrel{\$}{\leftarrow} \{0,1\}^\ell$	OUTPUT S	ELSE RETURN 0
	OUTPUT R_b		

Figure 6.4. *Procedures in security game* FWD

DEFINITION 6.5 (Forward-security for a stateful PRNG).– A stateful PRNG $\mathbf{G}$ = (key, next, q_n) is called (t, q_n, ε)-*forward-secure*, if for any adversary $\mathcal{A}$ running in time at most t, making at most q_n calls to next-ror, followed by one call to get-state, which is the last call $\mathcal{A}$ is allowed to make, the advantage of $\mathcal{A}$ in game FWD is at most ε.

6.2.3. *Stateful pseudorandom generator with inputs*

Barak and Halevi (2005) proposed a security model for PRNGs based on an ideal source of random bitstrings. In addition of being used to seed the generator, the noise source also provides entropy to *refresh* its state. This allows it to recover from a compromise of the state, that is, even after a state compromise, if the PRNG state is refreshed, its following outputs are indistinguishable from random by a bounded adversary.

DEFINITION 6.6 (PRNG with inputs (*from Barak and Halevi (2005)*)).– A *PRNG with inputs* is a pair of algorithms (refresh, next) where refresh is a deterministic algorithm that, given the current state $S \in \{0,1\}^n$ and an input $I \in \{0,1\}^p$, outputs a new state $S' \leftarrow \mathsf{refresh}(S, I)$ where $S' \in \{0,1\}^n$ is the new state and next is a deterministic algorithm that, given the current state S, outputs a pair $(S', R) \leftarrow \mathsf{next}(S)$ where $S' \in \{0,1\}^n$ is the new state and $R \in \{0,1\}^\ell$ is the output of the generator.

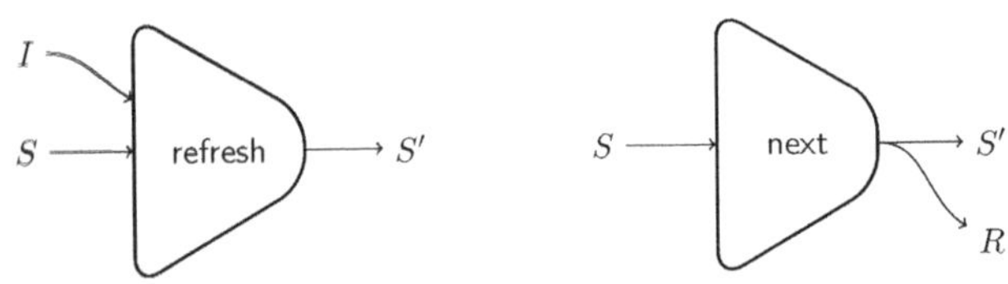

Figure 6.5. *PRNG with inputs (Barak and Halevi 2005)*

The security model captures the potential compromise of the internal state S and the inputs used to refresh the internal state. We present a simplified version of this security model that is based on the assumption that inputs are either controlled by the adversary (hence modeled by a bad-refresh procedure) or uniform (hence modeled by a good-refresh procedure).

Consider the security game described in Figure 6.6. Adversary $\mathcal{A}$ has access to the system where the generator is run, and can (a) get the output of the generator, (b) modify the data that are used to refresh the internal state of the generator and (c) have access to and can modify the internal state of the generator. The adversary $\mathcal{A}$ has two choices to refresh the generator, either with an uniform input, or with an input that $\mathcal{A}$ totally controls. In the first case, $\mathcal{A}$ uses procedure good-refresh: the challenger generates a uniform input and applies algorithm refresh with the previously generated input. In the second case, $\mathcal{A}$ uses procedure bad-refresh: $\mathcal{A}$ chooses an input that is directly used with algorithm refresh. Note also that the seeding of the generator is not performed in procedure initialize, but occurs through a call to good-refresh.

proc. initialize()	proc. good-refresh()	proc. set-state(S^*)	proc. next-ror
$S \leftarrow 0^n$; corrupt $\leftarrow$ true; $b \xleftarrow{\$} \{0,1\}$;	$I \xleftarrow{\$} \{0,1\}^n$; $S \leftarrow$ refresh(S, I); corrupt $\leftarrow$ false;	corrupt $\leftarrow$ true $S' \leftarrow S$ $S \leftarrow S^*$ OUTPUT S'	$(S, R_0) \leftarrow$ next(S) IF corrupt = true, OUTPUT R_0 ELSE $R_1 \xleftarrow{\$} \{0,1\}^\ell$ OUTPUT R_b
proc. finalize(b^*) IF $b = b^*$ RETURN 1 ELSE RETURN 0	proc. bad-refresh(I) $S \leftarrow$ refresh(S, I);		

Figure 6.6. *Procedures in security game* ROB

As in the original model from Barak and Halevi (2005), this security model uses a new important Boolean parameter, named corrupt, which is set to true when the generator is compromised and set to false otherwise. This parameter is part of the security game and is not a component of the generator. The state can be compromised through a call to set-state, which extends get-state by returning the current state but also setting the state to a value chosen by $\mathcal{A}$. Note that it is possible to obtain the effect of a get-state by calling twice set-state in order to reinject the learnt state in the generator.

The next-ror procedure differs from the equivalent procedure in the previous security models. Here, as the challenger maintains the flag corrupt, a challenge between the real output and a random one is sent to $\mathcal{A}$ only if corrupt = false. If corrupt = true, the adversary can mount an attack on the real output, so $\mathcal{A}$ will certainly distinguish it from a random one.

DEFINITION 6.7 (Robustness for a PRNG with inputs).– A PRNG with inputs $\mathcal{G}$: (refresh, next) is $(t, q_n, q_r, \varepsilon)$-*robust* if for any adversary running in time t, making at most q_r calls to bad-refresh and q_n calls to next-ror, the advantage of $\mathcal{A}$ in game ROB is at most ε.

In the original model from Barak and Halevi (2005), the input I used in procedure good-refresh is not uniform but is considered of high entropy, hence this model assumes that it is possible to *extract* this entropy from the input, before updating the internal state. Next section points challenges related to randomness extraction.

6.3. PRNG with imperfect noise sources

The assumption that a PRNG with inputs has an ideal noise source at its disposal may be too strong in some contexts. For example, a true random number generator is available but the assurance on its entropy rate is either too weak or too low. In other cases, only weak sources of randomness are available, such as user interface metadata or timings of interrupts. Their outputs are far from uniform, and the strongest property we can assume about them is that they provide some unpredictability, quantified for example by their min-entropy. In order to reduce these situations to the case of availability of an ideal source, the randomness contained in the outputs of weak sources needs to be extracted and accumulated. An additional security objective for PRNG with inputs in these contexts is that they are able to extract randomness from weak sources, even in the case where these sources are known or selected by an adversary.

6.3.1. *Extractors*

A map producing an output close to uniform when applied to the outputs of weak sources is called a *randomness extractor*. Some extractors are commonly used to improve the quality of the outputs of true random number generators. The "Von Neumann" extractor is an example of *deterministic extractor*.

DEFINITION 6.8 (Deterministic extractor).– Let p and m be integers, such that $p \geq m$. Let $\mathcal{C}$ be a class of sources on $\{0,1\}^p$. An ε-deterministic extractor for $\mathcal{C}$ is a function $\mathsf{Extract} : \{0,1\}^p \to \{0,1\}^m$, such that for every $X \in \mathcal{C}$, $\mathsf{Extract}(X)$ and $\mathcal{U}_m$ are ε-close, that is, their statistical distance is smaller than ε.

The link between min-entropy and extraction comes directly from the definition, as a necessary condition to extract m bits of randomness from a distribution X is that $\mathbf{H}_\infty(X) \geq m$. Ideally, we would like to consider only this condition: a PRNG with inputs dealing with imperfect noise sources should use a deterministic extractor to extract the entropy contained in their outputs, without considering further knowledge on their distribution. Unfortunately, it can be shown that no mapping can act as a good extractor for all weak sources. Consider for example an extraction function from $\{0,1\}^p \to \{0,1\}$. The inverse image of one of its admissible output has size greater than 2^{p-1}, and a source having uniform distribution on this set has min-entropy greater than $p-1$ while its image by the extraction function is constant.

6.3.1.1. *Seeded extractors*

In order to overcome this impossibility result, two paths have been studied. The first one consists in relaxing the notion of extractor by considering randomized extractors. If we allow it to choose the extraction function *at random*, then, with a high probability, it will become possible to extract the randomness from *each* k-source (a k-source X has $\mathbf{H}_\infty(X) \geq k$). To choose the extractor at random, we will assume that it belongs to a *family* of functions and we *uniformly* select a random element from this family. The selection process implies choosing a random parameter called seed $\in \{0,1\}^s$ and setting the extraction function as $\mathsf{Extract}_{\mathsf{seed}} = \mathsf{Extract}(., \mathsf{seed})$, hence the notion of *seeded extractor*. However, this can only improve the situation if the seed and the randomness source are independent, as illustrated by a straightforward extension of the example given above.

Hence, we need to consider further situations where the seed or the environment may be controlled by an adversary, and situations where a potential correlation between the randomness source and seed may be exploited to mount an attack against the scheme. This may occur in a hardware device that extracts from physical sources of randomness of a computer (e.g. timing of various events). These sources may be modified by the device and hence this behavior implies correlations between seed and the randomness sources. In order to implement a convenient entropy extraction, we need to add additional assumptions, either on the independence between the source and seed or on the capabilities of the adversary.

Suppose now that the independence between the source and seed cannot be ensured and we want to model situations where we need to perform randomness extraction. To overcome the impossibility result, we mainly have two options: (a) restrict the randomness source to a given family of k-sources (which is a similar strategy as for deterministic extractors) or (b) restrict the adversary $\mathcal{A}$.

The first option leads to the notion of *resilient extractor*. This notion of extractor is used in the model of Barak and Halevi (2005): a finite family of k-sources is first chosen, then the random parameter seed is chosen and finally a source is adversarially chosen (and therefore *without* independence with seed). Then when an input of high entropy is given to the PRNG, this entropy is first extracted before being used to update the PRNG's internal state.

If we do not want to restrict the class to which the randomness sources belong (and use potentially illimited sources), we need to use a different notion of extractor (named *strong extractor*). This notion of extractor has an additional parameter seed, which is used as an index to select the extractor from a family. This ensures that once a random parameter seed is chosen and made public, extraction is processed and the same parameter can be reused for the next extraction. This notion of extractor is used in the model of Dodis et al. (2013).

6.3.1.2. *Idealized extractors*

A second path explored to overcome the impossibility of generic extractors is to consider idealized cryptographic primitives as extractors. For example, a cryptographic hash function can be modeled as a public random oracle.

A first difficulty arising from this modelization is that if the source and the ideal primitive are assumed independent, the ideal primitive can be interpreted as introducing a large seed, which makes the extraction trivial. Another difficulty is that giving access to the ideal primitive to the source opens up the possibility of extractor-fixing attacks, where the source samples a large random value, performs the extraction and leaks a part of the extracted value. In order to avoid these pitfalls, and achieve a meaningful modelization, Coretti et al. (2019) proposes to consider an adapted notion of min-entropy, which is conditioned by a state representing a leakage as well as by the list of calls made the adversary to the ideal function. Random sources are considered to be *legitimate* if they provide a sufficient amount of this conditional min-entropy. It is expected that random sources occurring in implementations do not obtain their variability from computations of cryptographic primitives but rather gain it from the difficulty of predicting some information, such as the lower bits of fine-grained timings of random events. Thus such sources should satisfy the legitimacy requirement.

An extractor will the be considered secure if an adversary, generating its input according to a random procedure having access to the ideal primitive, and forgetting the details of the generation except some limited leakage and the calls performed to the ideal primitive, cannot distinguish the output of the extractor from random, provided that the conditional entropy of the input to the extractor is large enough.

6.3.2. *Robustness model of Coretti et al. (2019)*

In Coretti et al. (2019), a PRNG with inputs is defined by the two algorithms $\mathsf{refresh}^P$ and next^P, parameterized by an ideal primitive P.

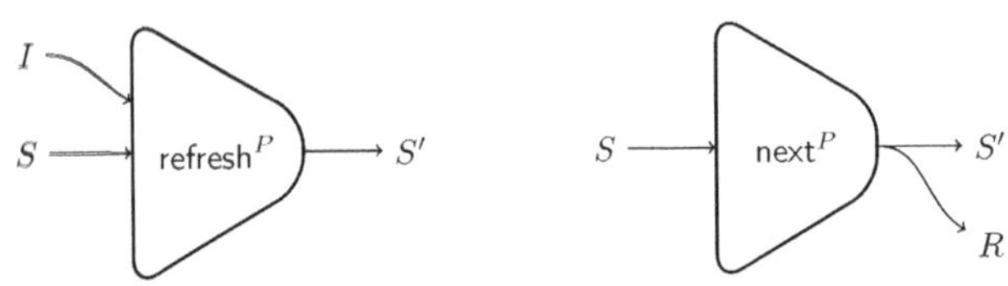

Figure 6.7. *PRNG with inputs (Coretti et al. 2019)*

DEFINITION 6.9 (PRNG with inputs (*from Coretti et al. (2019)*)).– A *PRNG with inputs* is a pair of algorithms $\mathcal{G} = (\mathsf{refresh}^P, \mathsf{next}^P)$ with access to an ideal primitive P. $\mathsf{refresh}^P$ is a deterministic algorithm that, given a state $S \in \{0,1\}^n$ and an input $I \in \{0,1\}^p$, outputs a new state $S' \leftarrow \mathsf{refresh}^P(S, I) \in \{0,1\}^n$ and next is a deterministic algorithm that, given a state $S \in \{0,1\}^n$, outputs a pair $(S', R) \leftarrow \mathsf{next}^P(S)$ where $S' \in \{0,1\}^n$ is the new state and $R \in \{0,1\}^\ell$ is the output.

The robustness security game uses procedures described in Figure 6.8. It uses the adv-refresh procedure to refresh the current state S using input I; the next-ror procedure, where it provides $\mathcal{A}$ with either the real-or-random challenge or the true generator output; the get-state/set-state procedures that provide $\mathcal{A}$ with the ability to either learn the current state S, or set it to any value S^*.

At the start of the game and after get-state/set-state oracle calls, the adversary knows the state of the PRNG. Likewise, when the adversary calls get-next while not enough entropy has been provided to the PRNG, it can recover the state of the PRNG. Such events are called entropy drains. An adversary is said to be γ^* legitimate, if it does not perform calls to get-next/next-ror unless the min-entropy of the inputs provided to the PRNG through adv-refresh since to most recent entropy drain, conditioned by the state of the adversary, the calls it performed to the ideal primitive P, and the state of the PRNG at the latest entropy drain, is greater than γ^*.

proc. initialize	proc. adv-refresh(I)	proc. get-state	proc.set-state(S^*)
$S \leftarrow 0^n$;	$S \leftarrow \text{refresh}^P(S, I)$	OUTPUT S	$S \leftarrow S^*$
$b \xleftarrow{\$} \{0,1\}$;			
proc. finalize(b^*)	**proc.next-ror**	**proc.get-next**	
IF $b = b^*$ RETURN 1	$(S, R_0) \leftarrow \text{next}^P(S)$	$(S, R) \leftarrow \text{next}^P(S)$	
ELSE RETURN 0	$R_1 \xleftarrow{\$} \{0,1\}^\ell$	OUTPUT R	
	OUTPUT R_b		

Figure 6.8. *Procedures in Security Game* ROB(γ^*)

Informally, a PRNG with inputs is secure if a legitimate adversary has only small advantage in distinguishing its outputs from random values.

DEFINITION 6.10 (Robustness for a PRNG with inputs (*from Coretti et al. (2019)*)).– A PRNG with inputs $\mathcal{G} = (\text{refresh}^P, \text{next}^P)$ is called $(\gamma^*, q, t, \ell, \varepsilon)$-*robust*, if for any γ^* legitimate adversary $\mathcal{A}$ performing at most q calls to the primitive P, ℓ calls to adv-refresh between any entropy drain and the next call to next-ror or get-next and making at most t calls to any oracle of the robustness game other that adv-refresh, the advantage of $\mathcal{A}$ in game ROB is at most ε.

6.4. Standard PRNG with inputs

We have presented in the previous sections the desirable security properties of a PRNG with inputs. Designing a PRNG with inputs together with providing an assessment of its robustness is not an easy task. Thus, implementing standard mechanisms is usually recommended. The current de facto standard for PRNG with inputs is by Barker and Kelsey (2015), since it is the recommended standard in FIPS evaluations. This document specifies three designs, Hash-DRBG, HMAC-DRBG and CTR-DRBG, based, respectively, on a hash function, an HMAC message authentication code, and a block cipher.

6.4.1. *General architecture of NIST PRNG with inputs*

This standard has known several iterations, but its terminology dates back from its first publication in 2006. As a result, it does not perfectly align with the latest academic works that have been published since. In particular, the specified mechanisms are called *deterministic random bit generators (DRBG)* and are defined by four functions: Instantiate, Reseed, Generate and Uninstantiate. Their descriptions are implementation oriented and contain much administrative information and optional arguments that would not appear in a streamlined design with a focus on security proof. This increases the complexity of their formal analysis.

From a security point of view, entropy is injected in the internal state of these PRNG during the Instantiate and Reseed functions, which thus correspond to the refresh function. In both cases, Barker and Kelsey (2015) assume that the PRNG has access to a source of randomness, providing a bitstring containing a sufficient amount of entropy. It does not however assume that this input is (close to) uniformly distributed, since NIST PRNG with inputs can make use of so-called *derivation functions* to extract the entropy of the obtained inputs.

The random outputs of the PRNG are obtained by calls to the Generate function, whose interface also differs slightly from that of the next function. First, Generate can produce outputs of variable length. Second, Generate offers the possibility to provide an additional input to the PRNG. This additional input is optional and may be used to provide additional entropy to the PRNG. The PRNG security guarantees rely however on the fact that the call to Instantiate and the calls to Reseed perform a full refresh of the state of the PRNG.

All in all, the features of the specified mechanisms show that they share a lot of the security objectives formalized in the latest models of PRNG with inputs. In particular, a non-invertible step immediately after the generation process targets forward security. Also, inputs are not assumed uniformly random and NIST PRNGs with inputs embed extraction functions based on cryptographic primitives.

6.4.2. *Security analysis and good practices*

At the time of their publication, NIST PRNG with inputs were not supported by formal security arguments. Academic publications have tried to address this shortcoming. A first step, described in the previous sections, has been to define the security game describing the security of PRNG with inputs. Informally, as soon as enough entropy has been injected in the PRNG, its outputs and states should be indistinguishable from random. Then, security proofs need to be developed specifically for the NIST PRNGs. It happens that their specificities require to make adaptations in the security models.

Several papers, such as Woodage and Shumow (2019) and Hoang and Shen (2020), have tackled this task. In general, they operate in an idealized model, where the analysis replaces the underlying cryptographic primitive by an idealized primitive.

On the whole, they conclude on the soundness of these standard PRNG with inputs. However, these works also raise some concerns and identify some formal issues. We list here some of theses problems and the recommended measures that enables to alleviate them.

– *Long requests*: to allow for variable output length, the Generate functions of all NIST DRBGs have an iterative structure. Every iteration consists of applying the underlying primitive to compute an output block, and then to update the state lightly, either by a simple incrementation or by replacing part of the state by the new output block. In a preliminary step, additional data can be incorporated in the state. In a final step, the state is updated more thoroughly through additional calls to the underlying cryptographic primitives. This leads to a tradeoff between security and performance. On the one hand, it is more efficient to request a large number of bits at every call to Generate, since this reduces the performance penalty incurred by the application of the final update of the state in Generate. The fact that the standard allows for the generation of up to 2^{19} bits by calls to the Generate function somewhat makes way for implementations that buffer a large amount of output bits and only call Generate when the buffer has been consumed. On the other hand, the lightweight update of the state during the iteration weakens the forward security of the scheme. Indeed, the generation of output bits cannot be considered atomic anymore due to the length of the output bitstring, and we must consider the effect of a state compromise during this process. We observe that the output block produced by Generate before the compromise can be recovered, either by undoing invertible state updates or by reassembling a past state from the compromise and a previous output to recover all of the intermediate outputs. In order to reduce the impact of a state compromise, it is important to ensure that the generation of output bits is as atomic as possible, that is to say not to abuse of long Generate outputs and allow for the final update of the state in Generate to execute as often as possible.

– *Forward security in HMAC-DRBG*: the optional use of additional inputs is also the source of concerns, since it leads to introduce notable differences in the schemes. A noteworthy example is the case of HMAC-DRBG update function. At the end of the Generate function, the state is updated thoroughly. When additional inputs have been provided to the update function, the key part and the message part of the state are updated twice. Though, when no additional input is provided, they are only updated once. In this case, it becomes possible to distinguish the last block V output by Generate together with the state (K', V') obtained by state compromise from a random bitstring. It suffices to test whether $HMAC(K', V) = V'$. This breaches the forward security property formalized in the robustness security games. It is disturbing that the absence of use of an optional parameter changes the status of the security analysis. This also calls for to systematically use additional inputs when calling the Generate function of HMAC-DRBG.

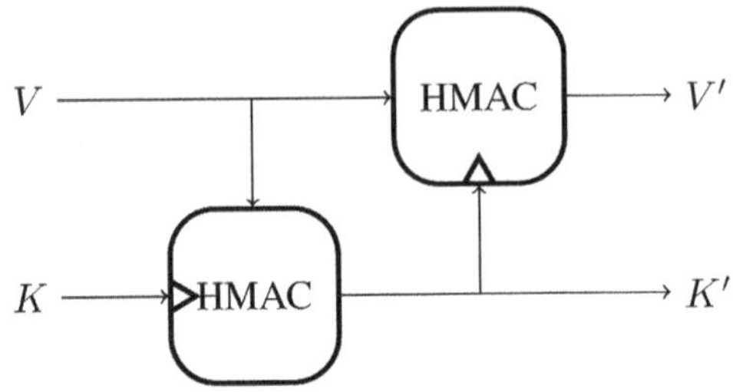

(a) No additional input

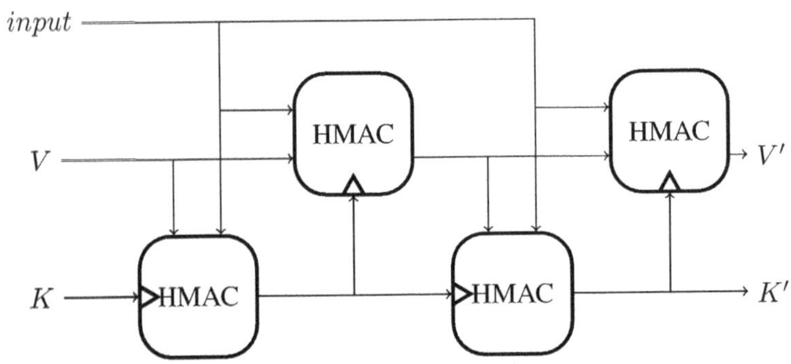

(b) With additional input

Figure 6.9. *Update function of HMAC-DRBG. When no additional input is provided, the state is only updated once*

6.5. Notes and further references

Several modelizations of the security of PRNGs with inputs have been proposed in the literature. A first model capturing the potential compromise of the internal state is given in Barak and Halevi (2005). Models trying to capture the imperfect nature of the noise sources and assessing the security of the extraction operations performed by PRNGs with inputs have been proposed later based on seeded extractors in Dodis et al. (2013), or idealized extractors in Coretti et al. (2019).

The de facto standard for PRNGs with inputs is Barker and Kelsey (2015). Its security analysis requires adaptations of the previous security models, that have been performed, for example, in Woodage and Shumow (2019); and Hoang and Shen (2020).

6.6. References

Barak, B. and Halevi, S. (2005). A model and architecture for pseudo-random generation with applications to /dev/random. In *ACM CCS 2005: 12th Conference on Computer and Communications Security*, Atluri, V., Meadows, C., Juels, A. (eds). ACM Press, New York.

Barker, E. and Kelsey, J. (2015). *Recommendation for Random Number Generation Using Deterministic Random Bit Generators*. National Institute of Standards and Technology, Gaithersburg.

Bellare, M. and Rogaway, P. (2006). The security of triple encryption and a framework for code-based game-playing proofs. In *Advances in Cryptology – EUROCRYPT 2006*, Vaudenay, S. (ed.). Springer, Berlin, Heidelberg.

Bellare, M. and Yee, B.S. (2003). Forward-security in private-key cryptography. In *Topics in Cryptology – CT-RSA 2003*, Joye, M. (ed.). Springer, Berlin, Heidelberg.

Blum, M. and Micali, S. (1982). How to generate cryptographically strong sequences of pseudo random bits. In *23rd Annual Symposium on Foundations of Computer Science*. IEEE, Chicago.

Coretti, S., Dodis, Y., Karthikeyan, H., Tessaro, S. (2019). Seedless fruit is the sweetest: Random number generation, revisited. In *Advances in Cryptology – CRYPTO 2019, Part I*, Boldyreva, A. and Micciancio, D. (eds). Springer, Berlin, Heidelberg.

Dodis, Y., Pointcheval, D., Ruhault, S., Vergnaud, D., Wichs, D. (2013). Security analysis of pseudo-random number generators with input: /dev/random is not robust. In *ACM CCS 2013: 20th Conference on Computer and Communications Security*, Sadeghi, A.-R., Gligor, V.D., Yung, M. (eds). ACM Press, New York.

Hoang, V.T. and Shen, Y. (2020). Security analysis of NIST CTR-DRBG. In *Advances in Cryptology – CRYPTO 2020, Part I*, Micciancio, D. and Ristenpart, T. (eds). Springer, Berlin, Heidelberg.

Woodage, J. and Shumow, D. (2019). An analysis of NIST SP 800-90A. In *Advances in Cryptology – EUROCRYPT 2019, Part II*, Ishai, Y. and Rijmen, V. (eds). Springer, Berlin, Heidelberg.

7

Prime Number Generation and RSA Keys

Marc JOYE and Pascal PAILLIER
Zama, Paris, France

7.1. Introduction

A positive integer q is said to be *prime* if $q > 1$ and if q has no positive divisors except 1 and q.

Numerous cryptographic primitives rely on prime numbers, a good representative being the RSA cryptosystem used for encryption or digital signatures. Let $\mathcal{M}$ denote the message space. In its simplest form, the RSA cryptosystem requires two distinct primes p and q to form a modulus $N = pq$, an exponent e that is co-prime with $\lambda(N) = \operatorname{lcm}(p-1, q-1)$,[1] and an injective (randomized) padding function $\mu\colon \mathcal{M} \to \mathbb{Z}_N$. There is also an exponent d satisfying $ed \equiv 1 \pmod{\lambda(N)}$. Modulus N and exponent e are made public while exponent d is kept private. A message $m \in \mathcal{M}$ is encrypted as $C \overset{\$}{\leftarrow} \mu(m)^e \bmod N$. The secrecy of primes p and q is primordial to guarantee the security as they allow recovering $d \leftarrow e^{-1} \bmod \operatorname{lcm}(p-1, q-1)$. Indeed, from d, the plaintext message m can be recovered in two steps as $m^* \leftarrow C^d \bmod N$ and $m \leftarrow \mu^{-1}(m^*)$. For digital signatures, the roles of e and d are exchanged. For a deterministic padding function μ, the signature σ on a message

1 LCM denotes the “lowest common multiple”. In particular, $\operatorname{lcm}(p-1, q-1) = (p-1)(q-1)/\gcd(p-1, q-1)$.

Embedded Cryptography 3,
coordinated by Emmanuel PROUFF, Guénaël RENAULT,
Matthieu RIVAIN and Colin O'FLYNN.

$m \in \mathcal{M}$ is given by $\sigma \leftarrow \mu(m)^d \bmod N$. The validity of σ is then verified by checking that $\sigma^e \equiv \mu(m) \pmod N$ using public exponent e.

A native way to produce an n-bit prime consists of generating an odd n-bit integer and testing it for primality. The process is iterated until a prime is found. The expected number of trials is asymptotically equal to $(\ln 2^n)/2 \approx 0.347n$. Generating a random 1,024-bit prime thus requires about 355 trials on average. The naïve prime generator can be made more efficient by selecting n-bit integers that are already co-prime with small primes, instead of just being co-prime with 2. For example, we can define Π as the product of the first 10 primes, $\Pi = 2 \cdot 3 \cdot \dots \cdot 29$, and randomly select an n-bit prime candidate q satisfying $\gcd(q, \Pi) = 1$. The expected number of trials before a prime is found then drops heuristically to $(\ln 2^n)\frac{\varphi(\Pi)}{\Pi} \approx 0.109n$, where φ denotes Euler's totient function. For 1,024-bit primes, this amounts to about 112 trials. The complexity can be further reduced by including more primes in the definition of Π. This methodology however requires an efficient way to generate random n-bit integers co-prime with Π.

The rest of this chapter is devoted to describing efficient methods for producing random primes in a prescribed interval along those lines:

1) A prime candidate $q \in [q_{\min}, q_{\max}]$ is *constructively* generated so as to be co-prime with Π, a product of many (small) primes.

2) q is tested for primality. If q is not prime, then it is updated in a way that its updated value remains co-prime with Π and lies within $[q_{\min}, q_{\max}]$. This step is repeated until q is found to be prime.

The output distribution of the primes that are generated also matters. In 2012, two independent teams of researchers collected RSA public keys from a wide variety of sources. Quite surprisingly, a non-negligible fraction of the collected RSA moduli exhibited a common prime factor. Sharing a common factor for non-duplicate RSA moduli completely compromises the security as calculating their greatest common divisor (GCD) reveals the secret factors and thus enables computing the private keys. These vulnerabilities apparently originated from the use of poor entropy in the generation of prime numbers p and q forming an RSA modulus $N = pq$. An important lesson is to generate RSA keys only after a proper initialization of the source of randomness. In particular, the initial random seed must be fresh and at least twice longer than the targeted security level.

The performance of algorithms highly depends on the hardware capabilities and specifics of the architecture implementing them. The methods developed in this chapter target embedded platforms allowing for super-fast evaluation of (modular) additions/subtractions/multiplications over large integers, which renders other types of computations comparatively prohibitive in the absence of integrated hardware to support these. Examples include high-end smart cards equipped with an arithmetic crypto-coprocessor. In such a setting, algebraic tricks involving (modular) arithmetic operations on large numbers are largely preferred over glue instructions such as register switches, loop control, pointer management, etc.

REMARK.– Cryptographic implementations should resist side-channel attacks as well as fault attacks. The different algorithms presented in this chapter are given in pseudocode for the sake of clarity. Actual implementations should however ensure full security against these attacks, whose specifics are architecture dependent. This de facto excludes schoolbook GCD algorithms, which leak a lot of information through the observation of their control flow. This chapter also assumes the availability of a secure cryptographic random number generator for producing uniformly random integers in a given range.

7.2. Primality testing methods

Primality testing has been an active research topic for many years. Computationally, two types of outputs are distinguished by nature: true primes and probable primes. The difference rests in the way these are generated. A *probable* prime (also known as *pseudoprime*) is usually obtained through a compositeness test, which is typically weaker but faster than a primality test. When such a test declares that a number is composite, then it is indeed with probability 1. However, if the test finds it to be prime, it is truly a prime with some probability < 1. Hence repeatedly running the test gives increasing confidence in the so-generated (probable) prime. Typical examples of compositeness tests include Fermat's test, the Solovay–Strassen test and the Miller–Rabin test.

There also exist (actual) primality tests, which tell apart prime numbers from composite numbers with a strictly null error probability (e.g. Pocklington's test and its elliptic curve analogue, and the Jacobi sum test). These tests are generally more expensive and intricate to implement.

7.3. Generation of random units

Let $\mathbb{Z}_{\Pi}^*$ denote the set of integers modulo Π that are co-prime with Π. The prime generation algorithms presented in this chapter require the random selection of an element $k \in \mathbb{Z}_{\Pi}^*$, that is, of a unit modulo Π. This section provides an algorithm that efficiently produces such an element with uniform output distribution. The design is based on the next two propositions, making use of Carmichael's function λ. Another approach based on quadratic residuosity – simpler but not strictly uniform – is also described.

DEFINITION 7.1.– The *Carmichael function* λ of an integer $\Pi \geq 2$, $\lambda(\Pi)$, is defined as the smallest positive integer t such that $a^t \equiv 1 \pmod{\Pi}$ for every integer a that is co-prime with Π.

In other terms, $\lambda(\Pi)$ denotes the exponent of the multiplicative group $\mathbb{Z}_\Pi^*$. Letting $\Pi = \prod_{i=1}^{L} {p_i}^{\delta_i}$ with p_i prime and $\delta_i \geq 1$, it can be shown that:

$$\lambda(\Pi) = \mathrm{lcm}(\lambda({p_1}^{\delta_1}), \ldots, \lambda({p_L}^{\delta_L}))$$

where

$$\lambda({p_i}^{\delta_i}) = \begin{cases} 2^{\delta_i - 2} & \text{if } p_i = 2 \text{ and } \delta_i > 2 \\ {p_i}^{\delta_i - 1}(p_i - 1) & \text{otherwise} \end{cases}$$

PROPOSITION 7.1.– Let $\Pi > 1$ and let k be an integer modulo Π. Then $k \in \mathbb{Z}_\Pi^*$ if and only if $k^{\lambda(\Pi)} \equiv 1 \pmod{\Pi}$.

Proof.– This follows from the definition of Carmichael's function. If $k \in \mathbb{Z}_\Pi^*$, then $k^{\lambda(\Pi)} \equiv 1 \pmod{\Pi}$ since $\lambda(\Pi)$ is the exponent of $\mathbb{Z}_\Pi^*$. Conversely, if $k^{\lambda(\Pi)} \equiv 1 \pmod{\Pi}$ then, for all primes p_i dividing Π, it follows that $k^{p_i - 1} \equiv 1 \pmod{p_i} \iff \gcd(k, p_i) = 1$, and thus $\gcd(k, \Pi) = 1 \iff k \in \mathbb{Z}_\Pi^*$. □

PROPOSITION 7.2.– Let k, r be integers modulo Π and assume that $\gcd(r, \Pi) = 1$. Then,

$$[k + r(1 - k^{\lambda(\Pi)}) \bmod \Pi] \in \mathbb{Z}_\Pi^*. \quad [7.1]$$

Proof.– Let $\prod_i {p_i}^{\delta_i}$ denote the prime factorization of modulus Π. Define $\omega(k, r) := [k + r(1 - k^{\lambda(\Pi)}) \bmod \Pi] \in \mathbb{Z}_\Pi$. Let p_i be a prime factor of Π. Suppose that $p_i \mid k$, then $\omega(k, r) \equiv r \not\equiv 0 \pmod{p_i}$ since $\gcd(r, p_i)$ divides $\gcd(r, \Pi) = 1$. Suppose now that $p_i \nmid k$ then $k^{\lambda(\Pi)} \equiv 1 \pmod{p_i}$ and so $\omega(k, r) \equiv k \not\equiv 0 \pmod{p_i}$. Therefore, for all primes $p_i \mid \Pi$, we have $\omega(k, r) \not\equiv 0 \pmod{p_i}$ and thus $\omega(k, r) \not\equiv 0 \pmod{{p_i}^{\delta_i}}$, which, invoking Chinese remaindering, concludes the proof. □

Benefiting from these facts, the unit generation method illustrated in Algorithm 7.1 can be devised.

As computed, the generation of units is self-correcting in the following sense: as soon as k is co-prime with some factor of Π, it remains co-prime with this factor after the updating step $k \leftarrow k + rU \pmod{\Pi}$. This follows from equation [7.1]. Put simply, what happens is that viewing k as the vector of its residues $k \bmod {p_i}^{\delta_i}$ for all

${p_i}^{\delta_i} \mid \Pi$ (i.e. an RNS[2] representation of k based on Π), non-invertible coordinates of k are continuously re-randomized until invertibility is reached for all of them. This ensures that the output distribution is strictly uniform, provided that the random number generator outputs uniform integers over $[1, \Pi)$.

Algorithm 7.1. Unit generation algorithm

Input: $\Pi \geq 2$ and $\lambda(\Pi)$
Output: a uniformly random unit $k \in \mathbb{Z}_{\Pi}^*$

1 Select $k \xleftarrow{\$} [1, \Pi)$ uniformly at random
2 Set $U \leftarrow (1 - k^{\lambda(\Pi)}) \bmod \Pi$
3 **if** $(U \neq 0)$ **then**
4   Select $r \xleftarrow{\$} [1, \Pi)$ uniformly at random
5   Set $k \leftarrow k + rU \pmod{\Pi}$
6   Go to Step 2
7 **end if**
8 **return** k

The above algorithm is particularly well suited to devices (e.g. smart cards) equipped with a coprocessor to efficiently perform multiplications modulo Π. This usually requires Π to lie within a certain range of supported values. For larger values of Π, the generation of units can be adapted as follows. Π is written as a product of pairwise co-prime integers $\Pi_i \geq 2$:

$$\Pi = \prod_{i=1}^{w} \Pi_i \quad \text{with } \gcd(\Pi_i, \Pi_j) = 1 \text{ for } i \neq j.$$

Algorithm 7.1 is then run with every couple $(\Pi_i, \lambda(\Pi_i))$ as inputs. This yields a sequence of M units $(k_1, \ldots, k_w)$ where $k_i \in \mathbb{Z}_{\Pi_i}^*$. There is no need to strictly apply Chinese remaindering to get a unit modulo Π from $(k_1, \ldots, k_w)$ as long as the resulting value is invertible modulo Π. For example, we can compute iteratively:

$$\begin{cases} K_0 = k_1 \\ K_j = \Pi_{j+1} K_{j-1} + \left(\prod_{i=1}^{j} \Pi_i\right) k_{j+1} \quad \text{for } 1 \leq j \leq w-1 \end{cases} \qquad [7.2]$$

and set $k \leftarrow K_{w-1} \bmod \Pi$. Letting $\epsilon_i := \frac{\Pi}{\Pi_i} \in \mathbb{Z}$, it can be verified that the so-defined k satisfies $k \equiv \epsilon_i\, k_i \pmod{\Pi_i}$ and thus $(k \bmod \Pi_i) \in \mathbb{Z}_{\Pi_i}^*$ since $\epsilon_i, k_i \in$

2 RNS stands for "residue number system". This system represents integers by their values modulo several pairwise co-prime integers.

$\mathbb{Z}^*_{\Pi_i}$. It can also be verified that k remains uniform over $\mathbb{Z}^*_{\Pi}$, again assuming a uniform random number generator.

Another method used to obtain units is to leverage the properties of quadratic residuosity. Given an odd prime p_i, an integer $-V$ is by definition a quadratic non-residue modulo p_i if there exists no integer t such that $-V \equiv t^2 \pmod{p_i}$. This implies that $t^2 + V$ is co-prime with p_i for every integer t. Let $\Pi' = \prod_i {p_i}^{\delta_i}$ with p_i prime, $p_i \neq 2$, and $\delta_i \geq 1$. With (Π', V) precomputed such that $-V$ is a quadratic non-residue for every prime $p_i \mid \Pi'$, a unit $k \in \mathbb{Z}^*_{\Pi'}$ can be simply obtained as:

$$k = (r^2 + V) \bmod \Pi' \quad \text{for some random } r \xleftarrow{\$} [0, \Pi').$$

Such a unit k is not uniform over $\mathbb{Z}^*_{\Pi}$. For each prime-power ${p_i}^{\delta_i}$, about half of the units in $\mathbb{Z}^*_{{p_i}^{\delta_i}}$ are covered. Hence, if Π' is made of w prime-power divisors ${p_i}^{\delta_i}$, about a subset of $\varphi(\Pi')/2^w$ units can be attained instead of the full set of $\varphi(\Pi')$ possible units. This can be mitigated by considering a product of J independent units, namely,

$$k = \prod_{j=1}^{J} \left({r_j}^2 + V\right) \bmod \Pi' \quad \text{where } r_j \xleftarrow{\$} [0, \Pi').$$

In practice, the value of J is typically set to 6, which results in a min-entropy loss of at most 0.11 bits.

7.4. Generation of random primes

This section describes a generic sieving algorithm for generating a random prime q in some arbitrary interval $[q_{\min}, q_{\max}]$. The algorithm requires as inputs a smooth integer $\Pi = 2^\delta \Pi'$ (with $\delta \geq 0$ and Π' odd) and a bound $c_{\max} \geq 1$ on a counter that indicates the maximum number of re-uses of a fresh unit. Optionally, it further requires (i) the Carmichael's value $\lambda(\Pi)$ for generating (uniform) units modulo Π and (ii) a pre-computed unit $U \in \mathbb{Z}^*_{\Pi}$ and/or a quadratic non-residue $-V$ modulo Π' for quickly sampling units in $\mathbb{Z}^*_{\Pi}$. It also assumes some fast (pseudo-)primality testing function T, which returns 1 when a candidate q is found to be prime and 0 otherwise.

The **repeat** loop involves the generation of a (uniform) unit modulo Π when $c = 0$. This can, for example, be achieved using Algorithm 7.1. If $c \neq 0$, unit $k \in \mathbb{Z}^*_{\Pi}$ is updated as another unit $k \in \mathbb{Z}^*_{\Pi}$ (the product of two units is a unit). A prime candidate q is next formed. Remark that by construction q is co-prime with Π since $q \equiv k \pmod{\Pi}$ and $k \in \mathbb{Z}^*_{\Pi}$. The process is iterated until $q \in [q_{\min}, q_{\max}]$ is declared prime.

Algorithm 7.2. Prime generation algorithm in $[q_{\min}, q_{\max}]$

Input: Π, $c_{\max}$ [optionally: $\lambda(\Pi)$, U and V]
Output: A random prime $q \in [q_{\min}, q_{\max}]$

Set $c \leftarrow 0$ and $M \leftarrow \left\lfloor \frac{q_{\max} - q_{\min}}{\Pi} \right\rfloor$
repeat
  if $(c = 0)$ **then**
    Generate $k \xleftarrow{\$} \mathbb{Z}_\Pi^*$
  else
    Sample $v \leftarrow \mathbb{Z}_\Pi^*$
    Update k as $k \leftarrow kv \bmod \Pi$
  end if
  Increment c as $c \leftarrow c + 1$
  if $(c \geq c_{\max})$ **then** $c \leftarrow 0$
  Set $L \leftarrow q_{\min} + \left((k - q_{\min}) \bmod \Pi\right)$
  Draw a random integer $m \xleftarrow{\$} [0, M]$ and set $q \leftarrow m\Pi + L$
until $(q \leq q_{\max})$ *and* $(\mathsf{T}(q) = 1)$
return q

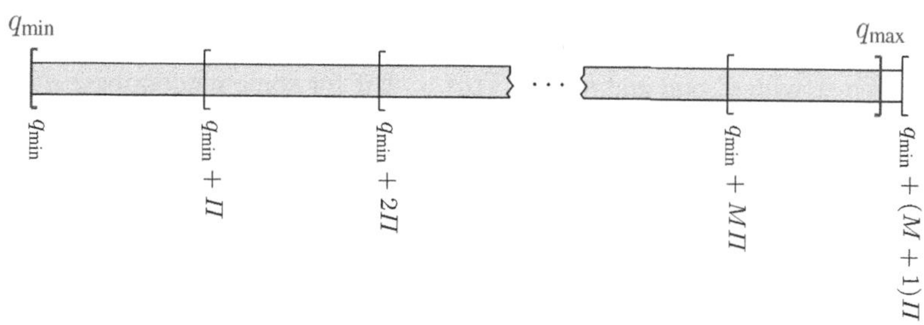

Figure 7.1. *Output domain*

Parameter $c_{\max}$ controls the distribution of the output primes. In the case of $c_{\max} = 1$, a fresh unit $k \in \mathbb{Z}_\Pi^*$ is generated for each tested prime candidate. If this unit is selected uniformly at random (e.g. with Algorithm 7.1), the prime q returned by Algorithm 7.2 is uniformly distributed on the set of primes in $[q_{\min}, q_{\max}]$ (provided that T is correct in identifying q as a prime).

Larger values for $c_{\max}$ enable various trade-offs running-time/uniformity for having units in $\mathbb{Z}_\Pi^*$. Several methods are available:

– The simplest way to update k consists of predetermining a fixed unit $U \in \mathbb{Z}_\Pi^*$ and replacing k with $k \leftarrow kU \bmod \Pi$ (i.e. $v = U$).

– Write $\Pi = 2^{\delta}\Pi'$ with $\delta \geq 0$ and Π' odd. A random unit u is first sampled in $\mathbb{Z}^*_{\Pi'}$ as $u \leftarrow (r^2 + V) \bmod \Pi'$ for a random integer $r \xleftarrow{\$} [0, \Pi')$. If $\delta = 0$, then $v = u$. Otherwise, $u \in \mathbb{Z}^*_{\Pi'}$ is extended as a unit v in $\mathbb{Z}^*_{\Pi}$ as:

$$v \leftarrow u + \big(2t + 1 - \mathrm{lsb}(u)\big)\Pi' \quad \text{for a random integer } t \xleftarrow{\$} [0, 2^{\delta-1} - 1].$$

It can be checked that $v \in \mathbb{Z}^*_{\Pi}$ since $v \equiv u \pmod{\Pi'}$ and $u \in \mathbb{Z}^*_{\Pi'}$, $v \equiv 1 \pmod 2$, and $v \in [1, \Pi)$. Next, unit $k \in \mathbb{Z}^*_{\Pi}$ is updated as another unit $k \in \mathbb{Z}^*_{\Pi}$ as $k \leftarrow kv \bmod \Pi$.

The second method offers the advantage of being probabilistic. The output distribution for the resulting primes is expected to be statistically closer to the uniform distribution. Note also that the two methods can be combined.

7.4.1. *Probable primes*

The choice of function T dictates the type of primes that are generated. For probabilistic tests T, numbers that pass the test are called *probable primes* or *pseudoprimes* as there is a nonzero probability that a composite number is falsely classified as prime. An example of such a function T is Fermat's test: $\mathsf{T}(q) = 1$ if $a^{q-1} \equiv 1 \pmod q$ for some random base $a > 1$. Miller–Rabin is usually preferred as it is more discriminative. The Miller–Rabin test writes (odd) prime candidate q as $q = 2^D q' + 1$ with q' odd and returns $\mathsf{T}(q) = 1$ if for some random base $a > 1$, it holds that

1) $a^{q'} \equiv 1 \pmod q$;
2) $a^{2^d q'} \equiv -1 \pmod q$ for some $0 \leq d < D$.

Let $P(n, t)$ denote the probability that an n-bit odd integer is composite if it successfully passes t iterations of the Miller–Rabin test. It can be shown that $P(n, 1) \leq n^2 4^{2-\sqrt{n}}$ for all $n \geq 2$, and $P(n, t) \leq 4^{1-t} P(n, 1)/(1 - P(n, 1))$ for every $n \geq 2, t \geq 2$. Stronger estimates for $P(n, t)$ are provided in the next table.

Hence, by defining function T as the repetition of Miller–Rabin with t random bases a, an odd composite n-bit integer q will be incorrectly declared prime with probability at most $P(n, t)$. From Table 7.1, it turns out that $P(n, t)$ is already $< 2^{-80}$ with $t = 2$ Miller–Rabin trials for prime candidates of bit-length $n \geq 600$.

The Miller–Rabin test can also be coupled with the Lucas test.

7.4.2. *Provable primes*

Deterministic tests T guarantee that the tested number is prime. They are however not truly practical. An alternative is to rely on methods derived from Pocklington's criterion. Unlike the Fermat's or Miller–Rabin tests, those methods provide sufficient conditions for primality. This is exemplified by the following proposition.

$n\backslash t$	1	2	3	4	5	6	7	8	9	10
100	5	14	20	25	29	33	36	39	41	44
150	8	20	28	34	39	43	47	51	54	57
200	11	25	34	41	47	52	57	61	65	69
250	14	29	39	47	54	60	65	70	75	79
300	19	33	44	53	60	67	73	78	**83**	88
350	28	38	48	58	66	73	**80**	86	91	97
400	37	46	55	63	72	**80**	87	93	99	105
450	46	54	62	70	78	**85**	93	100	106	112
500	56	63	70	78	**85**	92	99	106	113	119
550	65	72	79	**86**	93	100	107	113	119	126
600	75	**82**	88	95	102	108	115	121	127	133

Table 7.1. *Lower bounds for* $-\log_2 P(n,t)$

PROPOSITION 7.3.– Let $p > 2$ be an odd prime and let $q = 2rp + 1$ for some positive integer $r \leq p^2 + p + 1$. If there exists an integer a such that

(i) $a^{q-1} \equiv 1 \pmod q$ and $a^{2r} \not\equiv 1 \pmod q$

(ii) $r = up + s$ for some $1 \leq s < p$ and u odd

then q is prime.

Proof.– Suppose that $q = 2rp + 1$ is composite. Hence, it must have an odd prime divisor q_0 and so can be written as $q = q_0 q_1$ where $q_1 = q/q_0$ is odd. Assume that $a^{q-1} \equiv 1 \pmod q$ and $a^{2r} \not\equiv 1 \pmod q$ for some integer a. Define $b = a^{2r} \bmod q_0$. From $q_0 \mid q$, this yields $b^p \equiv 1 \pmod{q_0}$ with $b \not\equiv 1 \pmod{q_0}$. Furthermore, since q_0 is prime, it also holds that $b^{q_0-1} \equiv 1 \pmod{q_0}$. Lagrange's theorem and the primality of p imply that $p < q_0 - 1$ and in turn that $p \mid (q_0 - 1)$ (see Exercise 4). Therefore, prime q_0 must be of the form $q_0 = 2xp + 1$ for some integer $x \geq 1$. As a result, co-factor q_1 satisfies $q_1 = q \bmod (q_0 - 1) = (2rp + 1) \bmod 2xp = 2(r \bmod x)p + 1$. Letting $y = r \bmod x$, the product $q = q_0 q_1$ then leads to $q = 2(2xyp + x + y)p + 1$ and so $r = (2xy)p + (x + y)$, which contradicts the parity of $u := 2xy$. Note that $s := x + y$ verifies $1 \leq s < p$ since $x + y = x + (r \bmod x) < 2x = (q_0 - 1)/p$ and $q_0 \leq \sqrt{q} \leq \sqrt{2(p^2 + p + 1)p + 1} < p^2$ for $p > 2$. □

This proposition suggests a constructive method for generating (nonuniform) provable primes. We start with a prime p and – provided that conditions (i) and (ii) are met – obtains a prime $q = 2(up + s)p + 1$ that is about two to three times longer. Iterating the process eventually leads to a prime of the desired length. The initial prime can be chosen as any integer in the range $[2, 2^{32})$ that successfully passes the Miller–Rabin test with the three bases $(2, 3, 61)$. All of these integers are known to be prime.

In order to increase the likelihood that $q = 2rp + 1$ with $r = up + s$ verifies conditions (i) and (ii) and so is actually a prime, it is constructed in a way to be automatically co-prime with many small primes. Specifically, let $\Pi' \leq p^2 + p + 1$ be an odd smooth integer, with $p \nmid \Pi'$. If $r \equiv k - \frac{1}{2p} \pmod{\Pi'}$ for some $k \xleftarrow{\$} \mathbb{Z}^*_{\Pi'}$, it follows that $q \bmod 2 = 1$ and $q \equiv 2pk \pmod{\Pi'}$, and thus $\gcd(q, 2\Pi') = \gcd(q, \Pi') = 1$ since $2pk \in \mathbb{Z}^*_{\Pi'}$.

7.5. RSA key generation

An RSA modulus $N = pq$ is the product of two large prime numbers p and q. If ℓ denotes the bit-length of N, then, for some $1 < \ell_0 < \ell$, p must lie in the range $\left[\lceil 2^{\ell-\ell_0-\frac{1}{2}}\rceil, 2^{\ell-\ell_0}\right]$ and q in the range $\left[\lceil 2^{\ell_0-\frac{1}{2}}\rceil, 2^{\ell_0}\right]$, so that $2^{\ell-1} < N = pq < 2^{\ell}$. For security reasons, so-called balanced moduli are generally preferred, which means $\ell = 2\ell_0$. This corresponds to primes p and q being drawn at random in the interval $[q_{\min}, q_{\max}]$ where $q_{\min} = \lceil 2^{\ell_0-\frac{1}{2}}\rceil$ and $q_{\max} = 2^{\ell_0}$. Furthermore, for an RSA modulus $N = pq$, the primes p and q being generated must verify the condition $\gcd(p-1, e) = \gcd(q-1, e) = 1$ for a selected public exponent e. Matching private exponent d is given by an integer that is congruent to e^{-1} modulo $\mathrm{lcm}(p-1, q-1)$. In practice, d is often set to $d \leftarrow e^{-1} \bmod (p-1)(q-1)$.

NOTE.– A reminiscence of history is the use of so-called safe, strong, or X9.31 RSA primes. The reason for using such primes was to prevent certain classes of attacks. In particular, they were introduced to better resist cycling attacks and the $(p-1)$ and $(p+1)$ factoring attacks. Cyclic attacks were shown to have a negligible chance of succeeding, whatever the form of the RSA primes. The $(p-1)$ and $(p+1)$ factoring attacks are now obsolete owing to new factorization algorithms, particularly the elliptic curve method (ECM). It is therefore recommended to generate random RSA primes rather than special primes.

By construction, the prime generation algorithms of section 7.4 output a prime candidate $q \in [q_{\min}, q_{\max}]$ such that $q \equiv k \pmod{\Pi}$ for some random unit $k \in \mathbb{Z}^*_{\Pi}$. The product of primes, $\Pi = \prod_i p_i$, is chosen so as to minimize the ratio $\varphi(\Pi)/\Pi$ subject to $\Pi < q_{\max} - q_{\min}$. Euler's totient function $\varphi(\Pi)$ represents the group order (i.e. the number of elements) of $\mathbb{Z}^*_{\Pi}$. The minimality of $\varphi(\Pi)/\Pi$ lowers the expected number of trials before a prime is identified. This is achieved by ensuring that Π contains a maximum number of distinct primes and that these primes are as small as possible. For example, for the generation of 1,024-bit RSA primes, we can select $\Pi = 2 \cdot 3 \cdot 5 \cdots 739$ as the product of the first 131 primes, namely:

$$\Pi_{1024} = \texttt{0x 0590 bff0 e1e4 97d0 1ec5 6374 d841 7ae5}$$
$$\texttt{706f dfbe 2424 0db0 fb6a d6fa d3f4 9804}$$
$$\texttt{3820 f879 440d fd1f 4e10 1dea eddf f905}$$
$$\texttt{f362 1eae a0ca d6ef 2962 d5fa e132 dd23}$$
$$\texttt{5ded c15a 2bd2 360e 3593 649b 3164 675b}$$
$$\texttt{0ddc 0aaa 31cb 1cac c71d e317 58b8 e996}$$
$$\texttt{6b77 6dcb b5c4 f07b a381 9cfb d89f 8e1c}$$
$$\texttt{a30d a823 be6c 6d1e 0c35 46c0 23e6 02f2}$$

Companion parameters are Carmichael's value $\lambda(\Pi_{1024})$ and quadratic non-residue $-V_{1024}$ modulo $\Pi_{1024}/2$. We have $\lambda(\Pi_{1024}) = \texttt{0x0009 220e 37a8 2cbb 6007 a9de e07d e852 b1fd 11d7 5946 8826 4f7f 40e7 1355 f33b 7ebf c100}$. Observe that the bit-length of $\lambda(\Pi_{1024})$ is much smaller than that of Π_{1024}: $|\lambda(\Pi_{1024})|_2 = 276$ while $|\Pi_{1024}|_2 = 1019$. For V_{1024}, we can take:

$$V_{1024} = \texttt{0x 005b fdb1 a66b f64b f262 42fc b803 1844}$$
$$\texttt{ca3a 2182 ad42 294e 294d 40d7 61e8 552f}$$
$$\texttt{2051 4fae 12e2 e3ae 6e1d e402 4b68 4d98}$$
$$\texttt{5548 1fd9 c208 fd89 839c ff93 37a3 f8f9}$$
$$\texttt{2c16 6dff d1a7 ce2f 3b14 2ca0 8121 68f2}$$
$$\texttt{aaa6 e720 a340 2108 7bb9 71a3 5edc 796d}$$
$$\texttt{ed2f ef6d 1651 a9bc 6a23 4693 254b 7b2f}$$
$$\texttt{1cd1 2053 c4e6 6755 c506 8c07 479c 3310}$$

The private operation in RSA (i.e. decryption or signature generation) can be sped up through Chinese remaindering: the private operation is carried out modulo each prime factor of modulus N and these partial results are then recombined. In more detail, if $N = pq$ and d denotes the private exponent, we define:

$$d_p = d \bmod (p-1)\,, \quad d_q = d \bmod (q-1)\,, \quad i_q = q^{-1} \bmod p$$

and, given C, computes $C^d \bmod N$ as $\mathrm{CRT}(x_p, x_q) := x_q + q\big[i_q(x_p - x_q) \bmod p\big]$ from $x_p \leftarrow C^{d_p} \bmod p$ and $x_q \leftarrow C^{d_q} \bmod q$. This mode of operation is referred to as *CRT mode* and the private parameters are $\{p, q, d_p, d_q, i_q\}$. Compared to the standard (i.e. non-CRT) mode, the computation time is expected to be quartered.

It remains to demonstrate (i) how to ensure that primes p and q verify the additional constraint $e \nmid (p-1)$ and $e \nmid (q-1)$, (ii) how to get private key d and

(iii) how to get CRT parameters (d_p, d_q, i_q). *The rest of this section assumes that public exponent* e *is a (small) prime as is usually required in the vast majority of embedded implementations.* The most frequently used public exponent is $e = 2^{16} + 1$. Other popular exponents are $e = 3$ and $e = 17$.

The conditions $e \nmid (p-1)$ and $e \nmid (q-1)$ when e is a small prime translate into $p, q \not\equiv 1 \pmod{e}$. As a reminder, prime p is constructed in a way of being congruent to some unit k modulo Π, and similarly for prime q. There are two cases to consider:

1) $e \mid \Pi$: in this case, the candidate unit k is initialized as $k \leftarrow k_0 + er \pmod{\Pi}$ with $k_0 \xleftarrow{\$} [2, \ldots, e-1]$ so that $k \equiv k_0 \not\equiv 0, 1 \pmod{e}$. In doing so, the output of Algorithm 7.1 is a unit $k \in \mathbb{Z}_{\Pi}^{*}$ such that $k \not\equiv 1 \pmod{e}$.

2) $e \nmid \Pi$: a verification step has then to be explicitly added on the prime candidates, namely, are $p, q \not\equiv 1 \pmod{e}$? When applicable, this verification can be done before or after (pseudo)primality test T is applied.

Given public exponent e, corresponding private exponent d can be set as any value that is congruent to e^{-1} modulo $\lambda(N)$. In order to avoid computing $\gcd(p-1, q-1)$, d is usually defined as $d = e^{-1} \bmod \varphi(N)$ where $\varphi(N) = (p-1)(q-1)$. Observe that such a $d \equiv e^{-1} \pmod{\lambda(N)}$ since $\varphi(N) = \gcd(p-1, q-1) \cdot \lambda(N) \propto \lambda(N)$. Modular inverses can be obtained via Euclid's algorithm, which essentially amounts to compute a GCD. A method better suited to embedded platforms relies on Arazi's inversion formula. It enables expressing the inverse of e modulo f as a function of the inverse of f modulo e. This is stated in the next proposition.

PROPOSITION 7.4.– Let e and f be two positive integers. If $\gcd(e, f) = 1$ then

$$e^{-1} \bmod f = \frac{1 + f(-f^{-1} \bmod e)}{e}. \qquad [7.3]$$

Proof.– Define $U = e(e^{-1} \bmod f) + f(f^{-1} \bmod e)$. Since $U \equiv 1 \pmod{e}$ and $U \equiv 1 \pmod{f}$, it follows that $U \equiv 1 \pmod{ef}$. Hence, noting that $1 < e + f \leq U < 2ef$, this implies that $U = 1 + ef$ or, equivalently, that $e^{-1} \bmod f = \frac{1}{e}\big[(1 + ef) - f(f^{-1} \bmod e)\big] = \frac{1}{e}\big[1 + f(-f^{-1} \bmod e)\big]$, as desired. □

Taking $f := (p-1)(q-1)$, a valid value for private exponent d is therefore given by $d = \frac{1+f(-f^{e-2} \bmod e)}{e}$. Note that this requires e being prime. From d, private CRT exponents d_p and d_q are then directly obtained as $d_p = d \bmod (p-1)$ and $d_q = d \bmod (q-1)$. Since p is prime, CRT parameter i_q can be computed by an application of Fermat Little theorem as $i_q = q^{p-2} \bmod p$.

7.6. Exercises

1) Let w pairwise co-prime integers $\Pi_1, \ldots, \Pi_w$ with $\Pi_i \geq 2$ and let $\Pi = \prod_{i=1}^{w} \Pi_i$. Let also integers $\epsilon_i = \Pi/\Pi_i$. Given w integers $k_1, \ldots, k_w$ with $k_i \in \mathbb{Z}^*_{\Pi_i}$ (viewed as elements in $[1, \Pi_i - 1]$), define:

$$\begin{cases} K_0 = k_1 \\ K_j = \Pi_{j+1} K_{j-1} + \left(\prod_{i=1}^{j} \Pi_i\right) k_{j+1} \quad \text{for } 1 \leq j \leq w-1 \end{cases}.$$

Prove that $\gcd(K_{w-1}, \Pi) = 1$.

2) Factoring-based constructs typically make use of RSA moduli $N = pq$ with primes p and q that are congruent to 3 modulo 4. This is, for example, the case in the Fiat–Shamir identification protocol. Supposing that candidate prime p (respectively, q) always remains co-prime with some unit modulo Π, how to tweak the unit generation algorithm (Algorithm 7.1) so that the condition $p \equiv 3 \pmod 4$ (respectively, $q \equiv 3 \pmod 4$) is automatically satisfied? Can this be extended to support Rabin–Williams moduli, that is, moduli $N = pq$ with $p \equiv 3 \pmod 8$ and $q \equiv 7 \pmod 8$?

3) A DSA prime is an ℓ-bit prime q of the form $q = 1 + pr$ where p is also a prime. Given p and ℓ, the goal is to find an integer r such that $1 + pr$ is a prime in $[2^\ell, 2^\ell - 1]$. Let Π denote a product of prime numbers with $p \nmid \Pi$. Remark that if $r \equiv -1/p + k \pmod{\Pi}$ for some unit $k \in \mathbb{Z}^*_\Pi$, then $\gcd(1 + pr, \Pi) = 1$. Use this observation to design an efficient generator for DSA primes.

4) The order of an element $b \in \mathbb{Z}^*_q$ is the smallest positive integer n such that $b^n \equiv 1 \pmod q$. The order of a group is the number of its elements. Lagrange's theorem says that the order of an element always divides the order of its group. Let q be a prime and $b \in \mathbb{Z}^*_q$ with $b \not\equiv 1 \pmod q$. Prove that $b^p \equiv 1 \pmod q$ for some prime p implies that $p \mid (q-1)$.

5) Check that for each prime $p_i \neq 2$ dividing Π_{1024} (see section 7.5), the value of V_{1024} is such that $V_{1024} \bmod p_i \in \{1, 2, 5, 19\}$. Deduce a more compact representation for the pair of parameters (Π_{1024}, V_{1024}) and apply Exercise 1 for generating units modulo Π_{1024}.

6) Let $N = pq$ be an RSA modulus and let (e, d) denote the matching pair of public/private RSA exponents. Let also $d_p = d \bmod (p-1)$ and $d_q = d \bmod (q-1)$. Prove that $C^{d-1} \equiv p y_q + q y_p \pmod N$ where $y_q = \left(p(Cp)^{e-1}\right)^{q-1-d_q} \bmod q$ and $y_p = \left(q(Cq)^{e-1}\right)^{p-1-d_p} \bmod p$. Use this relation to derive a formula for computing $C^d \bmod N$ from CRT parameters $\{p, q, d_p, d_q\}$ (i.e. without using i_q). Estimate the incurred overhead compared to the usual CRT recombination when the public exponent is $e = 2^{16} + 1$.

7) Given an odd integer D, define the recurrence relation:

$$\begin{cases} x_0 = 1 \\ x_n = x_{n-1}(2 - Dx_{n-1}) \bmod 2^{2^n} \quad \text{for } n \geq 1 \end{cases}.$$

Show that $x_n = D^{-1} \bmod 2^{2^n}$. Explain how this can be used for quickly evaluating the integer division in Arazi's inversion formula (i.e. the integer division by e in equation [7.3]).

8) Find a way to reconstruct private exponent d from $d_p = d \bmod (p-1)$ and $d_q = d \bmod (q-1)$ without computing $\gcd(p-1, q-1)$.

7.7. Notes and further references

– Section 7.1. An excellent general reference to prime numbers is Crandall and Pomerance (2005). The RSA cryptosystem (Rivest et al. 1978) is named after its inventors Rivest, Shamir and Adleman. Widely used RSA padding functions are OAEP (Bellare and Rogaway 1995) for message encryption and FDH (Bellare and Rogaway 1993) or PSS (Bellare and Rogaway 1996) for digital signatures. The naïve prime generator is examined in Brandt and Damgård (1993). Its extension using a set of a small primes is described in Joye et al. (2000). Studies of RSA keys found in the wild were conducted in 2012 in two independent works: Heninger et al. (2012); and Lenstra et al. (2012). Setting the length of the initial seed to twice the security length associated with the RSA modulus is a NIST recommendation (NIST 2013, Appendix B.3.2). Methods for generating numbers from a sequence of random bits are provided in ISO/IEC (2011). Discussions regarding side-channel attacks can be found in Aldaya et al. (2019); Bauer et al. (2014); Clavier and Coron (2007); Finke et al. (2009); Weiser et al. (2018).

– Section 7.2. ANSI Standard ANSI X9.80-2020 (2020) is a useful reference on the different (pseudo)primality tests used in public-key cryptography, including for the RSA cryptosystem. An analysis of their strength under adversarial conditions is provided in Albrecht et al. (2018). Pocklington's test appears in Pocklington (1914) and its elliptic curve variant in Atkin and Morain (1993). The Jacobi sum test is described in Bosma and van der Hulst (1990).

– Section 7.3. A CRT sieve for sampling in $\mathbb{Z}_{\Pi}^*$ with $\Pi = \prod_{i=1}^{L} p_i^{\delta_i}$ using the Chinese remainder theorem (CRT) is given in Joye et al. (2000, section 4.1). It however requires pre-computing and storing a large sequence of constants $\{\theta_i\}_{1 \leq i \leq L}$ where $\theta_i \equiv 1 \pmod{p_i^{\delta_i}}$ and $\theta_i \equiv 0 \pmod{p_j^{\delta_j}}$ for $j \neq i$. The generation of units as per Algorithm 7.1 is presented in Joye and Paillier (2006, Figure 2). Advantageously, it only takes Π and $\lambda(\Pi)$ as pre-computed inputs. The method building units from a quadratic non-residue $-V$ modulo Π is presented in Hamburg et al. (2021, section 2.3). The pre-computed inputs in this case are Π and V.

– Section 7.4. The generation of prime numbers is covered in part in several cryptographic standards, including ISO/IEC 8032:2020 (ISO/IEC 2020) ANSI X9.80-2020 (ANSI 2020) and IEEE Standard 1363-2000 (IEEE 2000). The general presentation of Algorithm 7.2 is adapted from Joye and Paillier (2006, Figure 2). The main difference is the full coverage of the interval $[q_{\text{min}}, q_{\text{max}}]$ for prime candidates q. Rejection sampling is applied in the case $q > q_{\text{max}}$. As presented, Algorithm 7.2 also encompasses the prime generation algorithm given in Hamburg et al. (2021, Algorithm 5). See also Fouque and Tibouchi (2014) for a discussion on the output distribution. The failure probability of the Miller–Rabin test Rabin (1980) is discussed in Beauchemin et al. (1988); and Landrock (1999). Explicit functions that bound $P(n, t)$ are provided in Damgård et al. (1993). Table 7.1 is reproduced from Damgård et al. (1993, Table 2). The Lucas test is presented in Baillie and Wagstaff (1980). The main proposition in section 7.4.2 is a slight adaptation from (Landrock 1999, Theorem 1). It simplifies a special case of (Brillhart et al. 2002, Theorem 11, section III.B.2) used in Clavier et al. (2012) that requires an extra GCD computation. The corresponding prime generation methods reduce the number of iterations compared to earlier algorithms based on Pocklington's criterion Maurer (1995); Mihailescu (1994) (see also Brandt et al. 1993, section 3). Choices of Miller–Rabin bases that are necessary for proving primality up to a certain bound are given in Jaeschk (1993, section 5).

– Section 7.5. Good sources of practical information regarding the generation of RSA parameters are Joye and Paillier (2006); Joye et al. (2000). Arguments against the use of special RSA primes are clarified in Rivest and Silverman (2001). Lattice-based attacks against RSA keys using random primes with too few entropy are reported in Nemec et al. (2017). A frequency analysis of a large collection of public RSA exponents appears in Lenstra et al. (2012). Insider attacks against RSA key generation and mitigation measures are surveyed in Young (2004). Arazi's formula is named after Arazi who was the first to implement fast modular inversions of RSA exponents on a crypto-coprocessor. Its application to (small) prime exponents e is described in Fischer and Seifert (2002). Generalizations to arbitrary exponents e and various implementation tricks are detailed in Joye and Paillier (2003).

– Section 7.6:

1) Constructing a unit modulo $\Pi = \prod \Pi_i$ for pairwise co-prime moduli Π_i can be done easily from units modulo each Π_i using the CRT. The improved method that do not require pre-computing CRT constants is described in Hamburg et al. (2021, Algorithm 3).

2) This is an easy adaptation of Algorithm 7.1. The trick is to include 4 as a factor of Π. Variable k is initialized with $k \leftarrow 3 + 4r$ for some $r \xleftarrow{\$} [0, \Pi/4)$. Note that

$k \in [1, \Pi)$ and $k \equiv 3 \pmod 4$. Rabin–Williams moduli are supported analogously by including 8 as a factor of Π and initializing k accordingly.

3) An algorithm for generating DSA primes from units modulo Π is presented in Joye et al. (2000, section 7.1). Algorithms for the generation of safe, strong, and X9.31 RSA primes are also presented therein (see also Joye and Paillier 2006, section 4.2).

4) For a prime q, the order of $\mathbb{Z}_q^*$ is $q-1$. Let n denote the order of $b \in \mathbb{Z}_q^*$, $b \not\equiv 1 \pmod q$. Lagrange's theorem implies that $n \mid (q-1)$ and $n \mid p$ since $b^n \equiv 1 \pmod q$. As n cannot be 1, it follows that $n = p$ and thereby $p \mid (q-1)$.

5) Various compact representations for V (including CRT-based representations) are discussed in Hamburg et al. (2021, Appendix B).

6) The inversion-free CRT technique is demonstrated in Hamburg et al. (2021, section 3). As presented, it further includes a randomness step to blind the input: $C' \leftarrow Cr \bmod N$ with $r \xleftarrow{\$} \mathbb{Z}_N^*$ and $C^d \bmod N = C'(py'_q + qy'_p) \bmod N$ where $y'_q \leftarrow \left(pr(C'p)^{e-1}\right)^{q-1-d_q} \bmod q$ and $y'_p \leftarrow \left(qr(C'q)^{e-1}\right)^{p-1-d_p} \bmod p$.

7) The algorithm for computing $D^{-1} \bmod 2^{2^n}$ is presented in Joye and Paillier (2003, Figure 1) (note however that there is a typo: the modulus should read 2^{2^i}). Another algorithm can be found in Dussé and Kaliski (1991, section 3.2). As an application to equation [7.3] for an odd integer e, since $d := e^{-1} \bmod f < 2^{2^F}$ where $F := \lceil \log_2 \log_2 f \rceil$, d can equivalently be obtained as $d \leftarrow M \cdot e^{-1} \bmod 2^{2^F}$ with $M = (1 + f(-f^{-1} \bmod e)) \bmod 2^{2^F}$.

8) Let $\hat{d} := \frac{-(ed_p-1)(ed_q-1)+1}{e}$. It is easily verified that $e\hat{d} \equiv 1 \pmod{(p-1)}$ and $e\hat{d} \equiv 1 \pmod{(q-1)}$. Hence, $\hat{d} \bmod (p-1)(q-1)$ is a valid value for private exponent d in standard mode.

7.8. References

Albrecht, M.R., Massimo, J., Paterson, K.G., Somorovsky, J. (2018). Prime and prejudice: Primality testing under adversarial conditions. In *ACM CCS 2018: 25th Conference on Computer and Communications Security*, Lie, D., Mannan, M., Backes, M., Wang, X. (eds). ACM Press, New York.

Aldaya, A.C., García, C.P., Tapia, L.M.A., Brumley, B.B. (2019). Cache-timing attacks on RSA key generation. *IACR Transactions on Cryptographic Hardware and Embedded Systems*, 2019(4), 213–242.

ANSI (2020). ANSI X9.80–2020. Prime number generation, primality testing, and primality certificates. Standard, American National Standards Institute.

Atkin, A.O.L. and Morain, F. (1993). Elliptic curves and primality proving. *Mathematics of Computation*, 61(203), 29–68.

Baillie, R. and Wagstaff, S.S. Jr. (1980). Lucas pseudoprimes. *Mathematics of Computation*, 35(152), 1391–1417.

Bauer, A., Jaulmes, É., Lomné, V., Prouff, E., Roche, T. (2014). Side-channel attack against RSA key generation algorithms. In *Cryptographic Hardware and Embedded Systems – CHES 2014*, Batina, L. and Robshaw, M. (eds). Springer, Berlin, Heidelberg.

Beauchemin, P., Brassard, G., Crépeau, C., Goutier, C., Pomerance, C. (1988). The generation of random numbers that are probably prime. *Journal of Cryptology*, 1(1), 53–64.

Bellare, M. and Rogaway, P. (1993). Random oracles are practical: A paradigm for designing efficient protocols. In *ACM CCS 93: 1st Conference on Computer and Communications Security*, Denning, D.E., Pyle, R., Ganesan, R., Sandhu, R.S., Ashby, V. (eds). ACM Press, New York.

Bellare, M. and Rogaway, P. (1995). Optimal asymmetric encryption. In *Advances in Cryptology – EUROCRYPT'94*, Santis, A.D. (ed.). Springer, Berlin, Heidelberg.

Bellare, M. and Rogaway, P. (1996). The exact security of digital signatures: How to sign with RSA and Rabin. In *Advances in Cryptology – EUROCRYPT'96*, Maurer, U.M. (ed.). Springer, Berlin, Heidelberg.

Bosma, W. and van der Hulst, M.-P. (1990). Faster primality testing. In *Advances in Cryptology – EUROCRYPT'89*, Quisquater, J.-J. and Vandewalle, J. (eds). Springer, Berlin, Heidelberg.

Brandt, J. and Damgård, I. (1993). On generation of probable primes by incremental search. In *Advances in Cryptology – CRYPTO'92*, Brickell, E.F. (ed.). Springer, Berlin, Heidelberg.

Brandt, J., Damgård, I., Landrock, P. (1993). Speeding up prime number generation. In *Advances in Cryptology – ASIACRYPT'91*, Imai, H., Rivest, R.L., Matsumoto, T. (eds). Springer, Berlin, Heidelberg.

Brillhart, J., Lehmer, D.H., Selfridge, J.L., Tuckerman, B., Wagstaff, S.S. Jr. (2002). *Factorizations of* $b^n \pm 1$, $b = 2, 3, 5, 6, 7, 10, 11, 12$ *Up to High Powers*, 3rd edition. American Mathematical Society, Providence.

Clavier, C. and Coron, J.-S. (2007). On the implementation of a fast prime generation algorithm. In *Cryptographic Hardware and Embedded Systems – CHES 2007*, Paillier, P. and Verbauwhede, I. (eds). Springer, Berlin, Heidelberg.

Clavier, C., Feix, B., Thierry, L., Paillier, P. (2012). Generating provable primes efficiently on embedded devices. In *PKC 2012: 15th International Conference on Theory and Practice of Public Key Cryptography*, Fischlin, M., Buchmann, J., Manulis, M. (eds). Springer, Berlin, Heidelberg.

Crandall, R. and Pomerance, C.B. (2005). *Prime Numbers: A Computational Perspective*, 2nd edition. Springer, Berlin, Heidelberg.

Damgård, I., Landrock, P., Pomerance, C. (1993). Average case error estimates for the strong probable prime test. *Mathematics of Computation*, 61(203), 177–194.

Dussé, S.R. and Kaliski, B.S. Jr. (1991). A cryptographic library for the Motorola DSP56000. In *Advances in Cryptology – EUROCRYPT'90*, Damgård, I. (ed.). Springer, Berlin, Heidelberg.

Finke, T., Gebhardt, M., Schindler, W. (2009). A new side-channel attack on RSA prime generation. In *Cryptographic Hardware and Embedded Systems – CHES 2009*, Clavier, C. and Gaj, K. (eds). Springer, Berlin, Heidelberg.

Fischer, W. and Seifert, J.-P. (2002). Note on fast computation of secret RSA exponents. In *ACISP 02: 7th Australasian Conference on Information Security and Privacy*, Batten, L.M. and Seberry, J. (eds). Springer, Berlin, Heidelberg.

Fouque, P.-A. and Tibouchi, M. (2014). Close to uniform prime number generation with fewer random bits. In *ICALP 2014: 41st International Colloquium on Automata, Languages and Programming*, Esparza, J., Fraigniaud, P., Husfeldt, T., Koutsoupias, E. (eds). Springer, Berlin, Heidelberg.

Hamburg, M., Tunstall, M., Xiao, Q. (2021). Improvements to RSA key generation and CRT on embedded devices. In *Topics in Cryptology – CT-RSA 2021*, Paterson, K.G. (ed.). Springer, Berlin, Heidelberg.

Heninger, N., Durumeric, Z., Wustrow, E., Halderman, J.A. (2012). Mining your Ps and Qs: Detection of widespread weak keys in network devices. In *USENIX Security 2012: 21st USENIX Security Symposium*, Kohno, T. (ed.). USENIX Association, Berkeley.

IEEE (2000). IEEE 1361-2000. IEEE Standard Specifications for Public-Key Cryptography Standard.

ISO/IEC (2011). ISO/IEC 18031:2011. Information technology – Security techniques – Random bit generation. Standard, International Organization for Standardization.

ISO/IEC (2020). ISO/IEC 18032:2020. Information security – Prime number generation. Standard, International Organization for Standardization.

Jaeschk, G. (1993). On strong pseudoprimes to several bases. *Mathematics of Computation*, 61(204), 915–926.

Joye, M. and Paillier, P. (2003). GCD-free algorithms for computing modular inverses. In *Cryptographic Hardware and Embedded Systems – CHES 2003*, Walter, C.D., Koç, Ç.K., Paar, C. (eds). Springer, Berlin, Heidelberg.

Joye, M. and Paillier, P. (2006). Fast generation of prime numbers on portable devices: An update. In *Cryptographic Hardware and Embedded Systems – CHES 2006*, Goubin, L. and Matsui, M. (eds). Springer, Berlin, Heidelberg.

Joye, M., Paillier, P., Vaudenay, S. (2000). Efficient generation of prime numbers. In *Cryptographic Hardware and Embedded Systems – CHES 2000*, Koç, Ç.K. and Paar, C. (eds). Springer, Berlin, Heidelberg.

Landrock, P. (1999). Primality tests and use of primes in public key systems. In *Lectures on Data Security*, Damgård, I. (ed.). Springer, Berlin, Heidelberg.

Lenstra, A.K., Hughes, J.P., Augier, M., Bos, J.W., Kleinjung, T., Wachter, C. (2012). Public keys. In *Advances in Cryptology – CRYPTO 2012*, Safavi-Naini, R. and Canetti, R. (eds). Springer, Berlin, Heidelberg.

Maurer, U.M. (1995). Fast generation of prime numbers and secure public-key cryptographic parameters. *Journal of Cryptology*, 8(3), 123–155.

Mihailescu, P. (1994). Fast generation of provable primes using search in arithmetic progressions. In *Advances in Cryptology – CRYPTO'94*, Desmedt, Y. (ed.). Springer, Berlin, Heidelberg.

Nemec, M., Sýs, M., Svenda, P., Klinec, D., Matyas, V. (2017). The return of Coppersmith's attack: Practical factorization of widely used RSA moduli. In *ACM CCS 2017: 24th Conference on Computer and Communications Security*, Thuraisingham, B.M., Evans, D., Malkin, T., Xu, D. (eds). ACM Press, New York.

NIST (2013). Digital signature standard (DSS). Standard, Federal Information Processing Standards Publication, FIPS PUB 186-4.

Pocklington, H.C. (1914). The determination of the prime or composite nature of large numbers by Fermat's theorem. *Proceedings of the Cambridge Philosophical Society*, 18, 29–30.

Rabin, M.O. (1980). Probabilistic algorithm for testing primality. *Journal of Number Theory*, 12(1), 128–138.

Rivest, R. and Silverman, R. (2001). Are 'strong' primes needed for RSA. Cryptology ePrint Archive [Online]. Available at: https://eprint.iacr.org/2001/007.

Rivest, R.L., Shamir, A., Adleman, L.M. (1978). A method for obtaining digital signatures and public-key cryptosystems. *Communications of the Association for Computing Machinery*, 21(2), 120–126.

Weiser, S., Spreitzer, R., Bodner, L. (2018). Single trace attack against RSA key generation in intel SGX SSL. In *ASIACCS 18: 13th ACM Symposium on Information, Computer and Communications Security*, Kim, J., Ahn, G.-J., Kim, S., Kim, Y., López, J., Kim, T. (eds). ACM Press, New York.

Young, A. (2004). Mitigating insider threats to RSA key generation. *CryptoBytes*, 7(1), 1–15.

8

Nonce Generation for Discrete Logarithm-Based Signatures

Akira TAKAHASHI[1] **and Mehdi TIBOUCHI**[2]

[1] *J.P. Morgan AI Research & AlgoCRYPT Center of Excellence, New York, United States*[1]

[2] *NTT Social Informatics Laboratories, Japan*

8.1. Introduction

Discrete logarithm-based signature schemes, such as Schnorr signatures and elliptic curve digital signature algorithm (ECDSA) (Figure 8.1), are commonly used in today's real-world systems along with RSA. The signature generation algorithms in these schemes crucially rely on some ephemeral randomness, sometimes referred to as the *nonce*.

Clearly, the one-time randomness k in Figure 8.1 must not be reused, as otherwise, two signatures generated from the same nonce immediately leak a secret signing key. For example, given two Schnorr signatures (h_1, z_1) and (h_2, z_2) on distinct messages, the secret x can be easily found by computing $(z_1 - z_2) \cdot (h_1 - h_2)^{-1} \bmod q$. The reader may check that the same observation holds for ECDSA too. Nonce reuse has been a common vulnerability in practical implementations of discrete logarithm-based schemes: some high-profile attack examples include the extraction of leading technology company's ECDSA secret key for signing gaming software, or the stealth of Bitcoins associated with wallets that signed multiple transactions with repeated randomness.

---

1 Work partially done while Akira Takahashi was affiliated with University of Edinburgh.

Embedded Cryptography 3,
coordinated by Emmanuel PROUFF, Guénaël RENAULT,
Matthieu RIVAIN and Colin O'FLYNN.

Algorithm 8.1. EC Schnorr signing

Require: $x \in \mathbb{Z}_q$, $\mathsf{msg} \in \{0,1\}^*$
Ensure: (h, z)

$k \xleftarrow{\$} \mathbb{Z}_q$
$R := [k]G$
$h := \mathsf{H}(\mathsf{msg}, R)$
$z := k + h \cdot x \mod q$
return (h, z)

Algorithm 8.2. ECDSA signing

Require: $x \in \mathbb{Z}_q$, $\mathsf{msg} \in \{0,1\}^*$
Ensure: (r, s)

$k \xleftarrow{\$} \mathbb{Z}_q$
$(r_x, r_y) := [k]G$
$r := r_x \mod q$
$s := (\mathsf{H}(\mathsf{msg}) + r \cdot x) \cdot k^{-1} \mod q$
return (r, s)

Figure 8.1. *Comparison of two elliptic curve-based signature generation algorithms. In both schemes, $x \in \mathbb{Z}_q$ is a secret key, $\mathsf{msg} \in \{0,1\}^*$ is a message to be signed, G is a base point generating a subgroup of order q, and $\mathsf{H} : \{0,1\}^* \to \mathbb{Z}_q$ is a cryptographic hash function*

However, despite what their name may suggest, "nonces" in discrete logarithm-based signatures are much more sensitive than what is expected of a number only used once. If the randomness k fails to follow the uniform distribution in $\mathbb{Z}_q$, or if it is partially leaked, an attacker can completely bypass the discrete logarithm problem and recover the secret signing key by sufficiently collecting many signatures with this additional information.

Such randomness failures can occur in many different ways in real life. The majority of vulnerabilities pointed out in academic papers lurk in *nonconstant time* implementations of whatever operations involving k, such as scalar multiplication $[k]G$ or field inversion $k^{-1} \bmod q$ in case of ECDSA. More advanced *physical fault analysis* may also allow an attacker to artificially inject a fault into the base point G, such that scalar multiplication happens on a much smaller subgroup: for example, if a faulty base point $\tilde{G}$ has order $2^{\ell} \ll q$, the fault attacker can learn the ℓ least significant bits of k by checking the value of $[k]\tilde{G}$. Randomness bias has also been caused by simple *implementation mistakes*, including but not limited to a number of Bitcoin wallets producing secp256k1 ECDSA signatures using only 64-bit randomness Breitner and Heninger (2019), or the DSA implementation of the wolfSSL library fixing two consecutive bits of k to "11" for unknown reasons[2].

The goal of this chapter is to introduce practical attack methods exploiting randomness failures of Schnorr and ECDSA. It turns out that a small amount of leakage or bias of the one-time randomness k in both schemes allows an attacker to translate the key recovery problem to the so-called *hidden number problem (HNP)*.

2 CVE-2019-14317 discovered by Jàn Jančàr. The vulnerability was fixed in v4.2.0. See also https://github.com/wolfSSL/wolfssl/releases/tag/v4.2.0-stable.

In essense, the class of attacks described in this chapter follows the blueprint depicted in Figure 8.2. In section 8.2, we describe how to translate signatures with leaky or biased nonces to an instance of the HNP. We then go over two distinct approaches to solve the HNP: *lattice attack* (section 8.3) and *Fourier transform attack* (section 8.4). Finally, section 8.5 briefly discusses how to protect practical implementations from these devastating attacks.

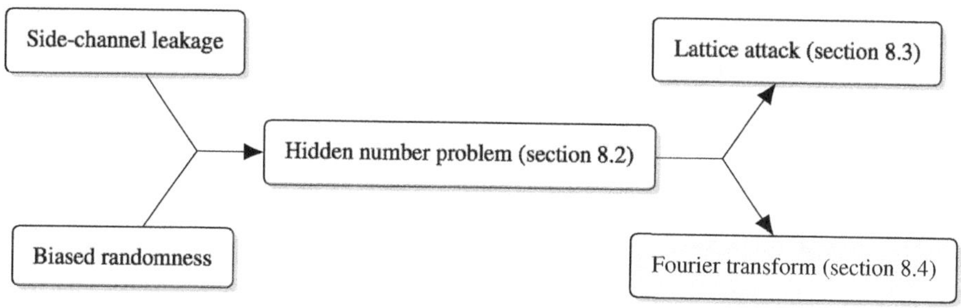

Figure 8.2. *Overview of key recovery attacks against Schnorr and ECDSA*

8.2. The hidden number problem and randomness failures

Let us first introduce the problem closely related to a key recovery of Schnorr and ECDSA.

DEFINITION 8.1.– (Hidden Number Problem ($\mathsf{HNP}_{q,\ell,n}$)).– Let q be a prime and $x \in \mathbb{Z}_q$ be a secret. Given uniformly random $h_i \in \mathbb{Z}_q$ and an approximation z_i of $h_i \cdot x$ such that $|h_i \cdot x - z_i|_q < q/2^\ell$ for $i = 1, \ldots, n$, find x. Here, $|a|_q$ denotes the unique integer in $\{0, 1, \ldots, q-1\}$ such that $a \equiv |a|_q \bmod q$.

8.2.1. *From Schnorr to HNP*

The reader may notice the similarity between Schnorr and the above formulation of HNP. In fact, it is rather straightforward to translate Schnorr with bad randomness to an instance of HNP. Assume for simplicity that the modulus q is close to a power of two 2^m (which is usually the case in elliptic curve-based instantiations). Then, in a secure implementation of Schnorr, the randomness k should be an (almost) uniform m-bit integer. Suppose that, instead, the top ℓ bits of k are fixed to a sequence of zeros. Due to the definition of z in Schnorr (Algorithm 8.1, Line 4), we have $z - h \cdot x \equiv k \bmod q$, and hence $|z - h \cdot x|_q = k < 2^{m-\ell} \approx q/2^\ell$. This expresses $(-h, -z)$ as a sample for the $\mathsf{HNP}_{q,\ell}$ problem associated with the secret x. A collection of n Schorr signatures sampled with nonces that have their top ℓ bits set to zero can thus be converted to an instance of $\mathsf{HNP}_{q,\ell,n}$ with the signing key as the secret (and solving the HNP therefore breaks the scheme).

Schnorr signatures with randomness *leakage* can also be turned into HNP samples with a simple modification. Suppose we have a signature (h, z) with side-channel information $0 \leq k_{\text{leak}} < 2^\ell$ representing the ℓ most significant bits (MSBs) of the nonce k. In other words, $k = k_{\text{leak}} \cdot 2^{m-\ell} + k'$ for some $k' < 2^{m-\ell}$. Then, we have:

$$z - k_{\text{leak}} \cdot 2^{m-\ell} - h \cdot x \equiv k' \bmod q$$

and thus $\left|(z - k_{\text{leak}} \cdot 2^{m-\ell}) - h \cdot x\right|_q < 2^{m-\ell} \approx q/2^\ell$. Hence, $(-h, -z + k_{\text{leak}} \cdot 2^{m-\ell})$ can be seen as an HNP sample.

If k_{leak} represents the ℓ least significant bits (LSBs) of k instead of the MSBs, then we can "shift" the cleared bit position to the top and obtain a similar result as follows. Since it holds that $(z - k_{\text{leak}}) \cdot 2^{-\ell} = k' + 2^{-\ell} \cdot h \cdot x \bmod q$, we can now treat $(-2^{-\ell} \cdot h \bmod q, (-z + k_{\text{leak}}) \cdot 2^{-\ell} \bmod q)$ as an HNP sample as well.

If the leakage information is on the middle bits of k, the conversion to an HNP instance is a bit more involved, but still possible. We refer the reader to further references at the end of this chapter for details.

8.2.2. *From ECDSA to HNP*

Although an ECDSA signature pair (r, s) satisfies a slightly more complex equation, we can essentially turn it into a "Schnorr form" with additional preprocessing. By rearranging the equation of Algorithm 8.2 (Line 4), we get:

$$k = \mathsf{H}(\mathsf{msg}) \cdot s^{-1} + r \cdot s^{-1} \cdot x \bmod q. \qquad [8.1]$$

Then redefining $h := -r \cdot s^{-1}$ and $z := \mathsf{H}(\mathsf{msg}) \cdot s^{-1}$ we obtain the equation equivalent to Algorithm 8.1 (Line 4) of Schnorr and we can therefore recast ECDSA with leaky/biased k as an HNP sample just as above. Although the distribution of $-r \cdot s^{-1}$ is not perfectly uniform in $\mathbb{Z}_q$, this will not impact the efficacy of the attacks that we will review in the following.

8.3. Lattice attacks

The best known attack on the hidden number problem (and by the transformations described in the previous sections, on discrete logarithm-based signatures with randomness failures) is most likely based on lattice reduction: it expresses the HNP as a so-called bounded distance decoding problem in a lattice. It was originally devised by Howgrave-Graham and Smart, and refined, improved and generalized in a number of papers afterwards. This section gives an overview of this attack, as well as some references to more recent work on this topic.

8.3.1. *Lattice basics*

For the purposes of this chapter, a *lattice* will be defined as a subgroup of the additive group $\mathbb{Z}^n$ for some $n \geq 0$, endowed with the standard Euclidean norm $\|(x_1, \ldots, x_n)\| = \sqrt{x_1^2 + \cdots + x_n^2}$. For any family of linearly independent vectors $\mathbf{b}_1, \ldots, \mathbf{b}_m$ of $\mathbb{Z}^n$, the set:

$$\mathcal{L}(\mathbf{b}_1, \ldots, \mathbf{b}_m) = \left\{ \sum_{i=1}^{m} c_i \mathbf{b}_i : c_i \in \mathbb{Z} \right\}$$

is a lattice, and conversely, any lattice $\mathcal{L} \subset \mathbb{Z}^n$ can be put in that form for some vectors $\mathbf{b}_1, \ldots, \mathbf{b}_m$. In that case, the family $(\mathbf{b}_1, \ldots, \mathbf{b}_m)$ is called a *basis* of $\mathcal{L}$. We can then represent the lattice $\mathcal{L}$ by the $m \times n$ matrix $\mathbf{B}$ whose rows are formed by the vectors $\mathbf{b}_i$ and write $\mathcal{L} = \mathcal{L}(\mathbf{B})$.

A given lattice $\mathcal{L}$ can infinitely have many distinct bases, but they all have the same cardinality $m \leq n$, called the *rank* of $\mathcal{L}$. In this chapter, we will only consider *full-rank* lattices, whose rank m is equal to n, the dimension of the ambient space. For a full-rank lattice $\mathcal{L}$ with basis matrix $\mathbf{B}$, we define the volume of $\mathcal{L}$ as the quantity $\mathrm{vol}(\mathcal{L}) = |\det(\mathbf{B})|$, which does not depend on the choice of $\mathbf{B}$.

The smallest Euclidean norm of a nonzero vector in $\mathcal{L}$ is called the first minimum of $\mathcal{L}$ and denoted by $\lambda_1(\mathcal{L})$. For a "random" n-dimensional lattice (for a natural distribution on lattices that is not important for our purposes), Ajtai proved that with high probability:

$$\lambda_1(\mathcal{L}) \approx \sqrt{\frac{n}{2\pi e}}\,\mathrm{vol}(\mathcal{L})^{1/n}. \qquad [8.2]$$

It is common to analyze lattice problems by heuristically assuming that the approximation above holds for a given lattice $\mathcal{L}$, even if that lattice is not random. This is a consequence of the more general *Gaussian heuristic*.

There are many computational problems related to lattices. The best-known one is the shortest vector problem (SVP for short): given a lattice $\mathcal{L}$, find a vector $\mathbf{v} \in \mathcal{L}$ such that $\|\mathbf{v}\| = \lambda_1(\mathcal{L})$. Using lattice reduction algorithms like BKZ, it can typically be solved exactly in practice for lattices of relatively small dimension n (say up to about $n = 100$), and approximately within good approximation factors for n below a few hundreds.

The lattice problem with the closest relationship to the HNP is *bounded distance decoding* (BDD): given a lattice $\mathcal{L}$ and a target vector $\mathbf{v}$ in the ambient space and a distance bound β, find a lattice point $\mathbf{u} \in \mathcal{L}$ such that $\|\mathbf{u} - \mathbf{v}\| \leq \beta$. When $\beta < \lambda_1(\mathcal{L})/2$, the triangular inequality shows that the solution $\mathbf{u}$ is unique if it exists.

If β is small compared to $\lambda_1(\mathcal{L})$, the problem is tractable in practice for lattice dimensions similar to SVP (e.g. applying Kannan's embedding technique sketched at the end of the next section).

8.3.2. *Expressing the HNP as a lattice problem*

Consider an instance of $\mathsf{HNP}_{q,\ell,n}$, given by n pairs (h_i, z_i) such that $|h_i \cdot x - z_i|_q < q/2^\ell$ for some secret $x \in \mathbb{Z}_q$. For each i, let $b_i = |h_i \cdot x - z_i|_q$. Since $h_i \cdot x - z_i \equiv b_i \bmod q$, there exists an integer c_i such that $h_i \cdot x - z_i + c_i \cdot q = b_i$. In particular, given the bound on b_i, we can write:

$$
\begin{aligned}
0 &\le h_i \cdot x - z_i + c_i \cdot q < q/2^\ell \\
-q/2^{\ell+1} &\le h_i \cdot x - z_i - q/2^{\ell+1} + c_i \cdot q < q/2^{\ell+1} \\
-q &\le 2^{\ell+1} \cdot (h_i \cdot x + c_i \cdot q) - 2^{\ell+1} \cdot z_i - q < q.
\end{aligned}
$$

Write $u_i = 2^{\ell+1}(h_i \cdot x + c_i \cdot q)$ and $v_i = 2^{\ell+1} \cdot z_i + q$, so that $|u_i - v_i| \le q$ for all i by the above. Then, consider the lattice $\mathcal{L}$ generated by the rows of the following $(n+1) \times (n+1)$ integer matrix:

$$
\mathbf{B} = \begin{bmatrix}
2^{\ell+1} \cdot q & 0 & \cdots & 0 & 0 \\
0 & 2^{\ell+1} \cdot q & & 0 & 0 \\
\vdots & & \ddots & & \vdots \\
0 & 0 & & 2^{\ell+1} \cdot q & 0 \\
2^{\ell+1} \cdot h_1 & 2^{\ell+1} \cdot h_2 & \cdots & 2^{\ell+1} \cdot h_n & 1
\end{bmatrix}. \qquad [8.3]
$$

Then the so-called *hidden vector* $\mathbf{u} = (c_1, \ldots, c_n, x) \cdot \mathbf{B} = (u_1, \ldots, u_n, x)$ belongs to the lattice $\mathcal{L}$. Moreover, it is *close* to the known vector $\mathbf{v} = (v_1, \ldots, v_n, 0)$, in the sense that the Euclidean norm $\|\mathbf{u} - \mathbf{v}\|$ satisfies:

$$
\|\mathbf{u} - \mathbf{v}\| = \sqrt{|u_1 - v_1|^2 + \cdots + |u_n - v_n|^2 + x^2} \le \sqrt{(n+1)q^2} = q\sqrt{n+1}.
$$

We can be more precise: in the HNP, each difference $u_i - v_i$ is essentially uniform in $[-q, q)$ (and x uniform in $[0, q)$), so that the expectation of $\|\mathbf{u} - \mathbf{v}\|^2$ becomes $\approx (n+1) \cdot q^2/3$, and standard results on concentration show that $\|\mathbf{u} - \mathbf{v}\|^2$ concentrates rapidly around that value as n grows.

As a result, recovering the hidden vector $\mathbf{u}$ (which reveals x and solves the HNP) from the known vector $\mathbf{v}$ becomes a BDD problem with radius $\approx q\sqrt{(n+1)/3}$. This is expected to be solvable with lattice reduction when this radius is small compared to the shortest vector $\lambda_1(\mathcal{L})$. Assuming the Gaussian heuristic, as equation [8.2] holds, we have:

$$
\lambda_1(\mathcal{L}) \approx \sqrt{\frac{n+1}{2\pi e}} |\det(\mathbf{B})|^{1/(n+1)} = \sqrt{\frac{n+1}{2\pi e}} \cdot \left(2^{\ell+1} \cdot q\right)^{n/(n+1)}.
$$

Thus, the condition for solvability is as follows:

$$\begin{aligned}
q\sqrt{\frac{n+1}{3}} &\ll \sqrt{\frac{n+1}{2\pi e}}(2^{\ell+1}\cdot q)^{n/(n+1)}\\
q\sqrt{\frac{2\pi e}{3}} &\ll (2^{\ell+1}\cdot q)^{n/(n+1)}\\
q^{n+1}\Big(\sqrt{\frac{2\pi e}{3}}\Big)^{n+1} &\ll (2^{\ell+1})^{n}\cdot q^{n}\\
q\Big(\sqrt{\frac{2\pi e}{3}}\Big)^{n+1} &\ll (2^{\ell+1})^{n}\\
q\sqrt{\frac{2\pi e}{3}} &\ll \Big(2^{\ell+1}\sqrt{\frac{3}{2\pi e}}\Big)^{n}\\
\log_2 q+\log_2\sqrt{\frac{2\pi e}{3}} &\lesssim n\cdot(\ell-\log_2\sqrt{\pi e/6})\\
n &\gtrsim \frac{\log_2 q+\log_2\sqrt{2\pi e/3}}{\ell-\log_2\sqrt{\pi e/6}}.
\end{aligned}$$

Ignoring the constants in the numerator and denominator, we see that the problem is expected to be solvable roughly when $n \gtrsim (\log_2 q)/\ell$, consistent with the intuition that each HNP samples reveals ℓ bits of information about the secret x, so that $(\log_2 q)/\ell$ in total is needed to recover the whole secret.

To solve the BDD problem concretely, a simple approach is to use Kannan's embedding technique: extend the lattice $\mathcal{L}$ to a new lattice $\widehat{\mathcal{L}}$ one dimension larger, with an abnormally short vector corresponding to the difference $\mathbf{u}-\mathbf{v}$. We can, for example, consider the lattice $\widehat{\mathcal{L}}$ generated by the rows of the following matrix:

$$\widehat{\mathbf{B}} = \begin{bmatrix}
2^{\ell+1}\cdot q & 0 & \cdots & 0 & 0 & 0\\
0 & 2^{\ell+1}\cdot q & & 0 & 0 & 0\\
\vdots & & \ddots & & \vdots & \vdots\\
0 & 0 & & 2^{\ell+1}\cdot q & 0 & 0\\
2^{\ell+1}\cdot h_1 & 2^{\ell+1}\cdot h_2 & \cdots & 2^{\ell+1}\cdot h_n & 1 & 0\\
-v_1 & -v_2 & \cdots & -v_n & 0 & \kappa q
\end{bmatrix}$$

for some constant κ. Note that the highlighted block corresponds to the basis $\mathbf{B}$ (equation [8.3]) of $\mathcal{L}$. This lattices contains the vector $(c_1,\dots,c_n,x,1)\cdot\widehat{\mathbf{B}} = (u_1-v_1,\dots,u_n-v_n,x,\kappa q)$ of norm $\approx q\sqrt{(n+1)/3+\kappa}$. If this norm is significantly smaller than the estimate for $\lambda_1(\widehat{\mathcal{L}})$ given by the Gaussian heuristic, then this vector should be the shortest vector with high probability, and if the dimension is small enough, an algorithm like LLL or BKZ should recover it as the first vector of a reduced basis for $\widehat{\mathcal{L}}$.

8.3.3. *Some recent developments*

The framework described above has been used essentially as-is in many physical attacks and randomness failure attacks in the literature. However, some refinements and generalizations have sometimes been necessary. Here, we give a short overview of some of these developments.

8.3.3.1. *Dealing with varying, not perfectly known leakage sizes*

One of the most common settings in which this attack applies is the case of non-constant time scalar multiplication on elliptic curves, where timing information reveals (albeit imperfectly) the bit length of the nonce k, and hence the number of contiguous zero MSBs. This is, for example, the type of side-channel information that the TPM–FAIL dataset provides. This setting deviates from the HNP model in two ways: first, not all samples have the same number of known bits of information (in other words, ℓ varies from one signature to the next); second, since the data are noisy, ℓ is not known with perfect accuracy either (we get, for each signature, some real number $\hat{\ell}$ essentially given by $\ell + \nu$ for some noise distribution ν).

There are ways to deal with these differences without modifying the attack. For example, we can discard most of the samples and keep only those for which $\hat{\ell}$ is large enough that we are confident that ℓ is at least 5 (depending on the standard deviation of the noise, this could mean keeping the signatures with $\hat{\ell} \geq 7$, and thus only keeping one signature in 2^7).

This approach is somewhat wasteful, however, and may be impractical depending on how difficult it is to obtain signature samples. Thus, several papers in the literature have strived to make the best possible use of a dataset like the above, by leveraging MSB leakages of different bit lengths, and proposing algorithms to best guess the actual number of zero MSBs from the noisy leakage. The state of the art along these lines is Minerva by Jančàr et al. (2020).

8.3.3.2. *Dealing with different rings*

Belgarric et al. (2016) considered the application of this lattice attack in side-channel attacks against Koblitz elliptic curves over fields of characteristic two. In that setting, the scalar multiplication is carried out using a so-called τ-adic representation for the nonce k, where τ is a certain element in the ring of integers of an imaginary quadratic field (representing the action of the Frobenius endomorphism on the Koblitz curve). As a result, the leakage is on the bits of the τ-adic expansion of k.

This setting is still amenable to a lattice attacks very similar to the one above, but the lattice construction has to take into account the structure of the ring in which computations are carried out.

While Belgarric et al. (2016) focused on Koblitz curves in particular, a unified treatment of such extensions of the HNP to different rings can be proposed. A systematic discussion is, for example, provided in Shani's PhD thesis (Shani 2017).

8.3.3.3. *Leveraging the knowledge of the public verification key*

For the HNP itself, the uniqueness of the solution x is not guaranteed if there are not sufficiently many samples. As alluded to above, there is an information-theoretic lower bound of $(\log_2 q)/\ell$ samples to ensure uniqueness, since each sample provides only ℓ bits of information on the secret. With fewer samples than that, we cannot hope to solve the problem.

Moreover, the analysis we gave of the lattice attack suggests that there is a hard limit to how small of a bias is tractable using the approach of this section. Indeed, the solvability condition was given as:

$$n > \frac{\log_2 q + \log_2 \sqrt{2\pi e/3}}{\ell - \log_2 \sqrt{\pi e/6}}.$$

This is impossible to achieve if ℓ is smaller than $\log_2 \sqrt{\pi e/6} \approx 0.255$ bits (note that our definition of the HNP still makes complete sense for ℓ an arbitrary positive real number).

Albrecht and Heninger recently showed how to overcome these theoretical limitations, at least in principle, in the case of attacks on signature schemes. The basic observation is that, for discrete logarithm-based signature schemes, there is *always* a unique, well-defined solution x regardless of the number of samples, because the attacker knows the public verification key g^x associated with x. Moreover, this knowledge can be used within lattice reduction, particularly in conjunction with lattice sieving. A lattice sieving algorithm will construct many small vectors in the lattice, and we can use the knowledge of the verification key to select, among those many candidates, the one that corresponds to the correct x. This approach turns out to also yield concrete efficiency improvements when applying the lattice attack to relatively small leakage sizes ℓ.

In a different direction, Sun et al. (2022) observed that if some bits of the secret x are known, we can easily adjust the lattice construction to take advantage of that knowledge and improve the attack. When we can check the validity of a solution using the public key, this gives rise to an interesting data–time trade-off for the lattice attack: guess some bits of x and use them to recover the remaining ones using a smaller lattice (and hence less data). An interesting feature of this approach is that this reduces the attack to solving many BDD instances with varying target vectors in the *same* lattice, making it possible to rely on various batch-CVP or CVP-with-preprocessing techniques to solve them. For example, carrying out an initial lattice reduction on the original BDD lattice, and then solving all of the BDD instances using Kannan's embedding technique, is typically much faster than without the original reduction.

8.4. Fourier transform attack

Independently of the lattice attack, a completely different approach to the HNP was proposed by Bleichenbacher in 2000. Bleichenbacher's method is known to work more effectively against HNP instances with smaller nonce leakages, such as 1-3-bit or even *less than* 1-bit, meaning that the most significant bit of nonces is known to the attacker with some probability $1 - \epsilon$. Albeit with much larger input data complexity compared to the lattice attack, Bleichenbacher's method has been used in the literature to break ECDSA, Schnorr and variants with small nonce leakages that seemed hard to exploit with the Howgrave-Graham–Smart method. This section serves as brief introduction to Bleichenbacher's framework, as summarized in Algorithm 8.3.

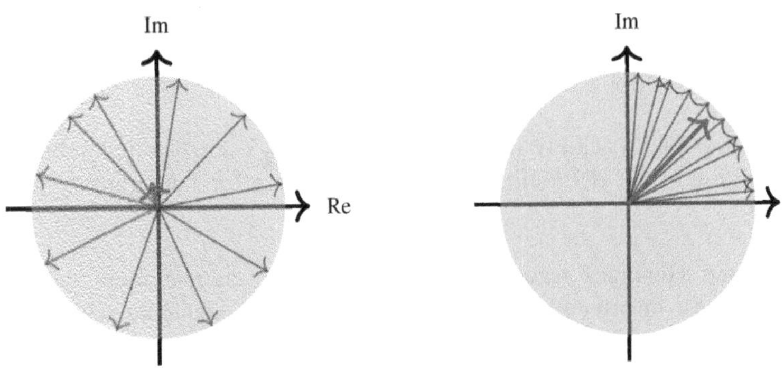

(a) k_i's are uniform in $[0, q)$ (b) k_i's are uniform in $[0, q/4)$

Figure 8.3. *Behavior of the bias function outputs. Gray arrows indicate input vectors. Green arrows are the normalized sum of input vectors. For a color version of this figure, see www.iste.co.uk/prouff/cryptography3.zip*

8.4.1. *Quantifying bias using discrete Fourier transform*

At the heart of Bleichenbacher's framework lies the so-called *bias function*. To get intuition about how the attack proceeds, assume for a moment the existence of some convenient function $f : \mathbb{Z}_q^n \to [0,1] \cap \mathbb{R}$, which takes a set of nonces $\{k_i\}_{i=1}^n$ as input and tells us how much these nonces are biased modulo q, by returning some real value between 0 and 1. If each k_i is distributed uniformly and independently in $\mathbb{Z}_q$, we have $f(k_1, \ldots, k_n) \approx 0$, and $f(k_1, \ldots, k_n) \approx 1$ otherwise. Then we can immediately come up with the following simple "attack" on the HNP: given a set of HNP samples $\{(h_i, z_i)\}_{i=1}^n$, for each candidate HNP solution $w \in \mathbb{Z}_q$, compute the corresponding set of nonces $K_w := \{k_{i,w} = z_i - h_i \cdot w \bmod q\}_{i=1}^n$ and the bias function $f(K_w)$. Return the value of w that maximizes the output of bias function as a solution to the HNP. Why does this work? If a candidate w does not match the actual solution x, that is, there exists some $\Delta \neq 0$ such that $w = x + \Delta$, then the bias function should output a value close to 0: as h_i samples are uniformly distributed in $\mathbb{Z}_q$, we obtain "wrong" nonces $k_{i,w} = z_i - h_i \cdot (x + \Delta) = k_i - h_i \cdot \Delta \bmod q$ that are uniform in $\mathbb{Z}_q$ no matter how the actual nonces k_i are biased. By contrast, if $w = x$, then the function f on input K_x should output a value close to 1, assuming that the input nonces are somewhat biased in $\mathbb{Z}_q$. Therefore, by observing the *peak* of the bias function, an attacker can distinguish whether their guess of the HNP solution is correct or not.

Of course, this naïve method is far from practical since it has to exhaustively check every possible candidate in $\mathbb{Z}_q$. But before dealing with this issue, let us first discuss how to instantiate the bias function. The essential idea of Bleichencher's approach is to quantify the modular bias of nonce k in the form of (inverse) discrete Fourier transform (DFT).

DEFINITION 8.2.– Let $\boldsymbol{K}$ be a random variable over $\mathbb{Z}_q$. The *modular bias* $B_q(\boldsymbol{K})$ is defined as:

$$B_q(\boldsymbol{K}) = \mathrm{E}\left[e^{(2\pi \boldsymbol{K}/q)\mathrm{i}} \right]$$

where $\mathrm{E}\left[\cdot\right]$ represents the mean and i is the imaginary unit. Likewise, the *sampled bias* of a set of points $K = \{k_i\}_{i=1}^n$ in $\mathbb{Z}_q$ is defined by:

$$B_q(K) = \frac{1}{n} \sum_{i=1}^{n} e^{(2\pi k_i/q)\mathrm{i}}.$$

Note that the sampled bias above outputs a complex number. Thanks to the factor $1/n$, the norm of its output is normalized to 0–1 range. The convenient function considered above thus can be instantiated as $f(K) := |B_q(K)|$. In practice, the sampled biases for q different sets $K_1, \ldots, K_q$ can be efficiently computed using the *fast Fourier transform* (FFT), which only takes $O(q \log q)$ operations instead of $O(q^2)$ as required by a naïve way.

To see why DFT tells us "how much the input nonces are biased", it is instructive to look at the output values mapped on the unit circle of complex plane, depicted in Figure 8.3. If the inputs are uniform in $\mathbb{Z}_q$ each "vector" $e^{(2\pi k_i/q)\mathrm{i}}$ contributing to the sum has a uniformly random angle, so the summed vector should have relatively small length. This is not the case anymore once these vectors have biased angles, leading to the norm close to 1 when summed together.

It is in fact possible to estimate the norm of the summed vectors depending on how many of most significant bits are fixed. Suppose ℓ MSBs of every k_i are fixed to some constant. Then, it is known that the norm of bias $|B_q(K)|$ converges to $2^\ell \cdot \sin(\pi/2^\ell)/\pi$ for sufficiently large modulus q and number of samples n. For example, if the first MSB of each k_i is fixed to a constant bit as in Figure 8.3(b), then the bias is estimated as $|B_q(K)| \approx 2\sqrt{2}/\pi \approx 0.9$. Moreover, if the k_i's follow the uniform distribution over $\mathbb{Z}_q$, then the mean of the norm of sampled bias is estimated as $1/\sqrt{n}$. This can be easily verified by computing the expected norm of a sum of n two-dimensional vectors with uniformly random angles.

8.4.2. *Stretching the peak width*

8.4.2.1. *Upper-bounding h_i values*

To avoid performing an exhaustive search in the entire $\mathbb{Z}_q$, it would be ideal if we could stretch the peak width, so that $B_q(K_w)$ with candidate $w = x + \Delta$ still shows a distinguishable value for sufficiently small Δ. Recall that for each candidate HNP secret $w = x+\Delta$ the corresponding nonce can be denoted as $k_{i,w} = k_i - h_i \cdot \Delta \bmod q$, where k_i is the actual nonce used for generating the ith signature. Intuitively, if Δ and every h_i are sufficiently small we can expect $k_{i,w} \approx k_i$ and thus $B_q(K_w) \approx B_q(K_x)$ with $K_w = \{k_{i,w}\}_{i=1}^n$. Therefore, by upper-bounding the value of h_i, we may be able to detect the peak of bias even if w does not match x exactly.

To see how much the peak width gets stretched let us take a look at how each vector gets "rotated" due to an error. The sampled bias value for a candidate w is:

$$B_q(K_w) = \frac{1}{n} \sum_{i=1}^{n} e^{(2\pi k_i/q)\mathrm{i}} \cdot e^{(-2\pi h_i \Delta/q)\mathrm{i}}. \qquad [8.4]$$

Of course, if $\Delta = 0$, the above coincides with the actual bias value $B_q(K_x)$. Recall that multiplication by $e^{\mathrm{i}\theta}$ can be seen as a rotation on the complex plane by an angle θ. If $\Delta \neq 0$, then each vector contributing toward the sum gets rotated by the angle $2\pi h_i \Delta/q$ on the circle. Hence, if $h_i < L \ll q$ and perturbation from the secret is $|\Delta| < q/(4L)$, we can observe that the rotation is at most $|\theta| < \pi/2$. Assuming $e^{(2\pi k_i/q)\mathrm{i}}$ have almost the same angles, it holds that the rotated vectors are still concentrated on the half of the circle, implying their sum still shows a value close to the peak. On the other hand, if the angle exceeds $\pi/2$, there will be vectors going toward opposite directions and thus they start canceling out. Therefore, by computing the bias for every $q/(2L)$th secret candidate in $[0, q-1)$, we should be able to observe the peak value. In practice, we can experimentally show checking every q/Lth value is sufficient to find the peak, that is, for $j = 1, \ldots, L$, let $w_j = j \cdot q/L$. Then the corresponding bias is:

$$B_q(K_{w_j}) = \frac{1}{n} \sum_{i=1}^{n} e^{(2\pi z_i/q)\mathrm{i}} \cdot e^{(-2\pi h_i w_j/q)\mathrm{i}} \quad [8.5]$$

$$= \sum_{t=0}^{L-1} \underbrace{\left(\frac{1}{n} \sum_{\{i: h_i = t\}} e^{(2\pi z_i/q)\mathrm{i}} \right)}_{Z_t} \cdot e^{(-2\pi t w_j/q)\mathrm{i}} \quad [8.6]$$

$$= \sum_{t=0}^{L-1} Z_t \cdot e^{(-2\pi t j/L)\mathrm{i}} \quad [8.7]$$

which is exactly the form of inverse DFT. Now a sequence of bias values $B_q(K_{w_0}), \ldots, B_q(K_{w_{L-1}})$ can be computed via FFT in time $O(L \cdot \log L)$ and $O(L)$ space. Then w_j leading to the maximum bias value should share its top $\log L$ bits with the secret x since w_j is within q/L distance of x. Figure 8.4 displays the effect of bounding h_i.

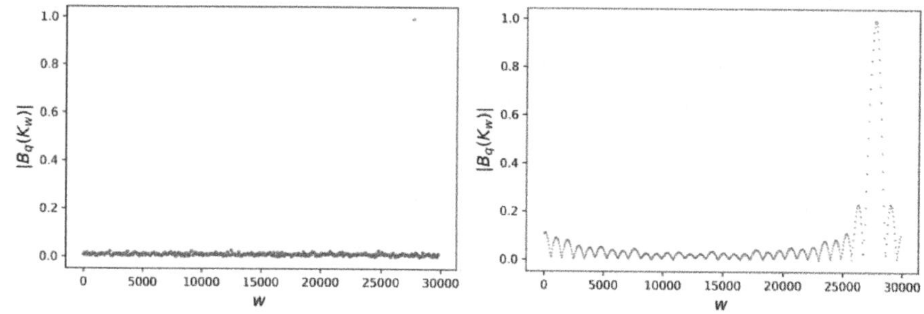

(a) $h_i \leq q$ (b) $h_i \leq q/2^{10}$

Figure 8.4. *Plotted sampled bias $|B_q(K_w)|$ for $q \approx 2^{15}$ and for $w \in [0, q)$. With a sufficiently small upper bound for h_i, we can observe the peak width gets stretched. For a color version of this figure, see www.iste.co.uk/prouff/cryptography3.zip*

8.4.2.2. *Small and sparse linear combinations*

In practice, the upper-bound L should be determined such that computation of FFT is tractable, for example, $L \leq 2^{38}$ in the literature. However, HNP samples constructed from actual signatures usually have a significantly larger initial bound on h_i. For instance, since a secure implementation of Schnorr derives challenge h_i through a hash function with sufficiently long output, such as SHA-256, just collecting signatures with $h_i < 2^{38}$ is not a viable option. How can we *reduce* the range of h_i while preserving the peak of nonce bias? The *range reduction* phase is a crucial preliminary step in Bleichenbacher's framework. This step takes *linear combinations* of input samples $\{(h_i, z_i)\}_{i=1}^{n}$ to obtain new samples $\{(h'_i, z'_i)\}_{i=1}^{n'}$ such that $h'_i < L \ll q$. In this way, we can "stretch" the peak width to q/L as observed above. But this comes at a cost: the peak height decays as we take linear combinations of more samples. To see why, suppose we take the sum of two samples (h_1, z_1) and (h_2, z_2), where the corresponding nonces $k_i = z_i - h_i \cdot x \bmod q$ are 2-bit biased, i.e. $k_i \in [0, q/4)$. Then the sum $(h', z') = (h_1 + h_2, z_1 + z_2)$ satisfies an HNP equation $k' := k_1 + k_2 = z' - h' \cdot x \bmod q$. Since k' may be within $[0, q/2)$, we end up with a new HNP sample with smaller bias. The prior analysis in fact indicates the value of bias peak decays exponentially: assuming all coefficients in the linear combinations are restricted to $\{-1, 0, 1\}$, we have $|B_q(K')| \approx |B_q(K)|^{\Omega}$, where $K' = \{k'_i\}_{i=1}^{n'}$ is a set of new nonces constructed via linear combinations of $K = \{k_i\}_{i=1}^{n}$ and Ω is the maximum L_1-norm of the coefficient vector. Since the noise floor for n' samples is approximated by $1/\sqrt{n'}$, for the decayed peak not to get lost in the noise we must keep Ω sufficiently small such that $1/\sqrt{n'} \ll |B_q(K)|^{\Omega}$. All in all, the major technical challenge of Bleichenbacher's attack is to efficiently find many *small* and *sparse* linear combinations of input samples.

Algorithm 8.3. Bleichenbacher's attack framework

Require:

$\{(h_i, z_i)\}_{i=1}^{n}$ - HNP samples over $\mathbb{Z}_q$.
n' - Number of linear combinations to be found.
L - FFT table size.

Ensure: Most significant bits of the HNP secret x

1: **Range reduction**
2: Generate n' samples $\{(h'_j, z'_j)\}_{j=1}^{n'}$, where $(h'_j, z'_j) = (\sum_i \omega_{i,j} h_i, \sum_i \omega_{i,j} z_i)$ is a pair of linear combinations with the coefficients $\omega_{i,j} \in \{-1, 0, 1\}$, such that for $j \in [1, n']$
   1) *Small*: $0 \leq h'_j < L$ and
   2) *Sparse*: $|B_q(\boldsymbol{K})|^{\Omega_j} \gg 1/\sqrt{n'}$ for all $j \in [1, n']$, where $\Omega_j := \sum_i |\omega_{i,j}|$.
3: **Bias Computation**
4: $Z := (Z_0, \ldots, Z_{L-1}) \leftarrow (0, \ldots, 0)$
5: **for** $j = 1$ to n' **do**
6: $\quad Z_{h'_j} \leftarrow Z_{h'_j} + e^{(2\pi z'_j/q)\mathrm{i}}$
7: **end for**
8: $\left\{B_q(K_{w_j})\right\}_{j=0}^{L-1} \leftarrow \mathrm{FFT}(Z)$, where $w_j = j \cdot q/L$.
9: Find the value j such that $\left|B_q(K_{w_j})\right|$ is maximal.
10: **return** most significant $\log L$ bits of w_j.

8.4.2.3. *Recovering the remaining bits*

Unlike the lattice attack Bleichenbacher's method does not recover the entire secret in one go. However, once the top $\beta = \lfloor \log L \rfloor$ bits of the secret x recovering the remaining $\alpha - \beta$ bits is straightforward, where $\alpha = \lceil \log q \rceil$. Suppose we have found $x_{\mathrm{Hi}} < 2^{\beta}$ such that $x = x_{\mathrm{Hi}} \cdot 2^{\alpha-\beta} + x_{\mathrm{Lo}}$ after running Algorithm 8.3, where $x_{\mathrm{Lo}} < 2^{\alpha-\beta}$ is an unknown lower bit string. Then by rewriting the input HNP samples as:

$$k_i = z_i - h_i \cdot x = \underbrace{z_i - h_i \cdot x_{\mathrm{Hi}} \cdot 2^{\alpha-\beta}}_{=\tilde{z}_i} - h_i \cdot x_{\mathrm{Lo}} \qquad [8.8]$$

we obtain new HNP samples $\{(h_i, \tilde{z}_i)\}_{i=1}^{n}$. Thus, we can repeat essentially the same procedures to recover the top bits of x_{Lo}. Note that the search space in the second run is much smaller, because one only needs to check L candidate values of secret x_{Lo} in $[0, 2^{\alpha-\beta})$. This means that the range reduction phase from the second run onwards can be carried out much faster since it only needs to find linear combinations with $h_i' < L^2$.

8.4.3. *Range reduction algorithms*

8.4.3.1. *The sort-and-difference method*

To illustrate the effect of range reduction, we introduce a simple sort-and-difference algorithm. Let $S = \{(h_i, z_i)\}_{i=1}^{n}$ be a set of input samples with $h_i < q$. The sort-and-difference with parameter γ proceeds as follows:

1) Sort $S = \{(h_i, z_i)\}_{i=1}^{n}$ by h_i. Initialize an empty set S'.

2) For $i = 2, \ldots, n$, let $(h_i', z_i') = (h_i - h_{i-1}, z_i - z_{i-1})$. If $h_i' < 2^{\log q - \log n + \gamma}$, push (h_i', z_i') to S'.

3) Output S'.

An analysis from order statistics suggests that the above algorithm outputs a reduced set of samples with $|S'| \approx (1 - e^{-2^{\gamma}})n$ assuming the input h_i are uniformly distributed. For instance, by setting $\gamma = 2$, we can expect 98% of the successive differences to be below the threshold value. We provide an example attack using this simple method against the parameters in supplementary material.

8.4.3.2. *More advanced algorithms*

Note that the number of samples after running sort-and-difference is bounded by the number of input signatures n. Hence, we can only clear at most $\log n$ bits of h_i per each iteration to keep the number of samples close to n (which is crucial for suppressing the noise floor). As this highly impacts a *input data complexity* for a large modulus q, a natural question would be how to clear more bits while maintaining the sparsity of linear combinations. One approach would be to use lattice reduction as in the previous section. However, linear combinations constructed via lattice reduction are not guaranteed to be sparse, and as such, the approach is not ideal once the available bias is so small that the sparsity condition is more stringent. A better approach in that case is to employ variants of the knapsack problem solver. An interested reader is encouraged to look at the supplementary Jupyter notebook to try running more advanced range reduction algorithms. These more involved algorithms have advantages in that (1) they can clear approximately $3 \cdot \log n$ bits by composing linear combinations of 4 per each iteration, and (2) they offer much more flexible time–space-data complexity tradeoffs. The latter in particular favors practical side-channel attack scenarios because we could minimize the number of input signatures (that is, data complexity) depending on the computational budgets (that is, time and space complexities) available for Bleichenbacher's attack. We refer the reader to Aranha et al. (2020a) for detailed tradeoff studies.

8.5. Preventing randomness failures

As mentioned above, the ephemeral randomness of discrete log signatures is subject to full key recovery attacks once it slightly deviates from the uniform distribution. It is therefore paramount to correctly implement a random number generator (RNG) as discussed in previous Chapter 5 and 6. An alternative solution would be to entirely avoid the use of RNG: a signer can *deterministically* derive randomness by hashing the secrete key x and msg to an element in $[0, q)$ as:

$$k := \mathsf{H}(x, \mathsf{msg}). \tag{8.9}$$

The assumption here is that (1) an output of the hash function H nearly follows the uniform distribution (the so-called *indifferentiability* property) and (2) an attacker cannot predict the value of x. The deterministic randomness derivation has been widely adopted in practical systems due to its simplicity. Have we finished? Not yet if we care about the risk of fault attacks (e.g. see, Volume 1 Part 3). Notice that a deterministic signer reuses k and thus $R := [k]G$ if the same msg is signed.

A fault attacker $\mathcal{A}$ can abuse this determinism to reproduce the randomness reuse attack we looked at in the beginning of the chapter. $\mathcal{A}$ first obtains a legitimate signature (h, z) on msg. Then $\mathcal{A}$ asks the signer to sign msg once again, but this time $\mathcal{A}$ injects a random fault during the computation of second hash $\mathsf{H}(R, \mathsf{msg})$, causing a signer to output a faulty signature (h', z') satisfying $z' = k + h' \cdot x \bmod q$.

Since both (h, z) and (h', z') rely on the same randomness k, the attacker can immediately recover the secret x.

To counter such a devastating attack at low cost, let us introduce some noise ρ in the hash input to avoid complete determinism, that is, the randomness is now computed as:

$$k := \mathsf{H}(x, \mathsf{msg}, \rho). \quad [8.10]$$

This approach is called *hedged* or *nonce-based* randomness derivation. On the one hand, it hedges randomness failures if, for example, ρ is sampled using a poor RNG: the signature scheme retains its security even if ρ is not completely uniform. On the other hand, its fault resilience essentially relies on ρ being nonce: k is derived uniformly and independently per every signing attempt as long as ρ does not repeat. Since the noise ρ cheaply mitigates the risk of simple fault attacks while it is much less sensitive than k directly generated via RNG, it is advisable to generate the signature randomness as in equation [8.10] in practical implementations.

8.6. Notes and further references

– Section 8.1. The broken random number generator used in leading technology company's ECDSA implementation was discovered by the fail0verflow (2010) team. The team successfully recovered the secret key after discovering gaming software had been signed under a fixed nonce k. A number of nonconstant time operations involving k have been discovered in the literature. For the most recent vulnerabilities found in deployed ECDSA/Schnorr implementations, (see for example, Ryan (2018); Dall et al. (2018); Jančàr et al. (2020); Aldaya et al. (2019); Ul Hassan et al. (2020); Moghimi et al. (2020); Aranha et al. (2020a); Weiser et al. (2020)). Takahashi et al. (2018) combined invalid curve attacks and physical fault injection to artificially cause randomness leakages in a variant of Schnorr. Breitner and Heninger (2019) discovered how many cryptocurrency wallets and SSH hosts are generating ECDSA signatures from significantly biased randomness and thus are subject to the lattice attack.

– Section 8.2. The hidden number problem (HNP) was originally defined by Boneh and Venkatesan (1998) in the context of Diffie–Hellman key exchange. Merget et al. (2021) recently found the first real-world implementations of Diffie–Hellman key exchange susceptible to an attack on the HNP, exploiting a timing side channel leakage rooted in the TLS 1.2 specification. Following the works drawing a connection to the problem of recovering secret signing keys (Bleichenbacher (2000); Howgrave-Graham and Smart (2001); Nguyen (2001); Nguyen and Shparlinski (2002, 2003)), the attacks on the HNP have been extensively used to exploit vulnerabilities of (EC)DSA and Schnorr under various leakage models. De Micheli and Heninger (2020) explain how to construct an instance of the HNP from side-channel information about the middle bits of the nonce.

– Section 8.3. Howgrave-Graham and Smart (2001) first proposed the lattice attack against DSA. Their analysis was later refined and extended to ECDSA by Nguyen and Shparlinski (2002, 2003). It was generalized further to binary Koblitz curves by Belgarric et al. (2016), and put in a very general framework by Galbraith and Shani (2015); and Shani (2017). The TPM–FAIL vulnerability described by Moghimi et al. (2020) is a typical example of a real-world timing leakage on ECDSA, and the lattice analysis deals with varying and noisy leakage sizes. This was further improved in the Minerva paper by Jančàr et al. (2020). Albrecht and Heninger (2021) recently showed how to overcome the theoretical limits of lattice attacks on HNP in the signature setting using the knowledge of the public verification key, and obtained substantial improvements on concrete parameter settings as well. Sun et al. (2022) introduced the idea of guessing some bits of the secret key in those lattice attacks and analyzed the resulting tradeoffs and efficiency improvements.

– Section 8.4. The idea of exploiting Fourier transform was first discovered by Bleichenbacher. His presentation slides at IEEE P1363 working group meeting Bleichenbacher (2000) describe all of the essential ideas. In his study, Bleichenbacher used the method to point out insecurity of the DSA implementation specified in FIPS 186: it suggested uniformly sampling k from $[0, 2^{160})$ even though the modulus q is *not* close to 2^{160}. De Mulder et al. (2014) revisited his idea and analyzed behaviors of the bias function in detail. The formal analysis of the sort-and-difference algorithm was carried out by Aranha et al. (2014, Proposition 1), who successfully mounted a key recovery attack on 160-bit ECDSA with 1-bit nonce bias. De Mulder et al. (2014) addressed the data complexity issue by making use of lattice reduction to attack 384-bit HNP with 5-bit bias using only 4000 signatures, whereas they estimated about 2^{30} signatures would be required with the sort-and-difference method. The original presentations by Bleichenbacher (2000, 2005) already suggested the Schroeppel–Shamir knapsack algorithm Schroeppel and Shamir (1981) as a plausible approach to range reduction and the idea has been refined in recent works (Takahashi et al. (2018); Aranha et al. (2020a)) using more modern variants of Schroeppel–Shamir, such as Wagner (2002); Howgrave-Graham and Joux (2010); and Dinur (2019).

– Section 8.5. The deterministic randomness derivation has been a popular solution to preventing randomness failures, as adopted in EdDSA (Bernstein et al. 2012) and deterministic ECDSA (Pornin 2013). A number of recent works introduced fault-injection attacks on deterministic schemes and experimentally demonstrated the feasibility of full key recovery (Barenghi and Pelosi 2016; Romailler and Pelissier 2017; Ambrose et al. 2018; Poddebniak et al. 2018; Samwel and Batina 2018; Bruinderink and Pessl 2018; Ravi et al. 2019). XEdDSA (Perrin 2016) is a hedged version of EdDSA used in the signal messaging protocol. Aranha et al. (2020b) and Fischlin and Günther (2020) concurrently analyzed the fault resilience of hedged signatures using the methodology of provable security. At the time of writing the IETF draft, advocating hedged EdDSA and ECDSA (Mattsson et al. (2022)) is going through a call for adoption.

8.7. Acknowledgment

This chapter was prepared in part for information purposes by the Artificial Intelligence Research group of JP Morgan Chase & Co and its affiliates ("JP Morgan"), and is not a product of the Research Department of JP Morgan. JP Morgan makes no representation and warranty whatsoever and disclaims all liability, for the completeness, accuracy or reliability of the information contained herein. This document is not intended as investment research or investment advice, or a recommendation, offer or solicitation for the purchase or sale of any security, financial instrument, financial product or service, or to be used in any way for evaluating the merits of participating in any transaction, and shall not constitute a solicitation under any jurisdiction or to any person, if such solicitation under such jurisdiction or to such person would be unlawful.

8.8. References

Albrecht, M.R. and Heninger, N. (2021). On bounded distance decoding with predicate: Breaking the "lattice barrier" for the hidden number problem. In *EUROCRYPT 2021*, Canteaut, A. and Standaert, F.-X. (eds). Springer, Berlin, Heidelberg.

Aldaya, A.C., Brumley, B.B., Ul Hassan, S., García, C.P., Tuveri, N. (2019). Port contention for fun and profit. In *2019 IEEE Symposium on Security and Privacy*, San Francisco.

Ambrose, C., Bos, J.W., Fay, B., Joye, M., Lochter, M., Murray, B. (2018). Differential attacks on deterministic signatures. In *CT-RSA 2018*, Smart, N.P. (ed.). Springer, Berlin, Heidelberg.

Aranha, D.F., Fouque, P.-A., Gérard, B., Kammerer, J.-G., Tibouchi, M., Zapalowicz, J.-C. (2014). GLV/GLS decomposition, power analysis, and attacks on ECDSA signatures with single-bit nonce bias. In *ASIACRYPT 2014*, Sarkar, P. and Iwata, T. (eds). Springer, Berlin, Heidelberg.

Aranha, D.F., Novaes, F.R., Takahashi, A., Tibouchi, M., Yarom, Y. (2020a). LadderLeak: Breaking ECDSA with less than one bit of nonce leakage. In *ACM CCS 2020*, Ligatti, J., Ou, X., Katz, J., Vigna, G. (eds). ACM Press, New York.

Aranha, D.F., Orlandi, C., Takahashi, A., Zaverucha, G. (2020b). Security of hedged Fiat-Shamir signatures under fault attacks. In *EUROCRYPT 2020*, Canteaut, A. and Ishai, Y. (eds). Springer, Berlin, Heidelberg.

Barenghi, A. and Pelosi, G. (2016). A note on fault attacks against deterministic signature schemes. In *IWSEC 16*, Ogawa, K. and Yoshioka, K. (eds). Springer, Berlin, Heidelberg.

Belgarric, P., Fouque, P.-A., Macario-Rat, G., Tibouchi, M. (2016). Side-channel analysis of Weierstrass and Koblitz curve ECDSA on android smartphones. In *CT-RSA 2016*, Sako, K. (ed.). Springer, Berlin, Heidelberg.

Bernstein, D.J., Duif, N., Lange, T., Schwabe, P., Yang, B.-Y. (2012). High-speed high-security signatures. *Journal of Cryptographic Engineering*, 2(2), 77–89.

Bleichenbacher, D. (2000). On the generation of one-time keys in DL signature schemes. Presentation, IEEE P1363 Working Group Meeting, 15 November [Online]. Available at: https://web.archive.org/web/20051124031342/http://grouper.ieee.org/groups/1363/Research/contributions/Ble2000.tif.

Bleichenbacher, D. (2005). Experiments with DSA. Rump session at CRYPTO 2005 [Online]. Available at: https://www.iacr.org/conferences/crypto2005/r/3.pdf.

Boneh, D. and Venkatesan, R. (1998). Breaking RSA may not be equivalent to factoring. In *EUROCRYPT'98*, Nyberg, K. (ed.). Springer, Berlin, Heidelberg.

Breitner, J. and Heninger, N. (2019). Biased nonce sense: Lattice attacks against weak ECDSA signatures in cryptocurrencies. In *FC 2019*, Goldberg, I. and Moore, T. (eds). Springer, Berlin, Heidelberg.

Bruinderink, L.G. and Pessl, P. (2018). Differential fault attacks on deterministic lattice signatures. *IACR TCHES*, 2018(3), 21–43.

Dall, F., De Micheli, G., Eisenbarth, T., Genkin, D., Heninger, N., Moghimi, A., Yarom, Y. (2018). CacheQuote: Efficiently recovering long-term secrets of SGX EPID via cache attacks. *IACR TCHES*, 2018(2), 171–191.

De Micheli, G. and Heninger, N. (2020). Recovering cryptographic keys from partial information, by example. Cryptology ePrint Archive [Online]. Available at: https://eprint.iacr.org/2020/1506.

De Mulder, E., Hutter, M., Marson, M.E., Pearson, P. (2014). Using Bleichenbacher's solution to the hidden number problem to attack nonce leaks in 384-bit ECDSA: Extended version. *Journal of Cryptographic Engineering*, 4(1), 33–45.

Dinur, I. (2019). An algorithmic framework for the generalized birthday problem. *Des. Codes Cryptogr.*, 87(8), 1897–1926. doi: 10.1007/s10623-018-00594-6.

fail0verflow (2010). Console hacking 2010. PS3 epic fail. In *27th Chaos Communication Congress* [Online]. Available at: https://www.cs.cmu.edu/dst/GeoHot/1780_27c3_console_hacking_2010.pdf.

Fischlin, M. and Günther, F. (2020). Modeling memory faults in signature and authenticated encryption schemes. In *CT-RSA 2020*, Jarecki, S. (ed.). Springer, Berlin, Heidelberg.

Galbraith, S. D. and Shani, B. (2015). The multivariate hidden number problem. In *ICITS 15*, Lehmann, A. and Wolf, S. (eds). Springer, Berlin, Heidelberg.

Howgrave-Graham, N. and Joux, A. (2010). New generic algorithms for hard knapsacks. In *EUROCRYPT 2010*, Gilbert, H. (ed.). Springer, Berlin, Heidelberg.

Howgrave-Graham, N. and Smart, N.P. (2001). Lattice attacks on digital signature schemes. *Designs, Codes and Cryptography*, 23(3), 283–290.

Jančàr, J., Sedlacek, V., Svenda, P., Sys, M. (2020). Minerva: The curse of ECDSA nonces. *IACR TCHES*, 2020(4), 281–308.

Mattsson, J.P., Thormarker, E., Ruohomaa, S. (2022). Deterministic ECDSA and EdDSA signatures with additional randomness. Report, Network Working Group [Online]. Available at: https://www.ietf.org/id/draft-mattsson-cfrg-det-sigs-with-noise-04.html.

Merget, R., Brinkmann, M., Aviram, N., Somorovsky, J., Mittmann, J., Schwenk, J. (2021). Raccoon attack: Finding and exploiting most-significant-bit-oracles in TLS-DH(E). In *USENIX Security 2021*, Bailey, M. and Greenstadt, R. (eds). USENIX Association, Berkeley.

Moghimi, D., Sunar, B., Eisenbarth, T., Heninger, N. (2020). TPM-FAIL: TPM meets timing and lattice attacks. In *USENIX Security 2020*, Capkun, S. and Roesner, F. (eds). USENIX Association, Berkeley.

Nguyen, P.Q. (2001). The dark side of the hidden number problem: Lattice sttacks on DSA. In *Cryptography and Computational Number Theory*, Lam, K.-Y., Shparlinski, I., Wang, H., Xing, C. (eds). Birkhäuser, Basel.

Nguyen, P.Q. and Shparlinski, I.E. (2002). The insecurity of the digital signature algorithm with partially known nonces. *Journal of Cryptology*, 15(3), 151–176.

Nguyen, P.Q. and Shparlinski, I.E. (2003). The insecurity of the elliptic curve digital signature algorithm with partially known nonces. *Des. Codes Cryptogr.*, 30(2), 201–217. doi: 10.1023/A:1025436905711.

Perrin, T. (2016). The XEdDSA and VXEdDSA signature schemes. Technical Document, Signal [Online]. Available at: https://signal.org/docs/specifications/xeddsa/.

Poddebniak, D., Somorovsky, J., Schinzel, S., Lochter, M., Rösler, P. (2018). Attacking deterministic signature schemes using fault attacks. In *2018 IEEE European Symposium on Security and Privacy, EuroS&P 2018*, 24–26 April, London. doi: 10.1109/EuroSP.2018.00031.

Pornin, T. (2013). RFC 6979 – Deterministic usage of the digital signature algorithm (DSA) and elliptic curve digital signature algorithm (ECDSA). Informational Document, IETF Trust [Online]. Available at: https://tools.ietf.org/html/rfc6979.

Ravi, P., Jhanwar, M.P., Howe, J., Chattopadhyay, A., Bhasin, S. (2019). Exploiting determinism in lattice-based signatures: Practical fault attacks on pqm4 implementations of NIST candidates. In *ASIACCS 19*, Galbraith, S.D., Russello, G., Susilo, W., Gollmann, D., Kirda, E., Liang, Z. (eds). ACM Press, New York.

Romailler, Y. and Pelissier, S. (2017). Practical fault attack against the Ed25519 and EdDSA signature schemes. In *2017 Workshop on Fault Diagnosis and Tolerance in Cryptography, FDTC 2017*, 25 September, Taipei. doi: 10.1109/FDTC.2017.12.

Ryan, K. (2018). Return of the hidden number problem. *IACR TCHES*, 2019(1), 146–168.

Samwel, N. and Batina, L. (2018). Practical fault injection on deterministic signatures: The case of EdDSA. In *AFRICACRYPT 18*, Joux, A., Nitaj, A., Rachidi, T. (eds). Springer, Berlin, Heidelberg.

Schroeppel, R. and Shamir, A. (1981). A $t=o(2^{n/2})$, $s=o(2^{n/4})$ algorithm for certain NP-complete problems. *SIAM J. Comput.*, 10(3), 456–464. doi: 10.1137/0210033.

Shani, B. (2017). Hidden number problems. PhD Thesis, The University of Auckland, Auckland.

Sun, C., Espitau, T., Tibouchi, M., Abe, M. (2022). Guessing bits: Improved lattice attacks on (EC)DSA with nonce leakage. *IACR Trans. Cryptogr. Hardw. Embed. Syst.*, 2022(1), 391–413. doi: 10.46586/tches.v2022.i1.391-413.

Takahashi, A., Tibouchi, M., Abe, M. (2018). New Bleichenbacher records: Fault attacks on qDSA signatures. *IACR TCHES*, 2018(3), 331–371.

Ul Hassan, S., Gridin, I., Delgado-Lozano, I.M., García, C.P., Chi-Domínguez, J.-J., Aldaya, A.C., Brumley, B.B. (2020). Déjà vu: Side-channel analysis of Mozilla's NSS. In *ACM CCS 2020*, Ligatti, J., Ou, X., Katz, J., Vigna, G. (eds). ACM Press, New York.

Wagner, D. (2002). A generalized birthday problem. In *CRYPTO 2002*, Yung, M. (ed.). Springer, Berlin, Heidelberg.

Weiser, S., Schrammel, D., Bodner, L., Spreitzer, R. (2020). Big numbers – Big troubles: Systematically analyzing nonce leakage in (EC)DSA implementations. In *USENIX Security 2020*, Capkun, S. and Roesner, F. (eds). USENIX Association, Berkeley.

9

Random Error Distributions in Post-Quantum Schemes

Thomas PREST

PQShield, Paris, France

9.1. Introduction

Post-quantum cryptography is an umbrella term that covers cryptographic schemes conjectured to be secure in the presence of large-scale quantum computers. Post-quantum cryptography can be based on mathematical assumptions related to hash functions, (error-correcting) codes, lattices, isogenies, multivariate equations, etc.

Many code-based and lattice-based schemes require the ability to sample from distributions with specific shapes (see Figure 9.1) that are seldom encountered in classical RSA-based or curve-based cryptography. Since these samples are typically required to be small in some geometric sense, the terms "*random errors*", "*random noise*" or "*errors*" are often used when referring to them.

This chapter answers the following questions:

– Where do random errors arise in post-quantum cryptography?

– Why do we need them? What are the most appropriate error distributions?

– What sampling methods do we use, and how do we implement them securely?

Embedded Cryptography 3,
coordinated by Emmanuel PROUFF, Guénaël RENAULT,
Matthieu RIVAIN and Colin O'FLYNN.

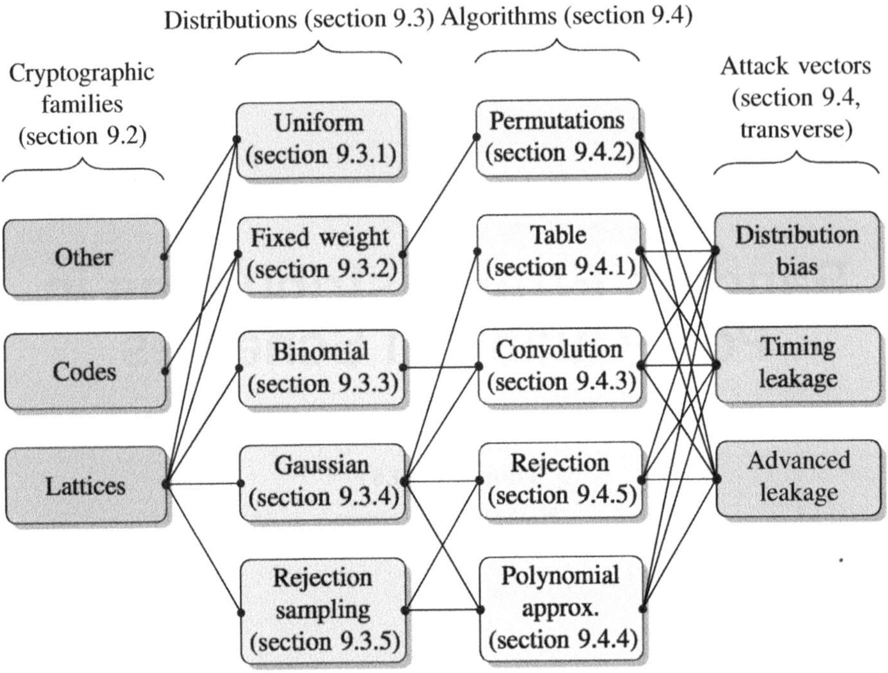

Figure 9.1. *Plan of this chapter. For a color version of this figure, see www.iste.co.uk/prouff/cryptography3.zip*

This chapter is organized as follows, and as summarized by Figure 9.1:

– In section 9.2, we illustrate the need for random errors by presenting two constructions for post-quantum encryption and signatures and explaining where and why they need random errors.

– In section 9.3, we describe in more detail the five main families of distributions which random errors are sampled from and highlight some of their key properties.

– In section 9.4, we discuss the five main algorithmic approaches that are used to sample the aforementioned distributions. For each of them, we point out their strengths and weaknesses in terms of efficiency, security, etc.

– In section 9.5, we provide pointers to additional references.

9.2. Why post-quantum schemes need random errors

The study of post-quantum cryptographic schemes could span an entire book. In this section, we only consider them through the prism of the random errors they require. We do so by selecting two classes of schemes that exemplify the issues that random errors solve and the ones that they raise: *noisy ElGamal* encryption (section 9.2.1) and hash-then-sign signature schemes (section 9.2.2).

9.2.1. *Example 1: noisy ElGamal*

RELEVANT SCHEMES.– Kyber (Schwabe et al. 2022), Saber (Schwabe et al. 2022), FrodoKEM (Naehrig et al. 2020), HQC (Aguilar Melchor et al. 2020), NewHope (Pöppelmann et al. 2019), NTRU Prime (Bernstein et al. 2020) (NTRU LPRime variant), BIKE (Aragon et al. 2019) (BIKE-2 variant).

The "noisy ElGamal" abstraction captures several post-quantum schemes. As implied by its name, at a high level it is similar to the classical ElGamal scheme: the generator group element g becomes a generator matrix $\mathbf{A}$, and the exponentiation action $(g, x) \mapsto g^x$ becomes a different action $(\mathbf{A}, (\mathbf{S}, \mathbf{E})) \mapsto \mathbf{A} \cdot \mathbf{S} + \mathbf{E}$. A more formal description is given in Figure 9.2.

The future standard Kyber, selected by NIST in July 2022, follows this framework.

Algorithm 9.1. KEYGEN()

Ensure: An encryption keypair (ek, dk)

Sample a public generator $\mathbf{A}$
Sample random errors $\mathbf{S}, \mathbf{E}$
$\mathbf{B} := \mathbf{A} \cdot \mathbf{S} + \mathbf{E}$
return ek $:= (\mathbf{A}, \mathbf{B})$, dk $:= \mathbf{S}$

Algorithm 9.2. ENCRYPT(ek, msg)

Require: An encryption key ek, a message msg
Ensure: A ciphertext ct

Sample random errors $\mathbf{R}, \mathbf{E}', \mathbf{E}''$
$\mathbf{U} := \mathbf{R} \cdot \mathbf{A} + \mathbf{E}'$
$\mathbf{V} := \mathbf{R} \cdot \mathbf{B} + \mathbf{E}'' + \text{ENCODE}(\text{msg})$
return ct $:= (\mathbf{U}, \mathbf{V})$

Algorithm 9.3. DECRYPT(dk, ct)

Require: A decryption key dk, a ciphertext ct
Ensure: A message msg

$\mathbf{M} := \mathbf{V} - \mathbf{U} \cdot \mathbf{S}$
return msg $:= \text{DECODE}(\mathbf{M})$

Figure 9.2. *Noisy ElGamal encryption*

ERRORS AND CORRECTNESS.– Let us study the correctness of Figure 9.2. Observe that:

$$\begin{aligned} \mathbf{M} &= \mathbf{V} - \mathbf{U} \cdot \mathbf{S} \\ &= \mathbf{R} \cdot (\mathbf{A} \cdot \mathbf{S} + \mathbf{E}) + \mathbf{E}'' + \text{ENCODE}(\mathsf{msg}) - (\mathbf{R} \cdot \mathbf{A} + \mathbf{E}') \cdot \mathbf{S} \\ &= \text{ENCODE}(\mathsf{msg}) + (\mathbf{R} \cdot \mathbf{E} + \mathbf{E}'' - \mathbf{E}' \cdot \mathbf{S}) \end{aligned} \qquad [9.1]$$

If we denote $\mathcal{E} := \mathbf{R} \cdot \mathbf{E} + \mathbf{E}'' - \mathbf{E}' \cdot \mathbf{S}$, correctness holds as long as, for any msg:

$$\text{DECODE}(\text{ENCODE}(\mathsf{msg}) + \mathcal{E}) = \mathsf{msg} \qquad [9.2]$$

At this point, a few specificities are apparent. In lattice-based schemes, by encoding msg in the most significant bits of $\mathbf{V}$, the decoding operation can recover msg as long as the L2 norm of $\mathcal{E}$ is not too high. For code-based schemes, encoding msg as a codeword allows us to recover it if the Hamming weight of $\mathcal{E}$ is small enough.

ERRORS AND SECURITY.– We now briefly discuss the security of Figure 9.2. If we set all coefficients of $\mathbf{E}, \mathbf{E}', \mathbf{E}''$ to zero, then the error term in equation [9.1] becomes zero and decryption is always successful. However, this also makes the scheme in Figure 9.2 insecure, since the decryption key $\mathbf{S}$ can then be recovered by inverting the overdetermined linear system $\mathbf{B} = \mathbf{A} \cdot \mathbf{S}$. The simple act of adding an error term $\mathbf{E}$ turns this linear system into a noisy linear system $\mathbf{B} = \mathbf{A} \cdot \mathbf{S} + \mathbf{E}$. When correctly parameterized, solving this linear system become an intractable problem with currently known techniques, even assuming large-scale quantum computers.

BALANCING CORRECTNESS AND SECURITY.– We can see by now two antagonistic constraints: error distributions with larger supports and entropy are helpful for security, whereas errors that are "short" are helpful for correctness. This explains the choice of distributions used in real-life instantiations of Figure 9.2: fixed-weight (section 9.3.2) for code-based schemes, and small-norm distributions – such as uniform (section 9.3.1), binomial (section 9.3.3), fixed-weight and Gaussians (section 9.3.4) – for lattice-based schemes.

9.2.2. *Example 2: hash-then-sign*

RELEVANT SCHEMES.– Falcon (Prest et al. 2022), Wave (Debris-Alazard et al. 2019).

In Figure 9.3, we describe a generic framework for post-quantum signatures that follows the "hash-then-sign" paradigm. Falcon, selected by NIST for standardisation in July 2022, follows this framework. For Falcon, Lines 2 to 4 require us to sample several times from Gaussian distributions (section 9.3.4) as a subroutine, and it is important for security that this operation is performed precisely and in constant time.

Similarly, in Wave, an operation called rejection sampling (section 9.3.5) is performed as part of Lines 2 to 4, and it also needs to be precise and constant time.

Algorithm 9.4. KEYGEN()

Ensure: A signature keypair (vk, sk)
1: Generate jointly a public matrix $\mathbf{A}$ and its trapdoor Trap
2: **return** vk := $\mathbf{A}$, sk := Trap

Algorithm 9.5. SIGN(sk, msg)

Require: A signing key sk = Trap, a message msg
Ensure: A signature sig
1: Compute an image $\mathbf{c} := H(\mathsf{msg})$
2: Using Trap, compute s such that:
3: $\quad \mathbf{A} \cdot \mathbf{s} = \mathbf{c}$, and
4: $\quad \mathsf{CheckCondition}(\mathbf{s}) = \mathsf{True}$
5: **return** sig := s

Algorithm 9.6. VERIFY(vk, msg, sig)

Require: A verification key vk, a message msg, a signature sig
Ensure: **accept** or **reject**
1: Accept if and only if:
2: $\quad \mathbf{A} \cdot \mathbf{s} = \mathbf{c}$, and
3: $\quad \mathsf{CheckCondition}(\mathbf{s}) = \mathsf{True}$

In Algorithms 9.5 and 9.6, CheckCondition checks a geometric constraint.

Figure 9.3. *Post-quantum signatures in the "hash-then-sign" paradigm*

9.2.3. *Example 3: Fiat–Shamir with aborts*

RELEVANT SCHEMES.– Dilithium (Lyubashevsky et al. 2022), qTESLA (Bindel et al. 2019), BLISS (Ducas et al. 2013).

In Figure 9.4, we describe the "Fiat-Shamir with aborts" paradigm. It can be interpreted as a transposition to the lattice setting of discrete logarithm-based Schnorr signatures.

A notable instantiation of this paradigm is Dilithium, selected for standardisation by NIST in July 2022. This paradigm requires sampling random errors during the key generation (Algorithm 9.7, Line 2) and signing (Algorithm 9.8, Line 1) procedures. In addition, it contains a rejection sampling subroutine (Algorithm 9.8, Line 6) that filters signatures before outputting them.

All these subroutines must be implemented in a way that prevents an adversary with side-channel capabilities from inferring information about their outcomes.

Algorithm 9.7. KEYGEN()

Ensure: A signature keypair (vk, sk)

```
Generate a uniformly random matrix A
Compute t := A · s + e, where (e, s) are random errors
return vk := (A, t), sk := (e, s)
```

Algorithm 9.8. SIGN(sk, msg)

Require: A signing key sk $= (\mathbf{e}, \mathbf{s})$, a message msg

Ensure: A signature sig

```
Sample random errors r, e'
Compute w := ⌊A · r + e'⌉
c := H(w, msg, vk)
z := c · s + r
y := A · z − c · t
if CheckCondition(z, y) = False then
    Restart
return sig := (c, z)
```

Algorithm 9.9. VERIFY(vk, msg, sig)

Require: A verification key vk, a message msg, a signature sig

Ensure: **accept** or **reject**

```
Accept if and only if:
    z is short
    H(⌊A·z−c·t⌉, msg, vk) = c
```

In Algorithm 9.8, CheckCondition is a *rejection sampling* step (section 9.3.5).

Figure 9.4. *Post-quantum signatures in the "Fiat-Shamir with Aborts" paradigm*

9.3. Distributions for random errors

We now review the main random error distributions used in practice: variants of uniform (section 9.3.1), fixed weight (section 9.3.2), binomial (section 9.3.3) and Gaussian (section 9.3.4) distributions. We conclude with randomized rejection sampling (section 9.3.5), which can either be interpreted as a special type of distribution or as a sampling method, and therefore allows us to segue into the section on sampling methods (section 9.4). A summary of all these distributions is given in Figure 9.5. Throughout the section, we assume access to a perfect source of uniformly random bits.

NOTATION 9.1.– We use the notation $x \leftarrow X$ to express that x is sampled from the distribution X, and we denote $X(x_0) = \mathbb{P}[x = x_0 | x \leftarrow X]$. The notation $x \sim X$ (respectively, $x \sim_s X$) means x is distributed exactly according to (respectively, statistically close to) X. For $a, b \in \mathbb{Z}$, $\{a, \ldots, b\}$ denotes the set $[a, b] \cap \mathbb{Z}$. Finally, given $\mathcal{S}$ a subset of the support of X, we denote by $X(\mathcal{S})$ the restriction of X to $\mathcal{S}$.

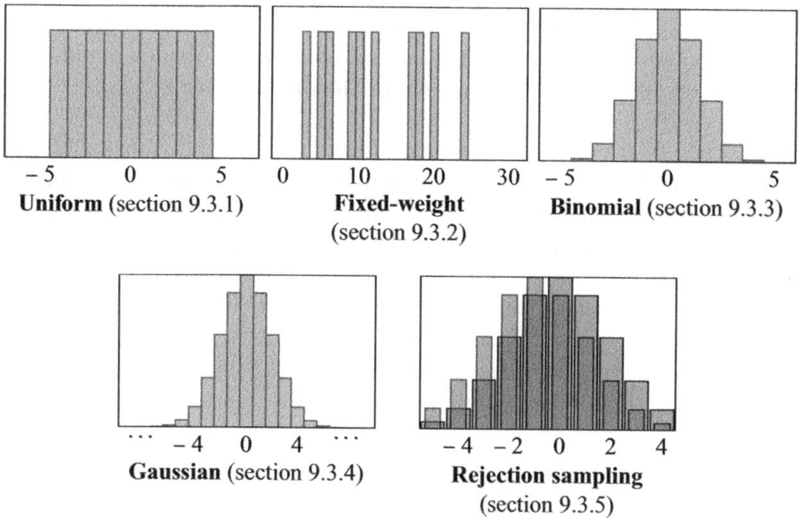

Figure 9.5. *The main distributions for random errors. Distributions add up to 1. For a color version of this figure, see www.iste.co.uk/prouff/cryptography3.zip*

9.3.1. *Uniform distributions*

USED IN.– Dilithium (Lyubashevsky et al. 2020), Saber (D'Anvers et al. 2020), qTESLA (Bindel et al. 2019), Picnic (Zaverucha et al. 2020).

DEFINITION 9.1.– Given a finite set $\mathcal{X}$, we denote by $U(\mathcal{X})$ the uniform distribution of support $\mathcal{X}$. We may also use the notation $x \leftarrow \mathcal{X}$ as a shorthand for $x \leftarrow U(\mathcal{X})$.

Uniform distributions are used mainly in lattice-based schemes. Compared to classical schemes (e.g. El Gamal encryption of ECDSA signatures), uniform distributions in lattice-based cryptography seldom use the underlying ring (e.g. $\mathbb{Z}_q$) as support. Rather, the support $\mathcal{X}$ will be a very narrow subset of $\mathbb{Z}_q$. For example, in Dilithium, the underlying ring is $\mathbb{Z}_q$ with $q = 2^{13}(2^{10} - 1) + 1$, whereas $\mathcal{X}$ may be equal to $\{-2, \ldots, 2\}$ (during key generation) or $\{-2^{17}, \ldots, 2^{17}\}$ (during signing). This has little impact if we simply need to implement a constant-time implementation, but it raises some delicate questions in the more complex context of masking (section 9.4.6).

9.3.2. *Fixed weight distributions*

USED IN.– BIKE (Aragon et al. 2020), Classic McEliece (Albrecht et al. 2020), HQC (Aguilar Melchor et al. 2020), NTRU (Chen et al. 2020), NTRU Prime (Bernstein et al. 2020).

DEFINITION 9.2.– Let us denote by $\mathcal{W}_{n,w}$ the subset of $\{0,1\}^n$ of vectors containing exactly w ones and $(n-w)$ zeroes. We call fixed-weight distribution of dimension n and weight w, and denote by $\mathcal{F}_{n,w}$ the uniform distribution over $\mathcal{W}_{n,w}$.

Fixed-weight distributions are a natural fit for code-based cryptography. Indeed, error-correcting codes are precisely designed to be able to decode errors, which are in $\mathcal{W}_{n,w}$ (as long as w is small enough), so it is unsurprising that such errors are used in code-based schemes such as BIKE, Classic McEliece or HQC.

A few lattice-based schemes (such as NTRU and NTRU Prime) use variants of these distributions, where -1 coefficients are allowed as well. Errors from these distributions have a Euclidean norm $\sqrt{w}$, which in the context of Figure 9.2 allows equation [9.2] to hold as long as $\sqrt{w}$ is small enough.

9.3.3. *Variants of the binomial distribution*

USED IN.– NewHope (Pöppelmann et al. 2019), Saber (D'Anvers et al. 2020), Kyber (Schwabe et al. 2022).

Binomial distributions for lattice-based cryptography were introduced by the NewHope scheme. They are essentially as easy to sample as uniform distributions (section 9.3.1) – if not more in a masked setting – while in terms of entropy versus variance trade-off, they are more similar to Gaussians (section 9.3.4). This means they provide an excellent compromise between both distributions when supported by the application.

DEFINITION 9.3.– The *binary binomial distribution* $\mathcal{B}_n$ of parameter n is the distribution of the sum $\sum_{i=1}^{n} b_i$, where each b_i is a uniformly random bit: $b_i \leftarrow \{0,1\}$. This is a special case of the binomial distribution $\mathcal{B}_{n,p}$, in which each bit b_i is 1 with a fixed probability $p \in [0,1]$, whereas $p = \frac{1}{2}$ in the case of the binary binomial distribution.

A related distribution is the *centered binomial distribution* CBD_n, which is defined in an algorithmic way. Sampling $x \leftarrow \mathsf{CBD}_n$ is done in three simple steps: (i) $y \leftarrow \mathcal{B}_n$, (ii) $z \leftarrow \mathcal{B}_n$ and (iii) $x := y - z$.

A CONVOLUTION PROPERTY.– We can see that given a (secure, efficient) sampling algorithm for $\mathcal{B}_n$, it is easy to obtain a (secure, efficient) sampling algorithm for CBD_n. The binomial distribution has plenty of interesting properties that provide other reductions between the two families of distributions. In particular, it follows from Definition 9.3 that the sum of two binomial distributions is a binomial distribution:

$$\mathcal{B}_m + \mathcal{B}_n \sim \mathcal{B}_{m+n} \qquad [9.3]$$

EXERCISE 9.1.– Show that sampling $x \leftarrow \mathsf{CBD}_n$ can equivalently be done as follows: $w \leftarrow \mathcal{B}_{2n}$; $x := w - n$.

SOLUTION 9.1.– $\mathcal{B}_n$ is symmetric around its mean $n/2$, so that (ii) is equivalent to computing $z' \leftarrow \mathcal{B}_n$; $z := n - z'$. Therefore, we may rewrite $x = y + z' - n$. It follows from equation [9.3] that the sum $w = y + z'$ of two samples of $\mathcal{B}_n$ is distributed as a sample of $\mathcal{B}_{2n}$, from which the result follows.

9.3.4. *Discrete and rounded Gaussians*

USED IN.– BLISS (Ducas et al. 2013), Falcon (Prest et al. 2020), FrodoKEM (Naehrig et al. 2020), qTESLA (Bindel et al. 2019) (key generation).

DEFINITION 9.4.– We call Gaussian function of center μ and deviation σ the function $\rho_{\sigma,\mu}$ defined over $\mathbb{R}$ as $\rho_{\sigma,\mu}(x) = \exp\left(-\frac{(x-\mu)^2}{2\sigma^2}\right)$, and also denote $\rho_\sigma(x) := \rho_{\sigma,0}(x)$. The discrete Gaussian distribution $D_{\mathbb{Z},\sigma,\mu}$ and the rounded Gaussian distribution $\Psi_{\mathbb{Z},\sigma}$ are both defined over $\mathbb{Z}$ by their probability functions:

$$D_{\mathbb{Z},\sigma,\mu}(z) = \frac{\rho_{\sigma,\mu}(z)}{\sum_{k\in\mathbb{Z}} \rho_{\sigma,\mu}(k)} \qquad [9.4]$$

$$\Psi_{\mathbb{Z},\sigma}(z) = \frac{\int_{\{x \mid \lfloor x \rceil = z\}} \rho_\sigma(x)dx}{\int_{x\in\mathbb{R}} \rho_\sigma(x)dx} \qquad [9.5]$$

We can see that discretized and rounded Gaussians are similar; the only difference is how the discretization process is done (point discretization versus rounding). In the rest of this section, we focus on discrete Gaussians, but most of our comments also apply to a large extent to rounded Gaussians.

ON THE NEED FOR GAUSSIANS.– We may note that both equations [9.4] and [9.5] are unwieldy, and indeed Gaussians are challenging to implement securely. The historical context in which they emerged provides a useful perspective. At least part of the inception of lattice-based cryptography can be traced back to works in mathematics and theoretical computer science, in which Gaussians played a key role as an analytic tool for studying lattices. This explains the prevalence of Gaussian distributions in several early works proposing lattice-based schemes, and raises a natural question:

Do we really need Gaussian errors in lattice-based cryptographic schemes?

As of today, the answer really depends on the type of scheme:

1) For encryption schemes, for example, the one in Figure 9.2, switching from Gaussians to simpler distributions incurs no degradation in concrete security, while providing a huge boost in computational efficiency.

2) For signatures schemes based on the Fiat–Shamir paradigm, moving away from Gaussians incurs a mild degradation of the parameters. For example, if signatures are short vectors in $\mathbb{Z}_q^n$, then using Gaussians (as in BLISS) increase the modulus q by a factor $O(\sqrt{n})$, whereas uniform distributions (as in Dilithium) increases it by $O(n)$. This is one reason why q is larger in Dilithium than in BLISS, and is offset by the fact that the distributions in Dilithium are much simpler to sample securely.

3) Lattice-based signatures employing the hash-then-sign paradigm (see Figure 9.3), as well as advanced constructions such as blind signatures or identity-based encryption, rely on an algorithmic tool called *trapdoor sampling*. Trapdoor sampling relies on Gaussian distributions as subroutines, and it is not known how to replace these with simpler distributions without a significant degradation of the parameters.

A CONVOLUTION PROPERTY.– An extremely useful property of Gaussians states that for appropriately chosen parameters, the integer linear combination $y = \sum_i z_i y_i$ of a finite number of discrete Gaussian samples $y_i \sim D_{\mathbb{Z},\sigma_i,\mu_i}$ is statistically close to a discrete Gaussian sample:

$$y \sim_s D_{\mathbb{Z},\sigma,\mu}, \quad \text{where} \quad \sigma = \sqrt{\sum_i z_i^2 \sigma_i^2} \quad \text{and} \quad \mu = \sum_i z_i \mu_i \qquad [9.6]$$

9.3.5. *Randomized rejection sampling*

USED IN.– BLISS (Ducas et al. 2013), Falcon (Prest et al. 2020) (subroutine).

Rejection sampling can be interpreted in two ways: (i) a technique for sampling distributions and (ii) a specific distribution that itself requires the leveraging of other techniques to be sampled from.

Suppose we wish to sample from a distribution P, and we have Oracle access to a related distribution Q and a constant M such that $\max_x \frac{M \cdot P(x)}{Q(x)} \leq 1$, which implies that the support of P is included in the support of Q. Algorithm 9.10 describes a way to sample from P: (i) sample $x \leftarrow Q$, (ii) a *rejection step* accepts x with probability $\frac{M \cdot P(x)}{Q(x)}$ and (iii) otherwise it restarts. At each trial, x is sampled with probability $Q(x) \cdot \frac{M \cdot P(x)}{Q(x)} = M \cdot P(x)$.

Algorithm 9.10. GENERICREJECTIONSAMPLER()

Require: Oracle access to a distribution Q, a constant M such that $\max_x \frac{M \cdot P(x)}{Q(x)} \leq 1$
Ensure: A sample from a distribution P

```
1: while True do
2:     x ← Q
3:     With probability M·P(x)/Q(x), return x
```

MOTIVATING THE SETTING.– Why assume access to Q and not P? The goal is to address situations where Q is the natural outcome of a construction, whereas P is the desired outcome. This is the case in lattice-based Fiat–Shamir signatures (section 9.2.3). If there was no rejection sampling, signatures would follow a "toxic" distribution Q that leaks information about the signing key sk. Performing rejection sampling during the signing process (Algorithm 9.8, Line 6) allows us to filter this dependency on sk out of the distribution and obtain a "clean" distribution P that no longer depends on sk.

DETERMINISTIC VERSUS RANDOMIZED.– Rejection sampling can be of two types. In the *deterministic* setting, $P = Q(\mathcal{S})$ is simply the restriction of Q to a subset $\mathcal{S}$ of its support, and the rejection step in Line 3 simply checks that $x \in \mathcal{S}$. This is the case in Dilithium and qTESLA. In the more general *randomized* setting, P can be any distribution, thus the rejection step becomes a probabilistic process. This is the case in BLISS. In the rest of this chapter, we focus on the *randomized* setting.

EXAMPLE WITH THE EXPONENTIAL DISTRIBUTION.– We illustrate (randomized) rejection sampling for the exponential distribution Exp (of density function $\exp(-x)$) restricted to the set $[0, 1]$, which we denote by $\mathrm{Exp}([0, 1])$. This is done in Algorithm 9.11, which is a specific instantiation of Algorithm 9.10 for $Q = U([0, 1])$ and $P = \mathrm{Exp}([0, 1])$.

Algorithm 9.11. EXPFROMUNIF()

Require: Oracle acccess to $U([0, 1])$
Ensure: $x \sim \mathrm{Exp}([0, 1])$

```
while True do
    x ← [0, 1]
    y ← [0, 1]
    if exp(−x) > y then
        return x
```

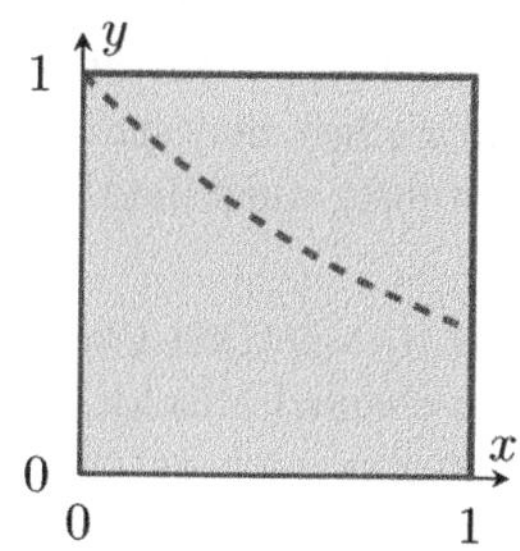

Figure 9.6. *On the left, an algorithm for sampling from* $\mathrm{Exp}([0, 1])$*. On the right, a visual interpretation:* (x, y) *is sampled uniformly in* $[0, 1]^2$ *(interior of ——), and* x *is accepted if and only if* (x, y) *is inside the hypograph ( ) of the function* $x \mapsto \exp(-x)$*) (- - -). The probability of restart is given by the area of ( ). For a color version of this figure, see www.iste.co.uk/prouff/cryptography3.zip*

PRECISION AND SIDE-CHANNEL LEAKAGE.– Note that Algorithm 9.10 does not completely solve the problem of sampling from P. Rather, it reduces it to Line 3, which can be seen as sampling a bit b from the Bernoulli distribution $\mathrm{Ber}_{f(x)}$ with $f(x) = \frac{M \cdot P(x)}{Q(x)}$. Algorithm 9.11 inherits this caveat, and it performs an on-the-fly computation of $f(x) = \exp(-x)$, a transcendental function which we cannot expect to have rational outputs for random values of x. This raises a first, two-stage question:

– How does the number of bits of precision k bias the distribution of sampling algorithms, and in turn, how does this bias impact the security of schemes that rely on these sampling algorithms?

A second natural concern is whether the computation of Line 3 in Algorithm 9.10 produces any side-channel leakage. This raises a second question:

– How do we implement rejection sampling in such a way that side-channel information does not leak anything about x (and possibly P or Q)?

9.4. Sampling algorithms

In this section, we present the main five algorithmic approaches that are used to sample random errors in post-quantum cryptography. These are based on probability tables (section 9.4.1), random permutations (section 9.4.2), convolution of distributions (section 9.4.3), polynomial approximations (section 9.4.4) and rejection-based methods (section 9.4.5), respectively. Finally, we revisit each approach in section 9.4.6 by discussing their compatibility with masking. Throughout the section, we will evaluate each approach using three metrics:

– EFFICIENCY.– Methods with low computational and storage requirements are in general better suited for adoption across a wide range of devices.

– PRECISION.– Given an error distribution, some algorithms may sample it exactly, while others may sample a related distribution that is close to it. The closeness can be rigorously quantified, for example, via the statistical distance or the Rényi divergence.

– SIDE-CHANNEL SECURITY.– Approaches may have different levels of resilience against side-channel attacks. These may vary from simple timing attacks to more advanced attacks such as cache-based timing, electromagnetic or power-analysis attacks.

Interestingly, many methods discussed here offer a three-dimensional trade-off between efficiency, precision and side-channel security, which allows some flexibility in their instantiations.

9.4.1. *Table-based algorithms*

USED FOR.– Virtually any distribution.

NOTATION 9.2.– Given a finite distribution P of support $\mathcal{S} = \{0, \ldots, n-1\}$, we call the cumulative distribution table of P the table $\mathrm{CDT}_P \in [0,1]^n$ defined for $\ell \in \mathcal{S}$ as $\mathrm{CDT}_P[\ell] = \sum_{i \leq \ell} P(i)$, and also add the convention $\mathrm{CDT}_P[-1] = 0$. Note that $\mathrm{CDT}_P[n-1] = 1$ by definition. We also denote by $\textsc{SecCmp}(x, y)$ an idealized comparison algorithm that takes as inputs $(x, y) \in [0,1]^2$ and outputs 1 if $x > y$, otherwise 0. We assume that SECCMP leaks no side-channel information about (x, y).

Table-based sampling is one of the most generic and versatile approaches for sampling distributions. Indeed, any distribution P of finite support is characterized by its cumulative distribution table CDT_P as defined in Notation 9.2 (assuming, without loss of generality, that its support is $\mathcal{S} = \{0, \ldots, n-1\}$). This observation provides a generic way to sample from P given CDT_P, which is described in Figure 9.7.

Algorithm 9.12. TABLESAMPLER()

$\ell := 0$
$x \leftarrow [0,1]$
while $x > \mathrm{CDT}_P[\ell]$ **do**
    $\ell := \ell + 1$
return ℓ

Algorithm 9.13. TABLESAMPLERSEC()

1: $\ell := 0$
2: $x \leftarrow [0,1]$
3: **for** $i = 1, \ldots, n$ **do**
4:     $\ell := \ell + \mathrm{SECCMP}(x, \mathrm{CDT}_P[i])$
5: **return** ℓ

Figure 9.7. *Two table-based sampling algorithms:* TABLESAMPLER *(not constant-time) and* TABLESAMPLERSEC *(constant-time). Both algorithms assume access to uniform randomness in* $[0,1]$ *and knowledge of* CDT_P

EXERCISE 9.2.– Show that both Algorithms 9.12 and 9.13 output ℓ such that $\ell \sim P$.

SOLUTION 9.2.– We first study Algorithm 9.12. Since $\mathrm{CDT}_P[n-1] = 1$, the **while** loop will have at most $n-1$ iterations and therefore the output ℓ is in $\{0, \ldots, n-1\}$. Inside the **while** loop, ℓ is incremented until $\mathrm{CDT}_P[\ell-1] < x \leq \mathrm{CDT}_P[\ell]$. Therefore, any viable output ℓ is output with probability $\mathrm{CDT}_P[\ell] - \mathrm{CDT}_P[\ell-1] = P(\ell)$.

In the **for** loop of Algorithm 9.13, ℓ is incremented only for the values i such that $x > \mathrm{CDT}_P[i]$. Thus, we can reuse the analysis of Algorithm 9.12 and derive the same conclusion.

SIDE-CHANNEL SECURITY.– Although Algorithms 9.12 and 9.13 are functionally identical, the former is not suited for environments where side-channels are a concern. Indeed, the number of iterations in the **while** loop is exactly the value of the output ℓ: Algorithm 9.12 is therefore not constant-time and can be vulnerable to timing attacks.

In contrast, Algorithm 9.13 reads all entries of CDT_P. This alone does not protect against timing attacks, since the comparison operator $(x > y)$ may not be leakage free. For example, the `memcmp()` function in the `string` library in C is not constant-time. This is why Line 3 of Algorithm 9.13 uses the secure function SECCMP (see Notation 9.2).

PRECISION AND BIAS.– In Example 2, we considered an idealized model where x and the entries of CDT_P are known with arbitrarily large precision. In practice, we need to fix the precision k, since the storage costs of Algorithms 9.12 and 9.13, as well as the running time of Algorithm 9.13, will be at least linear in k.

On the other hand, storing CDT_P with a finite precision discards some information about P and *biases* the output distribution, the same way a `.jpeg` image file loses information when compressed to a lower resolution. Striking a balance between minimizing k (thus maximizing the efficiency of Algorithms 9.12 and 9.13) and preserving meaningful security guarantees is a delicate exercise. However, a good rule of thumb is that if a table is used N times in a scheme that needs to preserve λ bits of security, then if suffices to set $k = \Omega(\lambda)$, or even $k = \Omega(\log N)$ in some cases.

9.4.2. *Random permutations*

USED FOR.– Fixed weight distributions (section 9.3.2).

Random permutations provide a simple and elegant way to sample fixed-weight distributions and their variants. Indeed, to sample $\mathbf{t} \in \{0,1\}^n$ from $\mathcal{F}_{n,w}$, it suffices to first set $\mathbf{t} := (1,\ldots,1,0,\ldots,0)$ with w ones and $(n-w)$ zeroes and shuffle (i.e. randomly permute) its entries.

A FIRST ATTEMPT.– We apply this idea with the Fisher–Yates shuffle (Algorithm 9.14); it runs in time $O(n)$, and we can show that it perfectly permutes the entries of $\mathbf{t}$. Unfortunately, it is not secure against side-channel attacks, as discussed below.

Algorithm 9.14. FISHERYATES($\mathbf{t}$)

Require: A table $\mathbf{t} = \{\mathbf{t}[1],\ldots,\mathbf{t}[n]\}$
Ensure: Apply a random permutation σ to the entries of $\mathbf{t}$
for $i \in \{1,\ldots,n-1\}$ **do**
  $j \leftarrow \{i,\ldots,n\}$
  Exchange $\mathbf{t}[i]$ and $\mathbf{t}[j]$

CACHE ATTACKS.– Cache attacks allow attackers to infer information about the position of data accessed during the execution of the algorithm. If there exists a dependency between this access pattern and some secret information, then the cache attack may expose some of this secret information. A more comprehensive overview of cache attacks is proposed in this book (see Volume 1, Part 1, Chapter 2: "Microarchitectural Attacks").

Let us see how cache attacks may impact Algorithm 9.14. If $\mathbf{t}$ is initialized to $(1,\ldots,1,0,\ldots,0)$ and the adversary infers via a cache attack that $\mathbf{t}[n]$ was not accessed during an execution of the algorithm, which happens with probability

$\prod_{i=1}^{n-1}\left(1 - \frac{1}{i+1}\right) = \frac{1}{n}$, then it is known that $\mathbf{t}[n]$ retained its initial value: $\mathbf{t}[n] = 0$. Depending on the context, this may have devastating consequences. For example, the output of Algorithm 9.14 may be used to add noise to a linear system, which is typical in code-based schemes. Knowing that the noise in the last equation is $\mathbf{t}[n] = 0$ may be exploited by the adversary to derive a noiseless linear system and recover some secret information.

OBLIVIOUS ALGORITHMS AND DATA STRUCTURES.– An algorithm $\mathcal{A}$ operating on a data structure $\mathbf{t}$ is said to be oblivious if its access pattern (i.e. the sequence of entries of $\mathbf{t}$ that were accessed) is independent of some sensitive information (e.g. the contents of $\mathbf{t}$ or the output of $\mathcal{A}$).

Oblivious algorithms are an elegant answer to cache attacks. If an algorithm applying a random permutation σ to $\mathbf{t}$ is oblivious with respect to the actual value of σ, then learning its access pattern provides the adversary with no information about σ. While Algorithm 9.14 is not oblivious, we will discuss two classes of algorithms that provide oblivious random permutations: sorting and switching networks.

Random permutations via sorting

HIGH-LEVEL IDEA.– We extend each entry $\mathbf{t}[i]$ of $\mathbf{t}$ with a random value $t_i' \leftarrow [0, 1]$, then sort the entries of $\mathbf{t}$ according to the t_i's. This provides a perfectly random permutation σ. This is illustrated in Figure 9.8.

PRECISION AND BIAS.– In practice, the t_i's are sampled with finite precision, say in the range $\{0, 1, \ldots, 2^k - 1\}$. This can slightly bias the distribution of σ. The relationship between k and this bias has been seldom studied in cryptography.

1	**1**	0	0	0	0	0
85	**173**	97	221	83	145	64

Sort w.r.t. bottom row ⟹

0	0	**1**	0	0	**1**	0
64	83	**85**	97	145	**173**	221

Figure 9.8. *Applying the sorting strategy to sample* $\mathbf{t} \leftarrow \mathcal{F}_{7,2}$ *(with* $k = 8$*)*

(NON-)OBLIVIOUS SORTING ALGORITHMS.– To guarantee security against cache attacks, the sorting algorithm must be oblivious, which is not always true.

Figure 9.9 illustrates this. MERGESORT has a runtime $O(n \log n)$ but is non-oblivious since its access pattern (bold red) depends on the input, whereas BUBBLESORT has a slower runtime $O(n^2)$ but is oblivious. The state of the art in oblivious sorting algorithms are the bitonic sort, with a runtime $O(n \log^2 n)$, and the bucket oblivious sort, with a runtime $O(n \log n)$ and an exponentially small but non-zero error probability.

Sorting networks are a subclass of oblivious sorting algorithms. A sorting network is a layered circuit composed of two types of components: (i) wires and (ii) comparator modules, which take (x, y) as input and output $(\min(x, y), \max(x, y))$. A secure comparator module is easily constructed from SECCMP (Notation 9.2). Most oblivious sorting algorithms (including BUBBLESORT and the bitonic sort) can be interpreted as sorting networks, and this abstraction is also useful in the context of masking.

MERGESORT ((1, 2, 3), (4, 5, 6))

1 2 3 4 5 6
1 2 3 4 5 6
1 2 3 4 5 6
1 2 3 4 5 6
1 2 3 4 5 6
1 2 3 4 5 6

MERGESORT ((1, 3, 5), (2, 4, 6))

1 3 5 2 4 6
1 3 5 2 4 6
1 3 5 2 4 6
1 3 5 2 4 6
1 3 5 2 4 6
1 3 5 2 4 6

BUBBLESORT (1, 2, 3, 4)

1 2 3 4
1 2 3 4
1 2 3 4
1 2 3 4
1 2 3 4
1 2 3 4
1 2 3 4

BUBBLESORT (4, 3, 2, 1)

4 3 2 1
3 4 2 1
3 2 4 1
3 2 1 4
2 3 1 4
2 1 3 4
1 2 3 4

Figure 9.9. *Two sorting algorithms:* MERGESORT *(non-oblivious) and* BUBBLESORT *(oblivious). For a color version of this figure, see www.iste.co.uk/prouff/cryptography3.zip*

Random permutations via switching networks

A switching network is a layered circuit composed of two types of components: (i) wires and (ii) random switches, which permute their input (x, y) with probability $\frac{1}{2}$. Figure 9.10 illustrates this idea by presenting a switching network called Beneš network, as well as an algorithmic description of a random switch (Algorithm 9.15).

An important property of a switching network is its mixing time, that is, the number of times it must be applied to an initial set of inputs before they can be considered to be (statistically) shuffled.

COMPARISON WITH SORTING.– Switching networks is a more direct approach than sorting (networks) to construct random permutations. At an algorithmic level, the main difference is that comparator modules are replaced with random switches.

OBLIVIOUSNESS AND BIAS.– Obliviousness is easily argued from their definition, since the position of each random switch is fixed in advance. The ability of a switching network to produce permutation σ that is (statistically) random depends on its mixing time, a property which is well studied for most common switching networks.

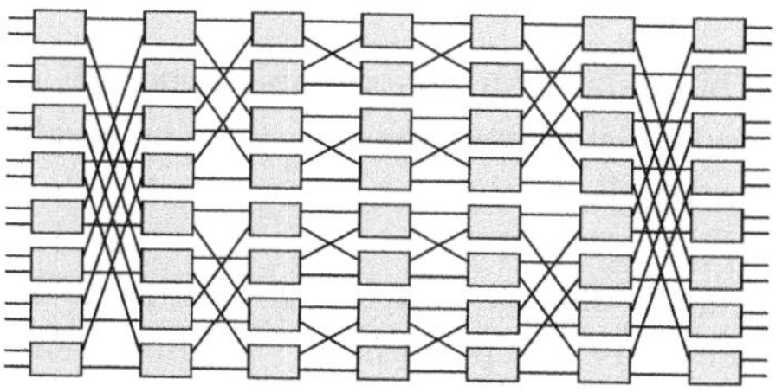

Algorithm 9.15. RANDOMSWITCH(x, y)

```
b ← {0,1}
x' = b · x + (1 − b) · y
y' = b · y + (1 − b) · x
return (x', y')
```

Figure 9.10. *On the left, a Beneš network with $n = 2^4$ inputs, $2 \log n$ layers and $n(2 \log n - 1)$ random switches (mint green nodes; see Algorithm 9.15 on the right). For a color version of this figure, see www.iste.co.uk/prouff/cryptography3.zip*

Summary

Random permutations provide an elegant way to sample from fixed-weight distributions (section 9.3.2). Multiple approaches for generating them exist, such as sorting networks (e.g. BUBBLESORT and bitonic sort), switching networks (e.g. Thorp shuffle and Beneš networks), sorting algorithms (e.g. the non-oblivious MERGESORT) or more direct approaches (e.g. the non-oblivious Fisher–Yates shuffle).

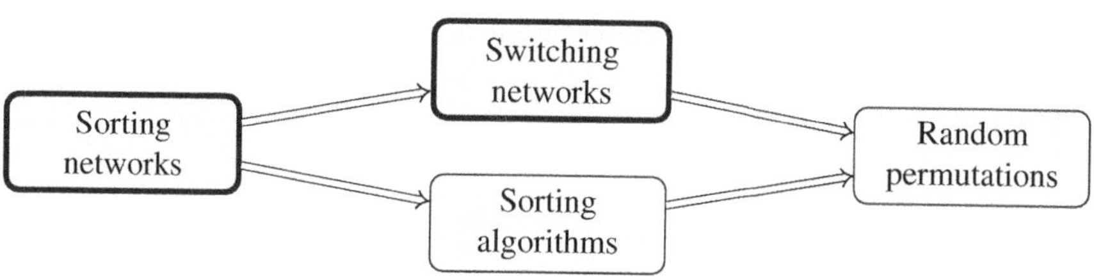

Figure 9.11. *Relationships between classes of algorithms for sampling random permutations. Classes that are always oblivious are drawn with thick boxes. For a color version of this figure, see www.iste.co.uk/prouff/cryptography3.zip*

9.4.3. *Convolution-based algorithms*

USED FOR.– Binomial (section 9.3.3) and discrete Gaussian (section 9.3.4) distributions.

This is a very simple approach, which takes advantage of the convolution properties that are specific to some distributions: equation [9.3] for binomial distributions and variations of equation [9.6] for discrete Gaussians. We explain the idea for binomials. To sample from CBD_n, we need to sample $2n$ uniformly random bits b_i and then apply either the formula from Definition 9.3 or Exercise 9.1. For Gaussians, the execution is slightly more complicated but still feasible.

BIAS.– When using convolution to sample binomial distributions, this approach is perfectly correct. When applied with discrete Gaussians, the bias can be made arbitrarily small by setting the parameters adequately.

SIDE-CHANNEL RESILIENCE.– This approach displays excellent resilience to side-channel attacks. Indeed, it simply consists of performing addition (and multiplications in the case of Gaussians), which can be easily implemented securely. This comes with the caveat that sampling from the base distribution ($U(\{0, 1\})$ in the case of binomials) needs to be implemented securely as well.

9.4.4. *Polynomial approximation*

USED FOR.– Randomised rejection sampling (section 9.3.5), Gaussians (section 9.3.4), etc.

Polynomial approximation provides a simple and generic solution for sampling distributions that entail dealing with functions that are expensive to compute. To showcase its potential, let us revisit the example of Figure 9.6. In Line 4 of Algorithm 9.11, we need to compute $f(x) = \exp(-x)$ for $x \in [0, 1]$. A simple way to do that with arbitrary precision is to truncate at a given degree d the Taylor series of $\exp(x)$:

$$\exp(x) = \sum_{n=0}^{\infty} \frac{x^n}{n!} \qquad [9.7]$$

PRECISON AND BIAS.– The precision of the approximation is an increasing function of two elements: the degree d of the truncated Taylor series of f, and the number of bits of precision k in the (fixed- or floating-point) computation. This depends on the use case; however, for some concrete example (e.g. Falcon), it seems sufficient to take $d = 10$ and $k = 53$.

SIDE-CHANNEL RESILIENCE.– Since evaluating a polynomial consists only of additions and multiplications, this approach has good side-channel resilience properties if we assume that both operations can be performed in constant-time.[1]

1 In some constrained environments, even integer multiplication may not be constant-time; see: https://www.bearssl.org/ctmul.html.

9.4.5. *Rejection methods*

USED FOR.– Gaussians (section 9.3.4), randomised rejection sampling (section 9.3.5), etc.

This class of methods derives from a work by von Neumann, which presented an elegant way to sample *exactly* from Exp given Oracle access to $U([0,1])$, using only simple operations such as comparisons. It was subsequently refined in several papers, but in Algorithm 9.16, we describe a simplified version that samples from $\mathrm{Exp}([0,1])$.

Algorithm 9.16. EXPFROMUNIFTWO()

Require: Oracle access to $U([0,1])$
Ensure: $x \sim \mathrm{Exp}([0,1])$

1: $\ell := 0$
2: $x := u_0 \leftarrow [0,1]$
3: **do**
4: $\quad \ell := \ell + 1$
5: $\quad u_\ell \leftarrow [0,1]$
6: **while** $u_\ell > u_{\ell-1}$
7: **if** ℓ is odd **then**
8: $\quad$ **goto** Line 1
9: **return** x

While both Algorithms 9.11 and 9.16 output $x \sim \mathrm{Exp}([0,1])$, they could not be more different. It might even seem surprising that Algorithm 9.16 is correct; however, we show in Exercise 9.3 that it is indeed true, and the proof leverages equation [9.7] in an unexpected way.

EXERCISE 9.3.– The goal of this exercise is to prove the correctness of Algorithm 9.16.

1) For a given x, show that, the probability $p_\ell(x)$ that the loop in Lines 3 to 6, terminates at a given value ℓ is equal to $\frac{x^{\ell-1}}{(\ell-1)!} - \frac{x^\ell}{\ell!}$.

2) Deduce from Item 1 that the output distribution of Algorithm 9.16 has support $[0,1]$ and probability density function $p(x) = \frac{\exp(-x)}{1-\exp(-1)}$.

SOLUTION 9.3.– We prove both items successively.

1) We first observe that:

$$\Pr[x > u_1 > \cdots > u_\ell] = \frac{\Pr[x > \max_{1 \le i \le \ell}\{u_i\}]}{\ell!} = \frac{x^\ell}{\ell!} \qquad [9.8]$$

The left equality in [9.8] stems from the fact that $\Pr[u_1 > \cdots > u_\ell] = \frac{1}{\ell!}$. This is true since there are $\ell!$ permutations of the $(u_i)_{1 \leq i \leq \ell}$, only one of which corresponds to a strictly decreasing sequence. Thus, the probability p_ℓ is given by:

$$\begin{aligned} p_\ell(x) &= \Pr[x > u_1 > \cdots > u_{\ell-1} < u_\ell] & [9.9] \\ &= \Pr[x > u_1 > \cdots > u_{\ell-1}] - \Pr[x > u_1 > \cdots > u_{\ell-1} > u_\ell] & [9.10] \\ &= \frac{x^{\ell-1}}{(\ell-1)!} - \frac{x^\ell}{\ell!} & [9.11] \end{aligned}$$

2) The support of the output distribution is obvious from Line 2. We now study the density function p. Given x sampled at Line 2, then depending on the parity of ℓ, it will be "accepted" or "rejected" (restarting the algorithm). More precisely, x is accepted if and only if ℓ is odd, which happens with probability:

$$\sum_{\ell \text{ odd}} p_\ell(x) = \sum_{\ell \text{ odd}} \left(\frac{x^{\ell-1}}{(\ell-1)!} - \frac{x^\ell}{\ell!} \right) = \exp(-x) \qquad [9.12]$$

We can see the Taylor series of exp equation [9.7] appear magically in equation [9.12]. Note that $\int_{[0,1]} \exp(-x)dx = 1 - \exp(-1)$, meaning that for each iteration of Lines 1 to 6, the algorithm will restart with probability $\exp(-1)$.

PRECISON AND BIAS.– The beauty of Algorithm 9.16 is that it samples $\text{Exp}([0,1])$ exactly, and similar remarks also apply for most algorithms based on the same idea. The only caveat is that sampling u_ℓ with finite precision k will bias the output; this can be circumvented by lazily increasing k when the condition $(u_\ell > u_{\ell-1})$ is undetermined.

SIDE-CHANNEL RESILIENCE.– The major flaw of this approach is that it suffers from poor side-channel resilience. For example, the number of iterations of the **while** loop is correlated to the output x, and several attacks have leveraged this kind of observation. It is possible to make the number of iterations constant, but this results in an algorithm that is more complex and costlier in bits of entropy than other methods.

9.4.6. *Masking the various algorithmic approaches*

We assume familiarity with masking. For an introduction, see the corresponding part (Volume 2, Part 1: "Masking"). We denote by d the masking order and k the bit-precision or number of bits per word. Recall that B2A conversion of k-bit values requires $O(d^2k)$ arithmetic operations in $\mathbb{Z}_{2^k}$, but 1-bit values require only $O(d^2)$ operations to convert, even if the result is in $\mathbb{Z}_{2^k}$. We now revisit the five main algorithmic approaches previously described, and ask the following question:

How amenable is each approach to masking?

TABLE-BASED ALGORITHMS.– Compatibility is average. The main bottleneck is the secure comparison operator $\textsc{SecCmp}(x, y)$ between two words in $\{0, \ldots, 2^k - 1\}$. In a masked setting, it requires a B2A conversion, which costs $O(d^2 k)$ word operations.[2]

RANDOM PERMUTATIONS.– Similarly to table-based algorithms, sorting networks suffer from an overhead $O(d^2 k)$ due to masked comparison. In contrast, switching networks use random switches as an atomic operation, and these are easy to mask with an overhead of $O(d^2)$, for example, by masking Algorithm 9.15.

All other things being equal, switching networks are therefore more amenable to masking than their sorting counterparts for generating random permutations.

CONVOLUTION-BASED ALGORITHMS.– Since they only use additions, convolution methods show great compatibility to masking as long as sampling from the base distribution can be easily masked.

POLYNOMIAL APPROXIMATION.– This method only uses additions and multiplications, and can therefore be masked with overhead $O(d^2)$ if we assume that the polynomial operate on integer values.

REJECTION METHODS.– There are no works on this topic. However, making these methods constant-time is already a challenging task, so we can expect masking to be highly non-trivial.

9.5. Notes and further references

The main application of the techniques described in this chapter is the secure implementation of post-quantum schemes. The most relevant ones are the first NIST PQC standards: Kyber (Schwabe et al. 2022), Dilithium (Lyubashevsky et al. 2022) and Falcon (Prest et al. 2022). Other relevant schemes are NIST candidates such as the code-based schemes Classic McEliece (Albrecht et al. 2020) and BIKE (Aragon et al. 2020), as well as the lattice-based schemes Saber (Schwabe et al. 2020), FrodoKEM (Naehrig et al. 2020), NewHope (Pöppelmann et al. 2019), NTRU (Chen et al. 2020) and NTRU Prime (Bernstein et al. 2020).

– Section 9.2. Due to space constraints, we did not mention some lattice- and code-based constructions which do not fall into the frameworks of section 9.2.1 and section 9.2.2 but still necessitate random errors. This is the case for (i) the code-based McEliece scheme (McEliece 1978) and its descendents such as Classic McEliece and

2 B2A conversion with complexity $O(d^2 \log k)$ exist, but with large constants.

BIKE, and (ii) the original NTRU encryption scheme (Hoffstein et al. 1998) and its descendents such as NTRU and NTRU Prime (in its StreamlineNTRU Prime variant).

– Section 9.2.1. The "*noisy ElGamal*" framework is inspired from the classical ElGamal scheme (Elgamal 1985). Early formalizations of what we call the noisy ElGamal framework were done in the context of lattice-based cryptography by Lyubashevsky et al. (2010); Lindner and Peikert (2011). Current instantiations of this framework include the lattice-based schemes Kyber, Saber, FrodoKEM (Naehrig et al. 2020), NewHope and NTRU Prime (in its NTRU LPRime variant), as well as the code-based schemes HQC and BIKE (in its BIKE-2 variant).

– Section 9.2.2. Modern lattice-based hash-then-sign schemes are descendents from the milestone work of Gentry et al. (2008). This includes Falcon as well as a few other schemes (Bert et al. 2018; Chen et al. 2019). The first code-based instantiation came was Wave (Debris-Alazard et al. 2019).

All concrete lattice-based instantiations use Gaussians. Works by Lyubashevsky and Wichs (2015) and Plançon and Prest (2021) explore the possibility of using other distributions, at the cost of degraded parameters.

– Section 9.2.3. Notable instantiation of the *Fiat–Shamir with aborts* framework is (Lyubashevsky 2009) and its descendents (Güneysu et al. 2012; Lyubashevsky 2012; Ducas et al. 2013; Bai and Galbraith 2014; Pöppelmann et al. 2014; Bindel et al. 2019; Lyubashevsky et al. 2020), including the standard Dilithium.

– Section 9.3.1. The first lattice-based signature (Lyubashevsky 2009) based on the *Fiat–Shamir with aborts* framework used uniform distributions, and this is also the case of one of its most recent incarnations, Dilithium (Lyubashevsky et al. 2020).

Uniform distributions can also be used in lattice-based encryption schemes; see the uSaber variant of Saber.

– Section 9.3.2. Fixed-weight distributions have been a staple of code-based cryptography for decades. The very first code-based cryptographic scheme (McEliece 1978) used these distributions. More recent code-based incarnations include the NIST (alternate) finalists BIKE, Classic McEliece and HQC. It has also been used in lattice-based NIST finalist NTRU and alternate finalist NTRU Prime.

– Section 9.3.3. The first occurrence of centered binomial distributions in lattice-based cryptography is due to Alkim et al. (2016), and motivated by the efficiency gain and ease of use that these distributions provide, compared to Gaussians. Notable uses include NewHope and the NIST finalists Saber and Kyber.

– Section 9.3.4. In mathematics and theoretical computer science, there is a rich and still ongoing history of using Gaussian distributions to study lattices (see, for example, Regev (2003); Micciancio and Regev (2004); Stephens-Davidowitz (2017)).

Gaussian distributions are also used in several cryptographic constructions, notably Falcon and FrodoKEM. In the case of FrodoKEM, Gaussians are sampled via a constant-time table lookup (section 9.4.1). In the case of Falcon, this table-based approach is combined with polynomial-based (section 9.4.4) rejection sampling.

– Section 9.3.5. Rejection sampling is an ubiquitous method in computer science; see (von Neumann 1950) for an early application. In the context of lattice-based cryptography, it was first proposed in the *Fiat–Shamir with aborts* framework (Lyubashevsky 2009) to prevent signing key leakage. In this context, rejection sampling has been applied both in deterministic (Lyubashevsky 2009; Lyubashevsky et al. 2020) and randomized (Ducas et al. 2013; Pöppelmann et al. 2014) form. Rejection sampling has also been used as a subroutine to sample from other distributions, for example, Gaussians in Falcon.

– Section 9.4. Several sampling methods not discussed in this chapter have adapted samples from discrete Gaussians, for example, Knuth-Yao trees (Dwarakanath et al. 2014; Karmakar et al. 2019) or the Ziggurat method (Buchmann et al. 2014).

– Section 9.4.1. Using a table to sample random errors for post-quantum schemes is a natural idea, as mentioned, for example, in Peikert (2010). Initially, a perceived need for high precision hampered the storage and computational efficiency of this approach. In recent years, its efficiency has been largely improved by borrowing algorithmic and information-theoretic tools from other fields, which allowed us to reduce both the number of elements and precision of tables. This is, for example, done via the use of guide tables and the Kullback–Leibler divergence (Pöppelmann et al. 2014), via the Rényi divergence (Bai et al. 2015; Prest 2017; Howe et al. 2020), and via the use of so-called conditional density tables (Prest 2017). Presently, the Falcon, FrodoKEM and Wave schemes use table-based sampling.

The FLUSH+RELOAD cache attack (Yarom and Falkner 2014) is applied in Bruinderink et al. (2016) to table-based sampling methods (notably the use of guide tables) used in BLISS. This attack worked in a somewhat idealized setting, a limitation lifted in subsequent work (Pessl et al. 2017).

– Section 9.4.2. There is a long history of oblivious sorting algorithms (including sorting networks) and switching networks that goes far beyond their cryptographic applications.

Sorting networks were first proposed by Batcher (1968), which also introduced the bitonic sort with its complexity $O(n \log^2 n)$. Sorting networks with complexity $O(n \log n)$ were proposed, but they have extremely large concrete $O(\cdot)$ constants due to their use of expander graphs: the AKS sort (Ajtai et al. 1983) and the Zig-Zag sort (Goodrich 2014). Recently, Asharov et al. (2020) proposed oblivious sorting and random permutation algorithms with complexity $O(n \log n)$ and small $O(\cdot)$ constants, with the caveat of an (exponentially) small failure probability.

A close but distinct notion is switching networks. This formalism encompasses the Thorp shuffle (Thorp 1973) and Benes networks (Gelman and Ta-Shma 2014). The "quality" of random permutations produced by switching networks is quantified by their *mixing* properties. Mixing properties of the Thorp shuffle and Benes networks have been studied in Morris (2008); Morris et al. (2009) and Gelman and Ta-Shma (2014), respectively. Using switching networks to sample random permutations has been studied in Czumaj (2015). See also (Bernstein 2020) for a focus on the formal verification of permutation networks, and (Bernstein 2017) for divergence bounds of sorting networks.

– Section 9.4.3. In lattice-based cryptography, sampling one-dimensional Gaussians by convolution was first done by Pöppelmann et al. (2014). This approach was then studied more in-depth by Micciancio and Walter (2017) and Zhao et al. (2020), making it both more generic and more efficient. Both Falcon (Prest et al. 2020) and qTESLA (Bindel et al. 2019) combine convolution with table-based sampling to sample Gaussians more efficiently during key generation.

– Section 9.4.4. Polynomial-based approximation was first proposed in the context of lattice-based cryptography by Aguilar Melchor et al. (2017) and Prest (2017), then adopted in a subroutine of Falcon. The idea was refined in subsequent works. Notably, Barthe et al. (2019) and Zhao et al. (2020) discuss tools for optimizing the search for polynomials that are "optimal" in the sense that for a given degree d, using a polynomial p of degree d instead of a transcendental function f would miminize the bias between some associated distributions $\mathcal{D}_p$ and $\mathcal{D}_f$.

– Section 9.4.5. Rejection methods to sample exponential-style distributions were pioneered by von Neumann (1950). Influential follow-up works include Forsythe (1972) and Ahrens and Dieter (1973). These methods were first applied in a cryptographic context by Ducas et al. (2013). Follow-up works are of Karney (2016) and Xie et al. (2021). It is notoriously difficult to make constant time.

Several side-channel attacks against rejection-based algorithms were proposed. For example, Espitau et al. (2017) propose such attacks either in the context of simple power analysis and an electromagnetic attack.

– Section 9.4.6. It has been shown in Schneider et al. (2019) and Coron et al. (2021) that B2A conversion for 1-bit values can be done using only $O(d^2)$ operations. As an application, Schneider et al. (2019) show how to sample masked binomials with an overhead $O(d^2)$.

Other attacks: a timing attack against a sampler in BLISS (Ducas et al. 2013) is proposed in Barthe et al. (2019). The attack exploits the fact that the running time of the sampler depends on the private signing key. Similarly, Tibouchi and Wallet (2021) put forward an attack exploiting non-constant-time bit-flips during noise generation.

Finally, Prest (2023) proposes a key-recovery attack against a variant of Falcon called Mitaka (Espitau et al. 2022).

9.6. References

Aguilar Melchor, C., Albrecht, M.R., Ricosset, T. (2017). Sampling from arbitrary centered discrete Gaussians for lattice-based cryptography. In *ACNS 2017*. Springer, Cham.

Aguilar Melchor, C., Aragon, N., Bettaieb, S., Bidoux, L., Blazy, O., Deneuville, J.-C., Gaborit, P., Persichetti, E., Zémor, G., Bos, J. (2020). HQC. Technical Report, National Institute of Standards and Technology [Online]. Available at: https://csrc.nist.gov/projects/post-quantum-cryptography/post-quantum-cryptography-standardization/round-3-submissions.

Ahrens, J. and Dieter, U. (1973). Extension of Forsythe's method for random sampling from the normal distribution. *Mathematics of Computation*, 27, 927–937.

Ajtai, M., Komlós, J., Szemerédi, E. (1983). An $O(n \log n)$ sorting network. In *Proceedings of the Fifteenth Annual ACM Symposium on Theory of Computing*. Association for Computing Machinery, New York.

Albrecht, M.R., Bernstein, D.J., Chou, T., Cid, C., Gilcher, J., Lange, T., Maram, V., von Maurich, I., Misoczki, R., Niederhagen, R. et al. (2020). Classic McEliece. Technical Report, National Institute of Standards and Technology [Online]. Available at: https://csrc.nist.gov/projects/post-quantum-cryptography/post-quantum-cryptography-standardization/round-3-submissions.

Alkim, E., Ducas, L., Pöppelmann, T., Schwabe, P. (2016). Post-quantum key exchange – A new hope. Report 2015/1092, Cryptology ePrint Archive [Online]. Available at: https://eprint.iacr.org/2015/1092.

Aragon, N., Barreto, P., Bettaieb, S., Bidoux, L., Blazy, O., Deneuville, J.-C., Gaborit, P., Gueron, S., Guneysu, T., Aguilar Melchor, C. et al. (2019). BIKE. Technical Report, National Institute of Standards and Technology [Online]. Available at: https://csrc.nist.gov/projects/post-quantum-cryptography/post-quantum-cryptography-standardization/round-2-submissions.

Aragon, N., Barreto, P., Bettaieb, S., Bidoux, L., Blazy, O., Deneuville, J.-C., Gaborit, P., Gueron, S., Guneysu, T., Aguilar Melchor, C. et al. (2020). BIKE. Technical Report, National Institute of Standards and Technology [Online]. Available at: https://csrc.nist.gov/projects/post-quantum-cryptography/post-quantum-cryptography-standardization/round-3-submissions.

Asharov, G., Chan, T.H., Nayak, K., Pass, R., Ren, L., Shi, E. (2020). Bucket oblivious sort: An extremely simple oblivious sort. In *Symposium on Simplicity in Algorithms*. SIAM, Alexandria.

Bai, S. and Galbraith, S.D. (2014). An improved compression technique for signatures based on learning with errors. In *Topics in Cryptology – CT-RSA 2014*. Springer, Cham.

Bai, S., Langlois, A., Lepoint, T., Stehlé, D., Steinfeld, R. (2015). Improved security proofs in lattice-based cryptography: Using the Rényi divergence rather than the statistical distance. *J. Cryptol.*, 31, 610–640.

Barthe, G., Belaïd, S., Espitau, T., Fouque, P.-A., Rossi, M., Tibouchi, M. (2019). GALACTICS: Gaussian sampling for lattice-based constant-time implementation of cryptographic signatures. Report 2019/511, Cryptology ePrint Archive [Online]. Available at: https://eprint.iacr.org/2019/511.

Batcher, K.E. (1968). Sorting networks and their applications. In *AFIPS Spring Joint Computing Conference*. Thomson Book Company, Washington, D.C.

Bernstein, D.J. (2017). Divergence bounds for random fixed-weight vectors obtained by sorting. Paper, University of Illinois at Chicago, Chicago.

Bernstein, D.J. (2020). Verified fast formulas for control bits for permutation networks. Report 2020/1493, Cryptology ePrint Archive [Online]. Available at: https://eprint.iacr.org/2020/1493.

Bernstein, D.J., Brumley, B.B., Chen, M.-S., Chuengsatiansup, C., Lange, T., Marotzke, A., Peng, B.-Y., Tuveri, N., van Vredendaal, C., Yang, B.-Y. (2020). NTRU prime. Technical Report, National Institute of Standards and Technology [Online]. Available at: https://csrc.nist.gov/projects/post-quantum-cryptography/post-quantum-cryptography-standardization/round-3-submissions.

Bert, P., Fouque, P.-A., Roux-Langlois, A., Sabt, M. (2018). Practical implementation of ring-SIS/LWE based signature and IBE. In *Post-Quantum Cryptography. PQCrypto 2018*, Lange, T. and Steinwandt, R. (eds). Springer, Cham.

Bindel, N., Akleylek, S., Alkim, E., Barreto, P.S.L.M., Buchmann, J., Eaton, E., Gutoski, G., Kramer, J., Longa, P., Polat, H. et al. (2019). qTESLA.Technical Report, National Institute of Standards and Technology [Online]. Available at: https://csrc.nist.gov/projects/post-quantum-cryptography/post-quantum-cryptography-standardization/round-2-submissions.

Bruinderink, L.G., Hülsing, A., Lange, T., Yarom, Y. (2016). Flush, gauss, and reload – A cache attack on the BLISS lattice-based signature scheme. In *Cryptographic Hardware and Embedded Systems*, Gierlichs, B. and Poschmann, A. (eds). Springer, Berlin, Heidelberg.

Buchmann, J., Cabarcas, D., Göpfert, F., Hülsing, A., Weiden, P. (2014). Discrete ziggurat: A time-memory trade-off for sampling from a Gaussian distribution over the integers. Report 2013/510, Cryptology ePrint Archive [Online]. Available at: https://eprint.iacr.org/2013/510.

Chen, Y., Genise, N., Mukherjee, P. (2019). Approximate trapdoors for lattices and smaller hash-and-sign signatures. In *Advances in Cryptology – ASIACRYPT 2019*, Galbraith, S. and Moriai, S. (eds). Springer, Cham.

Chen, C., Danba, O., Hoffstein, J., Hulsing, A., Rijneveld, J., Schanck, J.M., Schwabe, P., Whyte, W., Zhang, Z., Saito, T. et al. (2020). NTRU. Technical Report, National Institute of Standards and Technology [Online]. Available at: https://csrc.nist.gov/projects/post-quantum-cryptography/post-quantum-cryptography-standardization/round-3-submissions.

Coron, J.-S., Gérard, F., Montoya, S., Zeitoun, R. (2021). High-order table-based conversion algorithms and masking lattice-based encryption. Report 2021/1314, Cryptology ePrint Archive [Online]. Available at: https://eprint.iacr.org/2021/1314.

Czumaj, A. (2015). Random permutations using switching networks. In *STOC '15: Proceedings of the Forty-Seventh Annual ACM Symposium on Theory of Computing*. ACM, New York.

D'Anvers, J.-P., Karmakar, A., Roy, S.S., Vercauteren, F., Mera, J.M.B., Beirendonck, M.V., Basso, A. (2020). SABER. Technical Report, National Institute of Standards and Technology [Online]. Available at: https://csrc.nist.gov/projects/post-quantum-cryptography/post-quantum-cryptography-standardization/round-3-submissions.

Debris-Alazard, T., Sendrier, N., Tillich, J.-P. (2019). Wave: A new family of trapdoor one-way preimage sampleable functions based on codes. In *Advances in Cryptology – ASIACRYPT 2019*, Galbraith, S. and Moriai, S. (eds). Springer, Cham.

Ducas, L., Durmus, A., Lepoint, T., Lyubashevsky, V. (2013). Lattice signatures and bimodal Gaussians. In *Advances in Cryptology – CRYPTO 2013*, Canetti, R. and Garay, J.A. (eds). Springer, Berlin, Heidelberg.

Dwarakanath, N.C. and Steven, G.D. (2014). Sampling from discrete gaussians for lattice-based cryptography on a constrained device. *Appl. Algebra Eng. Commun. Comput.*, 25, 159–180.

Elgamal, T. (1985). A public key cryptosystem and a signature scheme based on discrete logarithms. *IEEE Transactions on Information Theory*, 31(4), 469–472.

Espitau, T., Fouque, P.-A., Gérard, B., Tibouchi, M. (2017). Side-channel attacks on BLISS lattice-based signatures: Exploiting branch tracing against strongSwan and electromagnetic emanations in microcontrollers. In *CCS '17: Proceedings of the 2017 ACM SIGSAC Conference on Computer and Communications Security*. ACM, New York.

Espitau, T., Fouque, P.-A., Gérard, F., Rossi, M., Takahashi, A., Tibouchi, M., Wallet, A., Yu, Y. (2022). Mitaka: A simpler, parallelizable, maskable variant of falcon. In *Advances in Cryptology – EUROCRYPT 2022*, Dunkelman, O. and Dziembowski, S. (eds). Springer, Cham.

Forsythe, G.E. (1972). von Neumann's comparison method for random sampling from the normal and other distributions. *Mathematics of Computation*, 26(120), 817–826 [Online]. Available at: http://www.jstor.org/stable/2005864.

Gelman, E. and Ta-Shma, A. (2014). The benes network is q*(q-1)/2n-almost q-set-wise independent. In *FSTTCS*. Schloss Dagstuhl – Leibniz-Zentrum für Informatik, Wadern.

Gentry, C., Peikert, C., Vaikuntanathan, V. (2008). Trapdoors for hard lattices and new cryptographic constructions. In *STOC '08: Proceedings of the Fortieth Annual ACM Symposium on Theory of Computing*. ACM, New York.

Goodrich, M.T. (2014). Zig-zag sort: A simple deterministic data-oblivious sorting algorithm running in $O(n \log n)$ time. In *STOC '14: Proceedings of the Forty-Sixth Annual ACM Symposium on Theory of Computing*. ACM, New York.

Güneysu, T., Lyubashevsky, V., Pöppelmann, T. (2012). Practical lattice-based cryptography: A signature scheme for embedded systems. In *Cryptographic Hardware and Embedded Systems*, Prouff, E. and Schaumont, P. (eds). Springer, Berlin, Heidelberg.

Hoffstein, J., Pipher, J., Silverman, J.H. (1998). NTRU: A ring-based public key cryptosystem. In *Algorithmic Number Theory. ANTS 1998*, Buhler, J.P. (ed.). Springer, Berlin, Heidelberg.

Howe, J., Prest, T., Ricosset, T., Rossi, M. (2020). Isochronous gaussian sampling: From inception to implementation. In *Post-Quantum Cryptography*, Ding, J. and Tillich, J.P. (eds). Springer, Cham.

Karmakar, A., Roy, S.S., Vercauteren, F., Verbauwhede, I. (2019). Pushing the speed limit of constant-time discrete Gaussian sampling. A case study on the falcon signature scheme. In *Proceedings of the 56th Annual Design Automation Conference 2019*. Association for Computing Machinery, New York. doi: 10.1145/3316781.3317887.

Karney, C.F.F. (2016). Sampling exactly from the normal distribution. *ACM Trans. Math. Softw.*, 42(1), 3:1–3:14. doi: 10.1145/2710016.

Lindner, R. and Peikert, C. (2011). Better key sizes (and attacks) for LWE-based encryption. In *Topics in Cryptology – CT-RSA 2011*, Kiayias, A. (ed.). Springer, Berlin, Heidelberg.

Lyubashevsky, V. (2009). Fiat–Shamir with aborts: Applications to lattice and factoring-based signatures. In *Advances in Cryptology – ASIACRYPT 2009*, Matsui, M. (ed.). Springer, Berlin, Heidelberg.

Lyubashevsky, V. (2012). Lattice signatures without trapdoors. In *Advances in Cryptology – EUROCRYPT 2012*, Pointcheval, D. and Johansson, T. (eds). Springer, Berlin, Heidelberg.

Lyubashevsky, V. and Wichs, D. (2015). Simple lattice trapdoor sampling from a broad class of distributions. In *Public-Key Cryptography – PKC 2015*, Katz, J. (ed). Springer, Berlin, Heidelberg.

Lyubashevsky, V., Peikert, C., Regev, O. (2010). On ideal lattices and learning with errors over rings. *Journal of the ACM (JACM)*, 60(6), 1–35.

Lyubashevsky, V., Ducas, L., Kiltz, E., Lepoint, T., Schwabe, P., Seiler, G., Stehlé, D., Bai, S. (2020). CRYSTALS-DILITHIUM. Technical Report, National Institute of Standards and Technology [Online]. Available at: https://csrc.nist.gov/projects/post-quantum-cryptography/post-quantum-cryptography-standardization/round-3-submissions.

Lyubashevsky, V., Ducas, L., Kiltz, E., Lepoint, T., Schwabe, P., Seiler, G., Stehlé, D., Bai, S. (2022). CRYSTALS-DILITHIUM. Technical Report, National Institute of Standards and Technology [Online]. Available at: https://csrc.nist.gov/Projects/post-quantum-cryptography/selected-algorithms-2022.

McEliece, R.J. (1978). A public-key cryptosystem based on algebraic coding theory. Progress Report, Jet Propulsion Laboratory, California Institute of Technology [Online]. Available at: https://ipnpr.jpl.nasa.gov/progressreport2/42-44/44N.PDF.

Micciancio, D. and Regev, O. (2004). Worst-case to average-case reductions based on Gaussian measures. In *45th Annual IEEE Symposium on Foundations of Computer Science*, Rome.

Micciancio, D. and Walter, M. (2017). Gaussian sampling over the integers: Efficient, generic, constant-time. Report 2017/259, Cryptology ePrint Archive [Online]. Available at: https://eprint.iacr.org/2017/259.

Morris, B. (2008). The mixing time of the thorp shuffle. *SIAM Journal on Computing*, 38(2), 484–504. doi: 10.1137/050636231.

Morris, B., Rogaway, P., Stegers, T. (2009). How to encipher messages on a small domain. In *Advances in Cryptology – CRYPTO 2009*, Halevi, S. (ed.). Springer, Berlin, Heidelberg.

Naehrig, M., Alkim, E., Bos, J., Ducas, L., Easterbrook, K., LaMacchia, B., Longa, P., Mironov, I., Nikolaenko, V., Peikert, C. et al. (2020). FrodoKEM. Technical Report, National Institute of Standards and Technology [Online]. Available at: https://csrc.nist.gov/projects/post-quantum-cryptography/post-quantum-cryptography-standardization/round-3-submissions.

von Neumann, J. (1950). Various techniques used in connection with random digits. *National Bureau of Standards, Applied Math Series*, 12, 36–38.

Peikert, C. (2010). An efficient and parallel Gaussian sampler for lattices. In *Advances in Cryptology – CRYPTO 2010*, Rabin, T. (ed.). Springer, Berlin, Heidelberg.

Pessl, P., Bruinderink, L.G., Yarom, Y. (2017). To BLISS-B or not to be: Attacking strongSwan's implementation of post-quantum signatures. In *CCS '17: Proceedings of the 2017 ACM SIGSAC Conference on Computer and Communications Security*. ACM, New York.

Plançon, M. and Prest, T. (2021). Exact lattice sampling from non-gaussian distributions. In *Public-Key Cryptography – PKC 2021*, Garay, J.A. (ed.). Springer, Cham.

Pöppelmann, T., Ducas, L., Güneysu, T. (2014). Enhanced lattice-based signatures on reconfigurable hardware. In *Cryptographic Hardware and Embedded Systems*, Batina, L. and Robshaw, M. (eds). Springer, Berlin, Heidelberg.

Pöppelmann, T., Alkim, E., Avanzi, R., Bos, J., Ducas, L., de la Piedra, A., Schwabe, P., Stebila, D., Albrecht, M.R., Orsini, E. et al. (2019). NewHope. Technical Report, National Institute of Standards and Technology [Online]. Available at: https://csrc.nist.gov/projects/post-quantum-cryptography/post-quantum-cryptography-standardization/round-2-submissions.

Prest, T. (2017). Sharper bounds in lattice-based cryptography using the Rényi divergence. In *Advances in Cryptology – ASIACRYPT 2017*, Takagi, T. and Peyrin, T. (eds). Springer, Cham.

Prest, T. (2023). A key-recovery attack against mitaka in the t-probing model. In *Public-Key Cryptography – PKC 2023*, Boldyreva, A. and Kolesnikov, V. (eds). Springer, Cham.

Prest, T., Fouque, P.-A., Hoffstein, J., Kirchner, P., Lyubashevsky, V., Pornin, T., Ricosset, T., Seiler, G., Whyte, W., Zhang, Z. (2020). FALCON. Technical Report, National Institute of Standards and Technology [Online]. Available at: https://csrc.nist.gov/projects/post-quantum-cryptography/post-quantum-cryptography-standardization/round-3-submissions.

Prest, T., Fouque, P.-A., Hoffstein, J., Kirchner, P., Lyubashevsky, V., Pornin, T., Ricosset, T., Seiler, G., Whyte, W., Zhang, Z. (2022). FALCON. Technical Report, National Institute of Standards and Technology [Online]. Available at: https://csrc.nist.gov/Projects/post-quantum-cryptography/selected-algorithms-2022.

Regev, O. (2003). New lattice based cryptographic constructions. *Journal of the ACM (JACM)*, 51(6), 899–942.

Schneider, T., Paglialonga, C., Oder, T., Güneysu, T. (2019). Efficiently masking binomial sampling at arbitrary orders for lattice-based crypto. In *Public-Key Cryptography – PKC 2019*, Lin, D. and Sako, K. (eds). Springer, Cham.

Schwabe, P., Avanzi, R., Bos, J., Ducas, L., Kiltz, E., Lepoint, T., Lyubashevsky, V., Schanck, J.M., Seiler, G., Stehlé, D. (2020). CRYSTALS-KYBER. Technical Report, National Institute of Standards and Technology [Online]. Available at: https://csrc.nist.gov/projects/post-quantum-cryptography/post-quantum-cryptography-standardization/round-3-submissions.

Schwabe, P., Avanzi, R., Bos, J., Ducas, L., Kiltz, E., Lepoint, T., Lyubashevsky, V., Schanck, J.M., Seiler, G., Stehlé, D. et al. (2022). CRYSTALS-KYBER. Technical Report, National Institute of Standards and Technology [Online]. Available at: https://csrc.nist.gov/Projects/post-quantum-cryptography/selected-algorithms-2022.

Stephens-Davidowitz, N. (2017). On the gaussian measure over lattices. PhD Thesis, New York University, New York.

Thorp, E.O. (1973). Nonrandom shuffling with applications to the game of Faro. *Journal of the American Statistical Association*, 68(344), 842–847 [Online]. Available at: https://www.tandfonline.com/doi/abs/10.1080/01621459.1973.10481434.

Tibouchi, M. and Wallet, A. (2021). One bit is all it takes: A devastating timing attack on bliss's non-constant time sign flips. *Journal of Mathematical Cryptology*, 15(1), 131–142. doi: 10.1515/jmc-2020-0079.

Xie, S., Zhuang, S., Du, Y. (2021). Improved Bernoulli sampling for discrete Gaussian distributions over the integers. *Mathematics*, 9(4) [Online]. Available at: https://www.mdpi.com/2227-7390/9/4/378.

Yarom, Y. and Falkner, K. (2014). FLUSH+RELOAD: A high resolution, low noise, L3 cache side-channel attack. In *SEC'14: Proceedings of the 23rd USENIX Conference on Security Symposium*. ACM, New York.

Zaverucha, G., Chase, M., Derler, D., Goldfeder, S., Orlandi, C., Ramacher, S., Rechberger, C., Slamanig, D., Katz, J., Wang, X. et al. (2020). Picnic. Technical Report, National Institute of Standards and Technology [Online]. Available at: https://csrc.nist.gov/projects/post-quantum-cryptography/post-quantum-cryptography-standardization/round-3-submissions.

Zhao, R.K., Steinfeld, R., Sakzad, A. (2020). FACCT: Fast, compact, and constant-time discrete gaussian sampler over integers. *IEEE Trans. Computers*, 69(1), 126–137.

PART 3

Real-World Applications

10

ROCA and Minerva Vulnerabilities

Jan JANCAR, Petr SVENDA and Marek SYS
Masaryk University, Brno, Czechia

ROCA and Minerva are two examples of real-world practically exploitable vulnerabilities found in cryptographic smartcards certified to high security levels under the Common Criteria certification scheme. Both vulnerabilities allow the extraction of the corresponding private key – RSA primes for The Return of Coppersmith's Attack (ROCA) and private scalar for ECDSA in the case of Minerva. The exploitation utilizes a lattice-reduction-based algorithm in both cases.

The Minerva vulnerability is caused by an *implementation weakness* providing an attacker with the knowledge of one or more most significant bits of an ECDSA nonce via timing side-channel leakage. The attack requires active monitoring of the computation of several thousand ECDSA signatures measured by a regular PC-based timer, or several hundred if precise power or EM analysis is available, followed by a cheap key extraction computation. The vulnerability affects Athena IDProtect smartcards that were certified to EAL4+ level and several types of tokens based on the AT90 security chip with the Atmel Toolbox cryptographic library. The same kind of weakness affected five other open-source cryptographic libraries.

On the contrary, the ROCA vulnerability is caused by a *design weakness* of a specific format of the used RSA primes. These primes are generated faster than if chosen completely randomly, but also taken from a smaller subset of all potential primes. While the internal entropy degradation was known, it was believed not to be exploitable. The attack only requires knowledge of an RSA public key, followed by a

Embedded Cryptography 3,
coordinated by Emmanuel PROUFF, Guénaël RENAULT,
Matthieu RIVAIN and Colin O'FLYNN.

somewhat expensive (several thousand dollars for 2048b RSA) but practical key extraction computation. The vulnerability affects a large range of chips produced by Infineon manufacturer and certified up to CC EAL 6+ level, manufactured between 2006 (at the latest) and 2017 in large quantities (estimated to 1–2 billion units) and deployed in a variety of scenarios, including electronic IDs, Trusted Platform Modules, full disk encryption, authentication tokens and protection of certification authorities signing keys.

As the impacted chips were certified under the Common Criteria scheme, the certification artifacts provide a trove of otherwise non-public information, which can help analyze the root cause of the vulnerabilities and identify other potentially vulnerable products and reasons for failed internal vulnerability notifications before the public disclosure.

10.1. The Return of Coppersmith's Attack

The ROCA vulnerability was discovered using large datasets of RSA keys generated by various smartcards and cryptographic libraries and used to identify the origin of RSA keys. In theory, properly generated RSA private keys are fully random primes; hence keys and also their sources are indistinguishable.

However, in practice, several choices are made by developers to simplify or speed up the key generation process, for example, if RSA keys (N) are generated to be of an exact size ($2n$ bits) with the corresponding primes P, Q of half size (n bits). Generation of a random RSA key is not as simple as generating two random primes of n bits because the product of two $n-$bit integers can produce a modulus with $2n-1$ or $2n$ bits. However, we can simplify the generation of primes by fixing their most significant bits (e.g. $P = 11 \cdots 1_2$). Such implementation choice creates an observable pattern in public keys (RSA modulus). This surprising fact was found by investigation of millions of RSA keys generated by range of smartcards and cryptographic libraries. As a result, we can identify a source of a given public modulus with high probability using only 8 bits (seven most and one second least significant). The bias of these bits also leaks some information about the private key (primes), but the leak is small and not sufficient for a successful attack.

Further analysis showed significantly different results from other sources for one specific card – Infineon JTOP 80K smart card. Specifically, the values of both primes P, Q and the corresponding modulus $N = P.Q$ modulo some small primes p_i are not distributed uniformly. For example, $P \mod 11 \in \{1, 10\}$ and $P \mod 37 \in \{1, 10, 26\}$ represent an entropy loss and leak information on the private key. Such an intriguing leak motivated further investigation, leading to the discovery of the structure of the primes and, finally, to the ROCA factorization vulnerability.

As the Infineon-generated RSA primes fall into two residue classes instead of 10 for $p_i = 11$, the entropy of primes is decreased by 2.3 bits ($2.3 = -log_2 2/10$). Similarly, primes lose additional 3.1 bits w.r.t $p_i = 37$ as the remainders for 11 and 37 are independent. We can estimate the entropy loss by analyzing the distribution of RSA primes P, Q modulo products of small primes p_i. Analysis showed that although the distribution of RSA primes is uniform (covers $Z^*_{p_i} - \{0\}$) for some of the primes (e.g. $p_i = 7$), they increase entropy loss even more when they are combined with others p_j. For example, RSA primes fall into six (two for $p_i = 11$ times three for $p_j = 37$) residue classes $P \mod 11{*}37 \in \{1, 10, 100, 186, 232, 285\}$ but for $7{*}11{*}37$, the number of classes remains six ($P \mod 7 * 11 * 37 \in \{1, 10, 100, 285, 1000, 1453\}$). Moreover, for some, moduli remainders form a multiplicative subgroup that is cyclic (generated by one element). This property was verified for modulus (maximal one) equal to product of all primes (up to some bound). Lastly, the smallest generator 65537 of the subgroup was found; hence, RSA primes generated by the vulnerable Infineon RSALib library have the following form:

$$P = k * M + (65537^a \mod M) \qquad [10.1]$$

for $k, a \in \mathrm{N}$ and product of small primes $M = \prod_{p_i < B} p_i$. The upper bound for value a is determined only by M which is fixed for range of key sizes. The upper bound for k is given by prime size and the size of M, that is, size of k is complement of size M w.r.t size of prime. The formula in equation [10.1] was a guarded secret until 2017.

10.1.1. *Fingerprinting*

The format of the RSA primes given by equation [10.1] is a specific fingerprint of the primes but also of the corresponding public modulus as shown by equation [10.2]:

$$N = \overbrace{(k * M + 65537^a \bmod M)}^{P} * \overbrace{(l * M + 65537^b \bmod M)}^{Q}, \qquad [10.2]$$

for $a, b, k, l \in \mathbb{N}$.

This specific form of modulus is equivalent to the existence of a corresponding discrete logarithm (DL) x for the base 65537 in Z^*_M. Concretely, N is of the form (equation [10.2]) if and only if $N \equiv 65537^x \mod M$ for some integer x. Hence, vulnerable keys can be easily identified by computing the DL of the public modulus N. DL x can be computed efficiently using the Pohlig–Hellman algorithm. The Pohlig–Hellman algorithm is applicable in situations where the order of a group (or a generator) is smooth (has small prime divisors), which is exactly the case for ROCA keys. Here, we benefit from the fact that M is smooth, which implies that the order $ord_M(65537)$ of the generator 65537 in Z_M^* is also smooth. The algorithm can correctly test a key for a vulnerability in milliseconds on a standard CPU. The probability of false positives is equal to the inverse of $r = |Z_M^*|/|G| = \phi(M)/ord_{65537}(M)$ and it is negligible (less than 2^{-154}). The ratio shows how small the set G of the remainders library can generate compared to set Z_M^* covered by correctly generated keys. The ratio r can be interpreted directly as entropy loss (at least 154 bits) of the primes. This huge entropy loss can be used to perform a practical factorization attack.

10.1.2. *Factorization attack*

The attack takes N as input and looks for its prime divisor P (or Q). For a given key size, the value of M is fixed and the primes differ only in their values a, k (see equation [10.1]). The values of M were computed by the authors of the attack. The values of M for selected keys sizes can be found in Nemec et al. (2017); Table 10.1.

Key size	Entropy loss (to random prime)	Initial attack cost (energy-only price)	Optimized cost (for 90% of keys)
512b	157.1b (61.4 %)	\$0.002	\$0.0007
1024b	340.2b (66.4%)	\$1.78	\$0.63
2048b	715.2b (69.8%)	\$944	\$336
3072b*	715.2b (46.6%)	$\$1.90 * 10^{26}$	$\$6.76 * 10^{25}$
4096b*	1527.5b (74.6%)	$\$8.58 * 10^{9}$	~\$3 billion

Table 10.1. *An estimation of entropy loss and factorization cost for different key lengths. As the attack is perfectly parallelizable, its run-time can be arbitrarily shortened using more CPUs in parallel. The energy cost is estimated for a standard Intel E5-2650v3@3GHz CPU with \$0.2/kWh electricity price*

A high-level description of the attack is as follows: the attack looks for a, k as their cumulative bit-size (e.g. 99 = 37 + 62 for 512b RSA keys) is much smaller than the bit-size of P (256 for 512b RSA). The attack iterates over a set of exponents a, utilizes Coppersmith's method (CM) to compute k and tests whether the corresponding P is a divisor of N. This naive approach is infeasible since a number of different a is large (see red line in Figure 10.1 representing $ord_M(65537)$). However, the approach could be optimized as the CM is able to compute k of larger sizes (up to half of the size of the RSA prime). The main idea of the optimization was that M can be replaced by any of its divisors M' ($M' \mid M$) in (equation [10.1]) and the values (primes and modulus) will still be of the same form. This observation allowed us to decrease M' and the number ($ord_{M'}(65537)$) of guesses for an alternative exponent a'. The dominant factor of the attack complexity:

$$Time = ord_{M'}(65537) * T(M', m, t)$$

is the order of the generator but when the size of k is close to the limits (half of the prime bits), the running time $T(M', m, t)$ of CM plays an important role too. The values m, t defines dimension $m + t$ of the matrix processed by LLL – celebrated lattice reduction algorithm used by CM. Order $ord_{M'}(65537)$ can be computed easily as $ord_{M'}(65537) = lcm(ord_{p_1}, ord_{p_2}, \cdots)$ based on orders $ord_{p_i}(65537)$ of all primes divisors $p_i \mid M'$. The running time $T(M', m, t)$ can be computed only empirically since it depends on chosen parameters m, t, and implementation of LLL.

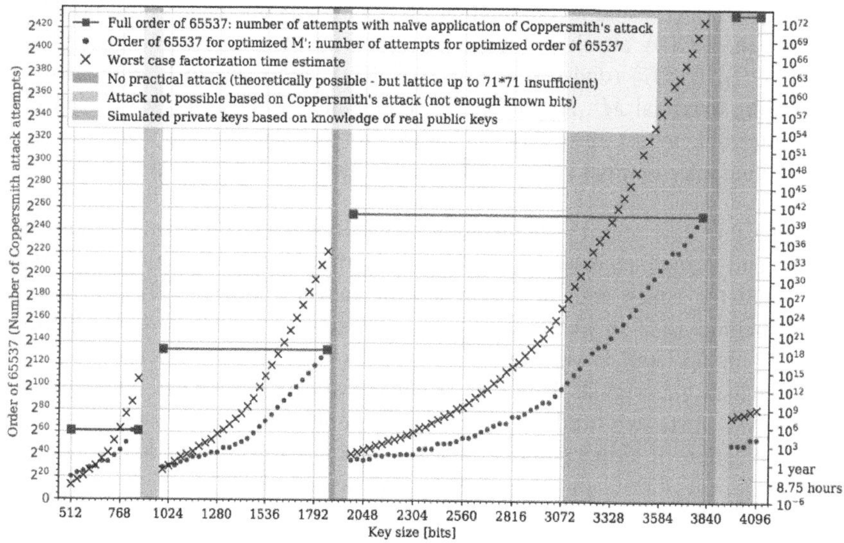

Figure 10.1. *Complexity of ROCA attack with respect to key length. The difficulty generally increases with a key length, but decreases significantly when parameter M is changed. Unfortunately, different M is used just before the practically important key lengths like 1,024 or 2,048 bits (Nemec et al. 2017). For a color version of this figure, see www.iste.co.uk/prouff/cryptography3.zip*

CM was proposed to find small root r_0 of polynomial $f(x)$ modulo some number b, that is, $f(x) \equiv 0 \mod b$ for some b. For the ROCA modulus, N and alternative guess a', it means that we look for the small root k' modulo P of the linear polynomial $f(x) = x + (M'^{-1} * 65537^{a'} \mod N)$. The idea of CM is to get rid of unknown modulus P and transform this modular equation to an equation over the integers solvable using standard algorithms. CM uses the LLL algorithm to find polynomial $g(x)$ with the same roots over Z as has $f(x)$ modulo b. Polynomial $g(x)$ is constructed as a linear combination of polynomials $f_i(x)$ for $0 \leq i < m + t$. The polynomials f_i are of the following forms: $f_i(x) = N^i f^{m-i}(x)$ for $0 \leq i < m$ and $f_{i+m}(x) = x^i f^m(x)$ for $0 \leq i < t$ and all share the same root k' modulo P^m. CM constructs polynomial $g(x)$ such that $g(k) < P^m$, which imply that k is root of $g(x)$ also over Z. CM applies LLL to $m + t \times m + t$ matrix B whose rows B_i encode polynomials $f_i(xX)$. The integer X creates a connection between the norms of the vectors B_i and upper bounds on $g(k)$ for $k < X$. Polynomial $g(xX)$ (which provides $g(x)$ directly) is found as a short (typically shortest) vector in a reduced matrix B' obtained from B by LLL.

Heuristic search on M', m, t aiming at 100% success rate to optimize the attack speed was performed using a combination of greedy heuristic and local brute force. Authors of the ROCA attack did not iterate directly over M' (as divisors of M) but over $ord_{M'}(65537)$ (divisors of $ord_M(65537)$), and then easily computed the corresponding maximal M'. Although this significantly reduced the search space, it was still infeasible to test all suitable candidates for M'. The authors that discovered the attack, guarantee optimal values of the parameters only for small key sizes.

Within a few days after the publication of the ROCA-detection tool, researchers Bernstein and Lange revealed the format of primes given by equation [10.1], re-discovered the attack and improved its efficiency by roughly 20–25% using a chaining method (one of the well-known strategies to speed up Coppersmith's method). A month later, Jannis Harder published in his blog an attack that is eight times faster than the original. However, it works only for small keys (demonstrated for 512b keys) where two-thirds (instead of half) of prime bits are known. The attack is a simplification of Coppersmith's attack – it looks directly for k, l as a small solution of $c_1 = c_2 * x + c_3 * y \mod M$ with c_i determined by a.

In 2019, Bruno Produit and Arnis Parsovs published another type of optimization. They analyzed the entropy of a, k for one million generated keys and found that there are four fixed bits (1 MSB of a and 3 MSB of k). This brought the worst-case time for the attack down from 140.8 CPU years to 35.2 CPU years for 90% of 2,048-bit keys. The remaining 10% keys require 70.4 CPU years.

10.1.3. *Practical impact and disclosure*

The ROCA factorization attack is a practical one – Masaryk University researchers factorized randomly selected 512b and 1024b keys. Estonian RIA later factorized a public key used in the real world, which turned out to be an "average" difficulty 2048b RSA key for "several thousand euros" in claimed energy cost. The resulting impact of the ROCA vulnerability is significant due to a combination of several factors: (1) the widely used key lengths, including 1024b and 2048b are practically factorable; (2) the weakness is on a design level; hence, it is not limited just to a particular range of physical devices; (3) the chip vendor is one of the top three secure integrated circuit (IC) producers with a large number of certified devices; and (4) the vulnerable algorithm for prime generation was used for a long time – introduced in the year 2006 at the latest (RSALib v1.02.013) and replaced only after vulnerability disclosure in 2017.

Vulnerable devices can be detected using two principal options: *(1) official device specification*: finding mentions of the ROCA-vulnerable library in its specification or certification documents; *(2) key fingerprint*: identifying the ROCA-specific bias in a modulus of a device-produced public key.

The Google-powered search of the Common Criteria portal of certified products for the string "RSA2048/4096 v1.02.013" (identifying the vulnerable library) returns 181 documents. An additional search of certificate references using the https://sec-certs.org project returns almost 300 potentially vulnerable certified products with direct or indirect references to vulnerable ones. Figure 10.2 shows the visualization of certificates relevant to a search based on the vulnerable library. The colors correspond to different certificate-issuing countries. The impacted domains naturally correlate with the utilization of cryptographic hardware and the usage of the RSA algorithm specifically. Still, assessing the real-world impact is difficult as a selection of a particular hardware vendor or an implementation used may not be public knowledge.

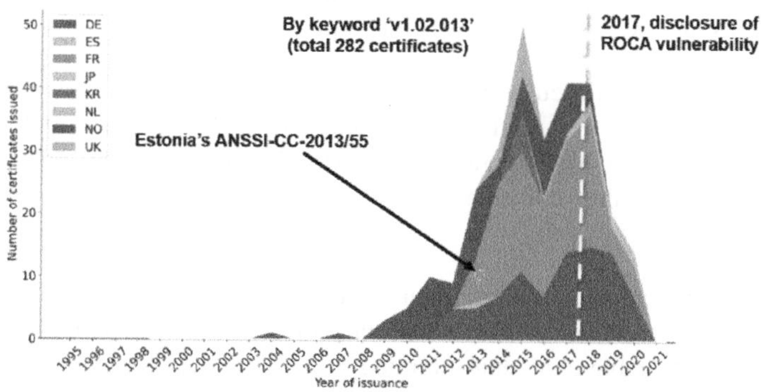

Figure 10.2. *The number of certified items under Common Criteria framework over the years as approved under different certificate issuing countries and mentioning the vulnerable library RSALib v1.02.013. For a color version of this figure, see www.iste.co.uk/prouff/cryptography3.zip*

Although the RSALib is neither mandatory to use nor automatically shipped with every chip, the developers are motivated to deploy it in order to benefit from ready-to-use higher level functions (such as the *RsaKeyGen()* method in question) and to get an implementation designed with protections against side-channel and fault injection attacks in mind.

Fortunately, the very fast detection algorithm can quickly test millions of keys using only the key's modulus with negligible false negative and false positive rates. The fast and accurate detection is beneficial both for an attacker as well as for a defender. While an attacker can broadly search for vulnerable keys and identify the vulnerable ones before attempting its costly factorization attempt, a defender can assess all the keys used and prevent the usage of vulnerable ones by revocation, update and filtering.

10.1.3.1. *Electronic identity documents*

Overall, the electronic identity documents (eIDs) domain was significantly affected as eIDs represent a large area for the application of cryptographic smartcards, such as biometric passports (ePassport, ICAO Doc 9303), eDriver licenses (ISO/IEC 18013) and country-specific identity documents. The card-based RSA keypair is typically utilized for holder authentication, the establishment of a secure channel (EAC-PACE) and the decryption of messages (OpenPGP, S/MIME). The use of the *RSALib* is referenced in multiple certification documents of electronic passports of several countries. While authentication and digital signing attacks are generally mitigated by the key revocation, the decryption of past eavesdropped messages remains an issue, unless perfect forward secrecy is guaranteed. Decryption attack is also getting progressively cheaper with the attack's factorization algorithmic improvements and overall speedup in computation.

Due to the general difficulty of obtaining relevant datasets with public keys from passports or eIDs, only two countries (Slovakia and Estonia) were initially reported as issuing documents with vulnerable keys. After public disclosure, other countries were found to use a vulnerable chip to various extend. Notably, Spain revoked around 18 million citizen certificates.

For Slovakia, only a small fraction of about 8% of citizens was issued with electronic ID, but all of them were vulnerable. Slovakia kept using the RSA algorithm on vulnerable chips but migrated to 3,072 bits keys (which are currently not practically factorable and are supported by their chip) and only revoked existing 2,048 bits keys.

The public lookup service of Estonia allowed for a random sampling of the public keys of citizens and revealed that more than half of the eIDs of regular citizens and all e-residents were vulnerable, counting roughly 750,000 certificates. Estonia migrated away from vulnerable RSA implementation to an ECC algorithm with 384 bits key length available on the same chip – a step that required an on-card update of the eID application (JavaCard applet). The update was performed remotely or at official kiosks for hundreds of thousands of cards. During the embargo period, the more important affected parties (which the Estonia government certainly is) were supposed to be notified before the full public disclosure, either directly by its local eID provider or via non-public memos distributed among the parties involved in EU-wide eIDAS directive for cross-board trust services. However, the vulnerability information was not propagated and received properly by the Estonian government until the beginning of September 2017 – again by ROCA's original researchers who coincidentally analyzed Estonian's repository of public keys and spotted freshly issued certificates still with vulnerable keys seven months after the initial private disclosure. As the Estonian national elections with widely used electronic voting via vulnerable *EstEID* cards were imminent, government officials were not only deciding how to technically fix issued *EstEID* cards but also how (and if) to carry online elections with votes being signed by (possibly) insecure private keys. The estimation of the factorization cost played a role; several thousand euros estimated to forge a single vote was deemed prohibitively expensive to carry meaningful voting fraud.

10.1.3.2. *Authentication tokens and code signing*

The use of two-factor authentication tokens and commit signing is recommended and on the rise, yet these approaches are still adopted only by a minority of developers – but usually for more significant projects. In some cases, application signing is mandatory and enforced by the platform (e.g. Android, iOS and OS drivers); elsewhere, voluntarily adopted by the developers. Hundreds of ROCA-fingerprinted keys for GitHub developers were found, more than half with a practically factorizable key length of 2,048 bits. Including keys with access to very popular repositories with up to 2,000 stars (users bookmarking the project) for user-owned repositories and more than 50,000 stars for organization-owned repositories. The impact is increased by the fact that some relevant repositories are libraries used in other projects and are essentially trusted by third-party developers. The large majority of vulnerable cases seemed to be caused by usage of a popular Yubico Yubikey 4 token (with vulnerable Infineon chip inside). Yubico updated vulnerable key generation on its own and offered a token replacement.

Usage domain	Public key availability	Misuse (examples)
TLS/HTTPS	Easy	MitM, eavesdropping (SCADA)
Message security	Easy	Message eavesdropping, forgery (PGP, Yubikey)
Trusted boot (TPM)	Limited	Decrypt/unseal data, forged attestation (IFX, BitLocker)
Electronic IDs	Limited	E-gov document forgery/cloning (EE, SK, ES, BE)
Payment cards (EMV)*	Limited	Clone card, fraudulent transaction (none)
Certification authorities	Easy	Forged certificates (ChamberSign, D-TRUST, DATEV)
Auth. tokens (FIDO2)	Limited	Unauthorized access or operation (Yubikey)
Software signing	Easy	Malicious application update (GitHub, Maven)
Programmable smartcard	Varies	Depends on usage

Table 10.2. *The summary of the impact of key factorization in the different usage domains. The ROCA-fingerprinted keys were found within all listed domains with exceptions marked with an asterisk (*)*

A similar analysis of packages and applications available via the Maven repository revealed only five keys (all with 4,096-bit moduli not considered practically factorizable by the method) and none for Android Playstore.

10.1.3.3. *Trusted Platform Modules and smartcards*

Trusted Platform Modules (TPMs) provide a secure hardware anchor for a trusted boot and key storage. The "sealed storage" is utilized by Microsoft BitLocker full disk encryption software to protect the volume master encryption key. The possibility to factorize TPM's 2,048-bit root storage key (SRK) directly leads to decryption of an unwrapping key necessary to decrypt the volume master key, thus bypassing the need for TPM to validate the correctness of a PIN. As a result, an attacker can decrypt a disk from a stolen laptop with a vulnerable TPM if encrypted by BitLocker in TPM-only or TPM+PIN mode. As mitigation, Microsoft deployed detection of vulnerable TPM-generated wrapping RSA key and migrated it under a new, non-vulnerable one.

The ROCA CVE vulnerability record lists four platform configurations (CPE) for vulnerable TPM firmware (v4.31, 4.32, 6.40, and 133.32) found in 130 different notebook and laptop platforms. Fortunately, the TPM firmware can be updated, and the corresponding patch was released.

Not all smartcards based on the Infineon hardware are vulnerable as many vendors use only the base hardware and libraries (e.g. SLE78 chip with RSA co-processor performing modular exponentiation) and choose not to deploy or use the vulnerable key generation. In contrast to TPM chips, an operating system and base libraries are typically stored in a card's read-only memory and cannot be updated later to remove the vulnerability, once a card is deployed. Vulnerable cards will be available for a prolonged time before eventually being sold or phased out, especially when dealing with low-volume markets. The vulnerable cards are still available for sale five years after the disclosure. The total number of chips produced with the vulnerable library is estimated to be 1–2 billion.

The chip-based payment cards used worldwide are backed by a set of protocols specified under the EMV standard and maintained by the EMVCo consortium. The *RSALib* was approved for use in EMV cards by EMVCo and is referenced in related certification reports, but no public database is available. Out of a small sample of RSA keys extracted from 13 payment cards issued by different banks in four European countries, six cards reported chips produced by Infineon, but none of them contained the ROCA fingerprint. Meaning that the vulnerable key generation method was not used in either one, possibly due to a key being generated outside the EMV card and imported later during a personalization phase. However, if used, the potential impact of factorizable keys would be particularly damaging to contactless payments due to the generally short RSA key lengths used, ranging between 768 and 1,280 bits only.

10.1.3.4. *Email, web and SCADA security*

The keys used for digital signatures and email encryption are easy to download from public PGP keyservers. Almost 3,000 fingerprinted keys with slightly less than 1,000 practically factorizable ones were found. The *Yubikey 4* token seems to be the origin for the majority of these keys, as hundreds even contain Yubikey-identifying strings in the keyholder information and the date of generation correlates with the release date of this token.

Despite analysis of more than 100 million certificates coming from whole IPv4 address space scans and Certificate Transparency logs, only a negligible number of 15 vulnerable keys was found in the TLS/HTTPS domain initially. However, all of the keys were tied to different pages with SCADA-related topics, which may point to a single provider of a SCADA remote connection platform. Following the public disclosure, a large number of certificates with vulnerable keys for SCADA-related domains like scada.emsglobal.net, alarms.realtimeautomation.net, and Belarusian Kapsch devices *.kapsch.by were revoked.

10.1.3.5. *Certification authorities*

The presence of vulnerable keys belonging to certification authorities would magnify the impact due to the possibility of key certificate forgery. Neither the browser-trusted certificates nor electronic passport signing certificates (ICAO) contained ROCA-fingerprinted keys among the 10,000 root and intermediate active authorities. However, retrospective analysis shows that several root certification authorities like ChamberSign Qualified CA and D-TRUST Qualified CA, CA DATEV ZSM had their certificates revoked and keys updated during (or shortly after) the embargo period. ENISA's annual report on trust services for the year 2017 showed that one-third of all notified breaches were due to the ROCA vulnerability, with 60% on the highest "disastrous" level. The currently largest certification authority for TLS/HTTPS certificates, Let's Encrypt refuses to certify any submitted certificate signing request (CSR).

10.1.4. *Notes and further references*

– Section 10.1. The ROCA (Nemec et al. 2017) vulnerability affects a range of certified devices by Infineon. The vulnerability was found using an already existing dataset of keys collected for the paper Svenda et al. 2016, doing origin library attribution based on the public key.

– Section 10.1.1. The details of the Pohlig–Hellman algorithm are provided in Pohlig and Hellman (2022). An open-source detection tool for vulnerable keys is available (Klinec and Svenda 2017) to study key patterns.

– Section 10.1.2. The blog describing rediscovery of an attack by Bernstein and Lange is described in Bernstein and Lange (2017). Another approach is described in

Harder (2017). The ROCA vulnerability is categorized under record CVE-2017-15361 in NIST National Vulnerability Database (NVD 2017). The ROCA attack was roughly 4x improved in Produit (2019), bringing overall energy cost down to several hundred dollars for a 2,048 bits key.

– Section 10.1.3.1 The European directive for trust services enables recognition of signatures between different EU countries and mandates disclosure of relevant vulnerabilities among the involved countries (EU 2014). ENISA issues an annual report with the summary for the issues which occurred in a given year (ENISA 2018).

– Section 10.1.3.3. Details of architecture and data format for Microsoft Bitlocker fulldisk encryption software are provided in Kumar and Kumar (2008); Kornblum (2009) and Microsoft (2013). EMVCo consortium is responsible for checking compatibility as well as security of the components like cards and terminals compatible under the EMV standard. The approved cards are issued a certificate under this scheme, which can be checked for presence of RSALib vulnerable library (EMVCo 2017a, 2017b).

– Section 10.1.3.5. The detection of the ROCA fingerprint was added to monitoring of issued certificates via Certificate Transparency, allowing for tracking of the revoked certificate https://misissued.com/batch/28/.

10.2. Minerva

The Minerva group of vulnerabilities was discovered in 2019. It affects a Common Criteria–certified smartcard and is used to affect five popular open-source cryptographic libraries. All of the affected implementations leak information on the most-significant bits (usually the bit-length) of the random nonce used in ECDSA signatures via a timing side-channel. This information collected over many signatures can be utilized to form an instance of the Hidden Number Problem (HNP), the solving of which recovers the private key used. This problem is usually solved by transforming it to the Closest Vector Problem (CVP) or the Shortest Vector Problem (SVP), two well-known problems on lattices, which have practical solutions for the cases encountered here via lattice-reduction algorithms. For more background on issues of ECDSA nonce leakage as well as the HNP, see Chapter 8 of this volume.

Concurrently with the discovery of the Minerva vulnerability, a different group of researchers found the same type of leakage in two TPMs, including a Common Criteria EAL4+ certified one, and dubbed it the TPM-Fail vulnerability.

10.2.1. *Discovery and leakage*

The discovery of the first vulnerable implementation, the Athena IDProtect smartcard, was made using ECTester, a tool for testing black-box elliptic curve cryptography implementations. A large-scale analysis of ECC operations from JavaCard-based smartcards and selected software cryptographic libraries, including the ECDSA signatures along with timing information, detected the leakage caused by a linear relationship between the bit-length of the ECDSA nonce and the duration of the signing operation, as visualized in Figure 10.3. Three other implementations exhibited the same linear bit-length leakage (libgcrypt, MatrixSSL and SunEC), with MatrixSSL also leaking the Hamming weight of the nonce via a similar linear relationship with the signing duration. Further, two implementations tested (wolfSSL and Crypto++) exhibited similar leakage but with a more complex dependency due to more complex scalar-multiplication algorithms used in these implementations.

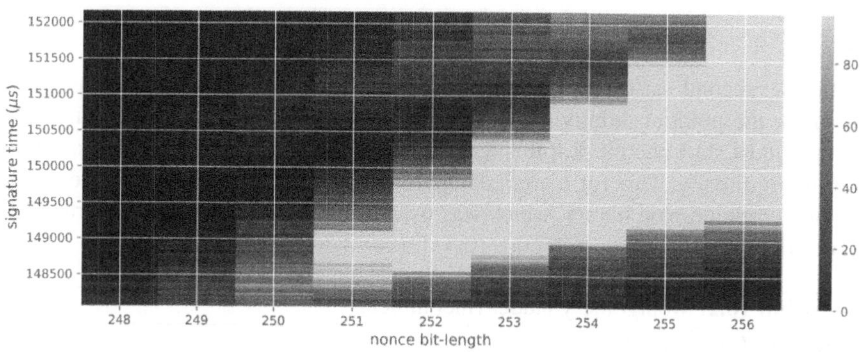

Figure 10.3. *The visible leakage of nonce's bit-length on signature times of the Athena IDProtect smartcard (on the secp256r1 curve) as measured by the host machine (Jancar et al. 2020). For a color version of this figure, see www.iste.co.uk/prouff/cryptography3.zip*

10.2.2. *Cause*

The exact cause of the vulnerability of each affected implementation differs slightly, as does the leakage itself, but the main issue is the same. The scalar multiplication implementation used in ECDSA is not constant time with respect to the bit-length of the scalar, as required by the constant-time criterion discussed in Chapter 7 of Volume 2. Implementing scalar multiplication that does not have this leak, yet uses incomplete addition formulas (that cannot correctly compute $\infty + Q$ or 2∞ in a side-channel indistinguishable way from $P + Q$ and $2P$), is very tricky. Even using a well-known constant-time algorithm for scalar multiplication, such as the Montgomery ladder (see Chapter 10 of Volume 2 for more background) can fail in this way when used with incomplete formulas. Using incomplete formulas, the two ladder variables are initialized either as $R_0 = \infty$, $R_1 = G$ (as in Algorithm 10.1) or as $R_0 = G$, $R_1 = 2G$ (as in Algorithm 10.2). In the first case, the computation can start at a fixed loop bound l, and thus it might seem that the bit-length will not be leaked through timing. However, all of the iterations processing the leading zero bits of k will input the point at infinity to incomplete formulas. As the formulas cannot handle this case, they need to be protected by detecting the input and short-circuiting, which obviously leaks via timing, as was the case in the libgcrypt implementation.

Algorithm 10.1. Montgomery ladder (complete)

function LADDER($G, k = (k_l, \ldots, k_0)_2$)
  $R_0 = \infty$; $R_1 = G$
  for $i = l$ **downto** 0 **do**
    $R_{\neg k_i} = R_0 + R_1$; $R_{k_i} = 2R_{k_i}$
  return R_0

In the second case, as in Algorithm 10.2, the incomplete formulas never encounter the point at infinity. However, the bit-length of k needs to be found, and the loop must start one bit past this length, thereby leaking the bit-length via timing even more directly. This (or a similar) approach was likely employed in the Atmel Toolbox cryptographic library, which was used in the Athena IDProtect smartcard as a collection of powertraces in Figure 10.4 shows.

Algorithm 10.2. Montgomery ladder (incomplete)

function LADDER($G, k = (k_l, \ldots, k_0)_2$)
  $R_0 = G$; $R_1 = 2G$
  for $i = |k| - 1$ **downto** 0 **do**
    $R_{\neg k_i} = R_0 + R_1$; $R_{k_i} = 2R_{k_i}$
  return R_0

10.2.3. *Attack*

As described in Chapter 8 of this volume, the knowledge of the most-significant bits of (EC)DSA can be used to mount a key recovery attack by first turning the knowledge into an instance of a Hidden Number Problem (HNP), then to an instance of the CVP and optionally the SVP. Hence, in this section, we will discuss the details specific to the Minerva vulnerability. Overall, the attack works as follows:

1) Collect N signatures (r_i, s_i) on messages m_i, while measuring the duration t_i.

2) Sort the signatures by t_i in ascending order and take d of the fastest.

3) Estimate the leading zero bits l_i of nonces of the fastest d out of N signatures.

4) Use the HNP to form a CVP instance based on l_i, r_i, s_i of the d signatures.

5) (Optionally) Transform the CVP instance into a SVP instance.

6) Solve the problem via lattice reduction methods (e.g. LLL and BKZ).

7) Extract and verify the correctness of the private key.

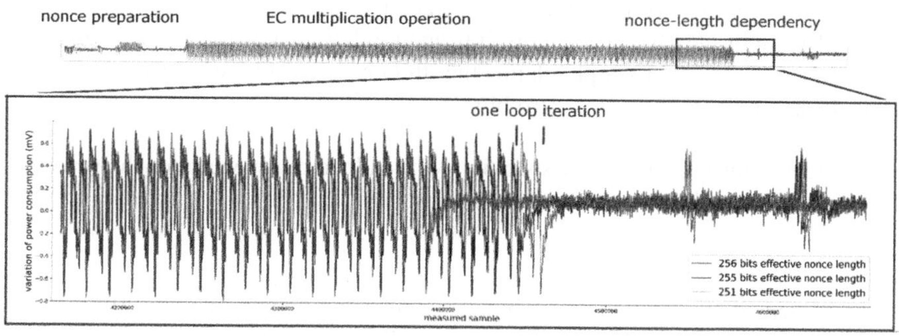

Figure 10.4. *The leakage of nonce bit-length on a power consumption trace of the Athena IDProtect smartcard as captured by an ordinary oscilloscope. The zoomed region displays the difference at the end of the scalar multiplication with nonces having 0, 1, and 5 leading zero bits. The pattern corresponding to a single iteration, and thus bit, is clearly discernible (Jancar et al. 2020). For a color version of this figure, see www.iste.co.uk/prouff/cryptography3.zip*

The first step of the attack is trivial. The only notable thing to mention is that the messages m_i only need to be distinct if deterministic nonce generation is used (see Chapter 8 of this volume); otherwise, they just need to be known to the attacker. This is because deterministic nonce generation would lead to the same nonce used for all of the signatures on the same message, and the leakage would not be useful.

In the second step, due to the nature of the linear relationship between nonce bit-length and signing duration, the attacker is sorting the signatures by the descending amount of leading zero bits l_i. The first (and fastest) signatures thus have the largest amount of leading zero bits in their nonces and thus usable information leaked to the attacker.

The third step computes the estimated leading zero bits l_i of unknown nonces k_i used in the fastest d out of N signatures by using the fact that nonces are generated uniformly at random modulo the curve order n. We can thus expect that the number of leading zero bits follows a sort of truncated geometric distribution with one-half of the nonces having $l_i = 0$, one-quarter having $l_i = 1$, etc. Then, taking into account the linear relationship between bit-length and signing duration t_i we obtain a clear method of estimating the l_i: sort them by duration and apply the above distribution. The slowest half of signatures would likely have nonces with full bit-length (thus $l_i = 0$), etc.

In the fourth step, the attacker needs to make a claim about the values of the most-significant bits of the nonces in order to form HNP inequalities and then the CVP lattice and target vectors. The attacker has a choice here; they can claim the most significant l_i bits to be zero, or they can include the $(l_i + 1)$-th bit and claim it is set to one. The latter clearly carries more information but also increases the probability of an error, as the former simply claims the ith nonce has at least l_i leading zero bits while the latter claims exactly l_i zero bits.

As steps 5 through 7 are not specific to the vulnerability, we refer the reader to Chapter 8 of this volume for more information.

10.2.3.1. *Improvements*

As presented above, the attack above is similar to one presented in 2011 against bit-length leakage in ECDSA in OpenSSL, discovered by Brumley and Tuveri. However, their attack did not compute the leading zero bit estimates l_i as above but simply put a constant bound l for all d signatures, which was not as effective. Their attack also introduced a method for handling errors in the claimed values of the most-significant bits, which often leads to a failure in extracting the correct private key. They proposed a change in step two of the attack by constructing random subsets of d signatures out of $d + e$ fastest (for some small values of $e \sim \frac{1}{4}d$) and repeating the attack, they could stumble upon an error-free subset and obtain the private key.

The Minerva authors discussed several possible attack improvements in their paper, including the above random subsets one, solving the CVP via transformation into SVP, as well as what they called a CVP + u-bitflips approach for solving errors.

Albrecht and Heninger (2021) focused on modifying steps 5 through 7 of the attack to not use lattice reduction techniques as a black-box but to incorporate the specifics of the attack in their internals. Concretely, they introduced a variant of the above lattice problems *with a predicate*, where the attacker has a way of verifying whether a private key guess is correct (by using the public key). They then gave efficient algorithms for these problems, either using lattice enumeration or sieving.

Sun et al. (2022) modified step four of the attack using an approach similar to CVP + u-bitflips but not with the goal of fixing errors; instead, guessing more bits of the secret material and thus obtaining the private key with a larger probability. They also investigated the properties of the transformation from CVP to SVP and its optimal parameterization.

10.2.4. *Impacted domains and disclosure*

The Minerva group of timing attack vulnerabilities in ECDSA signing coincided with (and exploited) the same type of leakage as TPM-Fail but targeted a different set of implementations, including smartcard certified under both CC and FIPS 140-2, the *Athena IDProtect*. Table 10.3 shows the list of analyzed libraries with scalar multiplication implementation used.

Type	Name	Version/Model	Scalar multiplier	Leakage
Library	OpenSSL	`1.1.1d`	Montgomery ladder[1]	no
	BouncyCasle	`1.58`	Comb method[2]	no
	SunEC	`JDK 7 - JDK 12`	Window-NAF	no
			Lopez-Dahab ladder	yes
	WolfSSL	`4.0.0`	Sliding window	yes[3]
	BoringSSL	`974f4dddf`	Window method	no
	libtomcrypt	`v1.18.2`	Sliding window	no
	libgcrypt	`1.8.4`	Double-and-add	yes
	Botan	`2.11.0`	Window method[4]	no
	Microsoft CNG	`10.0.17134.0`	Window method	no
	mbedTLS	`2.16.0`	Comb method	no
	MatrixSSL	`4.2.1`	Sliding window	yes
	Intel PP Crypto	`2020`	Window-NAF	no
	Crypto++	`8.2`	Unknown	yes
	IAIK ECCelerate	`6.0.1`	Unknown	no
Card	Athena IDProtect	`010b.0352.0005`	Unknown	yes
	NXP JCOP3	`J2A081, J2D081, J3H145`	Unknown	no
	Infineon JTOP	`52GLA080AL, SLE78`	Unknown	no
	G+D SmartCafe	`v6, v7`	Unknown	no

[1] Applies the fixed bit-length mitigation.
[2] Uses many scalar multiplication algorithms.
[3] Likely not exploitable, due to a small amount of leakage.
[4] Uses additive scalar blinding.

Table 10.3. *Libraries and devices analyzed in Jancar et al. (2020). For a color version of this table, see www.iste.co.uk/prouff/cryptography3.zip*

A manual analysis of the certificate reports and security targets from CC and FIPS 140-2 certificates about the vulnerable chip was used to report on the affected certified products. A single vulnerable CC certificate for the *Athena IDProtect* smartcard with ID https://sec-certs.org/cc/fca98ecd003e1b82/ was identified using CPLC (Card Production Life Cycle) data, which was also included in the certification report. However, the root cause of the vulnerability stemmed from another certified item, the *Atmel Cryptographic Toolbox 00.03.11.05* with certificate ID https://sec-certs. org/cc/49b4531177e9c3af/. Its security target describes two sets of functions for performing elliptic curve cryptography operations, *secure* and *fast*, with the fast functions not offering any SPA/DPA protection. It is likely that the vulnerable Athena IDProtect smartcard mistakenly decided to use the fast functions.

While the actual private key extraction demands non-trivial methods, the leakage itself is relatively easy to detect, showing surprising deficiencies in the testing of security devices and cryptographic libraries. The leakage can be detected using a computer timer only, with no need for power trace acquisition or similar SCA methods.

The vulnerabilities were responsibly disclosed to the affected vendors upon discovery, including assistance and patches fixing the vulnerability to several of them. All of the vulnerabilities in the software-only libraries are fixed in their newer versions. The state of the vulnerable chip AT90SC is unknown, as it is currently offered by the WiseKey company, which did not confirm or deny our findings regarding the chip. The Athena IDProtect card is no longer in production, and likely no new products are based on the vulnerable code after acquisition by NXP.

10.2.5. *Notes and further references*

– Section 10.2. The Minerva vulnerability presented in Jancar et al. (2020) was first found on the Athena IDProtect-certified smartcard ANSSI (2012) with cryptographic library. The authors provide a contentful web page for their attack at https://minerva.crocs.fi.muni.cz. The TPM-Fail vulnerability discovered by Moghimi et al. (2020) presented the same kind of leakage as Minerva in two separate TPMs.

– Section 10.2.1. ECTester, a tool by Jancar and Svenda (2018), was used to discover the vulnerability and collect data by the authors.

– Section 10.2.3.1. Brumley and Tuveri (2011) were the first to present the overall attack process on similar bit-length leakage, but targeting OpenSSL. Sun et al. (2022) presented the idea of guessing more bits of the secret and also investigated the CVP to SVP conversion step and its performance with different parameterization. Albrecht and Heninger (2021) introduced the bounded distance decoding with a predicate problem and gave efficient algorithms for solving it.

10.3. References

Albrecht, M.R. and Heninger, N. (2021). On bounded distance decoding with predicate: Breaking the "lattice barrier" for the hidden number problem. In *EUROCRYPT 2021, Part I*, Canteaut, A. and Standaert, F.-X. (eds). Springer, Heidelberg, Zagreb.

ANSSI (2012). Athena OS755/IDProtect v6 avec application IAS-ECC sur composant AT90SC28872RCU. Report [Online]. Available at: https://www.commoncriteriaportal.org/files/epfiles/ANSSI-CC2012-23fr.pdf.

Bernstein, D.J. and Lange, T. (2017). Reconstructing ROCA. Blog [Online]. Available at: https://blog.cr.yp.to/20171105-infineon.html.

Brumley, B.B. and Tuveri, N. (2011). Remote timing attacks are still practical. In *ESORICS 2011*, Atluri, V. and Díaz, C. (eds). Springer, Heidelberg, Leuven.

EMVCo (2017a). EMVCo product approval, ICCN0163, master component: M7892 A22/B11 [Online]. Available at: https://www.emvco.com/loase/EMVCoICCN0163R022017.pdf.

EMVCo (2017b). EMVCo product approval, ICCN0200, master component: M7893 B11 [Online]. Available at: https://www.emvco.com/loase/EMVCoICCN0200_R_02_2017.pdf.

ENISA (2018). Trust services security incidents 2017. Annual Report [Online]. Available at: https://www.enisa.europa.eu/publications/annual-report-trust-services-security-incidents-2017.

EU (2014). Regulation (EU) no 910/2014 of the European parliament and of the council of 23 July 2014 on electronic identification and trust services for electronic transactions in the internal market. Official Journal of the European Union [Online]. Available at: https://digital-strategy.ec.europa.eu/en/ policies/eidas-regulation.

Harder, J. (2017). Not even Coppersmith's attack. Blog [Online]. Available at: https://jix.one/not-even-coppersmiths-attack/.

Jancar, J. and Svenda, P. (2018). ECTester. Software [Online]. Available at: https://github.com/crocs-muni/ECTester.

Jancar, J., Sedlacek, V., Svenda, P., Sys, M. (2020). Minerva: The curse of ECDSA nonces. *IACR TCHES*, 2020(4), 281–308 [Online]. Available at: https://tches.iacr.org/index.php/TCHES/article/view/8684.

Klinec, D. and Svenda, P. (2017). ROCA: Infineon RSA key vulnerability. Software [Online]. Available at: https://github.com/crocs-muni/roca.

Kornblum, J.D. (2009). Implementing BitLocker drive encryption for forensic analysis. *Digital Investigation*, 5(3), 75–84 [Online]. Available at: http://www.sciencedirect.com/science/article/pii/S1742287609000024.

Kumar, N. and Kumar, V. (2008). Analysis of window vista bitlocker drive encryption. Presentation, NVLabs [Online]. Available at: http://www.nvlabs.in/uploads/projects/nvbit/nvbit_bitlocker_presentation.pdf.

Microsoft (2013). Technet: BitLocker overview [Online]. Available at: https://technet.microsoft.com/en-us/library/hh831713(v=ws.11).aspx.

Moghimi, D., Sunar, B., Eisenbarth, T., Heninger, N. (2020). TPM-FAIL: TPM meets timing and lattice attacks. In *USENIX Security 2020*, Capkun, S. and Roesner, F. (eds). USENIX Association, Berkeley.

Nemec, M., Sýs, M., Svenda, P., Klinec, D., Matyas, V. (2017). The return of Coppersmith's attack: Practical factorization of widely used RSA moduli. In *ACM CCS 2017*, Thuraisingham, B.M., Evans, D., Malkin, T., Xu, D. (eds). ACM Press, New York.

NVD (2017). CVE-2017-15361. Standard, National Vulnerability Database, National Institute of Standards and Technology [Online]. Available at: https://nvd.nist.gov/vuln/detail/CVE-2017-15361.

Pohlig, S.C. and Hellman, M.E. (2022). An improved algorithm for computing logarithms over GF(p) and its cryptographic significance. In *Democratizing Cryptography: The Work of Whitfield Diffie and Martin Hellman*, Slayton, R. (ed.) ACM, New York.

Produit, B.D. (2019). Optimization of the ROCA (CVE-2017-15361) attack. Master's Thesis, University of Tartu [Online]. Available at: https://comserv.cs.ut.ee/home/files/produitcybersecurity2019.pdf?study=ATILoputoo&reference=2ABC6CF8AB89C13221B4FAD657192FF787E425C1.

Sun, C., Espitau, T., Tibouchi, M., Abe, M. (2022). Guessing bits: Improved lattice attacks on (EC)DSA with nonce leakage. *IACR Trans. Cryptogr. Hardw. Embed. Syst.*, 2022(1), 391–413. doi: 10.46586/tches.v2022.i1.391-413.

Svenda, P., Nemec, M., Sekan, P., Kvasnovský, R., Formánek, D., Komárek, D., Matyás, V. (2016). The million-key question – Investigating the origins of RSA public keys. In *USENIX Security 2016*, Holz, T. and Savage, S. (eds). USENIX Association, Austin.

11

Security of Automotive Systems

Lennert WOUTERS, Benedikt GIERLICHS and Bart PRENEEL
COSIC, KU Leuven, Belgium

11.1. Introduction

The vast automotive ecosystem has an inherently large attack surface arising from its complexity and connectedness (Checkoway et al. 2011; Miller and Valasek 2014). In the automotive context, embedded attacks can be standalone, but often enable the discovery of a more scalable attack that can be more widely deployed.

For example, security vulnerabilities arising from the long-range wireless connectivity of vehicles are often the most severe. Such vulnerabilities can result in a large-scale remote attack, potentially affecting the safety of the vehicle's user and nearby road users. In their seminal work, Checkoway et al. (2011) presented the first publicly documented remote vehicle compromise. They demonstrated a remote vehicle compromise through its long-range cellular interface by calling the car's Telematics Control Unit (TCU) and playing a prerecorded audio file containing the exploit code. As a proof-of-concept their payload would force the car to reach out to an Internet Relay Chat (IRC) server, allowing the researchers to send commands to compromised vehicles. This command and control interface allowed to inject arbitrary packets on the compromised vehicle's internal controller area network (CAN).

The role of embedded attacks in such remote attacks should not be underestimated. Attackers often leverage physical access to a similar target vehicle or subsystem (e.g. an Electronic Control Unit (ECU)) to obtain secret information or to

Embedded Cryptography 3,
coordinated by Emmanuel PROUFF, Guénaël RENAULT,
Matthieu RIVAIN and Colin O'FLYNN.

accelerate the discovery of a scalable attack. In other words, attacks targeting the hardware components can allow us to obtain an initial foothold into the system or to extract the software being executed on the device. Obtaining this information accelerates vulnerability research.

This book covers a wide range of techniques that can be used to analyze and/or defeat the security of some embedded devices. It is not always clear how relevant these techniques are in real-world scenarios where the attacker may not have the same level of control as what is assumed in many research papers. Nevertheless, the applicability of these techniques in the real-world cannot be underestimated. The automotive sector is one of many sectors where such embedded attacks are relevant. In this chapter, we cover some attacks with real-world impact that target automotive systems. We will specifically focus on those works that use some of the techniques discussed in this book.

11.2. The embedded automotive attacker

Embedded automotive attackers apply the methods and techniques from embedded attacks to target automotive systems. The term "attacker" often has a negative connotation associated with it, which does not always reflect their goals. The motives to attack automotive systems can vary widely and are often without malicious intent.

The most widely imagined automotive attacker is someone who wants to steal cars, remotely harm a target or compromise a user's privacy. However, in practice it is likely that these are not the most common goals. Instead, embedded attackers may want to reverse engineer an ECU or other automotive components for various reasons. They may want to repair (or preserve older) vehicles for which the manufacturer is not offering spare parts or service manuals, or they may want to create a compatible (open-source) product or ECU with additional features. Legitimate owners may want to unlock software-locked features in their own vehicles. Researchers may want to demonstrate a technique, warn manufacturers of a security issue or simply want a fun challenge; all without malicious intent.

In some cases, an original equipment manufacturer (OEM) or car manufacturer may resort to the same offensive techniques to reverse engineer products of their competitors, often with the aim of so-called competitive analysis. Several companies offer competitive analysis as a service. These same techniques can be used by an OEM to steal intellectual property and to save time and money on the development of a competing product. Law enforcement agencies may want to retrieve forensic data from car systems or they may want to (briefly) gain access to a car.

The same techniques can thus be used for a broad range of end goals with different underlying incentives. Similarly, the same techniques are employed by a wide range of parties ranging from individual researchers to law enforcement agencies, each of which we can assume to have varying resources.

11.3. An overview of automotive attacks

This section provides a high-level overview of several types of attacks that target automotive systems. Here, we distinguish attacks that require physical proximity to the target vehicle, attacks that can be carried out remotely and attacks that do not target the vehicle directly.

11.3.1. *Proximity vehicle attacks*

A malicious attacker who is able to physically access a target vehicle has many tools at their disposal and can have multiple goals. The goal can be as simple as physically removing components from the vehicle. Tires, wheels, air bags and catalytic converters are among the most commonly stolen components. Alternatively, a car thief may try to use off-the-shelf locksmith and automotive repair tools to steal a vehicle, or items contained within. Similarly, some adversaries may attempt to gain access to the vehicle's interior with the goal to install privacy and/or safety compromising devices.

In some cases, car thieves remove a component (e.g. a radar module, headlight or mirror) to access the vehicle's CAN-bus wiring. By injecting specific CAN frames, it may then be possible to unlock the doors and to bypass the immobilizer (Hoppe et al. 2008). Tindell and Tabor (2023) reverse engineered a commercially available CAN injection tool disguised as a Bluetooth speaker that is being actively used to steal cars (Clatworthy 2023).

Furthermore, it may be possible to exploit vulnerabilities in diagnostic protocols to overwrite ECU firmware or to pair a new key fob to the car (Van den Herrewegen and Garcia 2018; Wouters et al. 2021). This same intimate knowledge of the CAN frames or the diagnostic authentication protocols for a specific vehicle can also be used to repair or modify vehicles.

Other attack vectors that can require some form of proximity include attacks that target tire pressure monitoring systems (Rouf et al. 2010), global navigation satellite system jamming and spoofing attacks (Tippenhauer et al. 2011; Zeng et al. 2017), machine learning systems (Song et al. 2018; Eykholt et al. 2018), and other relatively short range wireless interfaces such as Bluetooth and WiFi (Weinmann and Schmotzle 2020; Nie et al. 2017). Keyless entry systems are among the most widely researched automotive subsystems that use a short range wireless interface.

11.3.1.1. *Keyless entry and immobilizer attacks*

For almost 20 years, researchers have investigated the security of automotive keyless entry and immobiliser systems, yet many vulnerable systems remain and are still being deployed in brand new vehicles. For example, back in 2005 Bono et al. (2005) reverse engineered a cryptographically enabled transponder that used a proprietary 40-bit cipher named DST40. Almost 14 years later, Wouters et al. (2019) found that the same cipher was still being deployed in brand new vehicles. Similarly, Courtois et al. (2009) demonstrated the first cryptanalytic attacks targeting the HITAG2 stream cipher back in 2009. Multiple works improved upon those initial results and presented more practical attacks (Sun et al. 2011; Stembera and Novotný 2011; Verdult et al. 2012). Nevertheless, HITAG2 is still being used for remote keyless entry in recent vehicles (Garcia et al. 2016; Benadjila et al. 2017; Verstegen et al. 2018), meaning that vulnerable cars are likely to remain fielded for many years to come. Another example is the widely deployed KeeLoq block cipher, a proprietary block cipher owned by Microchip. The first cryptanalytic attacks targeting the KeeLoq block cipher were published in 2007 and 2008 (Bogdanov 2007a, 2007b; Courtois et al. 2008; Indesteege et al. 2008). These cryptanalytic attacks were followed by physical side-channel attacks that allowed us to recover the manufacturer key (Eisenbarth et al. 2008; Kasper et al. 2009). While KeeLoq does not appear to be widely deployed in newer vehicles these days, there are still many garage door openers and similar remote control systems that rely on KeeLoq.

Many car manufacturers and OEMs are adopting new products (e.g. DSTAES, HITAG-AES and KeeLoq-AES) that do implement standardized cryptographic primitives. Instead of opting for components specifically aimed at keyless entry systems, some manufacturers use certified secure elements. Unfortunately, a secure cipher (even in a secure implementation) is, by itself, not sufficient to guarantee practical security. Over the years, several weak key diversification schemes have been exposed in keyless entry systems (Kasper et al. 2009; Verdult et al. 2013; Garcia et al. 2016; Müllner et al. 2017; Wouters et al. 2020). In most cases, these key diversification issues allowed us to clone a key fob after recording only a small number of radio frequency (RF) transmissions.

Even in the absence of weak proprietary ciphers and key diversification issues, many of these systems remain vulnerable to protocol level attacks, including relay attacks (Desmedt et al. 1988; Hancke et al. 2009; Francis et al. 2010; Francillon et al. 2011; Yingtao Zeng and Li 2017) and jamming-and-eavesdropping attacks (Kasper et al. 2009; Kamkar 2015; Csikor et al. 2022). According to the Allgemeiner Deutscher Automobil-Club (ADAC) in January 2023, only 29 out of 567 evaluated car models were not vulnerable to a straightforward relay attack (ADAC 2023). Relay attack defenses are being adopted in the newest vehicles, most of these rely on the use of ultra-wideband (Gezici et al. 2005) and/or distance-bounding protocols (Brands and Chaum 1994; Abidin et al. 2021).

Recently some manufacturers have started adopting bluetooth low energy (BLE) as a communication standard for their keyless entry systems. Presumably this move to BLE is motivated by the introduction of smartphone applications that implement the same functionality as the key fob. This increased functionality and complexity results in a larger attack surface. Wouters et al. (2021) attacked the Tesla Model X keyless entry system by first compromising the BLE microcontroller in the key fob using a malicious firmware update. This allowed them to use the BLE interface to query the secure element in the key fob for a valid token that could be used to unlock the target vehicle. This case study will be covered in more detail in section 11.5. Similar to more classical implementations, these newer BLE keyless entry systems have also been shown vulnerable to protocol level attacks such as relay attacks (Jasek 2016; Herfurt 2022; Khan 2022).

Note that the weaknesses exposed in these systems are not only used with malicious intent: they can also be used to create compatible products or to repair vehicles (Wilson 2017). For example, weaknesses in immobilizer implementations are used to create aftermarket remote start devices. A vulnerability in a key fob pairing protocol can also be used by legitimate garage owners (who may not be able to access official manufacturer tools) to help customers who have lost their key fobs.

11.3.2. *Remote vehicle attacks*

Attacks targeting vehicles that do not require physical proximity are remote attacks. These can be the most devastating type of attack as they can typically scale more easily. Checkoway et al. (2011) presented the first publicly documented remote vehicle compromise in 2011. They demonstrated a remote vehicle compromise through its long-range cellular interface by calling the car's TCU and playing a prerecorded audio file containing the exploit code. As a proof-of-concept, their payload would force the car to reach out to an IRC server, allowing the researchers to send commands to compromised vehicles. This command and control interface allowed them to inject arbitrary packets on the compromised vehicle's internal CAN. In 2015, Miller and Valasek demonstrated a remote attack that allowed them to remotely compromise Jeep's in-vehicle infotainment (IVI) systems over the cellular network. Having compromised the IVI, they managed to upload malicious firmware to a Renesas V850 microcontroller, allowing to inject arbitrary CAN messages (Miller and Valasek 2015). Researchers from the Keen Security Lab at Tencent have performed several practical security evaluations of modern vehicles (Nie et al. 2017; Keen Security Lab 2018; Cai et al. 2019; Keen Security Lab 2021). Notably they identified remotely exploitable vulnerabilities in Tesla and BMW vehicles (Nie et al. 2017; Cai et al. 2019).

Broadcastable radio transmissions can be a potentially disastrous attack vector. Specifically, digital audio broadcasting (DAB), and to a lesser extent, the radio data system (RDS) are of interest. These systems allow us to transmit text, pictures and other data that are handled by the receiving vehicle. We are aware of attempts to use DAB and RDS as an attack vector, but not of any successful remote exploits (Davis 2015; Keen Security Lab 2021). However, there has been one report of Mazda IVI systems getting bricked due to an unintentionally malformed radio station broadcast (Gitlin 2022).

Modern vehicles often come with companion applications that allow for remote monitoring and control by the owner. These applications often interact with the vehicle through web application-based cloud services. Such applications publicly expose an intrinsically large attack surface. This attack surface has been explored by several researchers. Notably, Hunt (2016) revealed several vulnerabilities in the Nissan LEAF application programming interface (API) that was used by the companion mobile application. This research demonstrated that remote vehicle commands could be issued unauthenticated and only required the (enumerable) VIN of the target vehicle. In 2023, a team of web application security researchers identified several critical vulnerabilities in the web infrastructure of several car manufacturers such as Kia, Nissan, Mercedes-Benz, Hyundai, Ferrari, Porsche, Toyota, Land Rover and others (Curry et al. 2023). The vulnerabilities identified included account takeover, remote vehicle unlock and start, disclosure of personal data, access to administrator interfaces and remote code execution on production servers.

11.3.3. *Infrastructure attacks*

While we mainly cover direct vehicle attacks, it should be noted that an adversary can also opt to indirectly target vehicles through the attack surface of a related infrastructure. Such attacks could involve the automotive and general electronics supply chains or the critical infrastructure we rely on to safely navigate public roads.

For example, researchers have demonstrated flaws in traffic light controllers (Ghena et al. 2014) and traffic light emergency preemption systems (Williams 2017). Vehicle-to-everything (V2X) communication infrastructure also received substantial research attention, and Yoshizawa et al. (2023) provide a comprehensive review of the existing research in this field.

The increasing number of electric vehicles results in a rapid deployment of electric vehicle charging infrastructure. Johnson et al. (2022) provide an extensive overview of both the offensive and defensive electric vehicle charging research. For example, Baker and Martinovic (2019) demonstrated electromagnetic side-channel attacks that allowed us to eavesdrop on the power-line communication system used in the combined charging system. Besides academic research interest, the zero day initiative (ZDI) announced the inclusion of multiple electric vehicle chargers for their

2023 PWN2OWN competition, awarding up to $60,000 for vulnerabilities reported and demonstrated during the competition (Gorenc 2023).

11.4. Application of physical attacks in automotive security

All physical attacks that target a (micro-)processor or other electronic component are likely to be relevant for the automotive sector. Unfortunately, it is impossible for us to cover all such physical attacks in this section. Instead, we highlight research that includes physical attacks directly applied in the automotive context.

11.4.1. *Side-channel analysis*

In an offensive context, we consider as a passive, and typically a noninvasive analysis technique that can allow us to recover secret information from a device through the analysis of a physical observable (e.g. time, power consumption and electromagnetic emissions). In most cases, the attacker attempts to recover a secret cryptographic key from a device.

In the context of automotive applications, side-channel analysis typically requires physical access to the target device. Such physical side-channel attacks can scale when an attack performed on a single devices reveals secret information that allows them to easily compromise other devices. For example, researchers have shown that it is possible to retrieve the manufacturer key from a KeeLoq remote keyless entry receiver using side-channel analysis (Eisenbarth et al. 2008; Kasper et al. 2009). Recovery of this manufacturer key made it straightforward to recover the unique cryptographic key for any key fob made by the same manufacturer. Numerous similar key diversification issues have been identified over the years (Verdult et al. 2013; Garcia et al. 2016; Wouters et al. 2020), hence, it is likely that many of these can be exploited using side-channel analysis.

Researchers have also explored the application of side-channel analysis in scenarios where the attacker may be able to obtain physical access to the target device for a limited amount of time (i.e. an evil maid or evil valet type of scenario). For example, Eisenbarth et al. (2008) demonstrated KeeLoq key recovery by targeting the ICs used in key fobs, requiring as little as six power side-channel traces or as little as 10 EM traces. Oswald and Paar (2011) demonstrated practical side-channel attacks on Mifare DESFire RFID access cards, including a template attack that targets a key transfer. Wouters et al. (2010) performed side-channel attacks on DST80 key fob transponder ICs. Their profiled attack also targets a key transfer scenario and additionally considers the profiling of multiple devices to help overcome the portability problem.

Additionally, researchers have shown that side-channel analysis can be applied to recover the structure and weights of trained machine learning models (Wei et al. 2018;

Batina et al. 2019). It is possible that such attacks will become more prevalent in the automotive sector to extract the machine learning models used for autonomous driving capabilities. This could be done for competitive analysis purposes, or with the goal of IP theft.

Similar side-channel analysis techniques can also be applied for defensive purposes. For example, physical layer fingerprinting has been used to establish the authenticity of network nodes (Brik et al. 2008). Both physical layer fingerprinting and side-channel analysis are similar in that they apply statistical (time-series) analysis techniques to retrieve information from a physical observable. Researchers have applied these ideas in the automotive context in the form of intrusion detection systems (IDS) that can detect when a malicious ECU is present on the vehicle's internal networks (Cho and Shin 2016; Choi et al. 2018).

11.4.2. *Fault Injection*

Fault injection can be performed using multiple techniques: in this chapter, we assume an adversary with physical access to the target device, hence we will limit the discussion to physical fault-injection techniques that do not require code execution.

In practice, fault injection appears to be the most commonly applied physical attack. In many cases, fault injection allows us to retrieve the same or more information from the device under attack when compared to side-channel analysis. Additionally, a fault injection attack targeting a specific microcontroller can be developed once and applied to many different products using that same microcontroller regardless of the product specific firmware. For example, extracting a cryptographic key stored in flash memory may be achieved by performing a side-channel attack that targets the implementation of a cryptographic cipher. However, in practice it may be easier to circumvent debug security features using fault injection. In many cases, this would allow us to read all flash memory, including the cryptographic key. This is also reflected by commercially available device programmers that include the capability to bypass debug security features for some microcontrollers.

Many fault injection techniques exist (Bar-El et al. 2006), but voltage fault injection (Kömmerling and Kuhn 1999) and electromagnetic fault injection (Dehbaoui et al. 2012) are currently among the most widely applied in the automotive context. Researchers have demonstrated debug security feature bypasses using various fault injection techniques on a wide range of microcontrollers (Skorobogatov 2005; Bozzato et al. 2019; Van den Herrewegen et al. 2021). Similar techniques have proven useful in the automotive context. For example, voltage fault injection was used to extract firmware from a Renesas 78K0 microcontroller used in a body control module (Wouters et al. 2020). This allowed us to recover the proprietary DST80 cipher and revealed weak key derivation implementations used in immobilizer systems. O'Flynn (2020) demonstrated how the debug security features of the widely used MPC55xx and MPC56xx series PowerPC microcontrollers could be bypassed using EMFI, and this without modification of the target device. Wouters et al. (2022) used voltage fault injection to extract firmware from Texas Instruments SimpleLink microcontrollers to obtain key fob firmware.

Some automotive microcontrollers adhere to the automotive safety integrity level (ASIL) specification as defined in the ISO 26262 standard (ISO 2018). These microcontrollers have safety and fault-tolerance features that can help to mitigate certain fault injection attacks. Nevertheless, these safety focused features are by themselves not sufficient to stop a determined attacker (Wiersma and Pareja 2017; Melching 2022). For example, Melching successfully performed a voltage fault injection attack on a ASIL-D (the highest ASIL level) Renesas RH850 microcontroller used in an electronic power steering module. This allowed them to extract the firmware stored in the RH850 microcontroller and to claim a community bounty through the openpilot project (Melching 2022; COMMA 2021).

Instead of targeting a microcontroller's debug security features, it is also possible to target an application protocol stack instead. For example, Pareja and Cordoba demonstrated firmware extraction by bypassing the authentication mechanism implemented in the unified diagnostic services (UDS) (Pareja and Cordoba 2018).

Buhren et al. (2021) performed voltage fault injection attacks targeting AMD's secure processor by sending carefully timed commands to the processor's voltage regulators over a bus interface. This technique was later applied by Werling et al. (2023) to load custom car configuration data, allowing them to enable certain software-locked features in Tesla vehicles.

Fault injection techniques can also be used during the development of automotive electronics, specifically when evaluating the safety of automotive components. O'Flynn (2021) demonstrated that electromagnetic fault injection can be used to evaluate the resilience of automotive components to naturally occurring faults in the context of the ISO 26262 standard ISO (2018).

11.5. Case study: Tesla Model X keyless entry system

This section provides a high-level overview of the Tesla Model X remote keyless entry system security evaluation performed in Wouters et al. (2021). In contrast to many other keyless entry system, this system employs secure symmetric-key and public-key cryptographic primitives implemented on a Common Criteria–certified secure element.

11.5.1. *The key fob*

Figure 11.1 shows a disassembled Tesla Model X key fob. This key fob is capable of receiving messages over a low frequency (22 kHz) channel as well as establish a BLE connection with the car. Additionally, this key fob uses a secure element for all cryptographic operations. For example, when the unlock button is pressed on the key fob, the secure element will use an AES key stored within to generate a one-time unlock token. Secure elements can contain vulnerabilities, but they are rarely the easiest way to compromise a system. In this key fob design, it is clear that the Texas Instruments CC2541 BLE SoC has a much larger attack surface. Furthermore, in this case a compromised CC2541 will allow an adversary to interact with the secure element and request an unlock token.

Figure 11.1. *The Model X key fob PCB (top side). The main components are (1) Texas Instruments CC2541 BLE SoC, (2) TI CC2590 BLE range extender, (3) Maxim integrated MAX2153E 22 kHz transponder, (4) analog devices ADXL362 MEMS accelerometer and (5) Infineon SLM97CFX1M00PE secure element. The red circle indicates the test point for the Secure Element's IO interface. This figure was taken from Wouters et al. (2021). For a color version of this figure, see www.iste.co.uk/prouff/cryptography3.zip*

During our security evaluation, we determined that the key fob exposes several security critical BLE characteristics. Notably, we found that it was possible to send certain allow-listed commands to the secure element through the BLE interface, however the commands required for an attack were not allowed. Additionally, we found that the BLE interface allowed for over-the-air firmware updates. However, this implementation did not properly verify the authenticity of a received firmware update. This vulnerability allowed us to wirelessly perform a firmware update of the BLE SoC in the key fob and this update allowed us to send arbitrary commands to the secure element. In other words, the malicious firmware update allowed us to request a valid unlock token from the secure element: this token could then be used to unlock the target vehicle. Starting the car using this same method was not as easy in practice, as a challenge response authentication protocol is performed between the car and the key fob.

The body control module (BCM) played a critical role in our ability to push a malicious firmware update to the key fob, as we used a modified BCM to force the key fob to wake-up and start advertising as a BLE peripheral.

11.5.2. *The body control module*

In normal operating conditions, the BCM in the Tesla Model X is responsible for unlocking the doors, controlling interior lightning and setting off the alarm siren among other things. Additionally, the BCM is also the component inside the car that communicates with the key fob and that allows us to pair additional key fobs to the car through its diagnostic interface.

As discussed in section 11.5.1, we were able to wirelessly compromise a key fob and then request a valid unlock token that could be used to gain access to the car's interior. But we could not easily use that same technique to start the car. To that end, we reverse-engineered the process of pairing a key fob to the car.

To reverse-engineer the key fob pairing and provisioning processes, we created a bench setup that allowed us to interact with a BCM over CAN as well as sniff relevant signals (e.g. communication with the secure element) using a logic analyzer. Additionally, we reverse-engineered parts of a proprietary tool used by Tesla for diagnostics and servicing. The overall reverse-engineering process is explained in more detail in Wouters et al. (2021).

Our analysis of the reverse-engineered pairing and provisioning protocols revealed that an adversary could pair an illegitimate key fob to the car without requiring access to Tesla's proprietary software tools. Someone who is able to gain physical access to the vehicle's interior can reach the diagnostic connector and can thus pair any key fob to the car. While this weakness in the pairing protocol can be abused by malicious actors, it can also be a valuable tool for independent repair shops that want to service these vehicles.

11.5.3. *Putting it all together*

The vulnerabilities we identified in the Tesla Model X key fob and the key fob pairing protocols can be combined to achieve a practical attack. To demonstrate this, we built a proof-of-concept (PoC) device, as shown in Figure 11.2, that allowed us to carry out the full attack within minutes.

Figure 11.2. *The PoC device consists of a battery and a DC-DC converter that is used to power the Raspberry Pi Model 3b+ with a two-channel CAN-BUS shield and the modified BCM. This figure was taken from Wouters et al. (2021). For a color version of this figure, see www.iste.co.uk/prouff/cryptography3.zip*

To summarize, as an attacker we could walk up to a target Tesla Model X and read its vehicle identification number (VIN) from the windshield. This VIN number, in combination with our modified BCM, could then be used to wirelessly wake up the target's key fob. Next, a malicious firmware update was pushed to the key fob, enabling us to retrieve a one-time unlock token. We could then go back to the target car and unlock it using this token, allowing us to access the vehicle's interior without setting off the alarm. Afterwards, we could connect our PoC device to the diagnostic connector. We used a Raspberry Pi combined with a CAN-shield to orchestrate the pairing process between the car's BCM and our modified key fob. With a paired key fob at our disposal, it was then possible to drive off with the car or to return to the car at any other point in time to access it.

As a mitigation strategy, Tesla pushed software updates to the affected key fobs, fixing the vulnerability in the firmware update process. However, as far as we know the vulnerability in the pairing protocol was not fixed. On the one hand, this means that a vulnerability remained unresolved in this system; on the other hand, this issue has been used by others to service vehicles.

11.6. Conclusion

This chapter provided an overview of automotive sub-systems that are often targeted by automotive attackers, the incentives that may exist to attack these sub-systems and the techniques that are used to do so.

The automotive ecosystem suffers from a large attack surface that is likely to become even larger in the foreseeable future due to the introduction of new technologies, more connected features and self-driving capabilities. The increasing connectedness of these vehicles also results in this attack surface being more widely exposed and reachable. It is thus not unlikely that flaws identified in companion apps will be (or have already been) exploited with malicious intent.

Vehicle owners often have a desire and should have the right to repair their own vehicles or to have their vehicle repaired by an independent technician. This often opposes the desire of manufacturers to protect their intellectual property and their desire for control over after-sales services. It could be interesting for the research community to help design methods and techniques that enable both repairability and IP protection.

As mentioned in section 11.3.2, we are not aware of any remote attacks that exploit broadcast radio systems such as DAB. This could indicate that this is an under-explored research direction. Similarly, we have not observed any remote side-channel attacks on automotive systems. Some key fobs may be vulnerable to screaming side channels (Camurati et al. 2018, 2020), but we are not aware of such attacks being demonstrated.

11.7. References

Abidin, A., El Soussi, M., Romme, J., Boer, P., Singelée, D., Bachmann, C. (2021). Secure, accurate, and practical narrow-band ranging system. *IACR TCHES*, 2021(2), 106–135.

ADAC (2023). Autos und Motorräder mit Keyless Schlßssel, die der ADAC illegal öffnen und wegfahren konnte [Online]. Available at: https://assets.adac.de/image/upload/v1674556739/ADAC-eV/KOR/Text/PDF/Keyless_Liste_2023_560_Autos_jeiyj6.pdf.

Baker, R. and Martinovic, I. (2019). Losing the car keys: Wireless PHY-layer insecurity in EV charging. In *USENIX Security 2019*, Heninger, N. and Traynor, P. (eds). USENIX Association, Berkeley.

Bar-El, H., Choukri, H., Naccache, D., Tunstall, M., Whelan, C. (2006). The sorcerer's apprentice guide to fault attacks. *Proc. IEEE*, 94(2), 370–382. doi: 10.1109/JPROC.2005.862424.

Batina, L., Bhasin, S., Jap, D., Picek, S. (2019). CSI NN: Reverse engineering of neural network architectures through electromagnetic side channel. In *USENIX Security 2019*, Heninger, N. and Traynor, P. (eds). USENIX Association, Berkeley.

Benadjila, R., Renard, M., Lopes-Esteves, J., Kasmi, C. (2017). One car, two frames: Attacks on Hitag-2 remote keyless entry systems revisited. In *11th USENIX Workshop on Offensive Technologies, WOOT 2017*, 14–15 August. USENIX Association, Berkeley [Online]. Available at: https://www.usenix.org/conference/woot17/workshop-program/presentation/benadjila.

Bogdanov, A. (2007a). Cryptanalysis of the keeloq block cipher. Report 2007/055, Cryptology ePrint Archive. [Online]. Available at: https://eprint.iacr.org/2007/055.

Bogdanov, A. (2007b). Linear slide attacks on the keeloq block cipher. *Information Security and Cryptology, Third SKLOIS Conference, Inscrypt 2007*, 31 August–5 September. Springer, Berlin, Heidelberg. doi: 10.1007/978-3-540-79499-8_7.

Bono, S., Green, M., Stubblefield, A., Juels, A., Rubin, A.D., Szydlo, M. (2005). Security analysis of a cryptographically-enabled RFID device. In *USENIX Security 2005*, McDaniel, P.D. (ed.). USENIX Association, Berkeley.

Bozzato, C., Focardi, R., Palmarini, F. (2019). Shaping the glitch: Optimizing voltage fault injection attacks. *IACR TCHES*, 2019(2), 199–224.

Brands, S. and Chaum, D. (1994). Distance-bounding protocols. In *EUROCRYPT'93*, Helleseth, T. (ed.). Springer, Berlin, Heidelberg.

Brik, V., Banerjee, S., Gruteser, M., Oh, S. (2008). Wireless device identification with radiometric signatures. In *Proceedings of the 14th Annual International Conference on Mobile Computing and Networking, MOBICOM*, 14–19 September. ACM Press, New York. doi: 10.1145/1409944.1409959.

Buhren, R., Jacob, H.N., Krachenfels, T., Seifert, J. (2021). One glitch to rule them all: Fault injection attacks against AMD's secure encrypted virtualization. In *CCS '21: 2021 ACM SIGSAC Conference on Computer and Communications Security*, 15–19 November. ACM Press, New York. doi: 10.1145/3460120.3484779.

Cai, Z., Wang, A., Zhang, W., Gruffke, M., Schweppe, H. (2019). 0-days & mitigations: Roadways to exploit and secure connected BMW cars. Black Hat USA [Online]. Available at: https://i.blackhat.com/USA-19/Thursday/us-19-Cai-0-Days-And-Mitigations-Roadways-To-Exploit-And-Secure-Connected-BMW-Cars-wp.pdf.

Camurati, G., Poeplau, S., Muench, M., Hayes, T., Francillon, A. (2018). Screaming channels: When electromagnetic side channels meet radio transceivers. In *ACM CCS 2018*, Lie, D., Mannan, M., Backes, M., Wang, X. (eds). ACM Press, New York.

Camurati, G., Francillon, A., Standaert, F.-X. (2020). Understanding screaming channels: From a detailed analysis to improved attacks. *IACR TCHES*, 2020(3), 358–401.

Checkoway, S., McCoy, D., Kantor, B., Anderson, D., Shacham, H., Savage, S., Koscher, K., Czeskis, A., Roesner, F., Kohno, T. (2011). Comprehensive experimental analyses of automotive attack surfaces. In *USENIX Security 2011*. USENIX Association, Berkeley.

Cho, K.-T. and Shin, K.G. (2016). Fingerprinting electronic control units for vehicle intrusion detection. In *USENIX Security 2016*, Holz, T. and Savage, S. (eds). USENIX Association, Berkeley.

Choi, W., Jo, H.J., Woo, S., Chun, J.Y., Park, J., Lee, D.H. (2018). Identifying ECUs using inimitable characteristics of signals in controller area networks. *IEEE Trans. Veh. Technol.*, 67(6), 4757–4770. doi: 10.1109/TVT.2018.2810232.

Clatworthy, B. (2023). Luxury cars are gone in 90 seconds with thief kit. *The Times* [Online]. Available at: https://www.thetimes.co.uk/article/luxury-cars-are-gone-in-90-seconds- with-thief-kit-z300g0njf.

COMMA (2021). openpilot/etc. on Toyota/Lexus/Subaru with TSK/ECU SECURITY KEY/SecOC [Online]. Available at: https://web.archive.org/web/20230918084549/ https://github.com/commaai/openpilot/discussions/19932.

Courtois, N., Bard, G.V., Wagner, D. (2008). Algebraic and slide attacks on KeeLoq. In *FSE 2008*, Nyberg, K. (ed.). Springer, Berlin, Heidelberg.

Courtois, N., O'Neil, S., Quisquater, J.-J. (2009). Practical algebraic attacks on the Hitag2 stream cipher. In *ISC 2009*, Samarati, P., Yung, M., Martinelli, F., Ardagna, C.A. (eds). Springer, Berlin, Heidelberg.

Csikor, L., Lim, H.W., Wong, J.W., Ramesh, S., Parameswarath, R.P., Chan, M.C. (2022). Rollback: A new time-agnostic replay attack against the automotive remote keyless entry systems. *arXiv:2210.11923v1* [Online]. Available at: https://arxiv.org/abs/2210.11923.

Curry, S., Rivera, N., Buerhaus, B., Robert, M., Carroll, I., Rhinehart, J., Shah, S. (2023). Web hackers vs. the auto industry: Critical vulnerabilities in Ferrari, BMW, Rolls Royce, Porsche, and more [Online]. Available at: https://web.archive.org/web/~20230919115348/https://samcurry.net/web-hackers-vs-the-auto-industry/.

Davis, A. (2015). Broadcasting your attack: Security testing DAB radio in cars [Online]. Available at: https://troopers.de/media/filerpublic/18/4f/184fa903-3610-4647-9cb0-bb7644d3f295/broadcastingyourattacksecuritytestingdabradioincars.pdf.

Dehbaoui, A., Dutertre, J., Robisson, B., Tria, A. (2012). Electromagnetic transient faults injection on a hardware and a software implementations of AES. In *2012 Workshop on Fault Diagnosis and Tolerance in Cryptography*, 9 September. IEEE, Leuven. doi: 10.1109/FDTC.2012.15.

Desmedt, Y., Goutier, C., Bengio, S. (1988). Special uses and abuses of the Fiat-Shamir passport protocol. In *CRYPTO'87*, Pomerance, C. (ed.). Springer, Berlin, Heidelberg.

Eisenbarth, T., Kasper, T., Moradi, A., Paar, C., Salmasizadeh, M., Shalmani, M.T.M. (2008). On the power of power analysis in the real world: A complete break of the KeeLoqCode hopping scheme. In *CRYPTO 2008*, Wagner, D. (ed.). Springer, Berlin, Heidelberg.

Eykholt, K., Evtimov, I., Fernandes, E., Li, B., Rahmati, A., Xiao, C., Prakash, A., Kohno, T., Song, D. (2018). Robust physical-world attacks on deep learning visual classification. In *2018 IEEE Conference on Computer Vision and Pattern Recognition, CVPR 2018*, 18–22 June, Salt Lake City [Online]. Available at: http://openaccess.thecvf.com/content_cvpr_2018/html/Eykholt_Robust_Physical-World_Attacks_CVPR_2018_paper.html.

Francillon, A., Danev, B., Capkun, S. (2011). Relay attacks on passive keyless entry and start systems in modern cars. In *NDSS 2011*. The Internet Society, Reston.

Francis, L., Hancke, G.P., Mayes, K., Markantonakis, K. (2010). Practical NFC peer-to-peer relay attack using mobile phones. In *Radio Frequency Identification: Security and Privacy Issues – 6th International Workshop, RFIDSec 2010*, 8–9 June. Springer, Berlin, Heidelberg. doi: 10.1007/978-3-642-16822-2_4.

Garcia, F.D., Oswald, D., Kasper, T., Pavlidès, P. (2016). Lock it and still lose it – On the (in)security of automotive remote keyless entry systems. In *USENIX Security 2016*, Holz, T. and Savage, S. (eds). USENIX Association, Berkeley.

Gezici, S., Tian, Z., Giannakis, G.B., Kobayashi, H., Molisch, A.F., Poor, H.V., Sahinoglu, Z. (2005). Localization via ultra-wideband radios: A look at positioning aspects for future sensor networks. *IEEE Signal Process. Mag.*, 22(4), 70–84. doi: 10.1109/MSP.2005.1458289.

Ghena, B., Beyer, W., Hillaker, A., Pevarnek, J., Halderman, J.A. (2014). Green lights forever: Analyzing the security of traffic infrastructure. In *8th USENIX Workshop on Offensive Technologies, WOOT '14*, 19 August. USENIX Association, Berkeley [Online]. Available at: https://www.usenix.org/conference/woot14/workshop-program/presentation/ghena.

Gitlin, J.M. (2022). Radio station snafu in seattle bricks some Mazda infotainment systems [Online]. Available at: https://web.archive.org/web/20230919145412/ https://arstechnica.com/cars/2022/02/radio-station-snafu-in-seattle-bricks-some-mazda-infotainment-systems/.

Gorenc, B. (2023). Revealing the targets and rules for the first PWN2OWN automotive [Online]. Available at: https://web.archive.org/web/20230919075401/ https://www.zerodayinitiative.com/blog/2023/8/28/revealing-the-targets-and-rules-for-the-first-pwn2own-automotive.

Hancke, G.P., Mayes, K., Markantonakis, K. (2009). Confidence in smart token proximity: Relay attacks revisited. *Comput. Secur.*, 28(7), 615–627. doi: 10.1016/j.cose.2009.06.001.

Herfurt, M. (2022). Project TEMPA [Online]. Available at: https://trifinite.org/stuff/projecttempa/.

Hoppe, T., Kiltz, S., Dittmann, J. (2008). Security threats to automotive CAN networks – Practical examples and selected short-term countermeasures. In *Computer Safety, Reliability, and Security, 27th International Conference, SAFECOMP 2008*, 22–25 September. Springer, Berlin, Heidelberg. doi: 10.1007/ 978-3-540-87698-4_21.

Hunt, T. (2016). Controlling vehicle features of Nissan LEAFs across the globe via vulnerable APIs [Online]. Available at: https://www.troyhunt.com/controlling-vehicle-features-of-nissan/.

Indesteege, S., Keller, N., Dunkelman, O., Biham, E., Preneel, B. (2008). A practical attack on KeeLoq. In *EUROCRYPT 2008*, Smart, N.P. (ed.). Springer, Berlin, Heidelberg.

ISO (2018). ISO 26262 – Road vehicles functional safety package – (Parts 1 to 12). Standard, International Organization for Standardization.

Jasek, S. (2016). GATTacking Bluetooth smart devices – Introducing a new BLE proxy tool. Document, Securing [Online]. Available at: https://www.blackhat.com/docs/us-16/materials/us-16-Jasek-GATTacking-Bluetooth-Smart-Devices-Introducing-a-New-BLE-Proxy-Tool-wp.pdf.

Johnson, J., Berg, T., Anderson, B., Wright, B. (2022). Review of electric vehicle charger cybersecurity vulnerabilities, potential impacts, and defenses. *Energies*, 15(11), 3931. doi: 10.3390/en15113931.

Kamkar, S. (2015). Drive it like you hacked it. In *DEF CON 23* [Online]. Available at: https://samy.pl/defcon2015/.

Kasper, M., Kasper, T., Moradi, A., Paar, C. (2009). Breaking KeeLoq in a flash: On extracting keys at lightning speed. In *AFRICACRYPT 09*, Preneel, B. (ed.). Springer, Berlin, Heidelberg.

Keen Security Lab (2018). Experimental security assessment of BMW cars: A summary report. Report, Keen Security Lab, Shenzhen [Online]. Available at: https://keenlab.tencent.com/en/whitepapers/ExperimentalSecurityAssessmentofBMWCarsbyKeenLab.pdf.

Keen Security Lab (2021). Mercedes-Benz MBUX security research report. Report, Keen Security Lab, Shenzhen [Online]. Available at: https://keenlab.tencent.com/en/whitepapers/MercedesBenzSecurityResearchReportFinal.pdf.

Khan, S.Q. (2022). Popping locks, stealing cars, and breaking a billion other things: Bluetooth LE link layer relay attacks. *Hardwear.io* [Online]. Available at: https://hardwear.io/netherlands-2022/speakers/sultan-khan.php.

Kömmerling, O. and Kuhn, M.G. (1999). Design principles for tamper-resistant smartcard processors. In *Proceedings of the 1st Workshop on Smartcard Technology, Smartcard 1999*, 10–11 May. USENIX Association, Berkeley [Online]. Available at: https://www.usenix.org/conference/usenix-workshop-smartcard-technology/design-principles-tamper-resistant-smartcard.

Melching, W. (2022). Bypassing the Renesas RH850/P1M-E read protection using fault injection. *I CAN Hack* [Online]. Available at: https://blog.willemmelching.nl/carhacking/2022/11/08/rh850-glitch/.

Miller, C. and Valasek, C. (2014). A survey of remote automotive attack surfaces. Technical White Paper, IOActive, Seattle [Online]. Available at: https://ioactive.com/pdfs/IOActive_Remote_Attack_Surfaces.pdf.

Miller, C. and Valasek, C. (2015). Remote exploitation of an unaltered passenger vehicle. Technical White Paper, IOActive, Seattle [Online]. Available at: https://ioactive.com/pdfs/IOActive_Remote_Car_Hacking.pdf.

Müllner, M., Kammerstetter, M., Kudera, C., Burian, D. (2017). Uncovering vulnerabilities in Hoermann BiSecur: An AES encrypted radio system. Chaos Communication Club [Online]. Available at: https://media.ccc.de/v/34c3-9029-uncoveringvulnerabilitiesinhoermannbisecur.

Nie, S., Liu, L., Du, Y. (2017). Free-Fall: Hacking Tesla from wireless to CAN bus. Black Hat Briefing, Keen Security Lab, Shenzhen [Online]. Available at: https://www.blackhat.com/docs/us-17/thursday/us-17-Nie-Free-Fall-Hacking-Tesla-From-Wireless-To-CAN-Bus-wp.pdf.

O'Flynn, C. (2020). BAM BAM!! On reliability of EMFI for in-situ automotive ECU attacks. Report 2020/937, Cryptology ePrint Archive [Online]. Available at: https://eprint.iacr.org/2020/937.

O'Flynn, C. (2021). EMFI for safety-critical testing of automotive systems. Report 2021/1217, Cryptology ePrint Archive [Online]. Available at: https://eprint.iacr.org/2021/1217.

Oswald, D. and Paar, C. (2011). Breaking Mifare DESFire MF3ICD40: Power analysis and templates in the real world. In *CHES 2011*, Preneel, B. and Takagi, T. (eds). Springer, Berlin, Heidelberg.

Pareja, R. and Cordoba, S. (2018). Fault injection on automotive diagnostic protocols: Bypassing the security of protected UDS implementations. White Paper, Riscure, Delft [Online]. Available at: https://riscureprodstorage.blob.core.windows.net/production/2018/06/RiscureWhitepaper Faultinjectiononautomotivediagnosticprotocols.pdf.

Rouf, I., Miller, R.D., Mustafa, H.A., Taylor, T., Oh, S., Xu, W., Gruteser, M., Trappe, W., Seskar, I. (2010). Security and privacy vulnerabilities of in-car wireless networks: A tire pressure monitoring system case study. In *USENIX Security 2010*. USENIX Association, Berkeley.

Skorobogatov, S.P. (2005). Semi-invasive attacks: A new approach to hardware security analysis. PhD Thesis, University of Cambridge, Cambridge [Online]. Available at: https://ethos.bl.uk/OrderDetails.do?uin=uk.bl.ethos.614760.

Song, D., Eykholt, K., Evtimov, I., Fernandes, E., Li, B., Rahmati, A., Tramèr, F., Prakash, A., Kohno, T. (2018). Physical adversarial examples for object detectors. In *12th USENIX Workshop on Offensive Technologies, WOOT 2018*, 13–14 August. USENIX Association, Berkeley. Available at: https://www.usenix.org/conference/woot18/presentation/eykholt.

Stembera, P. and Novotný, M. (2011). Breaking Hitag2 with reconfigurable hardware. In *14th Euromicro Conference on Digital System Design, Architectures, Methods and Tools, DSD 2011*, 31 August–2 September. IEEE, Oulu. doi: 10.1109/DSD.2011.77.

Sun, S., Hu, L., Xie, Y., Zeng, X. (2011). Cube cryptanalysis of Hitag2 stream cipher. In *CANS 11*, Lin, D., Tsudik, G., Wang, X. (eds). Springer, Berlin, Heidelberg.

Tindell, K. and Tabor, I. (2023). CAN Injection: Keyless car theft. *CANIS Automotive Labs* [Online]. Available at: https://kentindell.github.io/2023/04/03/can-injection/.

Tippenhauer, N.O., Pöpper, C., Rasmussen, K.B., Capkun, S. (2011). On the requirements for successful GPS spoofing attacks. In *ACM CCS 2011*, Chen, Y., Danezis, G., Shmatikov, V. (eds). ACM Press, New York.

Van den Herrewegen, J. and Garcia, F.D. (2018). Beneath the bonnet: A breakdown of diagnostic security. In *ESORICS 2018*. Springer, Heidelberg.

Van den Herrewegen, J., Oswald, D., Garcia, F.D., Temeiza, Q. (2021). Fill your boots: Enhanced embedded bootloader exploits via fault injection and binary analysis. *IACR TCHES*, 2021(1), 56–81.

Verdult, R., Garcia, F.D., Balasch, J. (2012). Gone in 360 seconds: Hijacking with Hitag2. In *USENIX Security 2012*, Kohno, T. (ed.). USENIX Association, Berkeley.

Verdult, R., Garcia, F.D., Ege, B. (2013). Dismantling megamos crypto: Wirelessly lockpicking a vehicle immobilizer. *USENIX Security 2013*, King, S.T. (ed.). USENIX Association, Berkeley.

Verstegen, A., Verdult, R., Bokslag, W. (2018). Hitag 2 hell – Brutally optimizing guess-and-determine attacks. In *12th USENIX Workshop on Offensive Technologies, WOOT 2018*, 13–14 August. USENIX Association, Berkeley [Online]. Available at: https://www.usenix.org/conference/woot18/presentation/verstegen.

Wei, L., Luo, B., Li, Y., Liu, Y., Xu, Q. (2018). I know what you see: Power side-channel attack on convolutional neural network accelerators. In *Proceedings of the 34th Annual Computer Security Applications Conference, ACSAC 2018*, 3–7 December. ACM Press, New York. doi: 10.1145/3274694.3274696.

Weinmann, R.-P. and Schmotzle, B. (2020). TBONE – A zero-click exploit for Tesla MCUs. Document, Comsecuris, Duisburg [Online]. Available at: https://kunnamon.io/tbone/tbone-v1.0-redacted.pdf.

Werling, C., Kßhnapfel, N., Jacob, H.N., Drokin, O. (2023). Jailbreaking an electric vehicle in 2023 or what it means to hotwire Tesla's x86-based seat heater. Black Hat Briefings [Online]. Available at: http://i.blackhat.com/BH-US-23/Presentations/US-23-Werling-Jailbreaking-Teslas.pdf.

Wiersma, N. and Pareja, R. (2017). Safety != security: On the resilience of ASIL-D certified microcontrollers against fault injection attacks. In *2017 Workshop on Fault Diagnosis and Tolerance in Cryptography, FDTC 2017*, 25 September. IEEE, Taipei. doi: 10.1109/FDTC.2017.15.

Williams, E. (2017). Mike Ossmann And Dominic Spill: IR, Pirates! *Hackaday* [Online]. Available at: https://hackaday.com/2017/11/29/mike-ossmann-and-dominic-spill-ir-pirates/.

Wilson, B.L. (2017). Saving my 97 chevy by hacking it. *International Journal of PoC||GTFO*, 0x16 [Online]. Available at: https://www.alchemistowl.org/pocorgtfo/.

Wouters, L., Marin, E., Ashur, T., Gierlichs, B., Preneel, B. (2019). Fast, furious and insecure: Passive keyless entry and start systems in modern supercars. *IACR TCHES*, 2019(3), 66–85.

Wouters, L., Van den Herrewegen, J., Garcia, F.D., Oswald, D., Gierlichs, B., Preneel, B. (2020). Dismantling DST80-based immobiliser systems. *IACR TCHES*, 2020(2), 99–127.

Wouters, L., Gierlichs, B., Preneel, B. (2021). My other car is your car: Compromising the Tesla Model X keyless entry system. *IACR TCHES*, 2021(4), 149–172.

Wouters, L., Gierlichs, B., Preneel, B. (2022). On the susceptibility of Texas Instruments SimpleLink platform microcontrollers to non-invasive physical attacks. In *Constructive Side-Channel Analysis and Secure Design – 13th International Workshop, COSADE 2022*, 11–12 April. Springer, Berlin, Heidelberg. doi: 10.1007/978-3-030-99766-3_7.

Yingtao Zeng, Q.Y. and Li, J. (2017). Chasing cars: Keyless entry system attacks. *HITB Security Conference*. Hack In The Box, Kuala Lumpur [Online]. Available at: https://conference.hitb.org/hitbsecconf2017ams/sessions/chasing-cars- keyless-entry-system-attacks/.

Yoshizawa, T., Singelée, D., Mühlberg, J.T., Delbruel, S., Taherkordi, A., Hughes, D., Preneel, B. (2023). A survey of security and privacy issues in V2X communication systems. *ACM Comput. Surv.*, 55(9), 185:1–185:36. doi: 10.1145/3558052.

Zeng, K.C., Shu, Y., Liu, S., Dou, Y., Yang, Y. (2017). A practical GPS location spoofing attack in road navigation scenario. In *Proceedings of the 18th International Workshop on Mobile Computing Systems and Applications, HotMobile 2017*, 21–22 February. ACM Press, New York. doi: 10.1145/3032970.3032983.

12

Practical Full Key Recovery on a Google Titan Security Key

Laurent IMBERT[1], Victor LOMNE[2], Camille MUTCHLER[1,2] and Thomas ROCHE[2]

[1]LIRMM, CNRS, Université de Montpellier, France

[2]NinjaLab, Montpellier, France

12.1. Introduction

This chapter presents a practical case study of side-channel analysis. It is based on the work entitled *A Side Journey to Titan* published at USENIX Security 2021. The original work studies the security of the *Google Titan Security Key*[1] (a hardware security token for two-factor authentication) and shows that its secure element, the `NXP A700x` chip, is susceptible to a side-channel attack (through the observation of its local electromagnetic (EM) activity). Given physical access to a *Google Titan Security Key* for around 10 hours, this allows us to retrieve a user-specific secret key (there is one key for each remote account) and therefore to clone the security device.

The vulnerability was acknowledged by Google and the chip manufacturer NXP (CVE-2021-3011 was assigned). It is present in other security keys and various NXP JavaCards products[2] (all based on similar secure elements).

1 Google (2021). Google titan key. Software [Online]. Available at: https://cloud.google.com/titan-securitykey/.

2 The full list of identified products is here: https://ninjalab.io/a-side-journey-to-titan/.

Embedded Cryptography 3,
coordinated by Emmanuel PROUFF, Guénaël RENAULT,
Matthieu RIVAIN and Colin O'FLYNN.

In this chapter, we go back over this work with a focus on the exploitation of the side-channel vulnerability. We expose the vulnerability without detailing the whole discovery path (the interested reader can find all of the details from Roche et al. (2021)) and show how a small, sensitive leakage can result in a catastrophic key-recovery attack.

12.2. Preliminaries

12.2.1. *Product description*

The *Google Titan Security Key* is a hardware FIDO U2F (universal second factor) device. It provides a complement to the login/password authentication mechanism, in order to sign into a Google account, or any other web applications supporting the FIDO U2F protocol. The *Google Titan Security Key* is available in three versions: (1) micro-USB, NFC and BLE; (2) USB type A and NFC; and (3) USB type C. The USB type C and type A (opened) versions are depicted in Figure 12.1.

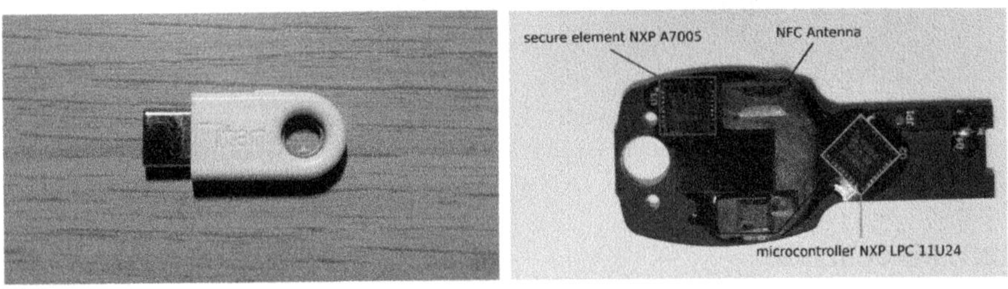

Figure 12.1. *Left: Google Titan Security Key USB type C version. Right: Google Titan Security Key PCB (USB type A version), with annotated main parts. For a color version of this figure, see www.iste.co.uk/prouff/cryptography3.zip*

The FIDO U2F protocol, when used with a hardware FIDO U2F device like the *Google Titan Security Key*, works in two steps: *registration* and *authentication*. Three parties are involved: the *relying party* (e.g. the Google server), the *client* (e.g. a web browser) and the *U2F device*.

The registration phase consists of the creation of a new ECDSA[3] keypair by the *U2F device* and the sending of the public key to the *relying party*.

During the authentication phase, the *relying party* sends a challenge to the *U2F device*, which uses it to perform an ECDSA signature and send it back to the

3 ECDSA is defined over the NIST P-256 elliptic curve (NIST 2001) in FIDO standard.

relying party. Thanks to the corresponding public key obtained during the registration phase, the *relying party* can verify the correctness of the ECDSA signature.

In this work, we expose a side-channel vulnerability in the ECDSA signature implementation and its exploitation in an evil maid attack scenario. Given physical access to a legitimate U2F device during a small amount of time (about 10 hours), an attacker can extract some side-channel information before giving the device back to the legitimate user. This critical information (side-channel traces) is then processed offline by the attacker in order to recover the ECDSA secret key.

12.2.2. Google Titan Security Key *Teardown*

Once plugged into a computer's USB port, `lsusb` outputs `Bus 001 Device 018: ID 096e:0858 Feitian Technologies, Inc.`. As a matter of fact, the company who designed the *Google Titan Security Key* is Feitian[4]. Indeed, Feitian proposes generic FIDO U2F security keys, with customization for casing, packaging and related services.

After removing the plastic casing with a hot air gun and a scalpel, we obtained the PCB depicted in Figure 12.1. The integrated circuit (IC) package markings allow us to guess the IC references; and our target is the secure authentication microcontroller from NXP (in red in Figure 12.1), the `A7005a` from the `A700x` family[5]. It acts as the secure element, generating and storing ECDSA key-pairs and performing the signatures.

Opening the `NXP A7005a` epoxy package necessitated a wet chemical attack. We protected the PCB with some aluminum tape and dropped hot fuming nitric acid on the `NXP A7005a` package until the die was revealed (see Beck (1998), Chapter 2 for a survey on IC package opening techniques).

12.2.3. *Matching the* Google Titan Security Key *with other NXP products*

The FIDO U2F protocol does not allow us to extract the ECDSA secret key of a given application account from a U2F device. With no control whatsoever on the secret key, understanding the details of a highly secured implementation (let alone attacking) can prove cumbersome. We had to find a workaround to study the implementation in a more convenient setting.

4 Feitian (2021). Feitian website. Software [Online]. Available at: https://www.ftsafe.com.

5 MOUSER (2013). NXP A700x datasheet, secure authentication microcontroller. Datasheet [Online]. Available at: https://www.mouser.fr/datasheet/2/302/a700x_fam_sds-1187735.pdf.

The NXP A700x public datasheet[6] provides interesting information: JCOP 2.4.2 JavaCard Operating System, JavaCard version 3.0.1 and GlobalPlatform version 2.1.1, technological node of 140 nm, CPU Secure_MX51, 3-DES and AES hardware co-processors as well as NXP FameXE public-key cryptographic co-processor with RSA and ECC available up to 2,048 and 320 bits, respectively.

These characteristics match with those of the NXP P5x secure microcontroller family. This is the first generation of NXP secure elements, also called SmartMX family[7]. Furthermore, the NXP P5x family is Common Criteria (CC) and EMVCo certified (last CC certification found in 2015).

Thanks to BSI and NLNCSA CC public certification reports[8], we were able to compile a (non-exhaustive) list of NXP JavaCard smartcards based on P5x chips. We selected the product NXP J3D081 (CC certification report BSI-DSZ-CC-0860-2013) since its characteristics were the closest to those of NXP A700x (JCOP 2.4.2 R2, JavaCard 3.0.1 and GlobalPlatform 2.2.1). We named it *Rhea*, in reference to the second largest moon of Saturn, right after *Titan*.

We developed and loaded a custom JavaCard applet allowing us to freely control the JavaCard ECDSA signature engine on *Rhea*. At this point, we were able to upload the long-term ECDSA secret keys of our choice, perform ECDSA signatures and verifications.

12.2.4. *Side-channel observations*

In order to perform EM side-channel measurements, we used a side-channel analysis hardware setup with a global cost of about US $12,000, made of a 500 μm diameter EM probe, a manual micro-manipulator and an oscilloscope with a 500 MHz frequency bandwidth and a sampling rate up to 5 GSa/s.

Figure 12.2 depicts the spatial position of the EM probe above the die of the *Google Titan Security Key* NXP A7005a and the die of *Rhea*. In Figure 12.3, we give the EM activities observed during the processing of the APDU command launching the ECDSA signature available in the JavaCard cryptographic API of *Rhea*.

The similarities between EM activities on *Titan* and *Rhea* confirm our hypothesis that the implementations are very similar. Note that the spatial probe positioning is sensitive to get a clear signal with sharp peaks, but the picture taken for *Rhea* (Figure 12.2, left) proved sufficient to replay the probe positioning on *Titan*.

6 See MOUSER (2013).

7 NXP (2014). NXP SmartMX family brochure. Brochure [Online]. Available at: https://www.nxp.com/ docs/en/brochure/75017515.pdf.

8 See: https://www.bsi.bund.de/EN/Topics/Certification/certified_products/Archiv_reports.html.

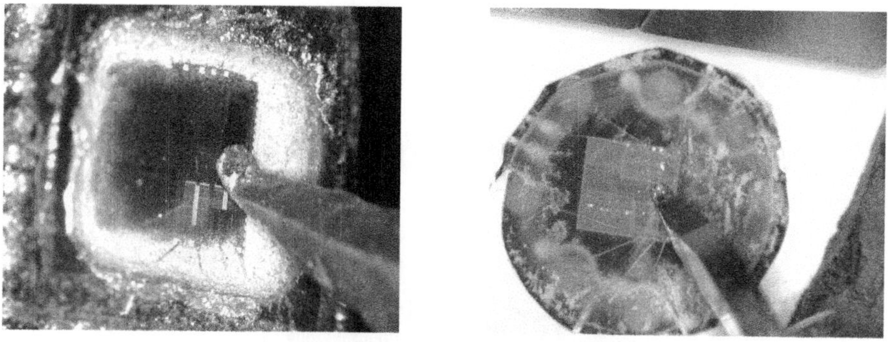

Figure 12.2. *EM probe positions on Titan (left) and Rhea (right). For a color version of this figure, see www.iste.co.uk/prouff/cryptography3.zip*

12.3. Reverse-engineering and vulnerability of the ECDSA algorithm

12.3.1. *Reverse engineering the ECDSA signature algorithm*

Let us recall that we work on the elliptic curve P-256 defined over the finite field $\mathbb{F}_p$ (as standardized by NIST in NIST (2001)).

We denote by G the base-point of the curve and by q its order. The ECDSA signature algorithm (Johnson et al. 2001) takes as inputs the hash of the message m to be signed $h = H(m)$ and a secret key d.

It outputs a pair (r, s) computed as follows:

1) randomly pick a nonce k in $\{0, \ldots, q-1\}$;

2) scalar multiplication[9] $Q = [k]G$;

3) compute $s = k^{-1}(h + rd) \bmod q$, where r denotes the x-coordinate of Q.

The different steps of the ECDSA algorithm are identified in Figure 12.3 over an EM trace. The scalar multiplication algorithm will be the target of our analysis, and we first need to understand its implementation and countermeasures.

The side-channel-based reverse engineering of the scalar multiplication algorithm is described in detail in Roche et al. (2021); we solely give here the final algorithm as well as the crucial information that led to this successful reverse.

9 In a secure implementation, this is usually done on randomized projective coordinates: $G = G_{(x,y)} \rightarrow G_{(xz \bmod p, yz \bmod p, z)}$ with z a fresh random from $\mathbb{F}_p$ (see, e.g. Coron 1999).

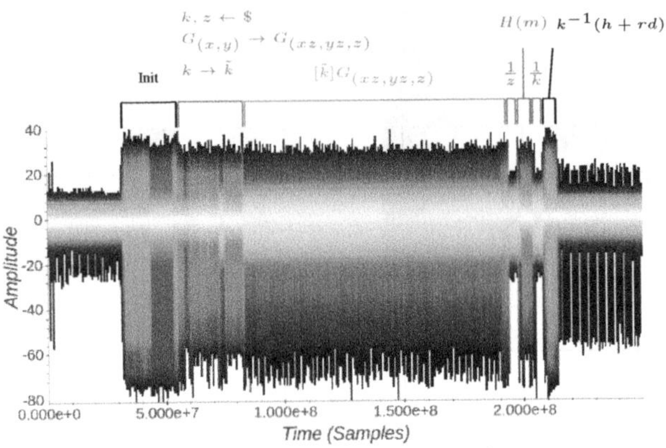

Figure 12.3. *Rhea EM Trace - ECDSA Signature (P-256, SHA-256). For a color version of this figure, see www.iste.co.uk/prouff/cryptography3.zip*

> *Rhea* allows us to choose the secret key of the ECDSA signature but also to execute the ECDSA signature verification algorithm. The verification algorithm includes two scalar multiplications but does not involve any secret. The developers then decided to remove the side-channel countermeasures. The unsecure scalar multiplication algorithm was then easily reversed and helped understand the countermeasures of the secure algorithm.

The secure scalar multiplication algorithm is a double-and-add always version of a *width-2 comb method* (see Lim and Lee 1994) plus tricks. The algorithms is presented in Algorithm 12.1, where $G_0 = G_1 = G$ (the elliptic curve base point), $G_2 = [2^{129}]G_1$, $G_3 = G_1 + G_2$ and $G_4 = [2^{128}]G_1$ are all pre-computed and stored on the device. In the *with-2 comb method*, the scalar $k = (k_1, \cdots, k_{258})$ is encoded as $\tilde{k} = (\tilde{k}_1, \ldots, \tilde{k}_{129})$, with:

$$\tilde{k}_i = 2 \times k_i + k_{i+129}, \forall i \in \{1, \cdots, 129\}.$$

It is easy to see that the scalar multiplication algorithm is constant time. It also involves a randomization of the dummy operation, and since $G_0 = G_1 = G$, we can check that the $Dummy \leftarrow S + G_{rand}$ addition is operated on G_1 half the time and on G_2 or G_3 the rest of the time. We would like to emphasize that this algorithm is only our interpretation of the real algorithm implemented on *Rhea*, which might differ slightly.

Details of the real implementation are not our concern here, and a high-level understanding of the countermeasures is good enough.

Algorithm 12.1. Secure Scalar Multiplication Algorithm

```
Input  : {k̃_1, ··· , k̃_i, ··· , k̃_129}: The encoded scalar
Input  : G_0, G_1, G_2, G_3, G_4: The pre-computed points
Output : [k]G: The scalar multiplication of scalar k by point G:

// Init Register S to the point G(= G_1)
S ← G_1
for i ← 2 to l_k/2 do
  | S ← [2]S
  | rand ← random element from {0, 1, 2, 3}
  | if k̃_i > 0 then
  |   | S ← S + G_{k̃_i}
  | else
  |   | Dummy ← S + G_rand
if k̃_1 = 0 then
  | S ← S − G_4
else
  | Dummy ← S − G_4
Return: S
```

12.3.2. *A sensitive leakage*

The research of sensitive leakage is a tedious task where many interdependent parameters have strong influence and should be set correctly for success. Many details of this study are provided in Roche et al. (2021), and we simply provide the important results here. The acquisition parameters are provided in Table 12.1.

Inputs	rand. inputs, const. key
# operations	4000
Length	100 ms
Sampling rate	5G Sa/s
# Samples/trace	500 M
EM probe	ICR HH 500-6 Langer (2019) position as in Figure 12.2
Channel conf.	DC 50 ohms, $\pm$50 mV
File size	2 TB
Acq. time	$\approx$ 4 hours

Table 12.1. *SCA acquisition parameters for Rhea*

The scalar multiplication contains a sequence of 128 double-and-add operations. The second argument of the add operation is G_v where v takes its value from

$\{0, 1, 2, 3\}$ depending on the current values of $\tilde{k}_i$ and $rand$ (see Algorithm 12.1). Inside the EM traces of the double-and-add operation (orange rectangle in Figure 12.4), we found a set of samples whose amplitude correlates with the choice of $v \in \{0, 1, 2, 3\}$. More precisely, the amplitude of the samples allows us to distinguish three cases among the four: the case $v = 0$ is not distinguishable from the case $v = 1$.

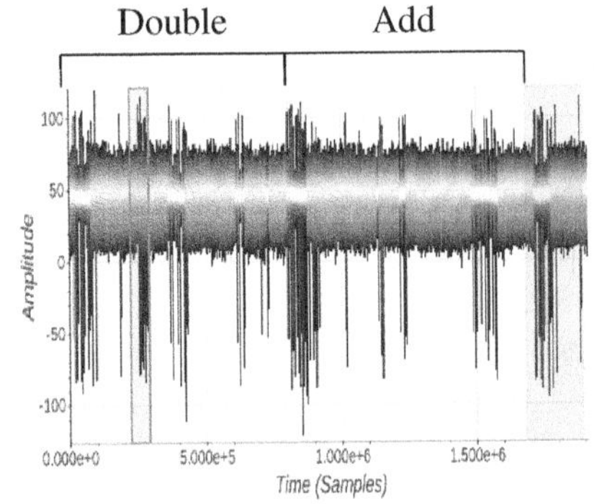

Figure 12.4. *Rhea EM Trace - ECDSA Signature (P-256, SHA-256) - Sensitive Leakage Area. For a color version of this figure, see www.iste.co.uk/prouff/cryptography3.zip*

> In Algorithm 12.1, let us assume that $G_0 = G_1, G_2, G_3$ are stored at three different register (or memory) addresses. Our leakage captures the address value when one of the three G_v is read.

Finally, the leakage shows that the sensitive value v leaks its two bits separately: v takes four possible values and then can be written as two bits. These two bits leak at different time samples and the most significant bit is leaking more often than the least significant bit. We therefore capture a more accurate information about it. In the following, we will then only consider the most significant bit of v (i.e. limiting ourselves to distinguish $v \in \{0, 1\}$ from $v \in \{2, 3\}$).

12.4. A key-recovery attack

In this section, we detail the process that resulted in the full recovering of the private keys embedded into the NXP's secure components of both *Rhea* and *Titan*. Our attack consists of two main steps: we first exploit the vulnerability observed in Algorithm 12.1 to recover some zero bits of the nonces with a very high confidence level. Then, from this partial knowledge on the nonces, we apply a lattice-based attack by reducing our problem to an instance of the extended hidden number problem (EHNP).

12.4.1. *Recovering scalar bits from the observed leakage*

As seen in section 12.3, Algorithm 12.1 leaks critical information whenever $\tilde{k}_i = 2k_i + k_{129+i}$ iz zero because the G-operand of the dummy addition is not chosen uniformly. If $\hat{k}_i \in \{1, 2, 3\}$ denotes the digit recovered from the observed leakage on $\tilde{k}_i$ in a noise-free scenario, the implementation choices lead to $P(\hat{k}_i = 1) = 3/8$, whereas $P(\hat{k}_i = 2) = P(\hat{k}_i = 3) = 5/16$. The case $\hat{k}_i = 1$ (i.e. $\mathrm{msb}(\hat{k}_i) = 0$) is of particular interest since it implies $k_i = \mathrm{msb}(\tilde{k}_i) = 0$. This observation led us to focus our analysis on the signal peaks resulting from the leakage on $\mathrm{msb}(\tilde{k}_i)$. We used a T-test together with an unsupervised clustering algorithm to classify our set of EM traces into two distinct subsets that correspond to the cases $\mathrm{msb}(\hat{k}_i) = 0$ and $\mathrm{msb}(\hat{k}_i) = 1$, respectively. At this stage, we were rather optimistic about the correctness of our clustering process since the respective sizes of the two output clusters did match the expected ratios $(3/8, 5/8)$. Moreover, preliminary experiments on *Rhea* allowed us to fine-tune some parameters (T-test threshold value, confidence level).

For the *Titan* attack, we acquired the side-channel execution traces of 6000 ECDSA signatures. After re-alignment, samples selection, signal processing, unsupervised clustering, pruning and nonces selection, we ended up with 156 nonces, each of which containing with very high probability a block of at least five consecutive zero bits at a known position[10].

12.4.2. *Lattice-based attack with partial knowledge of the nonces*

The second phase of the attack consists of recovering the unknown part of each nonce in order to deduce the secret key d. Following Howgrave-Graham and Smart (2001), this can be done using lattice reduction algorithms. The attack works as follows:

1) Run N ECDSA signatures and record the inputs $h^{(i)} = h(m^{(i)})$, the outputs $(r^{(i)}, s^{(i)})$ and the known information $\hat{k}^{(i)}$ on the nonces $k^{(i)}$. We denote by $u^{(i)}$ the unknown part of $k^{(i)}$ so that $k^{(i)} = \hat{k}^{(i)} + u^{(i)}$ for $i = 1, \ldots, N$.

2) Rewrite the ECDSA equations $s^{(i)} = {k^{(i)}}^{-1}(h^{(i)} + r^{(i)}d) \bmod q$ as linear equations of the form $A^{(i)}u^{(i)} + B^{(i)}d \equiv C^{(i)} \pmod{q}$.

3) Build a lattice $\mathcal{L}$ that contains the vector $\mathbf{u} = (u^{(1)}, u^{(2)}, \ldots, u^{(N)})$.

10 For each of the 156 nonces, there exists a bit position t such that $\forall i \in \{t, t+1, \cdots, t+4\}$, $\mathrm{msb}(\hat{k}_i) = 0$ and then $k_i = 0$.

4) If $\hat{k}^{(i)}$ is large enough, then the norm of $\mathbf{u}$ is small and we can expect to obtain the vector $\mathbf{u}$ by solving an instance of the shortest vector problem (SVP) in $\mathcal{L}$.

The literature mostly considers the case where the known part consists of some of the most significant bits of each nonce. In this case, the above attack amounts to finding a solution to the so-called *hidden number problem* (HNP) introduced in Boneh and Venkatesan (1996). We refer the reader to Chapter 8 for a very good introduction to HNP. A more general setting referred to as the *extended hidden number problem* (EHNP) allows the known part to be a sequence of several blocks of consecutive known bits scattered all over the nonce. In this case, the unknown $u^{(i)}$ is a vector whose elements are the unknown sections of each nonce. We note $u^{(i)} = (u_1^{(i)}, u_2^{(i)}, \ldots)$. This more general setting did not draw much attention (important papers are Howgrave-Graham and Smart (2001); Nguyen and Shparlinski (2002); Hlavác and Rosa (2007); Goudarzi et al. (2016)) but led to practical attacks nonetheless, mainly in the specific case of w-NAF implementations of the scalar multiplication (Fan et al. 2016; De Micheli et al. 2020). Our attack also relies on this extended version of the HNP.

The ECDSA equations $s^{(i)} = {k^{(i)}}^{-1}(h^{(i)}+dr^{(i)}) \bmod q$ can be rewritten as $k^{(i)} = A^{(i)}d - B^{(i)} \bmod q$, with $A^{(i)} = {s^{(i)}}^{-1}r^{(i)}$ and $B^{(i)} = -{s^{(i)}}^{-1}h^{(i)}$. If $k^{(i)}$ is small, then we can build a lattice $\mathcal{L}$ such that the closest vector to $\mathbf{v} = (B_1, \ldots, B_N, 0)$ in $\mathcal{L}$ reveals the nonces $k^{(1)}, \ldots, k^{(N)}$, hence the private key d. In this setting, the solution is obtained by solving an instance of the closest vector problem (CVP). A common variant makes it possible to reduce the problem to an instance of the SVP in $\mathcal{L}$. In general, this so-called embedding technique (Kannan 1987) provides a better probability of success.

In our case, the known part of each nonce k does not correspond to its most significant bits. Instead, we have $k = \hat{k} + \sum_{j=1}^{\ell} u_j 2^{\lambda_j}$, where the bits that form the known part $\hat{k}$ split the nonce k into ℓ unknown parts u_j. Note that the positions λ_j and number of chunks ℓ differ for each nonce.

After a few experiments on *Rhea*, we filtered out the 6,000 recorded signatures in order to keep only those for which the known part of $\hat{k}$ consisted of a single block of five consecutive zero bits surrounded by two unknown parts u_1, u_2.

We then reduced our problem to an instance to EHNP as sketched above. We applied several optimizations to increase both the efficiency and probability of success of the attack. In particular, we removed the secret key d from the equations and we used the already mentioned embedding technique. The details of our optimizations and lattice construction are given in Roche et al. (2021). To complete the attack, we ran our EHNP solver (using LLL) on random subsets of size 80 taken among the 156 selected nonces. The attack was successful after only a few tens of attempts.

Once the attacker gets hold of the *Titan* device, it should take less than 10 hours to replay the side-channel acquisition: two hours for preparing the device, one hour for preparing the side-channel acquisition setup, six hours for the side-channel acquisition and one hour for repackaging the device. After returning the device to the victim, the key recovery can then be performed offline in less than one day.

12.5. Take-home message

Some cryptographic primitive implementations require robustness against strong side-channel attackers (e.g. the so-called *secure elements*). Their security is ensured by building up layers of countermeasures such as de-synchronization techniques (jittering at the hardware level and/or shuffling and random delays at the software level) and masking/blinding mechanisms (at the algorithmic level). Often, one layer of countermeasure is the secrecy of the implementation (to our knowledge, and at the time of writing this chapter, there are still no secure chips with publicly disclosed cryptographic implementations).

While we are able to assess the strength of a known countermeasure (e.g. as it is done in CC evaluations), it is quite difficult to assess the level of security provided by the secrecy of the implementation. Smartcard CC evaluations do not assess the difficulty to reverse engineer a given implementation. It is however obvious, and the *Titan* case is a good illustration of it, that reverse engineering is greatly helped by some bad implementation choices: from the downgrading of countermeasures for public primitives (like the scalar multiplication in NXP ECDSA verification operation) to the creation of unbalanced behavior (e.g. by setting $G_0 = G_1$ in the NXP scalar multiplication algorithm).

Not assessing the reverse-engineer effort leads, in some cases, to overestimating the added security of secrecy. The safest place would be, of course, to finally get rid of this misleading security layer and open to public scrutiny the *real* layers of countermeasures.

12.6. References

Beck, F. (1998). *Integrated Circuit Failure Analysis: A Guide to Preparation Techniques*. John Wiley & Sons, New York.

Boneh, D. and Venkatesan, R. (1996). Hardness of computing the most significant bits of secret keys in Diffie-Hellman and related schemes. In *CRYPTO'96*, Koblitz, N. (ed.). Springer, Heidelberg.

Coron, J.-S. (1999). Resistance against differential power analysis for elliptic curve cryptosystems. In *CHES'99*, Çetin, K. and Koç, C.P. (eds). Springer, Heidelberg.

De Micheli, G., Piau, R., Pierrot, C. (2020). A tale of three signatures: Practical attack of ECDSA with wNAF. In *AFRICACRYPT 20*, Nitaj, A. and Youssef, A.M. (eds). Springer, Heidelberg.

Fan, S., Wang, W., Cheng, Q. (2016). Attacking OpenSSL Implementation of ECDSA with a few signatures. In *Proceedings of the 2016 ACM SIGSAC Conference on Computer and Communications Security, CCS '16, Association for Computing Machinery*. ACM, New York. doi: 10.1145/2976749.2978400.

Goudarzi, D., Rivain, M., Vergnaud, D. (2016). Lattice attacks against elliptic-curve signatures with blinded scalar multiplication. In *SAC 2016*, Avanzi, R. and Heys, H.M. (eds). Springer, Heidelberg.

Hlavác, M. and Rosa, T. (2007). Extended hidden number problem and its cryptanalytic applications. In *SAC 2006*, Biham, E. and Youssef, A.M. (eds). Springer, Heidelberg.

Howgrave-Graham, N. and Smart, N.P. (2001). Lattice attacks on digital signature schemes. *Des. Codes Cryptogr.*, 23(3), 283–290.

Johnson, D., Menezes, A., Vanstone, S. (2001). The elliptic curve digital signature algorithm (ECDSA). *International Journal of Information Security*, 1(1), 36–63.

Kannan, R. (1987). Minkowski's convex body theorem and integer programming. *Mathematics of Operations Research*, 12(3), 415–440 [Online]. Available at: http://www.jstor.org/stable/3689974.

Langer (2019). ICR HH 500-6. Product [Online]. Available at: https://www.langer-emv.de/en/product/near-field-microprobes-icr-hh-h-field/26/icr-hh500-6-near-field-microprobe-2-mhz-to-6-ghz/108.

Lim, C.H. and Lee, P.J. (1994). More flexible exponentiation with precomputation. In *CRYPTO'94*, Desmedt, Y. (ed.). Springer, Heidelberg.

Nguyen, P.Q. and Shparlinski, I. (2002). The insecurity of the digital signature algorithm with partially known nonces. *Journal of Cryptology*, 15(3), 151–176.

NIST (2001). FIPS 186-2, Digital Signature Standard (DSS) [Online]. Available at: https://csrc.nist.gov/csrc/media/publications/fips/186/2/archive/2000-01-27/documents/fips186-2.pdf.

Roche, T., Lomné, V., Mutschler, C., Imbert, L. (2021). A side journey to Titan: Revealing and breaking NXP's P5x ECDSA implementation on the way. In *30th USENIX Security Symposium (USENIX Security 21)*. USENIX Association, Berkeley.

13

An Introduction to Intentional Electromagnetic Interference Exploitation

José LOPES ESTEVES

Agence nationale de la sécurité des systèmes d'information, Paris, France

13.1. IEMI: history and definition

Part of the research in the field of electromagnetic compatibility (EMC) is dedicated to the understanding of the effects on electric or electronic devices, which are caused by electromagnetic (EM) interaction with their environment. The EMC of equipment is qualified through the characterization of their emission level (the impact of their activity on the EM environment) and their susceptibility level (the impact of the EM environment on their activity). The need for test procedures for the management of EM interference (EMI) has been in the scope of several standards committees since the early 1930s (Hoad 2007). At this time, sources of interference were unintentional, both natural (e.g. lightning and electrostatic discharge) and artificial (e.g. radio transceivers).

However, the potential offensive exploitation of such effects has gained interest, especially since the observations of collateral damage during Operation Starfish, a high altitude nuclear test in 1962 (Wikipedia 2023), which created a high-altitude nuclear EM pulse. Effects on electric and electronic devices were reported, such as input circuit troubles in radio receivers and street light failures, on the Hawaiian island of Oahu, at merely 14.00 km from the detonation (Vittitoe 1989). The evolution of

Embedded Cryptography 3,
coordinated by Emmanuel PROUFF, Guénaël RENAULT,
Matthieu RIVAIN and Colin O'FLYNN.

technology used for radars and their proliferation also introduced new sources of EMI, with potentially critical impacts as in the U.S.S. Forrestal case. A landing airplane was illuminated by a radar and an EMI triggered the accidental release of ammunition, according to a report from NASA (Leach and Alexander 1995). In order to evaluate equipment immunity against such EM environments, research was driven to build simulators focusing on the reproduction of these categories of waveforms.

In 1999, the URSI (Union de Radio Science Internationale) issued a resolution on criminal activities using EM tools, raising awareness about the offensive use of EMI and the need of scientific investment on protection and test methods (URSI 1999). In the same year, the IEC SC 77C subcommittee had added this topic in its standardization program (Lopes Esteves et al. 2021).

Intentional EMI (IEMI) was officially defined in 2005 as the following (ISO/IEC 2005):

> Intentional malicious generation of EM energy introducing noise or signals into electric and electronic systems, thus disrupting, confusing or damaging these systems for terrorist or criminal purposes.

The terms *intentional malicious* explicitly introduce an attacker, which is quite uncommon and surprising in a set of standards concerning the *compatibility* of equipment. The terms *disrupting, confusing or damaging* refer to functional safety and reliability issues. Together with the concept of an attacker, they also refer to information security issues, mostly on the availability of the information processed by the target system.

Furthermore, the definition encompasses the use of jammers, which are designed to overload antenna receiver circuits (ISO/IEC 2020). As a result, this new EMC field intersects with other technical fields such as electronic warfare, wireless communication, functional safety, information security and risk management.

This historical introduction to IEMI and the standard definition uncovers slightly the diversity and the complexity of the physical interactions, the targeted systems or the attack scenarios that can be considered in this field.

IEMI interaction can be modeled as shown in Figure 13.1, which provides a simplified version of the EM interaction model in Giri et al. (2020) and the EM pulse interaction models from Giri and Taylor (1994) and Lee (1986).

The attacker is in possession of a *source* which is able to generate EM energy destined to the target electric or electronic system. This EM energy, to reach the target, is subject to a *propagation* that can be radiated or conducted. It refers to the movement of currents, charges and/or electric and magnetic fields. Then the physical interaction with the conductive parts of the target, referred to as a *coupling*, occurs. The coupling produces physical effects, parasitic currents or voltages which, by reaching systems or components, can introduce physical or logical impacts.

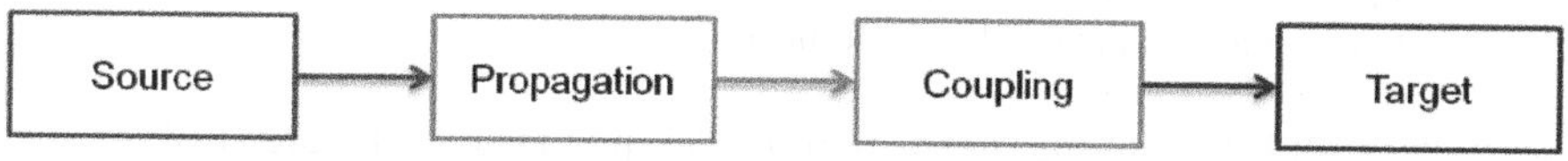

Figure 13.1. *Interaction model for IEMI (adapted from Lee (1986)). For a color version of this figure, see www.iste.co.uk/prouff/cryptography3.zip*

Depending on the complexity of the target topology, cascaded interactions may be considered, introducing other coupling, penetration and propagation steps (Giri and Taylor 1994).

13.2. Information security threats related to electromagnetic susceptibility

The physical or logical impacts on the target resulting from interaction with the electromagnetic environment can be interesting for an attacker. Several threat models can be considered and categorized according to the security criterion they impact as in Figure 13.2.

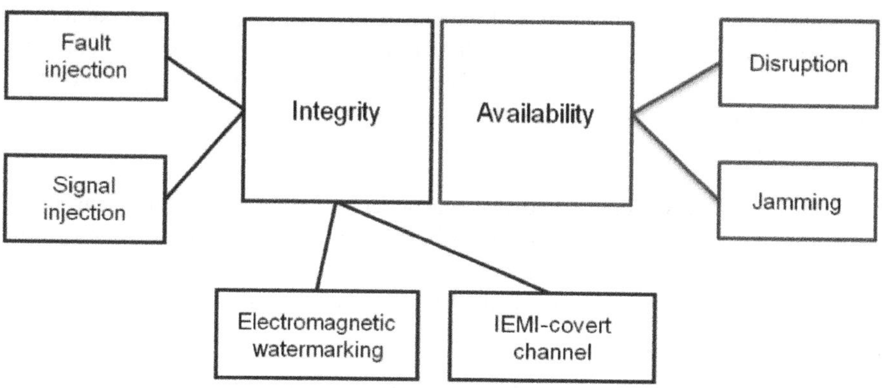

Figure 13.2. *Threats exploiting the electromagnetic susceptibility of a target electronic device and the impacted security criterion. For a color version of this figure, see www.iste.co.uk/prouff/cryptography3.zip*

In what follows, each threat model will be discussed and illustrated by exploitation examples from the literature. A special focus will be made on IEMI-covert channels and electromagnetic watermarking for which practical experiments are detailed.

13.3. Electromagnetic fault injection

Electromagnetic fault injection (EMFI) is a cybersecurity discipline dedicated to the investigation of attacks and defenses on integrated circuits (ICs), which is extensively covered in Chapter 9 of Volume 1.

While EMFI fits in the interaction model provided in Figure 13.1, some specificities regarding the attack goals and practical interactions with the target distinguish IEMI from EMFI.

The attacker is assumed to have a physical access to the target, enabling a preparation of the target's functional environment (e.g. printed circuit board (PCB)), physical measurements and a precise synchronization to the target's activity. The EM interactions are near-field over a localized area of the target, or conducted through the interfaces (pins) of the IC. Attack waveforms are mostly pulses, which are believed to target digital parts, and continuous waves (CW), for targeting analog functions.

The study of IEMI is an EMC-related field and it arises from EMC methodology. The attacker is considered as being at a variable distance from the target, potentially meters or even kilometers away. This implies a wide variety of potential sources and EM environments that increases the complexity of the dimensioning of the EMC problem. A consequence of this complexity is visible in the tailored test level derivation guidance (ISO/IEC 2020), which requires the determination of the EM environment from the operational deployment context (i.e. the practical conditions in which the target will evolve). The failure criteria can be measured for currents, voltages or EM fields on the target or effects, impacting the availability of the main function of the target. This makes the standard susceptibility assessment unfit for security analysis.

However, recently, in the context of sensor security, new attacks involving IEMI were proposed, with an attacker which can be closer to the target and use sources with less power. While detection is considered in EMC standards as a protective measure involving external devices, sensor security researchers proposed detection techniques included in the target.

The possibility of obtaining EMFI impacts on an IC through IEMI has been envisioned in Hayashi et al. (2011). A common mode conducted injection of 4–5.5 V 170 MHz sine waves on the power interface of a SASEBO-G board (3.3 V, 24 MHz clock frequency) implementing an AES encryption in FPGA resulted in the generation of faulty ciphertexts allowing a physical cryptanalysis. The possibility of obtaining similar results with a radiated injection was discussed but not demonstrated.

13.4. Destruction, denial of service

Several studies were dedicated to the determination of breakdown, burnout, destruction thresholds for different types and generations of electronic components (Backstrom and Lovstrand 2004; Giri et al. 2020; Hoad 2007; NASA/ADS 1978; Sabath and Nietsch 2006). In Mejecaze (2019), switch mode power supplies were tested against conducted high power (> 12 kW) signals in order to determine the destruction sequence of the components, showing that most impacted components were the fuses, the diodes, the pulse width modulation (PWM) controller and the MOSFET.

In Palisek and Suchy (2011), the functional performance of several network equipment was tested against high power (> 200 kW) radiated IEMI. Ethernet routers with different cables and WiFi routers showed impacts resulting mostly in a degradation or an interruption of the network traffic.

In Adami et al. (2014), electronic passport readers for automated border controls were tested against 1 µs pulsed signals with 1 kHz repetition rate at 150–3425 MHz and 13.56 MHz. Interference type effects reported included impacts on the image reading (no picture, failure in image recognition, failure in reading the machine-readable zone of the passport). Upset type effects included communication interruption on USB and RFID.

13.5. Denial of service on radio front-ends

A phase-locked loop (PLL) was studied in Dubois (2011) and the impact of its susceptibility when used as an oscillator in a quadrature phase shift keying (QPSK) radio receiver was assessed. Effects on the PLL were impacting the output signal frequency, phase and amplitude, resulting in demodulation errors. In case of a CW IEMI, impacts were significant when the CW frequency was close to the PLL output frequency (in this case, 3 GHz). In case of amplitude modulated (AM) CW, longer pulses and higher pulse repetition frequencies gave better results.

A 2.4 GHz radio front-end was studied in Payet et al. (2017), with a focus on effects impacting the low noise amplifier (LNA) and the power amplifier. It was illuminated by a $3\,\mathrm{kV} \cdot \mathrm{m}^{-1}$ 60 GHz pulsed CW with a pulse repetition rate of several kHz. The observed effect was a reduction of the amplitude or an extinction of the output signal during the pulses.

In Van de Beek (2016), CW IEMI effects on a TETRA receiver were studied, leading to a saturation of the front-end and a decrease of the receivers sensitivity, and showing that nonlinear interaction (harmonic distortion, cross modulation and intermodulation) with the LNA and desensitization due to a high power interferer could decrease the signal-to-noise ratio and degrade the demodulation efficiency.

The signals reradiated by radio frequency (RF) front-ends when illuminated with IEMI were also investigated in Martorell (2018). It was observed that the targets reemitted signals containing nonlinear distortion (harmonic and intermodulation products) when illuminated by mono-tone or two-tone CW signals. It was suggested to use nonlinear radar (H2 and IM3) signals to detect RF front end characteristics such as operating frequency and bandwidth.

13.6. Signal injection in communication interfaces

Signal injection in wired baseband communication cables was investigated in Dayanıklı et al. (2022a), targeting UART and I2C. Signals with a 65 MHz fundamental frequency were introduced by near field coupling using a signal generator, a 20 W amplifier and a small Vivaldi antenna at 10 cm. It was shown that an attacker was able to perform bit sets and bit resets in the serial communication frames if a prior synchronization was possible (e.g. by exploiting the EM emission of the serial communication) and cables were not twisted. A similar work was proposed in Jang et al. (2023), where the susceptibility of serial communication buses (I2C and SPI) between sensors and a system on chip (SoC) has been investigated, resulting in a random alteration of the transmitted data frames.

Signal injection in wired RF communication was also investigated. In Köhler et al. (2022b) and Nateghi et al. (2021), the possibility to disrupt power line communication (PLC) remotely with IEMI was shown. In Gardiner and Poore (2022), J2497, an in-vehicle UART over PLC communication protocol operating from 100–400 kHz was studied, and the possibility of remotely introduce frames into truck cables was demonstrated, using a software defined radio transmitter and a loop antenna to replay frames, needing 10 W at 45 cm.

13.7. Signal injection attacks on sensors and actuators

Both analog and digital sensors have been scrutinized under IEMI environments. Despite not being restricted to EM interactions, a very complete survey on signal injection into sensors is given in Giechaskiel and Rasmussen (2019). Most studies do not precisely identify if the observed effects are due to parasitic activity into the communication interfaces (post-transducer attack (Köhle et al. 2022a)) or into the sensing unit (pre-transducer attack (Köhle et al. 2022a)). However, a very thorough analysis of the different threats from IEMI against analog sensors is given in Kune et al. (2013). In particular, in order to introduce a parasitic signal with the characteristics of a target legitimate signal, a baseband IEMI or a modulated IEMI can be used.

The modulated IEMI can be demodulated in the target by nonlinear behavior of components, filters or distortion caused by analog digital converters (ADCs). As a result, the modulator signal gets interpreted by the digital logic reading the sensor values. With a modulated signal, the carrier frequency can be chosen so as to maximize the coupling efficiency. Several sensors are then targeted in practice, such as an analog microphone in a webcam that was targeted by an AM IEMI with a carrier around 825 MHz and an audio modulator signal (an actual song). Analog microphones have also been attacked with IEMI with scenarios exploiting smartphone voice assistants in Dai et al. (2022); Kasmi and Lopes Esteves (2015); Lopes Esteves and Kasmi (2018); Xu et al. (2021).

Optical sensors are studied in Köhle et al. (2022a), demonstrating the possibility to introduce an arbitrary image, with some quality limitations (e.g. colors), by a post-transducer interaction via a 190 MHz 100 mW AM IEMI. However, frame injection required a synchronization to the sensor activity. An exploitation without synchronization was also proposed by introducing enough noise to degrade an automated barcode recognition on the optical stream.

Interaction with smartphone capacitive touchscreens was also investigated, showing the possibility of injecting arbitrary touch events with varying precision (Jiang et al. 2022; Maruyama et al. 2019; Shan et al. 2022; Wang et al. 2022). In Jiang et al. (2022), a conducted CW IEMI introduced through the USB charging cables of target smartphones is used at a frequency close or related to the internal touchscreen excitation signal and with amplitudes of nearly 100 V (e.g. 300 kHz and 99 V on a Google Nexus 7). Again, a synchronization is necessary to inject arbitrary touch events, which precision depend on the exact moment and duration of the injection, and the exploitation of EM emission is proposed to this end. Without synchronization, random-touch events or a disruption of the touch-event detection are still achieved.

In Dayanıklı et al. (2022b), the possibility of injecting a signal into a PWM link between a SoC and an actuator (servomotor) is investigated. It is shown that an AM IEMI with a modulator signal corresponding to the intended PWM signal resulted in a good interpretation of the modulator signal by the actuator. A full control of the rotation of the actuator was achieved without the need of a synchronization, in contrary of previous work (e.g. Selvaraj 2018). A radiated test on a custom target setup mounted on a Cessna 150 unmanned aerial vehicle (UAV) showed a successful IEMI at 25 cm distance with a custom antenna, a 20 W amplifier and a 62 MHz carrier frequency, with a modulator of a few kHz.

13.8. IEMI-covert channel

This section focuses on a specific threat model aiming at the establishment of a covert communication channel by exploiting the electromagnetic susceptibility of the target. An extended version of this work is available in Lopes Esteves (2023). A practical application on a desktop computer is proposed, allowing for bridging an air gap[1]. A brief introduction to the air gap and some bypass techniques is first proposed, followed by an insight on the identification and the characterization of a covert channel with IEMI.

13.8.1. *The air gap*

Most critical infrastructures, organizations and companies have to compose with several information systems with different levels of trust. Good information system security practices (ANSSI 2020; Ross et al. 2022) involve a partitioning into security domains and the enforcement of security policies between security domains based on how data and information must be protected. This partitioning of security domains can include considerations of classification of the information and is the root of multi-level security (Anderson 2020). The permeability between security domains introduces security risks and several practices can be applied in order to mitigate this attack vector, such as firewalls, diodes, virtualization or air gaps.

The air gap is a security measure that consists of isolating physically a sensitive security domain from the other ones. The physical isolation usually involves a complete dedication of all information technology resources in order to avoid sharing hardware or software with other security domains and a suppression of communication interfaces with other security domains. A very common example involves a sensitive security domain dedicated to internal activities and internet connected resources dedicated to external interaction (e.g. emails).

13.8.2. *Bridging air gaps*

As the air gap consists of a physical and logical segregation of security domains, circumventing an air gap implies the introduction of a communication channel between computers belonging to two security domains. As the communication channel used for bridging an air gap is neither intentional nor legitimate, it is called a covert channel (Lampson 1973). With covert channels, entities on both sides of the communication are willing to communicate, to exploit the covert channel and are therefore usually considered as attacker-controlled. In other words, computers from each security domain are running a software implant, interacting with a covert exploit implementing the covert communication interface. Another possible scenario that could be considered is of an attacker using a dedicated device to communicate with a software implant (as it will be the case for IEMI-covert channels).

1 The IEMI-covert channel on a desktop computer was a joint work with Dr. Chaouki KASMI, Dr. Valentin HOUCHOUAS and Mr. Philippe VALEMBOIS.

In this framework, several techniques can lead to an air gap bridging. In case the targets possess wireless communication interfaces, they may be diverted by a covert exploit to send or receive information over the air. Techniques involving polyglot signals, hidden modulations (Bratus et al. 2016) and second-order soft-Tempest profit from an existing legitimate radio frequency communication (Lopes Esteves et al. 2017, 2018). Cross-technology communication can allow us to use a front end dedicated to a certain legitimate protocol (e.g. Zigbee) in order to send packets compatible with another protocol (e.g. Bluetooth low energy), as demonstrated in Cayre et al. (2021).

It can also be that both computers share simultaneously or alternatively peripherals. For example, there may be a need for exchanging data between A and B and a USB mass-storage peripheral could be used. Another common example is the temptation to share human interface devices, such as displays, keyboards and mice. However, peripherals are embedded systems that enclose persistent storage capabilities in order to store firmware or configuration data. When these storage capabilities can be read or written by the host, they can provide a covert storage channel.

Hardware implants can also be introduced into the targets to bridge the air gap. Several examples of such tooling were documented, such as the COTTONMOUTH implant family in the NSA offensive tooling catalog (EFF 2014) or red-team professional tooling (O.MG n.d.; USBNinja n.d.).

Last but not least, out-of-band covert channels, also referred to as physical covert channels, can also lead to a bypass of an air gap. Out-of-band covert channels are air gap covert channels that are enabled by semi-invasive and noninvasive covert exploits and have been extensively studied in Carrara (2016). In this category, the covert exploits provide an interface to a shared physical characteristic that can be modulated by the sender and measured by the receiver.

In other words, the practicality of attacks based on out-of-band covert channels is conditioned by the presence of resources on the sender side enabling the modulation (called the modulator) and by the presence of sensing resources on the receiver side enabling reception and demodulation (called the demodulator). Several studies were dedicated to out-of-band covert channels using acoustic signals (Guri 2021; Guri et al. 2020; Hanspach and Goetz 2013; Lee et al. 2016), light (Hasan et al. 2013; Loughry and Umphress 2002; Nassi et al. 2017), temperature (Guri et al. 2015) or radio-frequency signals (e.g. Kuhn and Anderson 1998). Most out-of-band covert channels were studied as an exfiltration threat, aiming at establishing an outgoing communication from an isolated target.

13.8.3. *Threat model*

When considering IEMI-covert channels, the attacker tries establishing an incoming covert communication channel by exploiting the electromagnetic susceptibility of a target isolated computer. On the target, a covert exploit implements the receiver side of the covert channel to provide a software implant with the capacity of receiving messages from the attacker. This threat model is illustrated in Figure 13.3.

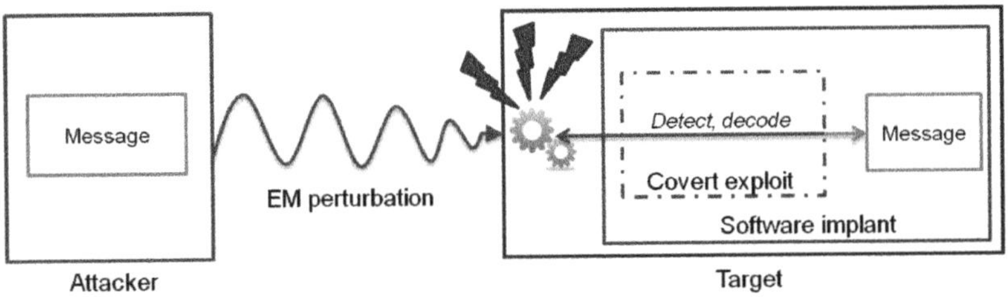

Figure 13.3. *IEMI-covert channel threat model. For a color version of this figure, see www.iste.co.uk/prouff/cryptography3.zip*

13.8.4. *Practical IEMI-covert channel on a PC*

13.8.4.1. *The target*

The target is a desktop computer equipped with a QDI Platinix 2-A motherboard, an Intel Pentium-IV CPU and a Winbond W83627HF-AW SuperIO controller. According to the documentation, the CPU encloses an on-die thermal diode (Intel 2004), which signal is routed toward the SuperIO chip and digitized with an 8-bit analog digital converter (ADC) (Winbond 2002).

The electromagnetic susceptibility of this electronic sub-circuit will show to be exploitable for an IEMI-covert channel.

13.8.4.2. *Experimental setup*

The target desktop computer was placed on a table inside a FARADAY cage, initialized in a nominal configuration with its keyboard, mouse and VGA display.

It has been connected to a monitoring computer located outside of the FARADAY cage with an ethernet link transiting through ethernet-optical transducers in order to forward the temperature readings in real time during susceptibility testing.

The full experimental setup is depicted in Figure 13.4.

13.8.4.3. *Susceptibility of the temperature sensor*

For an arbitrarily fixed carrier frequency of 2 GHz that has shown to produce effects on the temperature reading without side-effects, an analysis of the impact electric-field magnitude on the effect intensity has been done. An electric-field probe, placed inside the target computer chassis, was used to measure the electric-field magnitude. Figure 13.5 shows that the temperature offset is monotonically increasing with the electric-field magnitude. This observation confirms the possibility of performing an amplitude modulation of the temperature reading values by modulating the electric-field magnitude.

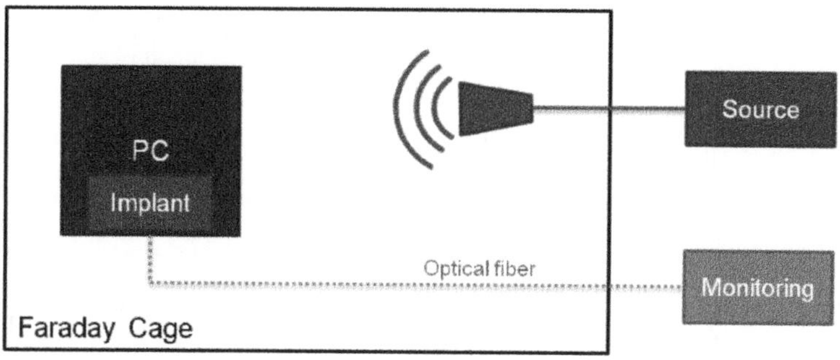

Figure 13.4. *IEMI-covert channel characterization setup. For a color version of this figure, see www.iste.co.uk/prouff/cryptography3.zip*

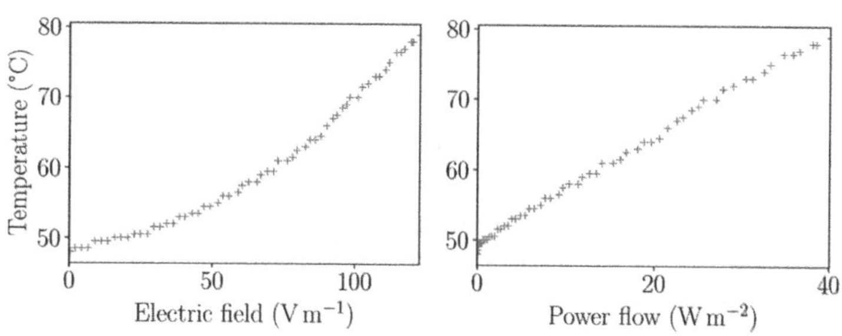

Figure 13.5. *Relationship between electric-field magnitude and temperature reading offset. For a color version of this figure, see www.iste.co.uk/prouff/cryptography3.zip*

13.8.4.4. *Covert exploit design*

Based on the possibility of inducing reading errors on the temperature sensor, a proof-of-concept receiver is first developed. In order to set-up a mono-directional communication link between the computer under test and the IEMI source, a covert exploit was implemented that monitors the temperature level and seeks for a known pattern. The covert exploit is in charge of high rate temperature readings, demodulation and decoding of the covert communication. Several modulation and coding schemes were tested, from simple on-off keying (OOK) to 4-level amplitude shift keying (4-ASK), leading to different theoretical communication rates.

Figure 13.6 shows a received 4-ASK frame along with the symbols sent, carrying the message "hello scientists!", at a bit rate of 10 bits per second.

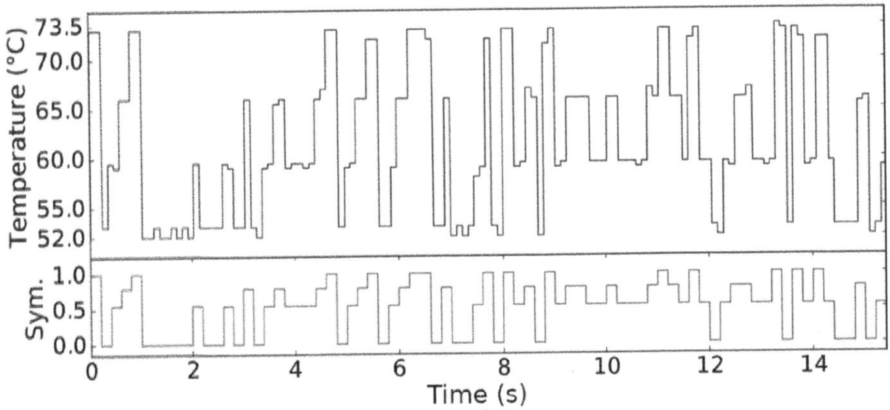

Figure 13.6. *An example 4-ASK frame as received by the covert exploit (top) and corresponding symbols coded before modulation by the sender (bottom). For a color version of this figure, see www.iste.co.uk/prouff/cryptography3.zip*

13.8.4.5. *Covert channel capacity*

Two proof of concept covert exploits were designed providing different communication channel characteristics. From an information security viewpoint, the maximum transmission rate is an interesting characteristic as it would allow us to determine the criticality of the presence of the covert channel. This theoretical upper bound for the transmission rate is called the channel capacity.

In Lopes Esteves (2023), an approach for applying the Shannon (1948) capacity formulation is proposed. Several approximations, resulting in an overestimation of the attacker profile, are made:

– the channel is considered a noiseless discrete channel;

– the maximum symbol rate is measured on the demodulator side;

– the maximum number of symbols is directly derived from the ADC specification.

The covert exploit was adapted to maximize the sampling rate of the temperature readings and a maximum symbol rate of $R_{sym} = 10$ samples per second was obtained. The maximum number of symbols has been derived from the maximum number of values sampled by the ADC, which is an 8-bit ADC according to the specification of the SuperIO chip (Winbond 2002). Therefore, the maximum number of representable symbols is $N = 2^8$. These considerations yield a worst case channel capacity $C = R_{sym} \cdot \log_2 N = 40$ bits per second[2].

This covert channel capacity is an overestimation of the actual channel capacity because of the approximations made, implying that considerations related to the IEMI source, the signal propagation, coupling and the quantization noise are discarded. However, this information can still be relevant for risk analysis.

13.9. Electromagnetic watermarking

This section is an introduction to electromagnetic watermarking (EMW), a threat model for IEMI first described more extensively in Lopes Esteves (2019). EMV is first be defined and explained. A practical application providing forensic-tracking capabilities on a civilian UAV is then detailed.

13.9.1. *Threat model*

EMV can be defined as the process of exploiting effects of IEMI that have persistent impacts on the target in order to remotely introduce (to store) a piece of information (the *watermark*) into a non-cooperating electronic target. Conceptually, this can be modeled as the combination of an IEMI-based covert communication channel and a storage channel (Figure 13.7).

In this framework, in can be viewed as a covert communication channel for which the covert exploit is not a software implant but, instead, a persistence mechanism intrinsic to the target. The *watermark* can then be detected and extracted later during a second phase in order to at least determine that the target has been in contact with an EMW environment.

13.9.2. *EMW for forensic tracking*

While traditional digital forensics aims at extracting evidence of criminal activities from electronic devices, forensic tracking consists in investigating the activity of a target in order to determine if it was at a specific location at a specific time (Al-Kuwari and Wolthusen 2011).

2 More details about the determination of the maximum symbol rate and the application of the Shannon capacity formulation are given in Lopes Esteves (2023).

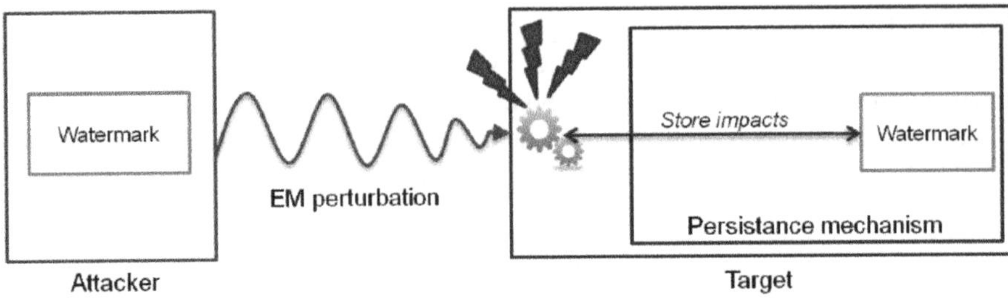

Figure 13.7. *Modeling of EMW as the combination of an IEMI-covert channel and a storage channel. For a color version of this figure, see www.iste.co.uk/prouff/cryptography3.zip*

Forensic tracking can be performed by extracting location traces inside the target such as a list of GPS coordinates (Sack et al. 2013) or by identifying traces of the target left on other devices (e.g. a network of CCTV cameras (Al-Kuwari and Wolthusen 2011)). In Zheng et al. (2017), a method of forensic tracking of audio recordings is proposed relying on the analysis of the variations of the electrical network frequency, which are consistent at different places of the same electrical power grid.

Forensic tracking using digital watermarking is widespread in digital cinema (Lee et al. 2009; van der Veen et al. 2007) determining the location in time and space of the recording of pirate copies of movies captured with a digital camera during the in-theater projection of the movie. In this case, the host signal is the motion picture and the watermark is an identifier of the theater and a timestamp. The embedding is performed in real time by the play back device. The processing channel would include the capture by the digital camera, the compression and format conversions that may have occurred between the capture and the share of a copy. The detection step will consist of searching for the watermark presence in a version of the motion picture and extracting the theater identifier and the timestamp, which will allow for further investigating on the piracy act.

As EMW allows us to introduce information into a target, it may be considered to be a potential embedding technique for forensic tracking. Similarly to DNA sprays used in some shops to mark people's body and clothes in case of robbery, EMW could allow for a digital marking of a target showing it has been colocated in time and space with the watermarking system. The main difference with the previous example is the control of the host signal in which the watermark is embedded. With EMW, the target is remote and non-cooperative and the host signal is not under the control of the watermarking entity.

13.9.3. *Practical EMW on a UAV*

During the last decade, UAVs have been spreading in both civilian and military contexts. The problem of their neutralization, called counter unmanned aerial systems (C-UAS), has become of high interest for security aware organizations. Among the proposed solutions, electromagnetic directed energy devices are also considered and commercial products already exist (HPEM 2019). In such context, EMW can be a relevant solution for forensic tracking of UAVs involved in unauthorized flights nearby critical infrastructures. The main principle would be to perform EMW in complement or as an alternative to a neutralization process.

13.9.3.1. *The target*

The targeted UAV is a common off the shelf quadcopter which is marketed as a photo and video acquisition device. The air segment is composed of the quadcopter aircraft equipped with a digital camera payload. The remote controller hosts a 2.4 GHz Wi-Fi access point and relays packets between all the components. A proprietary radio protocol is used for sending line of sight flight control commands from the remote controller to the aircraft.

The aircraft encloses a system on chip running *OpenWRT* (Brown 2016). Besides, other ICs are in charge of the avionics functions and real-time interactions with the sensors and the motors. Communicating with the main over an asynchronous serial link with a proprietary protocol means that both send telemetry data from the sensors and receive commands. The main microcontroller then forwards some of those packets through the Wi-Fi link to the remote controller and the mobile application.

13.9.3.2. *Experimental setup*

A susceptibility testing campaign was performed on the target in order to identify logical effects that were suitable for EMW. The target was placed on a table in a FARADAY cage together with the remote controller and a smartphone running the mobile application (Figure 13.8). The aircraft had its propellers removed in order to avoid difficulties due to flying or falling. The remote controller was started and the aircraft and the smartphone attached on the Wi-Fi network. A Raspberry Pi was also added and attached to the remote controller Wi-Fi network and configured to act as a Wi-Fi to ethernet bridge. All incoming packets on the Wi-Fi interface were forwarded to a monitoring computer outside the cage through a pair of ethernet to optical transducers. The source allowed generating pulsed CW signals in the 100–2.000 MHz range with pulse repetition frequencies between 1 kHz and 20 kHz with a maximum amplification of 50 W.

13.9.3.3. *Storage channel and watermark extraction*

After identifying effects from the right categories along with the IEMI waveforms that cause them, the determination of storage mechanisms for the selected effects had to be performed. For this, UAVs provide a genuine built-in feature that makes this kind of target suitable for EMW: the flight logs. On the target, the maximum logging frequency is 250 Hz, which means there is a new log entry every 4 ms. Each log entry contains a set of raw sensor values that have their own update rate. However, 250 Hz is the fastest sampling rate we can expect when reading the values from the flight logs. After each test, the flight logs were extracted from the internal storage of the target and analyzed.

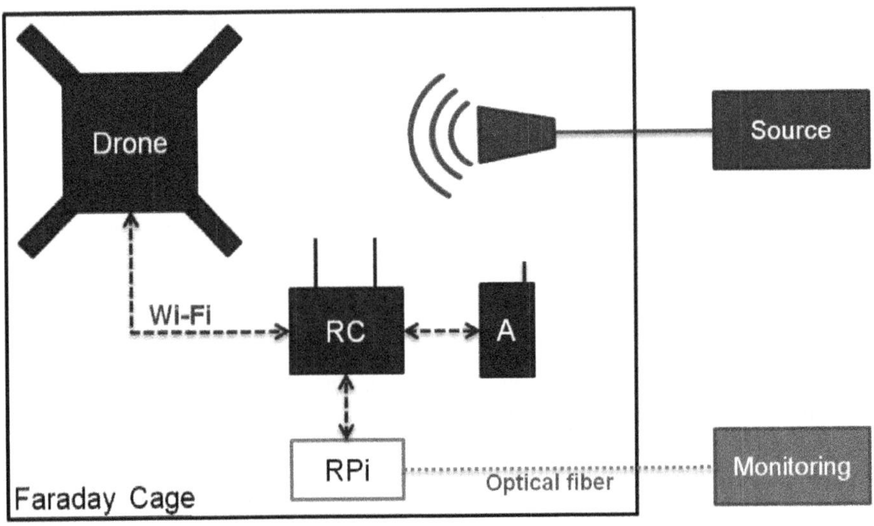

Figure 13.8. *Experimental setup for EMW on a UAV. For a color version of this figure, see www.iste.co.uk/prouff/cryptography3.zip*

13.9.3.4. *An EMW channel on the gimbal*

An IEMI effect on the gimbal has been observed with 282 MHz carrier frequency, 8 kHz repetition rate pulses. It had an impact on a value called "accel:z" in the flight logs, which is interpreted as the vertical acceleration in g. This value is sampled in the flight logs at a frequency of nearly 250 Hz.

It is a relevant example to document as the effect impacts several sensor values simultaneously, which might be a way to improve the watermark detection and extraction reliability.

This effect results in the appearance of a 15 Hz sinusoidal offset on the actual vertical acceleration value, as shown in Figure 13.9.

A proof of concept transmission based on an OOK modulation and a non-return to zero (NRZ) coding has been realized. Considering that one period of the 15 Hz signal is necessary to encode a symbol, a bit rate of 15 bps can be reached. Thus, considering a target flying at 60 km · h^{-1}, during the writing of a byte, the target will have moved approximately 8 m. Therefore, depending on the source power and the operational context, it will be possible to write one or several bytes in the target logs during illumination.

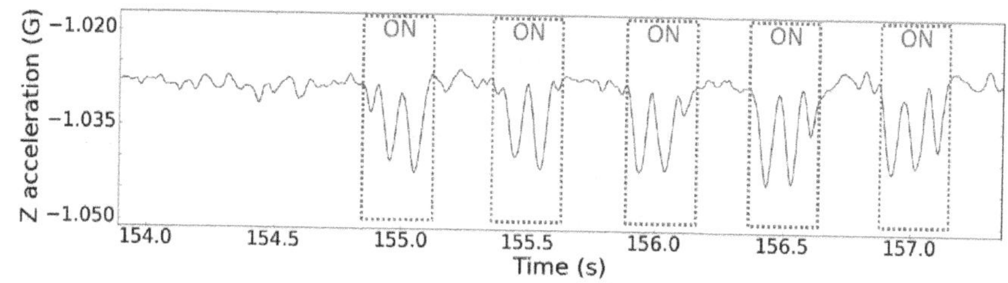

Figure 13.9. *Example EMW channel on the vertical acceleration, the effect occurs when the EMW source is on. For a color version of this figure, see www.iste.co.uk/prouff/cryptography3.zip*

Simultaneously, the roll and pitch angle values are also affected and the 15 Hz component is also present. Those effects appear as soon as the signal source is switched on.

The presence of the carrier signal in several observable values may allow for a robust detection and extraction of the embedded information. For example, when the effect was detected on the vertical acceleration curve, it could be confirmed by the switch of the slope sign of the pitch and roll curves to increase the probability of detection and reduce the false positive probability.

13.10. Conclusion

This chapter is dedicated to introducing intentional electromagnetic interference with an information security perspective. Among the techniques exploiting the electromagnetic susceptibility of electronic devices, IEMI was historically explored by the EMC scientific community. Methods for studying and modeling electromagnetic and electrical phenomena, evaluating and measuring the susceptibility of devices and designing protective measures were known for decades regarding unintentional EMI. Even the first intentional offensive uses of EMI were considering as well-defined EMI signals, with a focus on electronic warfare threat models tending to maximize distance to and damage on the target.

However, with IEMI, the range of threat models increased, from legacy long-range scenarios to very short-range scenarios considered in EMFI. The diversity of potential offensive signals considered also increased and the threat is nowadays qualified as proteiform. The introduction of the intentionality of IEMI raised the complexity of the problem, which can no longer be solely studied as an EMC problem, but also as an information security problem. With electromagnetic fault injection, threat and fault models, evaluation methods and countermeasures exist in the scope of component security.

But between historical EMI scenarios and EMFI, there is still room for exploration of mid-range mid-power threats as seen in recent studies on sensor security. In this research area between EMC, EMFI and sensor security, several open problems emerge concerning offensive and defensive aspects around threats exploiting the electromagnetic susceptibility of the targets for the quantification of the attacker profile and the attack rating, the security evaluation of products, the design of countermeasures, the approaches for detection and forensic analysis.

13.11. References

Adami, C., Suhrke, M., Pusch, T., Joester, M., Kolosnev, N., Neubauer, G., Preinerstorfer, A. (2014). Investigation of the impact of various IEMI sources to electronic passport readers. In *Future Security 2014*. Fraunhofer Verlag, Berlin.

Al-Kuwari, S. and Wolthusen, S.D. (2011). Fuzzy trace validation: Toward an offline forensic tracking framework. In *2011 Sixth IEEE International Workshop on Systematic Approaches to Digital Forensic Engineering*. Oakland.

Anderson, R.J. (2020). *Security Engineering: A Guide to Building Dependable Distributed Systems*, 2nd edition. John Wiley & Sons, New York.

ANSSI (2020). Recommandations relatives à l'interconnexion d'un système d'information à internet. Guide, ANSSI-PA-066, Paris.

Backstrom, M.G. and Lovstrand, K.G. (2004). Susceptibility of electronic systems to high-power microwaves: Summary of test experience. *IEEE Transactions on Electromagnetic Compatibility*, 46(3), 396–403.

Bratus, S., Goodspeed, T., Albertini, A., Solanky, D.S. (2016). Fillory of PHY: Toward a periodic table of signal corruption exploits and polyglots in digital radio. In *10th USENIX Workshop on Offensive Technologies (WOOT 16)*. USENIX Association, Berkeley.

Brown, R. (2016). Welcome to the OpenWrt Project [Online]. Available at: https://openwrt.org/start.

Carrara, B. (2016). Air-gap covert channels. PhD Thesis, University of Ottawa, Ottawa.

Cayre, R., Galtier, F., Auriol, G., Nicomette, V., Kaâniche, M., Marconato, G. (2021). WazaBee: Attacking Zigbee networks by diverting Bluetooth low energy chips. In *IEEE/IFIP International Conference on Dependable Systems and Networks (DSN 2021)*, Taipei.

Dai, D., An, Z., Yang, L. (2022). Inducing wireless chargers to voice out. In *Proceedings of the 28th Annual International Conference on Mobile Computing And Networking, MobiCom '22*. ACM Press, New York.

Dayanıklı, G.Y., Mohammed, A.Z., Gerdes, R., Mina, M. (2022a). Wireless manipulation of serial communication. In *Proceedings of the 2022 ACM on Asia Conference on Computer and Communications Security, ASIA CCS '22*. ACM Press, New York.

Dayanıklı, G.Y., Sinha, S., Muniraj, D., Gerdes, R.M., Farhood, M., Mina, M. (2022b). Physical-layer attacks against pulse width modulation-controlled actuators. In *31st USENIX Security Symposium (USENIX Security 22)*. USENIX Association, Berkeley.

Dubois, T. (2011). Étude de formes d'onde d'agressions électromagnétiques hyperfréquences sur la vulnérabilité de circuits électroniques. PhD Thesis, Polytechnique Montréal, Montreal.

EFF (2014). NSA ANT catalog [Online]. Available at: https://www.eff.org/document/20131230-appelbaum-nsa-ant-catalog.

Gardiner, B. and Poore, C. (2022). Talking PLC4TRUCKS remotely with an SDR. In *DefCon 30*, Las Vegas.

Giechaskiel, I. and Rasmussen, K.B. (2019). SoK: Taxonomy and challenges of out-of-band signal injection attacks and defenses. *arXiv:1901.06935 [cs]*.

Giri, D. and Taylor, C.D. (1994). *High-Power Microwave Systems and Effects*. Taylor and Francis, Washington, D.C.

Giri, D., Hoad, R., Sabath, F. (2020). *High-Power Electromagnetic Effects on Electronic Systems*. Artech House, London.

Guri, M. (2021). POWER-SUPPLaY: Leaking sensitive data from air-gapped, audio-gapped systems by turning the power supplies into speakers. *IEEE Transactions on Dependable and Secure Computing*, 20(1), 313–330.

Guri, M., Monitz, M., Mirski, Y., Elovici, Y. (2015). BitWhisper: Covert signaling channel between air-gapped computers using thermal manipulations. In *2015 IEEE 28th Computer Security Foundations Symposium*, Verona [Online]. Available at: https://www.computer.org/csdl/proceedings-article/csf/2015/7538a276/17D45WgziOb.

Guri, M., Solewicz, Y., Elovici, Y. (2020). Fansmitter: Acoustic data exfiltration from air-gapped computers via fans noise. *Computers & Security*, 91, 101721.

Hanspach, M. and Goetz, M. (2013). On covert acoustical mesh networks in air. *Journal of Communications*, 8(11), 758–767.

Hasan, R., Saxena, N., Haleviz, T., Zawoad, S., Rinehart, D. (2013). Sensing-enabled channels for hard-to-detect command and control of mobile devices. In *Proceedings of the 8th ACM SIGSAC Symposium on Information, Computer and Communications Security, ASIA CCS '13*. ACM Press, New York.

Hayashi, Y.-I., Homma, N., Sugawara, T., Mizuki, T., Aoki, T., Sone, H. (2011). Non-invasive EMI-based fault injection attack against cryptographic modules. In *2011 IEEE International Symposium on Electromagnetic Compatibility*, Long Beach.

Hoad, R. (2007). The utility of electromagnetic attack detection to information security. PhD Thesis, University of South Wales, Newport.

HPEM (2019). HPEM system from Diehl defence protects against mini-drones. Diehl Defence [Online]. Available at: https://www.diehl.com//defence/en/press-and-media/news/hpem-system-from-diehl-defence-protects-against-mini-drones/.

Intel (2004). Intel Pentium 4 processor with 512-KB L2 cache on 0.13 micron process datasheet. Intel Datasheet, 298643-012.

ISO/IEC (2005). ISO/IEC 61000-2-13:2005 – Electromagnetic compatibility (EMC) – Part 2–13: Environment – High-power electromagnetic (HPEM) environments – Radiated and conducted. Standard, International Organization for Standardization, Geneva.

ISO/IEC (2020). ISO/IEC 61000-4-36:2020 – Electromagnetic compatibility (EMC) – Part 4–36: Testing and measurement techniques – IEMI immunity test methods for equipment and systems. Standard, International Organization for Standardization, Geneva.

Jang, J., Cho, M., Kim, J., Kim, D., Kim, Y. (2023). Paralyzing drones via EMI signal injection on sensory communication channels. In *Proceedings 2023 Network and Distributed System Security Symposium*. Internet Society, San Diego.

Jiang, Y., Ji, X., Wang, K., Yan, C., Mitev, R., Sadeghi, A., Xu, W. (2022). WIGHT: Wired ghost touch attack on capacitive touchscreens. In *2022 IEEE Symposium on Security and Privacy (SP)*, Los Alamitos.

Kasmi, C. and Lopes Esteves, J. (2015). IEMI threats for information security: Remote command injection on modern smartphones. *IEEE Transactions on Electromagnetic Compatibility*, 57(6), 1752–1755.

Köhler, S., Baker, R., Martinovic, I. (2022a). Signal injection attacks against CCD image sensors. In *Proceedings of the 2022 ACM on Asia Conference on Computer and Communications Security, ASIA CCS '22*. ACM Press, New York.

Köhler, S., Baker, R., Strohmeier, M., Martinovic, I. (2022b). Brokenwire: Wireless disruption of CCS electric vehicle charging. *arXiv:2202.02104*.

Kuhn, M.G. and Anderson, R.J. (1998). Soft tempest: Hidden data transmission using electromagnetic emanations. In *International Workshop on Information Hiding*, Aucsmith, D. (ed.), Springer, Berlin, Heidelberg.

Kune, D.F., Backes, J., Clark, S.S., Kramer, D., Reynolds, M., Fu, K., Kim, Y., Xu, W. (2013). Ghost talk: Mitigating EMI signal injection attacks against analog sensors. In *2013 IEEE Symposium on Security and Privacy*, Berkeley.

Lampson, B.W. (1973). A note on the confinement problem. *Communications of the ACM*, 16(10), 613–615.

Leach, R.D. and Alexander, M.B. (1995). *Electronic Systems Failures and Anomalies Attributed to Electromagnetic Interference*. NASA, Washington, D.C.

Lee, K.S.H. (1986). *EMP Interaction: Principles, Techniques, and Reference Data (Revised Edition)*. Hemisphere Publishing, London.

Lee, M.-J., Kim, K.-S., Lee, H.-K. (2009). Forensic tracking watermarking against in-theater piracy. In *Information Hiding*, Katzenbeisser, S. and Sadeghi, A.-R. (eds). Springer, Berlin, Heidelberg.

Lee, E., Kim, H., Yoon, J.W. (2016). Various threat models to circumvent air-gapped systems for preventing network attack. In *Information Security Applications*, Kim, H.-W. and Choi, D. (eds). Springer, Cham.

Lopes Esteves, J. (2019). Electromagnetic watermarking: Exploiting IEMI effects for forensic tracking of UAVs. In *2019 International Symposium on Electromagnetic Compatibility-EMC EUROPE*, Barcelona.

Lopes Esteves, J. (2023). Electromagnetic interferences and information security: Characterization, exploitation and forensic analysis. PhD Thesis, HESAM Université, Paris.

Lopes Esteves, J. and Kasmi, C. (2018). Remote and silent voice command injection on a smartphone through conducted IEMI: Threats of smart IEMI for information security. System Design and Assessment Note, SDAN 48. Paper, ANSSI, Paris.

Lopes Esteves, J., Cottais, E., Kasmi, C. (2017). A ghost in your transmitter: Analyzing polyglot signals for physical layer covert channels detection. Document, Hardwear.Io, The Hague.

Lopes Esteves, J., Cottais, E., Kasmi, C. (2018). Second order soft-tempest in RF front-ends: Design and detection of polyglot modulations. In *2018 International Symposium on Electromagnetic Compatibility-EMC EUROPE*, Amsterdam.

Lopes Esteves, J., Kasmi, C., Arnaut, L., Degauque, P., Deniau, V., Giri, D., Gradoni, G., Gronwald, F., Hayakawa, M., Hobara, Y. et al. (2021). URSI Commission E: 100 years of URSI – The past, present, and future of commission E. In *100 Years of the International Union of Radio Science*, Wilkinson, P., Cannon, P.S., Stone W.R. (eds). URSI Press, Ghent.

Loughry, J. and Umphress, D.A. (2002). Information leakage from optical emanations. *ACM Trans. Inf. Syst. Secur.*, 5(3), 262–289.

Martorell, A. (2018). Détection à distance d'électroniques Par l'intermodulation. PhD Thesis, Université Montpellier, Montpellier.

Maruyama, S., Wakabayashi, S., Mori, T. (2019). Tap 'n ghost: A compilation of novel attack techniques against smartphone touchscreens. In *2019 IEEE Symposium on Security and Privacy (SP)*, San Francisco.

Mejecaze, G. (2019). Analyse des destructions d'alimentations électroniques soumises à un courant impulsionnel fort niveau. PhD Thesis, Université de Bordeaux, Bordeaux.

NASA/ADS (1978). Integrated circuit electromagnetic susceptibility handbook. Technical Report MDC-E1929, McDonnell Douglas Astronautics Company, St. Louis.

Nassi, B., Shamir, A., Elovici, Y. (2017). Oops!... I think I scanned a malware. *arXiv:1703.07751* [Online]. Available at: https://arxiv.org/abs/1703.07751.

Nateghi, A., Schaarschmidt, M., Fisahn, S., Garbe, H. (2021). Susceptibility of power line communication (PLC) channel to DS, AM and jamming intentional electromagnetic interferences. In *2021 Asia-Pacific International Symposium on Electromagnetic Compatibility (APEMC)*, Nusa Dua.

O.MG (n.d.). O.MG [Online]. Available at: https://o.mg.lol/.

Palisek, L. and Suchy, L. (2011). High power microwave effects on computer networks. In *10th International Symposium on Electromagnetic Compatibility*, York.

Payet, P., Raoult, J., Chusseau, L. (2017). Remote extinction of a 2.4 GHz RF front-end using millimeter-wave EMI in the near-field. *Progress In Electromagnetics Research Letters*, 68, 99–104.

Ross, R., Winstead, M., McEvilley, M. (2022). Engineering trustworthy secure systems. Special Publication, SP 800-160v1, National Institute of Standards and Technology, Gaithersburg.

Sabath, F. and Nietsch, D. (2006). Electromagnetic effects on systems and components. In *American Electromagnetics International Symposium, AMEREM 2006*. Summa Foundation, Santa Barbara.

Sack, S., Kröger, K., Creutzburg, R. (2013). Location tracking forensics on mobile devices. In *Multimedia Content and Mobile Devices*. SPIE Press, Bellingham.

Selvaraj, J. (2018). Intentional electromagnetic interference attack on sensors and actuators. PhD Thesis, Iowa State University, Ames.

Shan, H., Zhang, B., Zhan, Z., Sullivan, D., Wang, S., Jin, Y. (2022). Invisible finger: Practical electromagnetic interference attack on touchscreen-based electronic devices. In *2022 IEEE Symposium on Security and Privacy (SP)*, Los Alamitos.

Shannon, C.E. (1948). A mathematical theory of communication. *The Bell System Technical Journal*, 27(3), 379–423.

URSI (1999). Resolution on criminal activities using electromagnetic tools. Document, General Assembly and Scientific Symposium (URSI GASS), Toronto.

USBNinja (n.d.). USBNinja – Fast, stealth and ninja-like! [Online]. Available at: https://usbninja.com/.

Van de Beek, S. (2016). Vulnerability analysis of the wireless infrastructure to intentional electromagnetic interference. PhD Thesis, Universiteit Twente, Enschede.

van der Veen, M., Lemma, A., Celik, M., Katzenbeisser, S. (2007). Forensic watermarking in digital rights management. In *Security, Privacy, and Trust in Modern Data Management, Data-Centric Systems and Applications*, Petković, M. and Jonker, W. (eds). Springer, Berlin, Heidelberg.

Vittitoe, N,C. (1989). Did high altitude EMP cause the Hawaian streetlight incident? Sandia Report, Sandia National Laboratories, Albuquerque/Livermore.

Wang, K., Mitev, R., Yan, C., Ji, X., Sadeghi, A.-R., Xu, W. (2022). GhostTouch: Targeted attacks on touchscreens without physical touch. In *31st USENIX Security Symposium (USENIX Security 22)*. USENIX Association, Berkeley.

Wikipedia (2023). Starfish prime [Online]. Available at: https://en.wikipedia.org/wiki/Starfish_Prime.

Winbond (2002). W83627HF/F. Datasheet 2.0. Winbond Electronics Corp., Taichung City [Online]. Available at: http://bitsavers.informatik.uni-stuttgart.de/components/winbond/W83627HF_LPCIO_200211.pdf.

Xu, Z., Hua, R., Juang, J., Xia, S., Fan, J., Hwang, C. (2021). Inaudible attack on smart speakers with intentional electromagnetic interference. *IEEE Transactions on Microwave Theory and Techniques*, 69(5), 2642–2650.

Zheng, L., Zhang, Y., Lee, C. E., Thing, V. L.L. (2017). Time-of-recording estimation for audio recordings. *Digital Investigation*, 22, S115–S126.

14

Attacking IoT Light Bulbs

Colin O'FLYNN[1,2] and Eyal RONEN[3]
[1]*Dalhousie University, Halifax, Canada*
[2]*NewAE Technology Inc, Halifax, Canada*
[3]*Tel Aviv University, Israel*

14.1. Introduction

The Internet of Things (IoT) is a term given to the wide variety of connected devices, which now are inescapable in our daily lives. Examples of common IoT devices found in many homes and businesses include light bulbs, smart speakers, door locks and cameras. A key feature of these devices is that they have some ability to interconnect and interact. A user can talk to their smart speaker, which can lock the door and set all the exterior lights on for one hour.

Such devices typically have ad hoc networking capabilities, which allow them to communicate directly to each other. This "secondary" communication interface is rarely managed directly by the user, which means the user may be unaware of its capabilities. This also means there must be a high degree of trust in the implementation of any security on this secondary interface.

There are numerous attack vectors that IoT devices may be subject to, many of which depend on the capabilities and interfaces the device exposes. A device with a microphone or camera, for example, may be vulnerable to an attacker remotely turning on those features. The most fundamental vector is one, which allows an attacker to rewrite the software (firmware) running on the IoT device. Attacking the firmware

Embedded Cryptography 3,
coordinated by Emmanuel PROUFF, Guénaël RENAULT,
Matthieu RIVAIN and Colin O'FLYNN.

update is particularly powerful, as it provides an attacker with unlimited capability to rewrite the functionality of the device.

This firmware update capability is the main topic of this chapter, and in particular, it will be shown how an IoT device using AES-CCM to provide both encryption and authentication of a firmware image can be attacked with side-channel power analysis. The particular IoT device will be the Philips Hue smart bulbs.

This chapter is based on work by Ronen et al. (2017) presented in the paper *IoT Goes Nuclear: Creating a ZigBee Chain Reaction*. In addition, later work by Itkin (2020) is also discussed, which demonstrated attacks on the bridge device.

The attacks discussed in this chapter were reported to Phillips in 2016 and have been patched in various forms. Statements about the security features in place made in this chapter refer to the state of the devices in 2016.

The chapter will begin with an introduction to the specific IoT device and architecture, along with a discussion of the threat model and the bootloader and encryption used for firmware updates on this device. A side-channel attack on the bootloader will then be presented, allowing us to send firmware, which will be accepted by the device. A brief summary of the required work to form a complete attack is also presented, but the focus of this chapter is the demonstration of how knowledge about the attacks and AES implementation learned in earlier chapters is applied in "real life".

14.2. Preliminaries

A short overview of the general IoT specification used by these light bulbs will be presented, along with some specific details of the Philips Hue firmware update mechanism.

14.2.1. *ZLL (ZigBee Light Link) and smart light systems*

As seen in Figure 14.1, smart lamp systems enable users to control their lamps either from a remote control or from a smartphone application using a gateway. The gateway is used to bridge the IP world to the ZLL world, which is an industry standard developed and supported by most of the major home lighting manufacturers such as Philips, GE and OSRAM.

The Philips Hue lamps use hardware which is based on SoC (system on chip) that includes a microcontroller, flash memory for bootloader and code, SRAM memory for program data, AES hardware acceleration, 802.15.4 radio transceiver and various code protection mechanisms. We attacked a hardware version that uses the Atmel's ATmega2564RFR2 SoC.

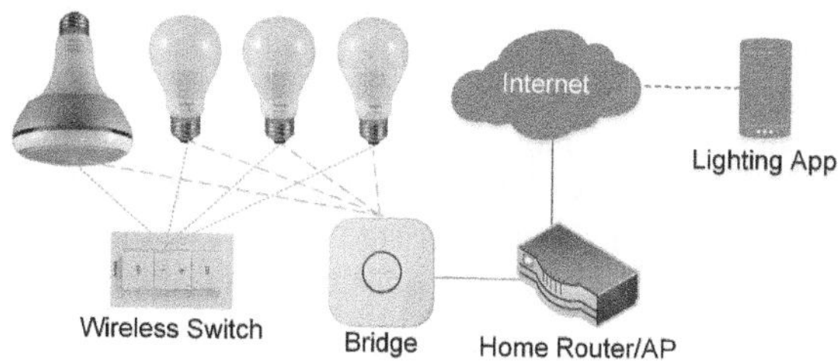

Figure 14.1. *The ZLL architecture. For a color version of this figure, see www.iste.co.uk/prouff/cryptography3.zip*

14.2.2. *Lamp hardware*

There are multiple versions of the lamp hardware, with different main microcontrollers. The original bulbs used a TI CC2530 (8-bit 8051) with an example of this board shown in Figure 14.2; later versions used a Microchip ATmega2564RFR2 (8-bit RISC) and then moved to a Microchip SAM based design (32-bit Arm).

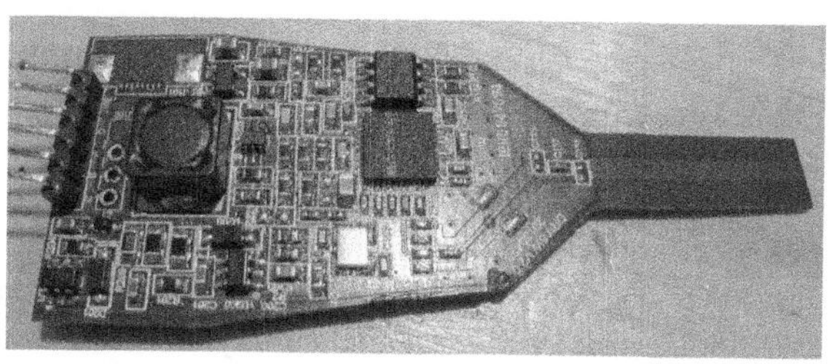

Figure 14.2. *The MegaRF-based bulb. For a color version of this figure, see www.iste.co.uk/prouff/cryptography3.zip*

14.2.3. *Firmware updates*

In order to securely update the firmware of both the bridge and lamp, firmware updates are downloaded from a Philips Hue server. This allows protection of the transfer using standard web security infrastructure. In order to update the bulbs, an additional mechanism is required, which sends the firmware over the ZLL protocol.

For the bulb firmware update, the encrypted and signed firmware files that were downloaded from the Philips server are sent in small chunks to the lamps. The lamps write each small chunk to an external SPI flash until all chunks are received. Finally, the bulb can verify the integrity of the firmware file and mark the file as ready for the bootloader to update.

As the bootloader is in a very limited memory space, the bootloader has no ability to use wireless features. It can only reprogram the firmware present in the SPI flash. If on boot, the bootloader detects a flag indicating the firmware should be programmed from SPI flash, the bootloader will first cryptographically verify the integrity and authenticity of the file. Once the bootloader starts the erase, the device will no longer function, so it is important that the bootloader does not attempt to program invalid firmware.

If the file passes the verification steps, the bootloader will then erase the application firmware and reprogram it from the SPI flash. The update file is decrypted on-the-fly, with each chunk decrypted as it is programmed. Once fully programmed, the authentication tag is checked, and if it passes, the bootloader now boots the new application firmware.

Critically, the authentication tag is part of the AES-CCM encryption used for the firmware update file. This means there is no separate PKI used to verify the bootloader, and the verification is entirely based on symmetric encryption.

14.2.4. *Hue Bridge hardware*

The Hue Bridge 2.0 uses a Qualcomm QCA4531, which is a MIPS 24Kc SoC. The bridge hardware runs a Linux kernel and has both ZigBee and Ethernet interfaces as previously mentioned. Attacks on this device will not be discussed in this chapter, but this brief overview is included for completeness. An attacker with access to the bridge can bypass the root password protection to install arbitrary code or otherwise modify the device. Having low-level hardware access to the device is often not protected against, since it is assumed such an attacker could easily install hardware bugs.

However, two other interesting attacks would be against the Internet infrastructure and the ZigBee interface. Eyal Itkin has presented research on the binary process running on the bridge (see the References section of this chapter). This resulted in an attack which happens from the ZigBee side and allows access to the Ethernet side. This will not be discussed further in this chapter, but highlights the multiple interfaces and vulnerabilities these IoT devices may contain.

14.3. Hardware AES and AES-CTR attacks

As the light bulbs under consideration have an Atmel ATMega2564RFR2 device, the first part of the attack is to explore the use of the hardware AES accelerator. We had previously demonstrated an attack against the AES accelerator in the closely related ATMega128RFA1 device, which is described in this section. See the Notes and further references section for a reference to this complete work and for more details of the attack on the hardware AES accelerator.

The first published attack of an Atmel product with hardware AES acceleration was the XMEGA attack by Kizhvatov (2009). Kizhvatov determined that for a CPA attack on the XMEGA device, a vulnerable sensitive value was the Hamming distance between successive S-box input values. These input values are the XOR of the plaintext with the secret key that occurs during the first `AddRoundKey`. This suggests a single S-box is implemented in hardware, with successive applications of the input values to the S-box.

The following notation considers P_j and K_j to be a byte of the plaintext and encryption key, respectively, where $0 \leq j \leq 15$. To determine an unknown byte K_j, we first assume we know a priori the value of P_j, P_{j-1} and K_{j-1}. The determination of K_{j-1} is presented later, but we can assume for now that byte K_{j-1} is known.

This allows us to perform a standard CPA attack, where the sensitive value is given by the Hamming weight of equation [14.1]. That is to say the leakage for unknown encryption key byte j is: $l_j = HW(b_j)$. Provided K_0 is known, this attack can proceed as a standard CPA attack, with only 2^8 guesses required to determine each byte.

$$b_j = (P_{j-1} \oplus K_{j-1}) \oplus (P_j \oplus K_j), \quad 1 \leq j \leq 15 \qquad [14.1]$$

If K_0 is unknown in practice, an attacker can simply proceed with an attack for all 2^8 possibilities of K_0. The attacker may then test each of the resulting 256 candidate keys to determine the correct value of K_0. This would entail a total of $2^8 \times (2^8 \times 15)$ guesses.

For the specific case of K_0, a more straightforward approach exists. Kizhvatov (2009) later determined that K_0 can be determined directly by using a leakage assumption based on the Hamming distance from the fixed value 0x00. This leakage function is shown in equation [14.2]:

$$l_0 = HW(b_0) = HW(P_0 \oplus K_0) \qquad [14.2]$$

This allows the entire encryption key to be attacked with a total of 16×2^8 guesses.

14.3.1. *Application to ATMega128RFA1*

The initial work was done on a development board for the ATMega128RFA1, the Dresden Elektronik radio board model number RCB128RFA1 V6.3.1. Power measurements were taken by inserting a resistor between the VCC_{core} power pin and decoupling capacitor. A differential probe was used to measure the voltage across this resistor. To sample the power measurements, the ChipWhisperer platform is used at 64 MS/s (which is 4 × the device clock of 16 MHz).

Examples of the correlation output versus sample point are shown in Figure 14.3, which shows the peaks at the output of the correlation function on the CPA attack for the "correct" key guess. The sign of the peak is not important – the sign will flip depending on probe polarity – but note that the correct key guess results in a larger magnitude correlation than the incorrect guess at certain points. These points are when the physical hardware is performing the operation in equation [14.1].

The majority of key bytes are recovered in under 10,000 traces on this setup, which suggests that the attack is viable in practical scenarios.

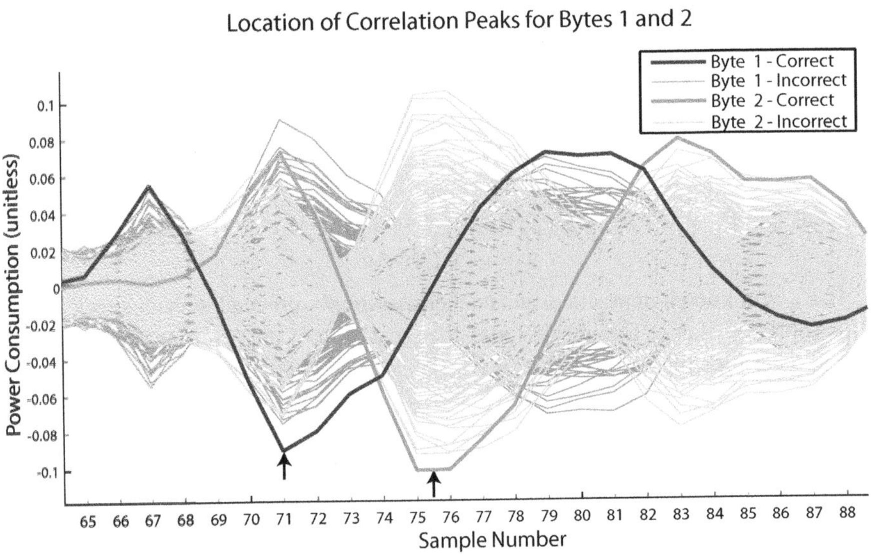

Figure 14.3. *Correlation peaks for byte $j = 1$ and $j = 2$. The "incorrect guess" means the $2^8 - 1$ guesses that are not the value of K_j. The sample number refers to the sample points since the start of the encryption operation, again sampling at 64 MS/s. For a color version of this figure, see www.iste.co.uk/prouff/cryptography3.zip*

14.3.1.1. *Guessing of K_{j-1}*

This attack used the leakage equation [14.2] of the first byte $j = 0$ to bootstrap the key recovery. Once we know this byte, we can use equation [14.1] to recover successive bytes.

Practically, we may have a situation where $j - 1$ is not recoverable. Previous work assumed either some additional correlation peak allowing us to determine $j - 1$, or the use of a brute-force search across all possibilities of the byte $j-1$. We can improve on this with a more efficient search algorithm, described next.

The leakage function equation [14.1] could be rewritten to show more clearly that the leaked value depends not on the byte values, but on the XOR between the two successive bytes, as in equation [14.3].

$$b_j = (K_{j-1} \oplus K_j) \oplus (P_{j-1} \oplus P_j), \quad 1 \leq j \leq 15 \qquad [14.3]$$

The side-channel attack can be performed with the unknown byte K_{j-1} set to 0x00, and the remaining bytes are recovered by the CPA attack described previously. These recovered bytes are not the correct value, but instead provide the value that has to be XOR'd with the previous byte to generate the correct byte.

The 256 candidate keys can then be generated with almost no computational work by iterating through each possibility for the unknown byte K_{j-1} and using the XOR values recovered from the CPA attack to generate the remaining byte values $K_j, k_{j+1}, \cdots, k_J$.

This assumes we are able to directly test those candidate keys to determine which is the correct value. As is described in the next section, we can instead use a CPA attack on the next-round key to determine the correct value of K_{j-1}.

14.3.2. *Later-round attacks*

Although previous work has been concerned with determining the first-round encryption key, information on later-round keys may also be required for a complete attack. For later rounds, the leakage assumption of equations [14.1] and [14.2] still holds, where the unknown byte K_j is a byte of the round key, and the known plaintext byte P_j is the output of the previous round. We can extend our notation such that the leakage from round r becomes $l_j^r = HW(b_j^r)$, where each byte of the round key is k_j^r, and the input data to that round is p_j^r.

As described in section 14.3.1.1, we can perform the CPA attack on byte K_j where K_{j-1} is unknown by determining not the value of the byte, but the XOR of each successive byte with the previous key. This means performing the attack first, where K_{j-1} is assumed to be 0x00.

By then enumerating all 2^8 possibilities for K_{j-1}, we can quickly generate 2^8 candidate keys to test. However, if we are unable to test those keys, we need another way of validating the most likely value of K_{j-1}.

If we know the initial (first-round) key, we can determine the input to the second round, and thus perform a CPA attack on the second-round key. In this case, we do not know the first-round key, but we have 256 candidates for the first round ($r = 1$), and want to determine which of those keys is correct.

To determine which of the keys is correct, we can perform a CPA attack on the first byte of the second round, K_0^2, repeating the CPA attack 256 times, once for each candidate first-round key. The correlation output of the CPA attack will be low for all guesses of K_0^2 where $\vec{K}^1$ is wrong, and only for the correct guess of K_0^2 and $\vec{K}^1$ will there be a peak. This allows us to use a CPA attack on the second round to determine which of the first-round keys is correct, without requiring us to have an oracle to verify the encryption key.

This can be useful in situations where we do not have both plaintext and ciphertext, or for attacking AES-ECB blocks that are used within parts of other AES modes.

So far, this attack is limited to the AES accelerator used in AES-ECB mode, so we can now apply this to the bootloader itself. We will first look at how the bootloader works, before looking at the exploitable leakage.

14.4. AES-CCM bootloader attack

This section will detail the bootloader attack, which relies on both CPA attacks and DPA attacks. A custom leakage model is used, and some form of leakage detection is used as part of the reverse engineering process. These are topics that were covered by earlier chapters of this book. In this section, we will first introduce the physical setup of the attack hardware, before discussing how the attack is used to recover the encryption key used by the bootloader.

The physical setup used for the power analysis work is shown in Figure 14.4. Note that a custom board was designed for the ChipWhisperer system, for the purpose of the attack the target chip was desoldered from the Hue Bulb, and soldered to the custom board. This provided a very low-noise and reliable method of performing the power analysis.

When the device boots, it can be forced to load an (encrypted) firmware image from SPI flash. The SPI flash data lines provide an excellent trigger source for this purpose. In addition, a SPI flash programmer is present in Figure 14.4. This is used to change the encrypted file to provide ciphertext control, which is used for work such as leakage detection, where specific controlled ciphertext input is required.

14.4.1. *Understanding Philips OTA image cryptographic primitives*

Our initial assumption was that Philips used the CCM encryption mode for the OTA image. This enables them to reuse the CCM code from the Zigbee encryption, which was also used in an old TI cryptographic bootloader implementation, which could have been used as a reference to their implementation in the older TI-based models. A summary of the AES-CCM mode is given in Figure 14.5.

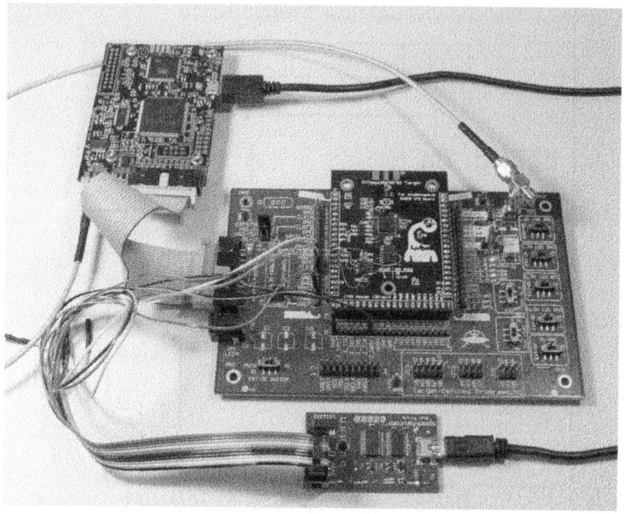

Figure 14.4. *Power analysis on the ATMega2564RFR2 from a Philips Hue bulb was done using a ChipWhisperer-Lite (top left) connected to a custom PCB with the ATMega2564RFR2 mounted (middle blue PCB) and using a Bus Pirate (bottom small PCB) to reprogram a SPI flash chip with various byte sequences. For a color version of this figure, see www.iste.co.uk/prouff/cryptography3.zip*

When we started this work, the newer bulbs based on the Atmel ATMega2564RFR2 did not have an OTA update released. Instead, we used an image for the CC2530 bulbs as a reference. To perform the bootload process, the new (encrypted) image is programmed in the SPI flash. On boot, the bulb will first check a flag to indicate if an OTA update is pending; if so, it reads the entire image to verify the signature. Then, it reads the image a second time to actually perform the flash programming. We determined this based on (1) modifying the image – which would invalidate the signature – causes the bulb to perform only the first read; and (2) the second read-through contain gaps where no SPI activity is occurring. These gaps align with the internal flash memory page-erase process required before performing a flash write.

As we knew the leakage mode for the ATMega2564RFR2 AES hardware engine, we targeted the newer hardware. The CC2530 OTA upgrade file was modified by changing the hardware type and image file size to fit the requirements of the bootloader on the new hardware, so the bootloader on the ATMega2564RFR2 would attempt the verification process. The actual verification will *fail* as this was not a valid OTA image for this platform, meaning we were able to perform this attack without having access to a valid firmware image.

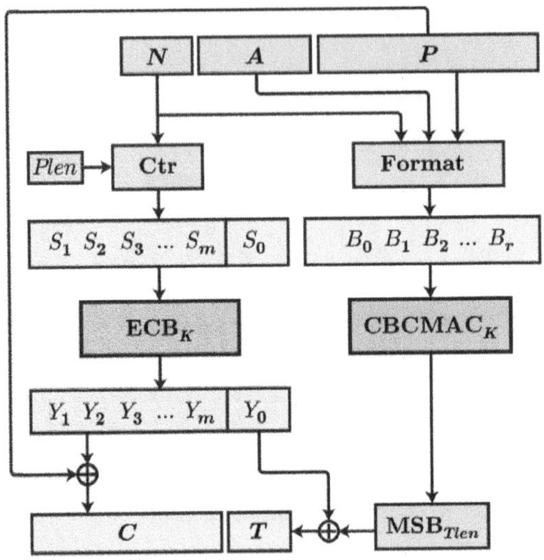

Figure 14.5. *CCM encryption mode. For a color version of this figure, see www.iste.co.uk/prouff/cryptography3.zip*

The hardware AES engine on the ATMega2564RFR2 has a unique signature, which makes detecting the location of AES straightforward. Looking at the power traces of the verification process, we could notice two AES operations for each 16 byte block, which supported the CCM assumption, as shown in the top portion of Figure 14.6.

In addition, we performed a DPA attack where the leakage assumption is simply the input data itself being loaded. This shows locations where the input data are manipulated (this will also track linear changes to the data, such as an XOR operation). We note that the input data are manipulated after the first AES operation and before the second AES operation, as in the lower part of Figure 14.6.

This would be consistent with the first AES operation being CTR mode, the output of CTR mode being a pad which is XORd with the input data to decrypt the block. The decrypted data are then fed into the CBC block. Note the XORs of the input data still generate the high difference spikes, as the input data are effectively being XORd with constants (either the AES-CTR output with the same CTR input, or the CBC output).

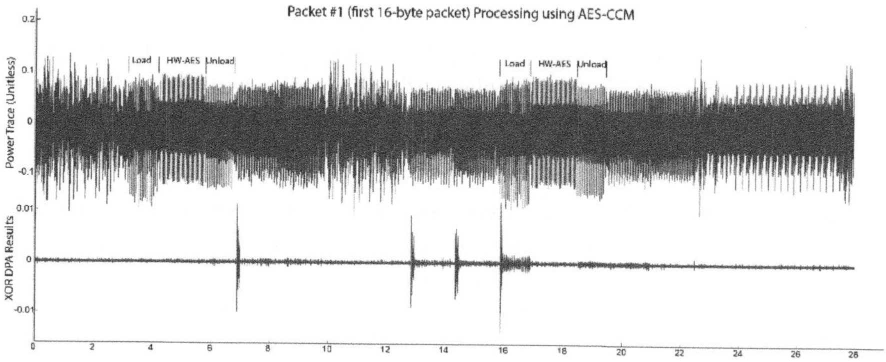

Figure 14.6. *Power analysis of processing a single 16-byte block by the cryptographic bootloader. HW-AES locations are marked based on comparison to a reference platform performing hardware AES encryptions. For a color version of this figure, see www.iste.co.uk/prouff/cryptography3.zip*

14.4.2. *CPA attack against the CCM CBC MAC verification*

Under the CCM assumption, we had to find a way to break the mode of operation under the following limitations:

1) We have no knowledge of the key.

2) We have no knowledge of the encryption nonce.

3) We have no knowledge of the signature IV or associated data.

4) We have no sample of a valid encrypted message.

5) Our target will not accept messages larger than around 2^{14} encryption blocks.

14.4.2.1. *Previous work on AES-CTR and AES-CCM*

Performing power analysis on AES-CTR mode is made more complicated as the majority of the bytes are constant (the nonce), and only the counter bytes vary. A standard first-order CPA attack is only able to recover the key-bytes where the associated input bytes vary, meaning that at most, two bytes of the counter are recovered. A solution to this was presented by Jaffe (2007), where Jaffe performs the attack over multiple AES rounds.

Jaffe's technique of performing the attack over multiple rounds allows recovery of a combination of the AES Round-Key XORd with either the constant plaintext or the output of the previous round. This allows us to ignore the unknown constant values, as they will eventually be removed. A similar technique was used in our description of the ATMega128RFA1 attack from section 14.3.

The AES-CTR attack requires 2^{16} encryptions to ensure power traces are recorded for all values of all 16 bits of the counter. While Jaffe (2007) reports that the attack may succeed with a smaller subset of these 2^{16} traces, the subset will include traces from throughout the set, such that even if a set of 2^{14} traces pulled from the larger set was sufficient, capturing only 2^{14} *consecutive* traces will not provide enough data.

The leakage observed by the hardware AES peripheral in section 14.3 is such that leakage occurs before the S-box operation, and it is not possible to reliably perform the attack using the output of the S-box. Had the output of the S-box leaked, it would have been possible to recover higher order bits of the key for which there is no associated toggling of higher order bits of input data due to the nonlinear property of the S-box.

A solution to the general problem of unknown counter inputs is also given by Hanley et al. (2009), where a template attack can be performed even with completely unknown input to the AES block. This attack has the downside of worse performance (in terms of number of traces required) compared to a known plaintext (or ciphertext) attack.

As our target only accepted about 2^{14} 16-byte blocks, we had limited ability to use the existing AES-CTR attacks. We were also unaware of the nonce format – if we had a known mapping of some input data field to AES-CTR nonce, additional attacks from the previous work could be used.

14.4.2.2. *Unknown plaintext with chosen differentials CPA attack against AES*

For our attack, we introduce a method of efficiently converting the most chosen plaintext CPA attack against ECB mode in the case of unknown plaintext with chosen differentials. Our attack works under the following assumptions:

1) We have a black-box chosen plaintext CPA attack that can break the first round of an ECB mode encryption implementation.

2) We do not know the input to our ECB mode encryption, but we can measure repeated encryptions with the same unknown input XORed to any chosen differential.

3) For each differential, we can measure the power trace of at least the first and second AES round.

As in previous works, we use the notion of a "modified key". We will use the following notation:

– P_i is the *i*th byte of the unknown plaintext input to the AES encryption.

– D_i is the *i*th byte of the chosen differential.

– $K_{j,i}$ is the *i*th byte of the jth round key of AES.

In the general case of first round of AES encryption, the key and plaintext bytes are used in calculation of the output of the S-box. The output of the S-box on byte i can be written as $Ouput_i = S(P_i \oplus K_{1,i})$. Any chosen plaintext CPA attack on the first round will be able to retrieve all of the bytes of K_1 by measuring traces of different inputs P. In our case, P_i is constant and we can choose D_i, and we get $Ouput_i = S(D_i \oplus P_i \oplus K_{1,i})$. We will denote our "modified key" as $K'_{1,i} = P_i \oplus K_{1,i}$, rewriting $Ouput_i = S(D_i \oplus K'_i)$.

We can now use our black-box CPA attack to retrieve all of the bytes of K'_1. Using D and K'_1, we can now calculate the input to the second AES round. As the first and second round of AES are identical, we can use the same black-box CPA attack against the second round with known inputs, and retrieve the real second round key.

In most CPA attacks, we can choose our inputs at random and use the same power traces we used for the first round attack. If real chosen plaintext is needed, we can use the invertible structure of the AES round and calculate the required differentials in the first round.

After getting the real second round key K_2, we can use the invertible AES key expansion algorithm to find K_1 and then all bytes of P_i. In the normal case where only random plaintext is needed for the CPA attack, we can break our ECB mode with unknown plaintext and chosen differentials in the same number of traces required to break ECB with chosen plaintext.

14.4.2.3. *Breaking AES-CCM*

For efficiently breaking the CCM mode, we attack the CBC MAC state calculation on two consecutive blocks. We will first summarize some notation for AES-CCM.

If we consider the AES-ECB function using key k as $E_k(x)$, we can write the CTR and CBC portions of the CCM mode as follows. The input will be in 16-byte blocks, where block m is the index. CTR mode requires some IV and counter which is input to an AES-ECB block, and we assume our input is $\{IV||m\}$, where IV is a 14-byte constant that is concatenated to the block number m. Counter mode first generates a "stream" based on the counter and IV:

$$CTR_m = E_k(\{IV||m\})$$

This stream is XORd with plaintext/ciphertext for encryption/decryption, respectively. Thus, decrypting block PT_m would be:

$$PT_m = CT_m \oplus CTR_m$$

In addition to decryption, CCM provides the authentication tag, which is the output of a CBC mode encryption across all PT_m (and possibly other) blocks. The internal state of this CBC mode after block m will be CBC_m, which can be written as:

$$\begin{aligned} CBC_m &= E_k(PT_m \oplus CBC_{m-1}) \\ &= E_k(CT_m \oplus CTR_m \oplus CBC_{m-1}) \end{aligned}$$

If we target a given block m, CTR_m and CBC_{m-1} will be constant. CT_m is the ciphertext we input to the block (e.g. by the firmware file we sent the device), allowing us to control the value of CT_m. We consider our unknown plaintext to be $CTR_m \oplus CBC_{m-1}$ and using the ciphertext as the chosen differential, and then we can use our CPA attack to recover the CBC MAC key k, and the value of $CTR_m \oplus CBC_{m-1}$. As the CCM mode reuses the key between encryption and verification, we also get the key used for encryption. We now repeat our attack for the first round of block $m+1$. From our attack on block m, we can calculate CBC_m, and from our attack on block $m+1$, we can retrieve $CTR_{m+1} \oplus CBC_i$ and from that CTR_{m+1}. We can now find the nonce used by decrypting CTR_{m+1} with the key we found.

14.4.2.4. *AES-CTR DPA recovery optimization*

Our attack on CCM requires twice the traces of ECB mode, since we must attack two blocks: both CBC_m and CBC_{m+1} in order to retrieve the CTR output. We can optimize our attack by using a bitwise difference-of-means DPA attack to recover the output of the AES-CTR encryption directly for block m. The DPA attack is attacking $CTR_m \oplus CT_m$ operation. An example of this on the actual bootloader power measurement is shown in Figure 14.7, where a single byte is being recovered.

Note that there may be multiple locations where a strong "difference" output is seen. These locations come about as any linear operations on the CT_m data will present such spikes (for example, not only the XOR we are targeting, but also the data loading, and when the AES-CTR output is used in the AES-CBC input). In addition, there will be both positive and negative spikes as the internal bus switches from precharge, to final state, back to precharge.

We found about 10 locations with such strong differences across the entire trace, giving us 10 possible guesses for the output of the AES-CTR on the first block on the same traces under the CPA attack. Using the key retrieved from the CPA attack, we tried decrypting the guesses, and simply chose the one that decrypted to the correct counter value in the last bytes.

The correct guess occurred in the window where the AES-CTR XOR operation was expected to occur (around sample point 6950 in Figure 14.6), meaning the additional guessing may not be required in most cases.

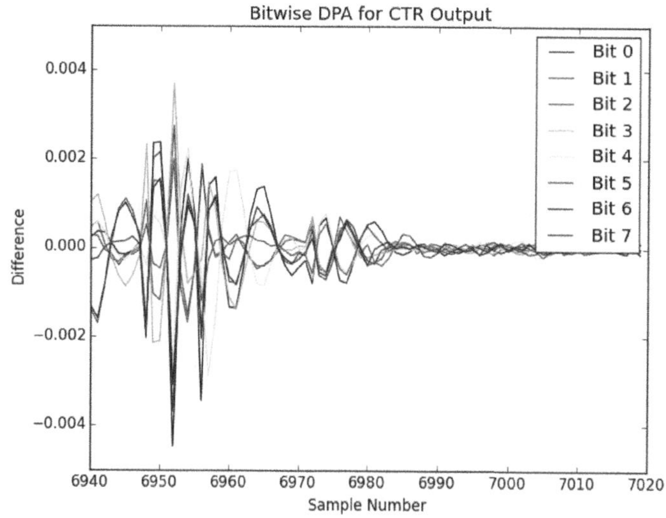

Figure 14.7. *Bitwise DPA attack on AES-CTR "pad", where all 8 bits are recovered. For a color version of this figure, see www.iste.co.uk/prouff/cryptography3.zip*

14.4.2.5. *Extending the CCM attack to other block ciphers*

By combining the CPA attack and DPA optimization, we can break any SPN (substitution–permutation network)-based cipher block algorithm regardless of the key expansion algorithm under the following assumptions:

1) We have a CPA attack that can break any round using chosen plaintext.

2) We can measure the power traces for all rounds.

3) The DPA attack provides a small number of possible guesses for the output of the CTR.

We use the CPA attack against block m to retrieve the CBC MAC state CBC_m. By using the DPA attack, we can retrieve the possible guess to the CTR output CTR_{m+1}. As the CBC MAC encryption in block $m+1$ is $E_k(CT_{m+1} \oplus CTR_{m+1} \oplus CBC_m)$, we can now do a chosen plaintext attack against block $m+1$ to retrieve all of the round keys, including the first round.

14.5. Application of attack

The previous sections in this chapter demonstrated how material in this book can be used to first break the AES hardware peripheral, and then the AES bootloader. The result of this attack is the AES bootloader key used to both encrypt and sign the firmware update. More effort is required to form a complete attack, which will be discussed here.

Finding the AES key for the bootloader is a critical step, as it allows signing of firmware images that will be accepted by the lamp. For a lamp to receive a firmware image, however, it must be associated with an attacker-controlled network. This means either the attacker first loads malicious firmware, or the attacker creates a malicious network.

Without any further vulnerabilities, this means bulbs could be reflashed without an external sign of tampering. This could be used in a supply-chain attack, where bulbs with malicious firmware have a permanent secondary function or backdoor. A backdoor would be limited to being accessed only from the 802.15.4 (ZigBee) radio link; the bulbs do not directly have access to the Internet.

A much more interesting vulnerability was disclosed by Ronen et al. (2017), where it is discovered that it is also possible to force a bulb to reassociate with a new attacker-controlled network. This immediately opens up a much more powerful attack: an IoT worm that spreads via the ZLL radio link, and will not be detected from the network side. Each bulb can easily force other nearby bulbs to join a new malicious network, and thus continue to spread the updated malicious firmware.

Practically, this also requires building firmware for the lightbulb. The firmware update in this case is not just a part of the firmware, but a complete replacement of the application. This means any desired functionality (including processing of ZLL packets) must be implemented. This also means the attacker has complete control of the hardware, including the choice of accepting future firmware updates.

Itkin (2020) demonstrated that a vulnerability in the Huge Bridge could allow access from the ZLL radio network to the user Ethernet network. This opens up new vulnerabilities, including allowing an "out-of-band" network to be formed between two networks that both have Philips Hue bridge interfaces on them. This shows that attacks on IoT devices have a long lifespan, as attacking the hardware opens up a wide range of possible attacks.

NOTE. The vulnerability allowing the worm to spread, the forced long-range re-association, has been fixed in a firmware patch distributed by Philips.

14.6. Notes and further references

This chapter work is based on the work published in Ronen et al. (2017) and O'Flynn and Chen (2016).

– Section 14.2. Some of the information about these networks is publically available, including the ZigBee Light Link (ZLL) specification and the datasheets of the various microcontrollers used in the products.

– Section 14.3. The leakage model for the hardware AES model was disclosed in Kizhvatov (2009). This was applied to the ATMega128RFA1 device in O'Flynn and Chen (2016), which is almost identical to the device used by the Philips Hue bulb. The specific attack is based on the AES-CTR attack presented in Jaffe (2007).

– Section 14.4. Attacking the bootloader uses the references from the previous section, especially previous work on AES-CTR in Jaffe (2007). Another solution to the problem is given in Hanley et al. (2009), which is not directly applicable here, but may be in other versions of the bootloader.

– Section 14.5. The full application of this attack is detailed in Ronen et al. (2017). Some additional details of the engineering work (including building the firmware for the bulb) are given in O'Flynn and Ronen (2017). A demonstration that it is possible to attack the local area network interface of the Huge bridge from the ZigBee interface is given in Itkin (2020).

14.7. References

Hanley, N., Tunstall, M., Marnane, W.P. (2009). Unknown plaintext template attacks. In *WISA 09*, Youm, H.Y. and Yung, M. (eds). Springer, Heidelberg.

Itkin, E. (2020). Don't be silly – It's only a lightbulb. Research Paper [Online]. Available at: https://research.checkpoint.com/2020/dont-be-silly-its-only-a-lightbulb/.

Jaffe, J. (2007). A first-order DPA attack against AES in counter mode with unknown initial counter. In *CHES 2007*, Paillier, P. and Verbauwhede, I. (eds). Springer, Heidelberg.

Kizhvatov, I. (2009). Side channel analysis of AVR XMEGA crypto engine. In *Proceedings of the 4th Workshop on Embedded Systems Security, WESS 2009*, Serpanos, D.N. and Wolf, W.H. (eds). ACM Press, New York.

O'Flynn, C. and Chen, Z. (2016). Power analysis attacks against IEEE 802.15.4 nodes. In *COSADE 2016*, Standaert, F.-X. and Oswald, E. (eds). Springer, Heidelberg.

O'Flynn, C. and Ronen, E. (2017). The lightbulb worm: A debriefing on philips hue attack. In *RECON 2017*. InfoconDB, Montreal.

Ronen, E., Shamir, A., Weingarten, A.-O., O'Flynn, C. (2017). IoT goes nuclear: Creating a ZigBee chain reaction. In *2017 IEEE Symposium on Security and Privacy*, San Jose.

List of Authors

Florent BERNARD
Jean Monnet University
Saint-Étienne
France

Viktor FISCHER
Jean Monnet University
Saint-Étienne
France
and
Czech Technical University in Prague
Czechia

Pierre GALISSANT
Laboratoire de Mathématiques
de Versailles
UVSQ, CNRS
Université Paris-Saclay
France

Benedikt GIERLICHS
COSIC
KU Leuven
Belgium

Louis GOUBIN
Laboratoire de Mathématiques
de Versailles
UVSQ, CNRS
Université Paris-Saclay
France

Patrick HADDAD
Rambus Cryptography Research
Rotterdam
Netherlands

Laurent IMBERT
LIRMM, CNRS
Université de Montpellier
France

Jan JANCAR
Masaryk University
Brno
Czechia

Marc JOYE
Zama
Paris
France

Stefan KATZENBEISSER
University of Passau
Germany

Victor LOMNE
NinjaLab
Montpellier
France

José LOPES ESTEVES
Agence nationale de la sécurité des systèmes d'information
Paris
France

Camille MUTCHLER
LIRMM, CNRS
Université de Montpellier
and
NinjaLab
Montpellier
France

Colin O'FLYNN
Dalhousie University
and
NewAE Technology Inc
Halifax
Canada

Pascal PAILLIER
Zama
Paris
France

Bart PRENEEL
COSIC
KU Leuven
Belgium

Thomas PREST
PQShield
Paris
France

Emmanuel PROUFF
LIP6
Sorbonne Université
Paris
France

Jean-René REINHARD
Agence nationale de la sécurité des systèmes d'information
Paris
France

Guénaël RENAULT
Agence nationale de la sécurité des systèmes d'information
Paris
France

Matthieu RIVAIN
CryptoExperts
Paris
France

Thomas ROCHE
NinjaLab
Montpellier
France

Eyal RONEN
Tel Aviv University
Israel

Sylvain RUHAULT
Agence nationale de la sécurité des systèmes d'information
Paris
France

Sebastian SCHRITTWIESER
University of Vienna
Austria

Petr SVENDA
Masaryk University
Brno
Czechia

Marek SYS
Masaryk University
Brno
Czechia

Akira TAKAHASHI
J.P. Morgan AI Research & AlgoCRYPT Center of Excellence
New York
United States

Philippe TEUWEN
Quarkslab
Paris
France

Mehdi TIBOUCHI
NTT Social Informatics Laboratories
Japan

Aleksei UDOVENKO
CryptoExperts and SnT
University of Luxembourg
Luxembourg

Lennert WOUTERS
COSIC
KU Leuven
Belgium

Index

A, B

C, D

E, F

G, H

I, J

K, L

M, N

O, P

R, S

T, U

W, Z

Summary of Volume 1

Chapter 4. Supervised Attacks
Eleonora CAGLI and Loïc MASURE

Chapter 5. Unsupervised Attacks
Cécile DUMAS

Chapter 12. Fault Countermeasures
Patrick SCHAUMONT and Richa SINGH

Summary of Volume 2

Chapter 13. Gate-Level Protection
Sylvain GUILLEY and Jean-Luc DANGER

Chapter 14. Physically Unclonable Functions
Jean-Luc DANGER, Sylvain GUILLEY, Debdeep MUKHOPADHYAY and Ulrich RUHRMAIR

Printed and bound by CPI Group (UK) Ltd, Croydon, CR0 4YY

13/09/2026

14961073-0005